EAGLE'S NEST

The Institute of Ismaili Studies
Ismaili Heritage Series, 10
General Editor: Farhad Daftary

Previously published titles:

1. Paul E. Walker, *Abū Yaʿqūb al-Sijistānī: Intellectual Missionary* (1996)
2. Heinz Halm, *The Fatimids and their Traditions of Learning* (1997)
3. Paul E. Walker, *Ḥamīd al-Dīn al-Kirmānī: Ismaili Thought in the Age of al-Ḥākim* (1999)
4. Alice C. Hunsberger, *Nasir Khusraw, The Ruby of Badakhshan: A Portrait of the Persian Poet, Traveller and Philosopher* (2000)
5. Farouk Mitha, *Al-Ghazālī and the Ismailis: A Debate on Reason and Authority in Medieval Islam* (2001)
6. Ali S. Asani, *Ecstasy and Enlightenment: The Ismaili Devotional Literature of South Asia* (2002)
7. Paul E. Walker, *Exploring an Islamic Empire: Fatimid History and its Sources* (2002)
8. Nadia Eboo Jamal, *Surviving the Mongols: Nizārī Quhistānī and the Continuity of Ismaili Tradition in Persia* (2002)
9. Verena Klemm, *Memoirs of a Mission: The Ismaili Scholar, Statesman and Poet al-Muʾayyad fiʾl-Dīn al-Shīrāzī* (2003)

EAGLE'S NEST

Ismaili Castles in Iran and Syria

PETER WILLEY

I.B.Tauris *Publishers*
LONDON • NEW YORK
in association with
The Institute of Ismaili Studies
LONDON

The final phases of research for this book were partially supported by grants from The Institute of Ismaili Studies and the Iran Heritage Foundation

To Adrianne
with love and grateful thanks

Published in 2005 by I.B.Tauris & Co Ltd
6 Salem Rd, London w2 4BU
175 Fifth Avenue, New York NY 10010
www.ibtauris.com

in association with The Institute of Ismaili Studies
42–44 Grosvenor Gardens, London sw1w oEB
www.iis.ac.uk

In the United States of America and in Canada distributed by
St Martin's Press, 175 Fifth Avenue, New York NY 10010

ISBN 1 85043 464 6
EAN 978 1 85043 464 1

A full CIP record for this book is available from the British Library
A full CIP record for this book is available from the Library of Congress

Library of Congress catalog card: available

Typeset in Minion Tra for The Institute of Ismaili Studies

Printed and bound in Great Britain by MPG Books Ltd, Bodmin

The Institute of Ismaili Studies

The Institute of Ismaili Studies was established in 1977 with the object of promoting scholarship and learning on Islam, in the historical as well as contemporary contexts, and a better understanding of its relationship with other societies and faiths.

The Institute's programmes encourage a perspective which is not confined to the theological and religious heritage of Islam, but seeks to explore the relationship of religious ideas to broader dimensions of society and culture. The programmes thus encourage an interdisciplinary approach to the materials of Islamic history and thought. Particular attention is also given to issues of modernity that arise as Muslims seek to relate their heritage to the contemporary situation.

Within the Islamic tradition, the Institute's programmes seek to promote research on those areas which have, to date, received relatively little attention from scholars. These include the intellectual and literary expressions of Shi'ism in general, and Ismailism in particular.

In the context of Islamic societies, the Institute's programmes are informed by the full range and diversity of cultures in which Islam is practised today, from the Middle East, South and Central Asia, and Africa to the industrialised societies of the West, thus taking into consideration the variety of contexts which shape the ideals, beliefs and practices of the faith.

These objectives are realised through concrete programmes and activities organised and implemented by various departments of the Institute. The Institute also collaborates periodically, on a programme-specific basis, with other institutions of learning in the United Kingdom and abroad.

The Institute's academic publications fall into a number of interrelated categories:

1.   Occasional papers or essays addressing broad themes of the relationship between religion and society in the historical as well as modern contexts,

with special reference to Islam.

2. Monographs exploring specific aspects of Islamic faith and culture, or the contributions of individual Muslim thinkers or writers.

3. Editions or translations of significant primary or secondary texts.

4. Translations of poetic or literary texts which illustrate the rich heritage of spiritual, devotional and symbolic expressions in Muslim history.

5. Works on Ismaili history and thought, and the relationship of the Ismailis to other traditions, communities and schools of thought in Islam.

6. Proceedings of conferences and seminars sponsored by the Institute.

7. Bibliographical works and catalogues which document manuscripts, printed texts and other source materials.

This book falls into category five listed above.

In facilitating these and other publications, the Institute's sole aim is to encourage original research and analysis of relevant issues. While every effort is made to ensure that the publications are of a high academic standard, there is naturally bound to be a diversity of views, ideas and interpretations. As such, the opinions expressed in these publications must be understood as belonging to their authors alone.

Contents

List of Illustrations   xi

Preface   xv

1   Introduction: Early History of the Ismailis   1

Part One: The Rise and Fall of the Nizari Ismaili State

2   Hasan Sabbah and the Ismailis of Iran   21

3   Rashid al-Din Sinan and the Ismailis of Syria   38

4   Organisation and Ethos of the Ismaili State   52

5   The Mongol Conquest   69

Part Two: The Castles of the Ismailis

6   The Strategy of Ismaili Castles   89

7   Castles of the Alamut Valley – I   103

8   Castles of the Alamut Valley – II   128

9   The Mountain Fortresses of Qumes   147

10   Castles of the Qa'inat   167

11   The Fortified Province of Qohistan   189

12   Castles of Isfahan and Arrajan   204

13   Citadels of the Syrian Mountains – I   216

14   Citadels of the Syrian Mountains – II   233

15   Badakhshan and Hunza   246

16   Epilogue   262

Appendices

I   Research Expeditions led by the Author   268

II   List of Ismaili Castles and Fortifications   270

III   Ismaili Pottery from the Alamut Period   277
       (by Rosalind A. Wade Haddon)
IV   Ismaili Coins from the Alamut Period   288
       (by Hussein Hamdan and Aram Vardanyan)

Bibliography   308
Index   312

List of Illustrations

The author expresses gratitude to all his friends and colleagues who have contributed illustrations to this publication. The copyright to the illustrations is held by the individuals or institutions mentioned in parenthesis.

Maps

1.   The Middle East in the 12th–13th centuries CE.
2.   Locations of major Ismaili castles in Iran.
3.   Locations of major Ismaili castles in Syria.

Plates

1.   The rock of Alamut. (*P. Willey*)
2.   Remains of fortifications on Alamut rock. (*P. Willey*)
3.   Tunnels and passages cut into the rock of Maymundez. (*P. Willey*)
4.   The site of the castle of Nevisar Shah. (*P. Willey*)
5.   A view of Alamut valley from Nevisar Shah. (*P. Willey*)
6.   The ruined towers and battlements of Lamasar. (*P. Willey*)
7.   Curtain walls of Samiran castle. (*P. Willey*)
8.   Artist's impression of Samiran before its destruction. (*Tony Garnett*)
9.   The fortified mountain of Gerdkuh rising above the plains. (*P. Willey*)
10.   Living quarters on the summit of Gerdkuh. (*P. Willey*)
11.   Remains of a water-cistern at Gerdkuh. (*P. Willey*)
12.   The main castle at Soru on a high rocky outcrop. (*Adrianne Woodfine*)
13.   A section of the subsidiary castle at Soru. (*Adrianne Woodfine*)
14.   A domed entrance at Soru castle. (*Isa Mirshahi*)
15.   The castle of Qa'in. (*P. Willey*)
16.   The castle of Furk, reconstructed in Safavid times. (*Adrianne Woodfine*)

17. The crumbling walls and towers of Shahanshah. (*P. Willey*)
18. The fortress of Khanlanjan. (*Andrew Dobson*)
19. A group of villagers dancing at Furk. (*P. Willey*)
20. Adrianne Woodfine with Ali Moradi (centre) and friends
     in search of Soru. (*P. Willey*)
21. The author, Peter Willey, with Adrianne Woodfine in Syria.
     (*Ahmed Yagi*)
22. The citadel of Masyaf in Syria, overlooking the old town. (*P. Willey*)
23. Main entrance to the citadel of Masyaf. (*P. Willey*)
24. Gateway at the castle of Qadmus. (*P. Willey*)
25. The castle of Rusafah, as seen from a nearby village. (*P. Willey*)
26. The castle of Kahf, set in a green lush valley. (*Adrianne Woodfine*)
27. Building housing the tomb of Sinan near al-Kahf. (*P. Willey*)
28. Remains of the central citadel at Khawabi castle. (*P. Willey*)
29. Shrine of Naser Khosraw in Badakhshan, Afghanistan. (*P. Willey*)
30. The renovated fort of Baltit in Hunza, northern Pakistan.
     (*The Aga Khan Trust for Culture*)
31. Pottery fragments from Alamut castle.
     (*Rosalind A. Wade Haddon, from Peter Willey's collection*)
32. Agate beads and fine moulded wares from Andej.
     (*Rosalind A. Wade Haddon, from Peter Willey's collection*)
33. A blue-glazed water pot, possibly from Hanarak.
     (*Rosalind A. Wade Haddon, from British Museum Collection,
     Box 367, reg. no. OA 15230 a & b; 15229*)
34. Fragments of glazed pottery, possibly from Nevisar Shah.
     (*Rosalind A. Wade Haddon, from British Museum collection,
     Box 128 of Alamut collection*)
35. Alamut region *sgraffiato*, possibly from Andej.
     (*Rosalind A. Wade Haddon, from British Museum collection,
     Box 128 of Alamut collection donated by P. Willey*)
36. Selection of *sgraffiato* sherds from al-Kahf, Syria.
     (*Rosalind A. Wade Haddon, from British Museum collection,
     Box 128 of Alamut collection donated by P. Willey*)
37. Exterior view of Samiran bowl.
     (*Rosalind Wade A. Haddon, from Peter Willey's collection*)
38. Interior view of Samiran bowl.
39. Exterior view of Ayiz bowl.
     (*Rosalind Wade A. Haddon, from Peter Willey's collection*)
40. Interior view of Ayiz bowl.

Figures

Fig. 1. Groundplan of Alamut castle. (*Capt. R. Dugmore*)

Fig. 2. A possible reconstruction of Maymundez castle. (*Andrew Garai*)

Fig. 3. Groundplan of Lamasar castle. (*Capt. R. Dugmore*)

Fig. 4. Sketch survey of Samiran castle. (*Tony Garnett*)

Fig. 5. Groundplan of Gerdkuh castle. (*Amin Dara*)

Fig. 6. Groundplan of the main Soru castle. (*Amin Dara*)

Fig.7. Groundplan of Qa'in castle. (*Andrew Dobson*)

Fig.8. Groundplan of Furk castle. (*Simon Furness and Tom Savery*)

Fig.9. Groundplan of Mo'menabad castle. (*Simon Furness*)

Fig.10. Groundplan of the citadel of Masyaf. (*Dr Michael Braune*)

Facsimiles

A 19th-century orientalist representation of Hasan Sabbah (*Enno Franzius*)

Nos. 1–43 of Ismaili coins from the Alamut period (Appendix IV).

Preface

The Ismaili Muslims of the Middle Ages are a classic example of how the teachings of a religious or political movement can so easily be distorted by its opponents and, as a consequence of ever more extravagant myths and legends, attract a totally ill-founded reputation for its supposedly malign and perverted ways. As the centuries pass, these legends are further embroidered until they become accepted as fact, even by scholars and academics who should know better. Such was the fate of the early Nizari Ismailis of Iran and Syria, who for centuries were portrayed as power-hungry and ruthless fanatics who would stop at nothing, including assassination, to achieve their ends, and hence became popularly known in the West by the name of 'Assassins'.

Most of the Western world first became aware of the 'Assassins' as a result of the publication by Rustichello of Pisa of Marco Polo's *Description of the World*, probably written in 1298, when the two men were prisoners of war of the Genoese. *The Travels of Marco Polo*, as the book later came to be known, became a 'bestseller' of the time and gave rise to a flood of travel literature. For a long time, the world accepted the *Travels* as authentic, but one of the most recent investigators of the subject, Frances Wood, throws serious doubts on the veracity of both Marco Polo and Rusticello in her fascinating book, *Did Marco Polo go to China?*[1] Almost reluctantly, she comes to the conclusion that there are too many inconsistencies and omissions in the work, and that the book is most likely to have been the product of the lively imagination of both men, based on the accounts of Marco's father and uncle, who did indeed make the journey to China. Marco himself had probably never been further east than Constantinople and the Black Sea.

Be that as it may, Marco Polo's description of the 'Grand Master of the Assassins', his lofty castle at Alamut and his famous 'Garden of Paradise' has been one of the most enduring oriental myths to have come down to us from medieval Europe. The story goes that the 'Grand Master', Hasan Sabbah, lived in a remote and impregnable castle where he conceived a plot to take over the Muslim world, and that in pursuit of this dream he sent out his fanatical devotees to assassinate his enemies. Before commencing their mission of death, so the story continues, the assassins were first given wine laced with hashish, served to them by beautiful damsels in an enchanted garden, in order to remind them of the delights awaiting them in Paradise after their death.

There are many similar and even wilder legends concerning the Ismailis that go back many centuries, spread first by their religious opponents among the Muslims, and then brought back to the West, further embellished, by the Crusaders and Christian chroniclers. It was mainly through their writings that the word 'assassin', in its various corrupted Arabic and Latin forms, came to be used for the Ismailis and thereafter passed into European languages as a synonym for a professional or political murderer. The ensuing demonology of the 'sect of Assassins' and the uncritical acceptance of such legends to the present day is an astonishing literary phenomenon. Even the prestigious *Oxford English Dictionary* (1989) repeats the incorrect derivation of the word 'assassin' as: 'A hashish eater, one addicted to hashish, both forms being applied in Arabic to the Ismaili sectarians, who used to intoxicate themselves with hashish or hemp, while preparing to dispatch some king or public man.' The tone of this entry, apart from the historical confusion, is interesting and indicative of how much we are still influenced by past myths.[2]

The study of Ismaili castles

One of the reasons for the persistence of such legends was the absence of any real scientific investigation of Islamic and especially Ismaili history, thought and literature until comparatively recent times. The first serious attempt in Europe to address the subject was in 1697, in a series of articles that appeared in Barthélemy d'Herbelot's encyclopaedic work, the *Bibliothèque Orientale*. This remained the main source of information for many years to come until Napoleon's invasions of Egypt and Syria in 1798–99, which stimulated oriental studies in France and other European countries. In 1809, the foremost French orientalist of the time, Silvestre de Sacy, delivered to the Institut de France his famous lecture, 'Mémoir sur la dynastie des Assassins', in which he examined various etymologies of the word 'assassin'. De Sacy went on to publish in 1838 his major work, *Exposé de la religion des Druzes*,[3] in which he examined the early history and doctrines of the Ismailis and one of their offshoots, the Druze people of Syria and Lebanon. Although de Sacy drew his information almost entirely from Sunni sources hostile to the Ismailis, his works influenced all subsequent Western scholarship on the Ismailis.

The first book to be devoted exclusively to the study of the Ismailis was produced in German by the Austrian diplomat and scholar, Joseph von Hammer-Purgstall in 1818. Von Hammer is well-known for having introduced Western readers to the poetry of the great Persian poet Hafez. He was also the first orientalist to examine in considerable detail the history of the Persian and Syrian Ismailis, in his *Die Geschichte der Assassinen*.[4] But he allowed himself to be carried away by his hostility to the Ismailis. He accepted without question all the medieval myths about the Ismailis, and in fact embellished his own version of the sinister intentions of Hasan Sabbah and his intoxicated band of murderers to destroy the Islamic world from within. Von Hammer's work was followed in the 19th century by several shorter studies by other orientalists such as Charles Defrémary, Reihart Dozy, M.J. de Goeje and Jean-Baptiste L.J. Rousseau, which advanced the study of the Ismailis somewhat but failed to clear the fog of myth, prejudice and ignorance surrounding their history and doctrines.

With the onset of the imperial era, the opportunity arose for Westerners to investigate Ismaili sites at first hand. The earliest study of this kind was undertaken by a British army officer, Colonel Monteith, who visited some of the ruins of fortifications near Alamut in 1832. He had some knowledge of the Persian Ismailis and knew that the castle of Alamut was in the mountains near Qazvin. From the town of Menjil he followed the course of the Shahrud, and eventually came to the entrance of the Alamut valley, though he did not reach the village of Gazor Khan above which the castle of Alamut is situated. He also seems to have confused the fort of Shirkuh, at the entrance to the valley, with the main castle. Shortly after his return to England, Colonel Monteith published his findings in the *Journal of the Royal Geographical Society*.[5] The honour of being the first Westerner to have correctly identified the castle of Alamut belongs, however, to Lieutenant-Colonel Shiel, who gave an account of his visit in the same journal in 1838.[6] A few decades later, in 1895, the Syrian castles of the Ismailis came under the scrutiny of the French archaeologist Max van Berchem, who studied mainly the inscriptions found in the walls and chambers of these fortresses.[7]

The name most frequently associated in this country with the 'Assassins' and their castles is that of Freya Stark, who published in her book, *The Valleys of the Assassins*, an account of her journey made in May 1930. Very courageously and at some risk to herself, this resourceful lady had actually visited the Alamut valley and described in considerable detail some of the Ismaili castles, particularly Alamut and Lamasar, which she had seen for herself. Her work, essentially a travelogue, is refreshingly devoid of myths and legends. She writes quietly and attractively and does not conceal her liking for the villagers she encountered in the course of her journeys. She states quite simply:

What I write here is for pleasure, for other people's, I hope, but in any case for my own, for it is always agreeable to go over the wandering days. History and geography, arguments and statistics are left out. I mention the things I like to remember as they come into my head.[8]

The great breakthrough in Ismaili studies came with the ground-breaking work of the Russian scholar Wladimir Ivanow (1886–1970). After completing his studies in Arabic and Persian at St Petersburg, Ivanow became a keeper of oriental manuscripts at the Asiatic Museum of the Imperial Russian Academy of Sciences. In the course of his work, he travelled widely in Central Asia and Iran to collect manuscripts for the Museum, and became familiar with some Ismaili texts acquired in Badakhshan. In the 1930s he decided to dedicate his scholarly life to the study of Ismailism and transferred his residence to Bombay, where he was instrumental in the foundation of the Ismaili Society. Thereafter he produced at regular intervals a series of scholarly studies on the Ismailis. Ivanow's works completely transformed the conventional orientalist view of the Ismailis and laid the foundation of all future studies on the subject. Among his many fine works, the one of special relevance to us is his *Alamut and Lamasar*, a product of an archaeological survey he conducted in the years 1957–1958.[9]

The pioneering contributions of Ivanow paved the way for the discovery and publication of many authentic Ismaili texts, preserved in the private libraries of the Ismailis themselves. The first comprehensive and scholarly study of the Ismailis of the Alamut period appeared in 1955 by Marshall G.S. Hodgson of the University of Chicago. His book, *The Order of Assassins*, remains to this day the standard reference work on this subject.[10] Hodgson was able for the first time to study the entire phenomenon of the Nizari Ismaili movement with a remarkable breadth of scholarship and insight. Nor is his work compromised by the accumulated myths and distortions of medieval Sunni authors or Crusader chroniclers. He was able, wherever possible, to consult original Ismaili sources in Persian and Arabic, many of which had been earlier discovered, transcribed and published by Ivanow.

In addition to Hodgson's seminal work, there have been several other major contributions to Ismaili studies in the later part of the 20th century. Through the writings of scholars such as Rudolf Strothmann, Louis Massignon, Samuel M. Stern, Henry Corbin and Wilferd Madelung, it is now possible to have more accurate knowledge of virtually every aspect of Ismaili history and thought. All this scholarship and much more besides has been consolidated more recently by Farhad Daftary in his comprehensive survey, *The Isma'ilis: Their History and Doctrines*.[11] This was followed in 1994 by *The Assassin Legends: Myths of the Isma'ilis*, in which he demonstrates conclusively the fictional and fantastical nature of many of the medieval reports about the Ismailis. As he points out:

Rooted in fear, hostility, ignorance and fantasy, however, the exotic tales of hashish, daggers and earthly gardens of paradise, have proved too sensational to be totally relegated to the domain of fiction by more sober investigations of modern times. That such legends have continued to fire the popular imagination of so many generations, and that they are still believed in many quarters, attest to the unfortunate fact that in both western and eastern societies the boundaries between fact and fiction, and reality and fantasy, are not always clearly definable. Now, finally, the time has come to recognise, once and for all, that the Assassin legends are no more than absurd myths, the products of ignorant, hostile 'imagination', and not deserving of any serious consideration, even though they have circulated for centuries as reliable narratives.[12]

Of course, these legends were rooted in 'fear, hostility, ignorance and fantasy', but what is astonishing is that they are still half-believed and popularised as fact by many who should know better. As the post-September 11 writings on the origins of political terrorism show, there is still quite a long way to go before the dross of seven centuries of myth and fiction is finally swept away.

I must not fail to mention here one other milestone in the study of Persian Ismailism in particular, and that is the publication in 1958 of the complete English version of the Persian Sunni historian 'Ata-Malik Juwayni's great historical narrative, *Ta'rikh-i jahan-gushay*. Translated by John Andrew Boyle as *The History of the World-Conqueror*, it provides a fascinating contemporary Mongol account of the Ismailis of the Alamut period, their history, doctrines and castles in Iran, culminating in the fall of Alamut and Maymundez in 1256.[13] Juwayni was in the entourage of the Mongol commander Hulegu Khan when he marched against the Ismailis. Later he was also to witness Hulegu's capture of Baghdad, the slaughter of its inhabitants and the murder of the last Abbasid caliph. In 1259 Hulegu appointed him governor of Baghdad and all the territory that was conquered by him in Iran and Iraq. Juwayni's account of the Ismailis is highly coloured by his animosity towards this Shi'i community, whom he condemns as 'heretics' deserving their destruction by the Mongols. But the epic sweep and vigorous invective of his narrative has been magnificently translated by Professor Boyle, and the book is a pleasure to read for its own sake.

Thus, from the 1930s onwards, a great deal of scholarly material has been published on the history, doctrines, literature and different traditions of the Ismailis.[14] But apart from the works of Freya Stark and Professor Ivanow, as well as one or two articles by Sir Auriel Stein, Dr Lawrence Lockhart and others on individual sites such as Alamut, Lamasar and Samiran, little attempt has been made to give an extensive account of the Ismaili castles and fortresses that survive today. The present volume seeks to fill this vacuum and present to the modern reader the findings of nearly forty years of research and fieldwork that I have conducted on the Ismaili sites in various parts of Iran and Syria.

My research on Ismaili castles

I first became interested in the Ismailis after reading Freya Stark's attractive and compelling book, *The Valleys of the Assassins*. When I was a schoolmaster Fellow of Balliol, I had the great fortune to meet Dr Samuel M. Stern, Fellow of All Souls College at Oxford, the eminent scholar of Islam and especially Ismailism. On hearing that I intended to accept the invitation of Sir Geoffrey Harrison, the British Ambassador to Iran, to spend my 1959 summer vacation in Tehran, Stern urged me to try and find the previously unlocated Ismaili castle of Maymundez near Alamut, where the Mongol armies under Hulegu Khan crushed the Ismaili resistance in 1256. An article in *The Times* of London described my first two expeditions in the following words:

> Two expeditions have recently been to northern Persia exploring the valleys of the Assassins. The first, in 1959, began as a light-hearted affair: a party of Oxford undergraduates setting off (in a bus labelled 'The Oxford Assassins') with no higher aim than to extract the maximum enjoyment from an adventurous summer vacation in Persia. But their unexpected success and discoveries led to a second expedition last year, which made a serious contribution to historical studies concerning the Assassins, as well as to the knowledge of a remote part of Persia.[15]

As a consequence of my first two expeditions to Alamut in 1959 and 1960, when my team was fortunate enough to locate for the first time the site of Maymundez, I embarked upon a long series of research expeditions in Iran until 1979, the year of the Revolution in Iran, and subsequently in Syria, Pakistan and Tajikistan until 2000. I must have visited Alamut eight or nine times, and the descriptions I give of the castles in this book are often the result of several visits to the same site. It would perhaps help the reader if I describe the main stages of my own investigations.

My research work falls into four distinct phases. The first from 1959 to 1963 was concerned with my initial investigations in Alamut and the Rudbar district, including the castle of Samiran, some 18 km west of Menjil. The most important task was the investigation of Maymundez, which in many ways was the most difficult and dangerous fortress I had to enter. In 1963 I published *The Castles of the Assassins*, which describes the work I had done thus far and gives a reasonably detailed account of the main Ismaili castles in the Alamut valley.[16] This book has remained until now the most comprehensive work on the subject, although I have in the meantime considerably modified the somewhat simplistic judgements I made in the book about the Ismailis themselves and reassessed their achievement in military architecture.

I was then urged by Dr Samuel M. Stern to continue my research work further east in the direction of Gerdkuh and Khorasan, where there were more castles to be investigated. From 1963 until 1979 I took every opportunity I could to use my summer vacations – I was then a housemaster at Wellington College in Berkshire – to continue my work. My first task was to examine the fortress of Gerdkuh, near Damghan in northern Iran. Some years previously, Dr Lawrence Lockhart of Cambridge University had climbed to the top of the mountain and shown me his photographs of the remarkable water cisterns he had found there. Gerdkuh has always remained in my mind as one of the most impressive Ismaili castles. I last visited it in 1997 and found it as compelling a site as ever. My research then took me to Khorasan and especially Qohistan in the south of the province, which contains the great fortresses of Qa'in, Ferdaws, Birjand, Mo'menabad, Furk and many others.

The work of my teams was made much easier during these years by the constant practical support we were given by the late Dr Bagher Mostofi. Through his influence and that of the Minister of Court, we received all possible assistance, including the loan of vehicles and the provision of petrol and other supplies. We could not have been more generously treated. The British Army, too, seconded on various occasions officers from the Royal Engineers (Military Survey) to help us with our work.

By 1979 I was approaching the end of my research work and was already thinking of writing another book in which I would radically reassess my previous views of the Ismailis, having seen for myself their remarkable skills in the construction of their castles, the development of agriculture and irrigation, and other areas such as pottery. There was still further work to do in the field and many more castles to describe. But the Islamic Revolution of 1979 forced me to break off my work and I was unable to return to Iran for many years.

In the middle of 1995, there was an improvement in relations between the governments of Iran and the United Kingdom. At a reception in London I asked the Iranian chargé d'affaires, Mr Ansari, if he thought I could now return to Iran to refresh my memory about the Ismaili castles and complete my research. Mr Ansari thought that there could be difficulties, but promised that he and his deputy, Dr Safaei, would support my application. There were indeed many hurdles to overcome but, thanks to Dr Safaei's genuine interest and support, I was given a visa to go to Tehran to consult the authorities there about my research. I had just had a major operation on my left leg (which had been badly wounded during the Battle of Anzio in 1944) and so I was on crutches. From my discussions with members of Iran Bastan, the main Iranian museum in Tehran, it seemed that I might be given permission to work in 1996, together with some Iranian archaeologists. Upon returning to Britain, I asked a friend, Adrianne Woodfine, if she would accompany me, and she agreed to come as my research assistant and help in any practical way I might need owing to my physical disability.

By the middle of 1996, the Iranian Embassy in London had still not received any definite reply from Tehran, but it was made clear to us by the Embassy that the Iranian Ministry of Foreign Affairs would support us. Consequently Adrianne and I decided to fly out to Tehran to see if we could get formal permission from the Ministry of Cultural Heritage and Islamic Guidance to work; and if we could not, we would still travel as far as we could on our tourist visas. The Ministry of Cultural Heritage was still unapproachable despite appeals to them from their own Foreign Ministry to help us. So Adrianne and I set off to Mashhad, armed with impressive looking documents from the Iranian Foreign Ministry. We were fortunate in having the addresses of two Ismaili contacts, Dr Abbas Badakhshani in Mashhad and Mr Isa Mirshahi in Tehran, who together with their families could not have been more helpful. We had waited many days in fruitless negotiations with the authorities, but were able to establish close relations with the Ismailis. After six weeks our visas, which had already been renewed once, were due to expire again. As the renewal process would be lengthy and protracted, we decided to return home and come back again the following year to complete our work.

Our 1997 expedition was even more productive than I had anticipated, thanks to a generous grant from the Iran Heritage Foundation, the constant support of The Institute of Ismaili Studies in London, and the assistance of our Ismaili friends in Iran. After ten weeks in the field we felt we had completed our mission to the best of our abilities. We estimated that we had identified over forty new castles, including the very important complex at Soru near Semnan in the Qumes area. Thus ended the third phase of my research work.

Encouraged by our success, in 1998 I went to Syria with Adrianne to study the Ismaili castles there. I had first been to Syria in 1970 and naturally wanted to refresh my memory and compare the Arab, especially Ismaili, castles with those of the Crusaders. The 1970 expedition was far from easy. It was a time of much political tension and the United Kingdom had broken off diplomatic relations with Syria. However, we were allowed into the country and had to register with the Swiss Embassy who were looking after British interests. We were warned that we would have to be very careful about photography, as even medieval castles were considered prohibited areas. We managed, however, to visit quite a few, though on several occasions we were peremptorily told to move elsewhere immediately or we would be arrested. In 1998 it was quite a different story. Everyone was very relaxed and friendly. Thanks to our Ismaili guide, Mr Ahmad Yagi, who was a teacher at the main school in Salamiyya, we were able to travel freely wherever we wished. Consequently our visit was very rewarding and happy.

While the focus of my research has always been Iran and Syria, we took the opportunity in 1968 and again ten years later to visit the Northern Areas of Pakistan and the Badakhshan province of Afghanistan. These regions are the home of considerable numbers of Ismailis with a long historical and cultural connection with their co-religionists in neighbouring Iran and Tajikistan. In 2000 Adrianne and I returned to northern Pakistan and were able to explore Hunza and other mountain valleys in the region. We made our way up the great Karakoram Highway to the Chinese border despite snow avalanches and dangerous rockfalls. Unfortunately we could not cross into China to visit the Ismaili communities there.

The present book, which is far more detailed and inclusive than my previous work, covers the work of over twenty expeditions to Iran and Syria from 1959 to 2000. I had originally intended to publish the book much earlier, before my research was completed, as there seemed so little chance of being allowed to return to Iran to work. But the delay was, in fact, a blessing in disguise, as it has enabled me to review my findings; and when I returned to Iran in 1996 and 1997, I was able to continue my study of the Ismaili castles there in greater depth and locate many others whose existence I had not expected. These discoveries influenced my whole approach to the study of the Nizari Ismailis and their long struggle for independence against the most formidable powers ruling the Middle East in the 12th and 13th centuries.

At the beginning of my work I had accepted more or less the conventional version of the 'Assassins' as a group of fanatic and somewhat rough and ready adventurers, led by their charismatic leader Hasan Sabbah, who established their power-base by building strong and well-supplied castles in the valley of Alamut and elsewhere. I took some of the more extreme legends with a pinch of salt, but did not realise how absurd they actually were. Once I had the opportunity of seeing for myself the very high quality of military architecture exhibited in their castles, which in many ways surpass the achievements of the Crusaders, I began to develop a greater appreciation of this remarkable community and the nature of the state they once created and defended, often against overwhelming odds, in the remote mountains of Iran and Syria for more than 150 years.

As a result of my research work, I believe that we now have for the first time an overall picture of the part played by the castles in the Ismaili state. From the study of these castles we can extrapolate much interesting and valuable information on the circumstances in which the Ismailis lived and the difficulties they faced. The structure of the castles, their architecture, provisions for water and food supplies, and other details tell us a great deal about the Ismailis themselves. On the basis of existing scholarship and my own research, it is now possible also to make a comparison between the Ismaili castles in Syria and those of the Crusaders. In contrast to the malevolent view of the Ismailis held by their opponents, we can now positively assert that they were a people of exceptional intelligence and determination with a sophisticated knowledge of military architecture, administration and logistics, as well as being highly successful agriculturalists and water engineers in a mostly arid and mountainous terrain. The spiritual, intellectual and cultural side of the Ismailis was the mortar that bound them together in a cohesive and energetic community with pride in their own achievements. The picture that finally emerges is the very opposite of the 'assassins' and 'terrorists' of popular imagination.

The primary purpose of this book to describe as fully as possible the principal castles and fortresses of the Ismailis in Iran and Syria, and by so doing also to define in some detail the extent of the areas they once controlled. In fact, the network of these castles numbering well over 250 strongholds – some large and imposing citadels, others smaller fortifications and outposts – played a vital role in protecting the Ismailis from their religious and political opponents. They also provided refuge to people of surrounding villages in times of attack, as well as willing assistance to scholars of different creeds to pursue their studies under Ismaili patronage. It had been assumed that this state largely consisted of Alamut and a few other castles in Quhistan and elsewhere in Iran. Now we know that a much larger portion of southern Khorasan was heavily fortified by the Ismailis, as were the areas around Semnan and Damghan in northern Iran. The Syrian highlands of the Jabal Bahra, now called Jabal Ansariyya, were also largely under the control of the Ismailis loyal to Alamut.

As well as describing the castles I have examined, I have occasionally tried to give a flavour of the conditions in which we worked by describing significant or unusual incidents that happened along the way. To help the reader, I have supplied a number of maps, photographs and other illustrations of various Ismaili castles and their sites. I have also listed in the Appendices I and II all the important Ismaili castles known to us together with their locations, as well as my various expeditions with their dates and the areas covered in case the reader wishes to work out in greater detail the chronology of my work. The title of this book, *Eagle's Nest*, is an approximate translation of the name Alamut, which in the local dialect signifies the great height at which the eagle soars above the rock on which the castle stands.

In the Introduction to this work, I have tried to place the Ismailis in their historical context within the Islamic tradition, and in Part I describe in some detail the complex circumstances that accompanied the rise and fall of their power in Iran and Syria. This account is intended to be a general guide and background to the more focused regional study of the Ismaili castles that appears in Part II of the book. As a result of this work, I hope that a more accurate picture of the Ismailis will emerge, free of the burden of the Assassin legends, as well as a proper understanding of their achievements, intellectual and cultural as well as in the field of military strategy and architecture, which are remarkable by any standard.

Acknowledgements

It is almost impossible for me to give a complete list of all those who helped me during my long period of research. In my *Castles of the Assassins* I gave details of all our very generous Iranian and British sponsors and helpers, academic, political, military and commercial. It would not be really appropriate to repeat this now, although our gratitude remains undimmed. But I would be unhappy if I did not reiterate the immense support I received from the late Dr Baghir Mostofi, an old friend and a wise counsellor, who did so much to help me personally and ease my path by persuading members of the Iranian government, army chiefs and commercial companies to donate liberally to our cause. I remain very grateful to the British Ambassadors in Tehran, especially the late Sir Denis Wright, and their staff, for all their help and concern.

I must also express my deep sense of gratitude to my chief academic advisor and mentor, the late Dr Samuel M. Stern of All Souls College, Oxford, who inspired and encouraged me to continue with what at times seemed an impossible task. Likewise I owe much to the late Dr Lawrence Lockhart of Cambridge University and Mr Ralph Pinder-Wilson, formerly a curator in the Department of Oriental Antiquities at the British Museum. It is also a great pleasure for me to thank Rosalind A. Wade Haddon for her valuable assessment, illustrated by photographs, of the pottery we discovered on our expeditions, which appears in Appendix III. Likewise, I am indebted to Hussein Hamdan and Aram Vardanyan for their account of Ismaili coins of the Alamut period in Appendix IV, the first catalogue of this kind.

Then, of course, are all the members of my expeditions without whom nothing could have been achieved. I thank them and salute them for their determination, helpfulness, good humour, intelligence and realism. In particular, I must pay tribute to Major Roddie Dugmore for the outstanding maps and sketches of the different sites we visited in my early expeditions. I am also most grateful to

Mr Mehdi Shalforushan who had visited the castle of Soru sometime ago with an American friend, James Whittaker, and who persuaded Mr Amin Dara, who lives in Tehran, to make two or three visits to Soru and Gerdkuh. Amin has let me have his superb plates and photographs of both sites. I am also very grateful to the members of my teams who have lent me their diaries and slides, especially Mr Andrew Dobson who was present on at least four expeditions. I must also thank Mr Simon Furness who drew the original map of Qohistan and its castles.

In my recent expeditions since 1995, my constant companion, helper, adviser and friend has been Adrianne Woodfine. Her contribution to my physical welfare, caused by the problems of my disability, and the ultimate success of our venture is beyond praise. And in addition she has undertaken cheerfully and with expertise, the demanding task of converting my disjointed calligraphy to a presentable script, which has involved the sufficient mastering of a computer, checking all the notes and relieving the author of almost everything apart from the writing.

As mentioned, we have had generous support from the Iran Heritage Foundation and The Institute of Ismaili Studies, and I must also acknowledge the assistance of the British Institute of Persian Studies and the Institut Français in Tehran. The names of others who have been generous with their time and advice are legion, but I must in particular mention Mr Kutub Kassam, my ever-patient and judicious editor at The Institute of Ismaili Studies who has always been a tower of strength. I must also mention Dr Farhad Daftary of the same Institute; Dr Michael Braune of Hanover, and especially Mr. Mike Shaw, my agent, with Jonathan Pegg of Curtis Brown, who never let me despair.

Peter Willey

Upavon Pewsey

Wiltshire, UK

August, 2004

Notes

1. Frances Wood, *Did Marco Polo go to China?* (London, 1995).

2. The legends of 'the Assassins' resurfaced more recently, following the attack on the World Trade Center in New York on 11 September 2001, in a spate of ill-informed articles in the popular media purporting to show that Hasan Sabbah and his followers were the originators of modern terrorism.

3. Silvestre de Sacy, 'Mémoire sur la dynastie des Assassins et sur l'étymologie der leur Nom,' *Mémoirs de l'Institut Royal de France*, 4 (1918), pp. 1–84. English trans., 'Memoir on the Dynasty of the Assassins, and on the Etymology of their Name,' in Farhad Daftary, *The Assassin Legends: Myths of the Isma'ilis* (London, 1994), pp. 136–182.

4. Joseph von Hammer-Purgstall, *Die Geschichte der Assassinen aus Morgenländischen*

Quellen (Stuttgart-Tübingen, 1818). English trans., O.C. Wood, *The History of the Assassins* (London, 1835).

5. W. Monteith, 'Journal of a Tour through Azerdbijan and the Shores of the Caspian,' *Journal of the Royal Geographical Society*, 3 (1833), pp. 15–16.

6. J. Shiel, 'Itinerary from Tehran to Alamut and Khurrem-abad in May 1837,' *Journal of the Royal Geographical Society*, 8 (1838), pp. 430–434.

7. M. van Berchem, 'Epigraphic des Assassins de Syrie,' *Journal Asiatique*, 9 série, 9 (1897), pp. 453–501.

8. Freya Stark, *The Valleys of the Assassins and other Persian Travels* (London, 1934), p. 228.

9. W. Ivanow, *Alamut and Lamasar: Two Mediaeval Ismaili Strongholds in Iran* (Tehran, 1960).

10. Marshall G.S. Hodgson, *The Order of Assassins: The Struggle of the Early Nizari Isma'ilis Against the Islamic World* (The Hague, 1955). See also his 'The Isma'ili State,' in *The Cambridge History of Iran*, Volume 5: *The Saljuq and Mongol Periods*, ed. J.A. Boyle (Cambridge, 1968), pp. 422–482, where Hodgson admits that *The Order of Assassins* was 'unfortunately mistitled' (p. 424, note 1).

11. Farhad Daftary, *The Isma'ilis: Their History and Doctrines* (Cambridge, 1990). See also his *A Short History of the Ismailis: Traditions of a Muslim Community* (Edinburgh, 1998).

12. Daftary, *The Assassin Legends*, p. 124.

13. 'Ata-Malik Juwayni, *Tarikh-i jahan gushay*, ed. M. Qazwini (Leiden-London, 1912–37). English trans., J.A. Boyle, *The History of the World-Conqueror* (Manchester, 1958).

14. The large and constantly growing scholarship on the Ismailis is impressively reflected in Farhad Daftary's *Ismaili Literature: A Bibliography of Sources and Studies* (London, 2004).

15. Peter Willey, 'New Finds in Valleys of the Assassins,' *The Times* (London, 25th Feb., 1961).

16. Peter Willey, *The Castles of the Assassins* (London, 1963).

CHAPTER 1

Early History of the Ismailis

While Western nations were still struggling to come to terms with the turmoil and fragmentation that followed the fall of the Roman Empire and the creation of the Christian imperium established by Constantine in Byzantium, a new empire of astonishing proportions was created by the followers of the Prophet Muhammad living in his native Arabia. The Prophet had died in 632, but such was the fervour and loyalty inspired by him that within a remarkably short time the Islamic empire stretched from Cordoba to Delhi, spanning almost the entire North African littoral including Egypt, the Levant, Syria, Yemen, Iraq, Iran and Transoxiana. By 720 the Muslims had conquered Spain and nearly succeeded in subduing France, until they were halted at Poitiers in 732. The Muslims made further conquests in India and Central Asia, reaching as far as the borders of China by 751.

There were several reasons for the outstanding success of the Muslim armies. Their commanders were the ruling elite of Medina, allied with the tribal aristocracy which had controlled Mecca since the early sixth century. Their primary aim was to extend Muslim rule from the Arabian peninsula to the neighbouring lands. These wars were not religious as such but economic and territorial in character. The vitality, energy and ingenuity of the conquerors is quite amazing, especially in view of their somewhat undistinguished bedouin origins. Equally remarkable was their tolerance of Christians, Jews and other religious minorities in the conquered territories. When the Muslim armies first appeared among the lands ruled by the Byzantine and Sasanid empires, they did not demand of the people their immediate acceptance of the new faith. Contrary to popular perception in the West, Islam was not spread at the point of the sword but it was a gradual process of conversion over several generations.[1] The Islamic faith appealed far more to the inhabitants of the Middle East than any other religious doctrine, especially the Byzantine and Orthodox traditions. The message of Islam was quite simple: There is one God, Muhammad was His Messenger, and the Qur'an His last and final message to mankind.

The Caliphate

After the death of the Prophet in Mecca, there was at first considerable uncertainty and rivalry about his succession. According to Muslim belief, Muhammad was the last of the prophets who had lived and taught before him. All Muslims accept the Biblical prophets Adam, Noah, Abraham, Moses and Jesus as messengers of God, but maintain that divine guidance to mankind became completed with Muhammad. The true faith and holy law had now been fully revealed in the Qur'an, and after Muhammad there would be no further need for a prophet. But as well as being the supreme religious authority, the Prophet at the end of his life was also the ruler of a large and important state in Arabia. It almost seemed as though there might be civil war between the supporters of various candidates for the leadership of the Muslim community. Eventually the tribal leaders of Mecca and Medina agreed to support the claim of Abu Bakr, chiefly on the basis of his seniority of age and companionship to the Prophet. There were others, however, who felt that legitimate authority belonged to 'Ali, the Prophet's cousin and son-in-law, because of his kinship and intimacy with the Prophet, as well as his deep knowledge of the faith. They also claimed that Muhammad had on several occasions designated 'Ali as his successor. In time, of course, these differences would crystallise and produce the Sunni and Shi'a branches of Islam.

Abu Bakr ruled for only two years and before his death in 634 nominated 'Umar as his successor. It was during 'Umar's caliphate that the great Muslim conquests began and by the time of his death in 644 the Islamic empire was well established. He appointed a council of six men to nominate his successor and their choice fell upon 'Uthman of the Umayyad clan. 'Ali, who had always claimed the right to leadership for himself, was rejected once again to the great dismay of his followers. The reign of 'Uthman was marked by much instability, caused mainly by the difficulties of governing a huge empire and the corruption it generated in the provinces. In 656 'Uthman was murdered in a popular uprising, making it possible for 'Ali finally to become the fourth caliph. But in light of the tragic circumstances, it was a position that he accepted reluctantly.

The appointment of 'Ali was opposed by various tribal factions who accused him unjustly of complicity in 'Uthman's murder and rose up in armed rebellion. 'Ali was able to crush the rebels in Mecca and Medina easily, but a more serious challenge to his leadership came from Mu'awiya, the governor of Syria and cousin of 'Uthman who coveted the caliphate for himself. After an inconclusive battle fought against the Syrian forces at Siffin on the banks of the upper Euphrates, 'Ali returned to his military base at Kufa near Basra in Iraq. It was in the mosque of Kufa, while he was at prayer, that 'Ali was mortally wounded by the sword of an assassin in 661. 'Ali is greatly revered by the Shi'i Muslims as their first Imam or spiritual leader after the Prophet, and his golden domed mausoleum at Najaf, near Kufa, has become a major focus of pilgrimage for the faithful from all over the world.

Despite these civil wars, the period from 632 to 661 is regarded by many Muslims as the golden age of a united, all-triumphant Islam. The four caliphs who presided over the destiny of Islam were close to Muhammad during his lifetime and thus familiar with his thinking and vision. Their great achievement was the preservation of the unity of Islam and the founding within three decades of a far-flung empire, spanning from the shores of the Atlantic to the steppes of Central Asia. As a result, these early caliphs are invested with great esteem and veneration among Muslims to this day.

The Umayyads and the Abbasids

The high office held by the first four caliphs was not a hereditary one and did not survive for more than thirty years. After the murder of 'Ali, the caliphate became a purely dynastic office held by the Umayyad clan, starting with Mu'awiya. He was first hailed as caliph in Syria and shortly afterwards was recognised all over the empire. Damascus was his capital. Although not noted for his piety or religious knowledge, Mu'awiya was an able military commander, and even his enemies paid tribute to his diplomatic and political skills.[2] The Umayyads retained the caliphate for less than a hundred years (661–750), during which time they strengthened as far as they could the power and prestige of their office. They minted their own gold coins, which until then had been the prerogative of the Byzantine emperors – the Muslims had previously contented themselves with minting silver coins. It was under Umayyad rule that the earliest expressions of a new Islamic civilisation began to emerge. Perhaps the most impressive monument today to the Umayyads is the Great Mosque of Damascus, which has a pre-eminent place in early Islamic architecture and majestically symbolises the vision and scale of the new world empire.

When the Arabs first conquered the lands of the Middle East, they had naturally sought to enlist the help of the local populations in setting up their new administration, but they soon began to encounter considerable resistance. This was particularly sharp in the case of the more sophisticated Persians, whose imperial history went back centuries to the days of Cyrus and Darius. The conflicts between the established landowners and the Arab settlers who had flooded into the more fertile lands of Mesopotamia also threatened to undermine the very existence of the new empire. Under the Umayyads, power and wealth came to be concentrated almost exclusively in the hands of the Arab tribal aristocracy. On the other hand, the non-Arab Muslims, the so-called *mawali*, suffered from much poverty and discrimination, causing them to rise up periodically in armed rebellion. Another source of discontent came from the more religious-minded Muslims who denounced what they deemed to be the profane and irreligious lifestyle of the Umayyad rulers. The Umayyads incurred much hostility too from their policy of persecuting the descendants of 'Ali and their supporters. The most infamous act of the Umayyads was the massacre of 'Ali's son, Husayn, together with his family at Karbala in 680. The murder of the Prophet's grandson caused enormous shock and revulsion among all Muslims. It united the opposition into a powerful force that eventually led to the violent overthrow of the Umayyad dynasty in 750. The tragedy of Karbala was the pivotal event that crystallised the division between the Shi'a and Sunni Muslims, and its echoes still reverberate today in the tragedy of the war in Iraq.

The revolt against the Umayyads was led by the Abbasid family who claimed descent from al-'Abbas, an uncle of the Prophet. They denounced the Umayyads as usurpers of the rights that belonged to the Prophet's family. This message attracted a large Shi'a following and thus ensured their victory over the Umayyads. The first Abbasid caliph, who took the forbidding throne-name of al-Saffah, 'the Blood-spiller', established his capital in Baghdad, which until then had been a small town of no particular consequence. But it was now to become the centre of a new empire, ruled for the next five centuries by the Abbasid dynasty (750–1258). The transfer of the capital to the east naturally increased the influence of Persian culture. The court ceremonial, the government administration and the army were all modelled on Persian lines, even though Arabic language and literature remained the dominant influence. This confluence of Arabic and Persian traditions resulted in an extraordinary cultural flowering in the following centuries. Baghdad became one of the leading centres of a new Islamic civilisation, surpassing the cities of medieval Europe in artistic and intellectual achievements. The most celebrated of the Abbasid caliphs was Harun al-Rashid (d. 809), whose fame is known to many Western readers mainly through the stories of *A Thousand and One Nights*, also known as *Arabian Nights,* where he is depicted roaming the streets of Baghdad in disguise at night to dispense justice and bring relief to the oppressed.

The Abbasid caliphs were at first absolute rulers, but later their power passed to a series of military leaders whose loyalty to the caliph was merely nominal. The power of the caliphate began to collapse alarmingly soon after the death of Harun al-Rashid. In the second half of the ninth century, the Abbasid empire began to disintegrate as Spain and North Africa challenged the rule of Baghdad. In 868 the governor of Egypt declared himself an independent ruler. The bedouin tribes of Syria and Iraq began to reassert their old freedom and at times even took control over their own areas. Everywhere in the empire, independence movements sprang up, particularly in Iran where Khorasan (which plays such an important part in our story) became a highly turbulent and rebellious region which the Abbasids struggled to subdue without much success.

The stability of the Abbasid caliphate was further undermined by the increasing polarisation between the Shi'a and Sunni Muslims. Although the Abbasids had initially come to power largely with Shi'a support, upon assuming office they began to make common cause with the majority Sunni population and to persecute the Shi'a. This policy provoked a series of violent insurrections among the Shi'a of Iraq and Iran which were brutally crushed by the Abbasid authorities. The most formidable challenge, however, came from the Ismaili Shi'a who had organised themselves into an underground revolutionary movement that won wide support in many parts of the Muslim world. The deepening political crisis considerably reduced the authority of the Abbasid caliphs and effective control passed into the hands of military generals. In 946 Baghdad was occupied by the Buyids (or Buwayhids), a pro-Shi'a military dynasty from the Daylam region of northern Iran (which is not far from Alamut). A century later the Buyids were driven out by the Sunni Saljuq Turks extending their empire from Central Asia into Iran and Iraq. Under these military regimes, the Abbasid caliphate was reduced to a titular institution and the caliphs became mere puppets of the military rulers who exercised all authority.[3]

The Shi'a and Sunni Muslims

The division of the Islamic faith into Shi'a and Sunni branches has its historic origins in differences over the question of leadership and authority within the Muslim community. Both Shi'a and Sunnis subscribe to the same articles of faith such as belief in one God and the Prophet Muhammad, as well as the basic duties of prayer, fasting, charity and pilgrimage to Mecca. The two are divided essentially around their differing views on the office of *khalifa* or caliph, the head of the Muslim community after Muhammad. According to Sunni doctrine (the name comes from *sunna*, the traditional way or practice of the Prophet), the caliphate was to be held by any competent member of the Meccan tribe of the Quraysh, to which the Prophet belonged. The Shi'a (from *Shi'at 'Ali*, the 'party of 'Ali') regard the Prophet's cousin and his descendants as his only rightful successors. They maintain that even when political power is usurped by others, the spiritual leadership of Muslims is divinely ordained to remain with the Prophet's family.

In later centuries several other differences emerged in the interpretation of faith between the two communities, which became codified into distinctive schools of thought. By the 10th century, the main tenets of Sunni Islam were already well established and systematically expounded by the great theologian Abu'l-Hasan al-'Ashari (d. 935). Sunni doctrine came to be based on the authority of the Qur'an, the *Sunna* or practice of the Prophet, as interpreted by scholarly opinion. The Shi'a, too, accept the authority of the Qur'an and the *Sunna*, but assert that only their Imams have inherited the true knowledge of faith to interpret the word of God authoritatively.

As we have seen, 'Ali was murdered in 661 and the caliphate was claimed by his rival, Mu'awiya, the governor of Syria. The Umayyad ruler forced 'Ali's son, Hasan, to renounce his own claim to the office. When Hasan died a few years later in suspicious circumstances, murder was suspected. His younger brother Husayn now left Medina for Kufa to lead the resistance, but he and his small force were cut to pieces at Karbala. To the horror of all Muslims, the Prophet's grandson was beheaded and his head sent to Damascus. It was afterwards buried with his body at Karbala, which is now one of the great Shi'i shrines. The murders of 'Ali and his son were in many ways the cement that united the Shi'a in opposition to the Sunnis. The psychological effect of martyrdom and sacrifice in the cause of justice has been of great significance to the Shi'a and still is today. The anniversary of Husayn's death, the tenth of Muharram, is always charged with intense religious fervour and emotion, and is observed with ten days of public mourning and lamentation throughout the Shi'i world.

The Shi'a began to emerge as a distinct branch of Islam under Husayn's successors, the Imams Zayn al-'Abidin, Muhammad al-Baqir and Ja'far al-Sadiq. Due to the hostility of the Umayyads and later the Abbasids, these Imams refrained from active political involvement and devoted their lives to piety, scholarship and guiding their followers. The consolidation of Shi'i Islam has been attributed mainly to Ja'far al-Sadiq who became Imam around 732. By all accounts Ja'far was a man of considerable religious learning and intellectual ability who attracted a wide circle of students and disciples to his residence in Medina. Drawing from the Qur'an and the Prophetic traditions, as well as the teachings of his predecessors, he was the first to articulate with some precision the nature of the Shi'a Imamate. The Imamate is a divinely ordained institution for the continuous guidance of mankind invested in the family of the Prophet Muhammad. All Imams have inherited from the Prophet the *nur* or Light of God and along with it the *'ilm* or true knowledge of religion. This means that the Imam is God's representative on earth, with the authority to interpret the inner meaning of the Qur'an and to guide his people according to the circumstances of time.

The next principle formalised by Ja'far al-Sadiq was that the appointment of each Imam was determined by a principle known as *nass*, a function inspired directly by God. This enables the Imam to designate his successor and transfer the imamate to him spiritually at the appropriate time. Thus, for the Shi'a, in every age there is always an Imam in existence, whether he possesses temporal power or not, and whether he openly declares his imamate or conceals himself from the public. The consequence of this is that even if the Muslims are in disarray and the caliphate is appropriated by political authorities of the day, the office of the Imam continues to abide on earth in perpetuity.

Another principle laid down by Ja'far was the observance of *taqiyya*, that is, concealment or dissimulation of one's beliefs in times of danger, so that the community may not be endangered or persecuted. Clearly the practice of *taqiyya* was, in part, a response to the persecution suffered by the Shi'a under the Umayyad and Abbasid caliphs. Thus, by virtue of these four propositions of *nur*, *'ilm*, *nass* and *taqiyya*, the Imam Ja'far al-Sadiq enunciated a distinctive and coherent doctrine of Shi'a Islam that was quite distinct from the Sunni interpretation of the faith.[4]

Some years before his death in 765, Ja'far had designated by *nass* his eldest son Isma'il to be his successor as Imam. Isma'il seems to have won a large personal following of devotees, but according to some sources he disappeared by the time of his father's death. Others claimed that he died before his father's death, and a further group maintained that he went into hiding to escape arrest by the Abbasid authorities. As no one could be sure whether or not Ja'far had designated another of his three surviving sons, there was a split among his followers. A number of factions emerged from which two major groups eventually prevailed. One remained loyal to the claim of Isma'il and his descendants, and became known as the Ismailis. The other gave their loyalty to Musa al-Kazim, another son of Ja'far, and came to be known as the Ithna'asharis or 'Twelvers', since they believe in a line of twelve Imams. Their last Imam is said to have disappeared in a cave in Samarra, Iraq, around 874 while still in his youth, but the Twelvers believe that he is still alive and will return on the Last Day to restore true religion to the world. The Twelvers constitute the majority of the Shi'a Muslims today and are found mainly in Iran and Iraq, with substantial communities also in Lebanon, Bahrayn, eastern Arabia, Pakistan and India.

The early Ismailis

It is quite beyond the scope and purpose of our book to recount the long and complex history of the Ismailis. The interested reader can do no better than consult our main source, Farhad Daftary's *The Isma'ilis: Their History and Doctrines*, for a scholarly and comprehensive account of this branch of Shiʻi Islam. In the course of their history, the Ismailis themselves became divided into a number of branches. The largest and most prominent of these today are the Nizari Ismailis, a prosperous and culturally diverse community scattered across the world and led by their 49th Imam, Prince Karim Aga Khan IV. Although the Ismailis are at present a small minority of the global Muslim population, in the early centuries of Islam they were a major religious, intellectual and political force who exercised a decisive role in the shaping of Islamic history.

The early history of the Ismailis is shrouded in a great deal of obscurity. This is mainly because for more than a century after the disappearance of Ismaʻil, the son of Jaʻfar al-Sadiq, he and his descendants are believed to have remained in concealment. To avoid persecution, they did not openly claim to be Imams and used various pseudonyms to hide their identities. But in the early part of the 9th century, the whereabouts of one of these leaders, ʻAbd Allah the Elder, came to be known to the Abbasids. ʻAbd Allah fled to Salamiyya, a small desert town in Syria, where he settled down in the guise of a wealthy merchant. From this relatively safe enclave, he and his successors set about expanding the work of the Ismaili *daʻwa* or 'mission', one of the most remarkable religio-political movements in Islamic history. As we shall read in another chapter, Salamiyya has remained to this day an important historical centre of the Syrian Ismailis.

We know little about the evolution of the Ismaili *daʻwa* as it operated mostly in secrecy and kept few written records. What can be gathered from the available sources is that it first came to prominence in parts of Iran and Iraq in the ninth century as a radical movement for social and religious reform conducted in the name of Ismaʻil and his son Muhammad. At the head of the organisation was the Ismaili leader in Salamiyya, recognised by his followers as the *hujja* or chief representative of the hidden Imam. The active agent of the *daʻwa* was the *daʻi* (literally meaning 'summoner'), often a highly educated and motivated man whose task was to propagate the Ismaili cause and create conditions for an Ismaili state. All those initiated into the faith were bound to secrecy by an oath of allegiance and required to practise *taqiyya* or dissimulation to protect themselves. The faithful were assured that the long-awaited Imam would soon appear openly in the world as the *Mahdi*, the 'rightly-guided one', to deliver mankind from injustice and oppression, and inaugurate a new era of universal peace and brotherhood.

In the chaotic socio-economic conditions of the time, the revolutionary message of the Ismaili *daʻi*s fell on fertile grounds and attracted popular support from different communities and groups. The messianic aspect of their doctrines appealed to the Imami Shiʻa who, following the murder of the Prophet's grandson Husayn, had been expecting the imminent return of their hidden twelfth Imam.

The idea of a more just social world appealed to the lower and dispossessed social classes, especially the peasants and the bedouins. The intellectuals too were attracted by the Ismaili interpretation of Islam. In contrast to the legalistic formalism of Sunni scholars, the Ismailis offered a more philosophical and spiritual understanding of Islam based on an esoteric interpretation of the Qur'an. According to Ismaili doctrines, every verse of the Qur'an has an outer, exoteric (*zahir*) meaning and an inner, esoteric (*batin*) one. The esoteric meaning can be glimpsed by a means of symbolic exegesis called *ta'wil*, but only the Imam has true knowledge of the word of God. The Ismailis further developed an elaborate metaphysical and cosmological system of thought based on prophetic history and a cyclical conception of time. They also adopted an ecumenical approach to other religions and traditions by citing Qur'anic as well as Biblical scriptures and Greek philosophers to support their arguments.[5]

As was to be expected, the popular response to the Ismaili teachings provoked the Abbasid authorities and the Sunni clergy to denounce the Ismailis as heretics and accuse them of seeking to destroy Islam. The Abbasids intensified their persecution of the Ismailis and began to hunt down their *da'is* mercilessly. Anyone suspected of sympathising with their views was likely to be arrested and executed. Despite this opposition, the Ismaili *da'wa* continued to gather force in various parts of the Muslim world, especially Iran, Iraq, Arabia and as far as North Africa to the west and the Indian region of Sind to the east. Very few details have survived of the many early Ismaili *da'is* involved in these activities, which were conducted mostly in great secrecy. But their efforts were gradually crowned with success: by 909 the Ismailis had succeeded at last in establishing their own independent states in Bahrayn, Yemen and North Africa.

The most decisive event in early Ismaili history occurred in 899 when their leader, 'Abd Allah II, the future founder of the Fatimid caliphate, decided to end his concealment and make public his claim to the Imamate. He informed his senior *da'is* that he was not only the representative of the hidden Imam but in reality the Imam himself. He also asserted that he was the Mahdi foretold by the Ismaili *da'wa* for more than a century. The majority of his *da'is* accepted 'Abd Allah's evidence of his descent from the Shi'i Imam Ja'far al-Sadiq and recognised his imamate. A small number, however, seceded to found their own movement known as the Qarmatis. Henceforth the Qarmatis, whose power base was confined mainly to Bahrayn in eastern Arabia, became implacable foes of the mainstream Ismailis loyal to 'Abd Allah. The bitter divisions caused by his claims could not fail to alert the ever-vigilant Abbasid agents, thus making 'Abd Allah's security in Salamiyya highly precarious. He knew that the Abbasids had issued orders for his capture and that the Qarmatis were gathering a force to attack Salamiyya. 'Abd

Allah had no choice but to abandon his home and in 902 he set out for North Africa, accompanied by his son and a few other trusted companions.

As 'Abd Allah and his group fled to Ramla in Palestine and from there to Egypt, they were pursued all the way by Abbasid agents. The Ismaili Imam's ultimate destination was Tunisia where his *da'is* had succeeded in converting the local Berber tribes to the Ismaili cause and were on the verge of defeating the ruling Aghlabid dynasty. Passing through Tripoli in Libya, 'Abd Allah proceeded to the town of Sijilmasa in eastern Morocco where he settled for a while in 905. But the governor of the town, acting upon instructions received from Baghdad, placed him under house arrest. Destiny, however, seemed to favour 'Abd Allah, for in 909 the Ismaili forces succeeded in overturning Aghlabid rule and marched to Sijilmasa to liberate their Imam. Soon afterwards in January 910, 'Abd Allah entered the capital Raqadda at the head of his victorious troops and was publicly proclaimed as the caliph. He formally took the regnal title of al-Mahdi bi'llah for himself and the dynastic name of Fatimids for his family – in honour of Fatima, the Prophet's daughter and wife of the Imam 'Ali. Such were the dramatic circumstances in which the Ismailis came to establish the Fatimid caliphate in North Africa.[6]

The Fatimid Ismailis

The remainder of this chapter will focus mainly on the Fatimids, the third major dynasty of caliphs after the Umayyads and the Abbasids who sought to unite the Muslim world under their imperium. Some familiarity with Fatimid history is essential for understanding the rise of the Nizari Ismailis in Persia led by Hasan Sabbah. The Nizaris regarded themselves as the true inheritors of the Fatimid legacy and, as we shall see, their emergence can be traced back firmly to crucial political events in Fatimid Egypt.

The foundation of the Fatimid state represents outwardly the first great political success of the Shi'a after 300 years in the wilderness. Fatimid Imam-caliphs always regarded themselves as true successors of the Prophet Muhammad and as such the sole legitimate authority in Islam. Their primary goal was to extend their power from North Africa into the heartlands of Islam and challenge the Abbasid empire. But the early years of the Fatimid state were beset with many difficulties. The caliph al-Mahdi and his successors, al-Qa'im and al-Mansur, were concerned chiefly with consolidating their rule and subduing Berber rebellions in North Africa. There were also periodic naval clashes with Spanish Umayyad and Byzantine fleets seeking to undermine the new state. It was not until 969, during the reign of al-Mu'izz, that the Fatimids were able to gain control of Egypt. Here

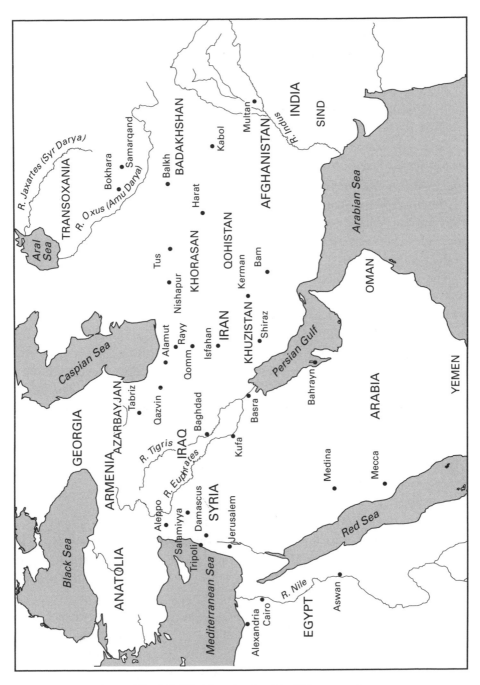

Map 1: The Middle East in the 12–13th centuries CE

they founded their new capital city of Cairo and embarked on a series of ambitious social and economic reforms. The prosperity generated in Egypt enabled the next caliph, al-'Aziz, to build a powerful army and navy capable of challenging both the Abbasids and the Byzantines for political supremacy in the Middle East.

The transformation of the Fatimid state into a major international power was quite rapid under al-'Aziz and his successor al-Hakim (996–1021). The empire reached its furthest extent during the long reign of the caliph al-Mustansir (1036–1094), extending westwards across the North African littoral from Cairo to Morocco, then eastwards through Palestine as far as Aleppo in Syria, and southwards along the Red Sea coast to Yemen and the holy cities of Mecca and Medina in Arabia. For a brief period in 1058 it seemed that the Fatimids would supplant the Abbasids when they occupied Baghdad. But as will be seen below, this victory proved to be at once the apogee as well as the beginning of the decline of the Fatimid empire.

The prosperity of Fatimid Egypt depended on two main factors, the river Nile and foreign trade. The annual inundation of the Nile has been the mainstay of Egyptian economy from time immemorial. Inadequate flooding of the river was invariably followed by food shortages and sometimes famine. This was the case for seven years during 1065–1072 when the Turkish troops plundered the countryside and people were reduced to eating cats and dogs.[7] The Fatimids had their own shipyards and naval bases at Alexandria, from where they were able to control most of the Mediterranean routes. The only other major sea-power in the region was, of course, Byzantium. Sicily was also a Fatimid dependency until it was lost to the Normans in 1070. The Fatimids established trade routes to India via the Red Sea and overland across the Sahara. As a result, they were able to import a variety of luxury goods from India and China as well as gold and silver from West Africa.

One interesting feature of Fatimid rule is that the Ismailis always remained a minority in all the lands they conquered and ruled. The majority continued to be Sunni, with smaller communities of Twelver Shi'i, Christians, Jews and others. In spite of their earlier avowed aim to spread their Shi'i faith, the Fatimids avoided imposing their beliefs on Sunnis or other subjects, and allowed them to continue their religious traditions without undue interference. The Fatimid caliphs made a clear distinction between the religious administration which remained in Ismaili hands, and the civilian administration which was run largely by other Muslims, both Shi'i and Sunni. Even Jews and Christians were not precluded from reaching the highest offices of state. In fact, the most capable and brilliant vizier of the Fatimids was originally a Jew, Ibn Killis (d. 991), whose long and distinguished service to the caliphs al-Mui'zz and al-'Aziz is confirmed in all sources.

The Fatimid policy of religious tolerance was not always easy to maintain as there was the constant danger of inter-religious conflicts between Muslims and Christians. On one occasion the caliph al-Hakim ordered the demolition of the Church of the Holy Sepulchre in Jerusalem. This church attracted great numbers of people from the Christian West to visit the places where Jesus had lived, preached and later faced death. Its destruction aroused much hostility in Europe and was later used as a pretext for the invasion of the Holy Land by the Crusaders. But contrary to Steven Runciman's assertion that al-Hakim forcibly converted Christians to Islam,[8] Heinz Halm maintains that there was no general persecution of the Christians. He explains al-Hakim's measure as an attempt to contain the rise of anti-Christian sentiment in Egypt because of their economic power and disregard for the *shari'a* or Islamic law. Halm observes further that al-Hakim was generally popular among both Muslims and Christians, and in the last years of his life he allowed the Byzantines to rebuild the Church of the Holy Sepulchre and encouraged Christian pilgrimages to their holy sites in Palestine.[9]

In any event, the enlightened policies of the Fatimids and the prosperity they brought to Egypt soon transformed Cairo into one of the great centres of artistic and intellectual life in the Islamic world. The Fatimid caliphs were generous in their patronage of learning, and established schools, colleges and libraries for the public. Additionally, the caliphs had their own palace libraries containing hundreds of thousands of books. The Ismaili thinkers of the Fatimid period were well acquainted with the Greek philosophical and scientific traditions, more so perhaps than in the Christian world. Scholars from all over the Muslim world were attracted to Cairo and the natural sciences, medicine and astronomy flourished, as well as architecture, poetry and philosophy.

The luxury and refinement of the Fatimid capital astonished every visitor. When the great Persian poet and Ismaili thinker Naser Khosraw visited Cairo in 1047, he was amazed by the high level of prosperity and the security enjoyed by its citizens. 'I saw such personal wealth there,' he records in his *Safarnameh* (*Book of Travels*), 'that were I to describe it, the people of Persia would never believe it.'[10] He goes on to report that 'the security and welfare of the people have reached a point that drapers, money changers and jewellers do not even lock their shops – they just lower a net across the front, and no one tampers with anything.'[11]

Although the Fatimid era is rightly regarded as a period of great achievement in commerce, arts and sciences, it is necessary to stress the importance that was attached to public education and learning. The Fatimids are credited with establishing in Cairo probably the world's first university. Founded in 970 as the mosque of al-Azhar (meaning 'House of Illumination'), it was transformed twenty years later into a university with its own curriculum, lecture halls and residences for teachers and students, all funded generously by the state. As a result, al-Azhar became the foremost Fatimid institution of higher learning, specialising in various religious sciences such as Qur'anic studies, theology and law. Admission was open to all, including women for whom special classes were organised.

Another important academic institution of the Fatimids was the Dar al-'Ilm (House of Knowledge), also known as Dar al-Hikma (House of Wisdom). Founded by the caliph al-Hakim in 1005, the Dar al-'Ilm specialised in the non-religious sciences, such as astronomy, medicine, mathematics, philosophy and logic. But we know little about the *majalis al-hikma* ('sessions of wisdom') which were organised in a section of the Fatimid palace exclusively for the Ismaili *da'i*s, since their content was regarded as of the greatest importance and to be jealously guarded from the uninitiated and unauthorised. It is very likely that Hasan Sabbah himself, the future founder of the Ismaili state in Iran, received some of his advanced education at this academy when he visited Cairo in 1078.

In the course of this work, I will often have the occasion to mention the work of the Ismaili *da'i*s. Under the Fatimids, the Ismaili *da'wa* or mission was a strictly hierarchical organisation. At the top was the Imam-caliph, believed by his followers to be a direct descendant of the Prophet and the vicegerent of God on earth, and as such the fount of all knowledge and wisdom – a very different concept from the authority of the Abbasid caliph. Each Imam was responsible for maintaining the cohesion and security of his community and ensuring the correct interpretation of the faith for his own time. Below him came the *da'i al-du'at* or chief *da'i*, who was often the head of the Fatimid judiciary. *Da'i*s of various ranks were assigned specific responsibilities in a part of the empire or territory elsewhere where missionary work was proceeding. The *da'wa* in each region, called a *jazira* or 'island', was under the control of a high ranking *da'i* called a *hujja*, meaning 'proof', that is, of the Imam. Officially there were twelve such 'islands', but the actual number is not really significant. There were two 'islands' in Iran, one based in Isfahan and the other in Khorasan, both of which were to play an important role in the Alamut period.

Great care was taken over the training of the Ismaili *da'i*s. They were required to possess an almost encyclopaedic knowledge of all subjects, including logic, theology, philosophy, history and geography. The *da'i*s were required to be skilled in argument, persuasive, perceptive, sensitive figures of authority and, of course, totally committed to their Imam and his cause. They often had to operate in disguise if they were working in unfriendly territory and resort to *taqiyya*, concealment of belief, in times of danger. One rare Fatimid treatise, composed towards the end of the tenth century, describes the qualities needed by a *da'i* in the following terms:

[T]he *da'i* must combine in himself all the ideal qualities and talents which may be found separately in people of different professions and standing. He must possess the good qualities of an expert lawyer because he often has to act as a judge; he must possess patience, good theoretical education, intelligence, psychological insight, honesty, high moral character, sound judgement, etc. He must possess the virtues of leaders, such as a strong will, generosity, administrative talent, tact and tolerance. He must be in possession of the high qualities of the priest, because he has to lead the esoteric prayers of his followers. He must be irreproachably honest and reliable, because the most precious thing, the salvation of the souls of many people, is entrusted to him. … He must have the virtues of the physician because he himself has to heal sick souls. Similarly he has to possess the virtues of an agriculturist, a captain of a ship, a merchant and the like, developing in himself the good qualities required in different professions.[12]

I have lingered on the education of the Ismailis *da'is* as it offers a fascinating insight into the aspirations and ethics of the Ismaili mission under the Fatimids. It is also illustrative of the kind of training to which Hasan Sabbah may have been exposed during his stay in Cairo, and which provided the model for the training of his own *da'is* when he returned to Persia and founded the independent Nizari Ismaili movement.

Emergence of the Nizari Ismailis

As we have seen, the empire of the Fatimids reached its furthest extent with the establishment of their sovereignty in Baghdad briefly in 1058. The troops supporting the Fatimid cause were expelled from the Abbasid capital a year later by the intervention of the Saljuqs. The Saljuqs were a militarised tribe of Turkish nomads from Central Asia who had invaded Iran in the early decades of the 11th century. In 1055 they entered Iraq and occupied Baghdad, overthrowing the Shi'i Buyid regime that had governed Iraq for a century and placing the Abbasid caliph under their own control and protection. This arrangement suited the Saljuqs well because the caliphate lent them legitimacy in the eyes of the majority Sunni population in the Middle East. It also enabled them to promote Sunni Islam as the state religion and to intensify persecution of the minority Shi'i communities, especially the Ismailis, in their domains.

The most renowned Saljuq sultan was Malekshah (1073–1092), whose territories spanned the huge landmass from Transoxania in the east to Syria in the west. In his governance of the empire, the sultan was ably assisted by his Persian vizier, Nezam al-Molk, who was by all accounts a learned and cultured man as well as a zealous champion of Sunni Islam. Both the sultan and his chief minister recognised that their foremost enemies in the west were the Fatimids of Egypt whom they were determined to crush. Hence, they mounted a vigorous propaganda campaign against the Fatimid caliphs as well as a major military offensive to wrest Syria from their control. At the same time, the Saljuq sultan intensified persecution of the Ismailis in his territories who were suspected, not without some justification, of collusion with the Fatimids.

For the Fatimids, the setbacks to their forces in Iraq and Syria were compounded by a serious deterioration in the internal conditions in Egypt. Mention was made earlier of the devastation caused to the Egyptian economy by seven years of famine during the reign of the caliph al-Mustansir. There was widespread hunger and disease in the population, followed by a complete breakdown in public order. The Turkish contingents of the Fatimid armies pillaged the land and fought against the Berber and Sudanese contingents. Even the Fatimid palaces were not secure from their looting which resulted in the destruction of parts of several libraries. In 1074 the caliph summoned his Armenian governor of Syria, Badr al-Jamali, to restore order, which he did ruthlessly, killing all the rebel commanders. After his victory, Badr al-Jamali was promoted to the two highest positions of state as commander-in-chief of the army and vizier to the caliph. During the next twenty years, he was able to reunify the army and restore Egypt to its previous level of prosperity. He was unable, however, to prevent the loss of most of Syria and Palestine to the Saljuq Turks. The remaining years of al-Mustansir's reign passed peacefully, but overall political authority had now passed irrevocably into the hands of Badr al-Jamali. The vizier even managed before his death in 1094 to pass all his functions to his son al-Afdal.

The caliph al-Mustansir himself died a few months after Badr, having already designated his eldest son Abu Mansur Nizar to succeed him as the next Fatimid Imam and caliph. Nizar was an independent-minded man of about fifty who resented the excessive military control over the state. Sensing his potential threat, the new vizier and military commander al-Afdal decided to impose his own candidate on the throne, Nizar's half-brother Musta'li, who was married to al-Afdal's sister. On al-Mustansir's death, al-Afdal arranged a ceremony in the palace where Nizar's younger brother al-Musta'li was declared the new caliph. The vizier maintained that al-Mustansir had changed his succession in favour of al-Musta'li. This *coup de théâtre* was completely unacceptable to Nizar and his followers, not least because they believed the Imam's *nass* or designation of his successor could not be overturned under any circumstances. Nizar fled to Alexandria where he received the support and allegiance of its citizens. But Nizar's revolt was short-lived. In 1095 al-Afdal's forces besieged Alexandria, captured Nizar and later had him executed or possibly buried alive.

These tragic events in Cairo shocked the Ismailis everywhere in the Fatimid dominions and beyond, splitting the *da'wa* between the Nizaris and the Musta'lis. From the time of al-Mustansir's death, the Fatimid state went into rapid political and economic decline. The new caliph al-Must'ali and his successors became completely subservient to the military authorities. In 1171 the Sunni general of Kurdish origin Salah al-Din (known to the West as Saladin, whom we shall meet again in this book) put an end to the Fatimid caliphate by imprisoning or killing the surviving members of the dynasty, and restoring Sunni Islam as the official religion of Egypt. In the chaos that followed, the great Fatimid libraries were destroyed and their countless books used as fuel in the streets of Cairo. As for the Ismailis of Egypt, many fled into exile, others perished in futile revolts in the provinces, and the remainder were eventually compelled to accept the Sunni faith.

As we have related, the unity of the Ismaili community was completely shattered by the dispute over the succession to al-Mustansir. Although eliminated from Egypt by Saladin (who subsequently established his own Ayyubid dynasty), the network of the Ismaili *da'wa* survived in other countries in one form or another. The followers of Musta'li continued their activities in Yemen and Gujarat in India, but became increasingly divided into small quarrelling factions. The situation was quite different for the followers of Nizar in Iran and other areas, for whom the murder of Nizar was a betrayal and violation of the most fundamental tenets of their faith. Coming under the leadership of Hasan Sabbah, the Persian Ismailis severed their relations with the Musta'lis and founded their own independent Nizari *da'wa*. At the same time, they embarked on a revolutionary path that was to leave a deep and lasting impact on Islamic history and beyond. The record of their struggle survives to this day in hundreds of ruined castles and fortresses to be found in the highlands of Iran and Syria. That story – dramatic and impressive by any standard – forms the backdrop of our study of Ismaili castles, which we must now consider in the following chapters.

Notes

1. W. Montgomery Watt, *The Majesty that was Islam: The Islamic World 661–1100* (London, 1974), p. 33.

2. Bernard Lewis, *The Middle East* (New York, 1995), p. 64.

3. Ibid., p. 81.

4. For more details see S. Husain M. Jafri, *Origins and Early Development of Shi'a Islam* (London, 1979), pp. 289–300.

5. For a detailed exposition of Ismaili cosmological doctrines, see in particular Henry Corbin, *Cyclical Time and Ismaili Gnosis*, trans. Ralph Manheim and James W. Morris (London, 1983).

6. A unique, first-hand account of the founding of the Fatimid state, the *Kitab al-Munazarat* by Ibn al-Haytham, has survived and was recently published as *The Advent of the Fatimids: A Contemporary Shi'i Witness*, ed. and trans. Wilferd Madelung and Paul E. Walker (London, 2000).

7. Daftary, *The Isma'ilis*, p. 203.

8. Steven Runciman, *A History of the Crusades*, Volume 1: *The First Crusade and the Foundation of the Kingdom of Jerusalem* (Cambridge, 1951), pp. 11–12.

9. Heinz Halm, *The Fatimids and their Traditions of Learning* (London, 1997), pp. 35–38.

10. Naser Khosraw, *Naser Khosraw's Book of Travels (Safarnama)*, ed. and trans. Wheeler M. Thackston, Jr. (Costa Mesa, CA, 2001), p. 72.

11. Ibid., p. 74.

12. Cited in Halm, *The Fatimids and their Traditions of Learning*, pp. 63–64.

PART ONE

The Rise and Fall
of the Nizari Ismaili State

A 19th-century orientalist representation of Hasan Sabbah

CHAPTER 2

Hasan Sabbah and the Ismailis of Iran

It was nearly noon on a hot day in the early summer of 1090. Mahdi, the lord of the castle of Alamut, was beginning to sweat a little. He had spent the last few weeks in Qazvin, a modest town some 60 km away in the Daylaman region of northern Iran. The purpose of his visit to Qazvin had been to talk with government officials about his plans to enlarge his castle and strengthen its fortifications. The castle had been built some 200 years earlier on one of the best defensive sites in the Rudbar highlands, and now it was in the hands of Mahdi in fief from the Saljuq sultan, Malekshah. While in Qazvin, he had received strict orders from the sultan's vizier, Nezam al-Molk, to arrest the Ismaili leader, Hasan Sabbah. The vizier had declared Hasan to be an outlaw and a villain now known to be hiding somewhere in Daylaman. Mahdi was determined to do his utmost to find this dangerous man and suppress his followers with all the powers at his command.

The lord of Alamut had arisen early that morning for the return to his castle so that he and his armed escort would not have to travel during the heat of the day. He was already past his prime and disliked travelling long distances on horseback. But today he quite enjoyed the long ride back to his castle over the foothills of the Alborz mountains. The track twisted and turned, rose and fell with the contours of the hills and valleys. Occasionally, Mahdi stopped to greet a few passing merchants and peasants, and ask them if they had seen any strangers or suspicious activities, a sight that might suggest the presence of Hasan Sabbah in the area. It did not seem long before they saw the great mass of the Taleqan range rising sharply before them in the clear blue sky. Soon they arrived at Shirkuh where the Taleqan and Alamut rivers join to form the fast-flowing Shahrud. This was the summer entrance to the valley of Alamut, and the escort rode through the clear blue waters that were only waist high. In winter it was impossible for any horse or foot soldier to cross the thundering stretch of water.

Once inside the gorge through which the track led, Mahdi felt more secure. The rock walls of the narrow opening towered up some 350 metres and guards, stationed at the fortifications built halfway up the rock walls, saluted their lord on his return. Having passed through the gorge, the valley at once opened out and on each side Mahdi noted with approval the well-tended fields of the peasants. There would be a good harvest and his garrison would be well supplied during the winter. His little party passed through the villages of Badasht and Shahrak, and after 15 km or so arrived at Shotorkhan. Here they crossed the river and climbed steeply northwards up to the village of Gazorkhan where directly ahead of them, firmly built on the outcrop of a great rock, stood the castle of Alamut, set proudly against the magnificent backdrop of the Hawdequan range. After a steep climb up the left-hand side of the rock, Mahdi and his escort rode through the imposing outer gateway of the castle, which overlooked a wide sweep of the valley.

After a pause for rest and refreshment, the governor and his deputy set off on a tour of inspection of the castle defences. To his surprise he found a number of new faces among the garrison and servants. When Mahdi inquired the reason for this, the deputy replied that quite a few men had been taken ill or had returned to their homes for various reasons, and so he had to employ others. Knowing that the lord intended to start rebuilding parts of the castle, he had also hired skilled men from neighbouring villages. Fortunately there had been no shortage of stonemasons and bricklayers to do the necessary work.

A sudden shaft of suspicion struck the governor's mind: 'Are you quite sure that these men are reliable,' he asked, 'and that they are not Ismailis connected with the accursed Hasan Sabbah? We must certainly have nothing to do with them. Before we know where we are, they will open the gates to him and seize the castle from us. I will not allow these people to play any tricks on us. Everyone knows that Alamut is the strongest fortresses in Daylaman and cannot be captured even by a thousand horsemen.'

Now that Mahdi's suspicions were thoroughly aroused, he ordered his deputy to arrest anyone in the castle suspected of associating with the Ismailis. 'In any case,' said Mahdi grimly to his deputy, 'the castle belongs to the Saljuqs and the mighty sultan Malekshah will never let these heretics take the castle.'

The capture of Alamut

The lord of Alamut had good reason to be fearful of Hasan Sabbah. But it was already too late. At the very time he was in Qazvin, Hasan was in fact hiding in another part of the town, finalising plans to take over his castle. Alamut was Hasan's obvious choice as the base from which to launch his revolution. The valley below the castle was fertile and its inhabitants were mostly Shi'i Muslims, including many Ismailis on whom Hasan could count for support. The castle itself was easily defensible, as it was located on top of a massive rock and surrounded on all sides by mountains. Since it was built, the castle had never been taken by military force. Legend has it that the site of the castle was first indicated to a local ruler by an eagle that soared above the great rock, hence its name 'Alamut', the 'Eagle's Nest'.

In the summer of 1090, when Hasan received word from his agents that all was ready at Alamut, he set out from Qazvin with the greatest circumspection. He knew very well that the vizier Nezam al-Molk had issued orders for his arrest. As a result Hasan avoided the direct route from Qazvin to Andej, but took the longer route northwards through Ashkavar and arrived over the mountains, by the back door so to speak. Hasan stayed for a while in Andej in the guise of a schoolteacher called Dehkhoda. Soon he was joined by a band of his most loyal supporters, whom he sent in small groups to Alamut, ostensibly to seek employment. Some of these men probably settled in the village of Gazorkhan just below the castle, ready to be summoned at short notice.

Finally, Hasan himself entered the castle officially as a teacher to the children of the garrison. Once inside the walls, Hasan and his men befriended the soldiers and converted some of them secretly to their cause. Mahdi's deputy himself was probably converted at some point and was waiting to help Hasan in his plan. The day arrived when Hasan was assured of significant support and minimum resistance from the garrison. He calmly went to Mahdi, revealed his true identity and announced that the castle was now in his possession. The governor was astounded at the so-called schoolmaster's impertinence and summoned the guards to arrest him, only to find them ready to obey the upstart and put Mahdi to the sword at his command. At that moment the governor came to recognise the true nature of the plot against him and that he had been tricked. The castle was lost to him and he was powerless to do anything about it. In his victory, Hasan was magnanimous. He allowed Mahdi to leave unharmed and even gave him a draft for 3,000 gold dinars as the price of the castle. The draft was payable in the name of Ra'is Mozaffar, a Saljuq government official and secretly an Ismaili, who later honoured the payment in full, much to Mahdi's astonishment.[1]

At first sight, Hasan Sabbah's capture of Alamut has all the qualities of a *coup de théâtre*. It appears almost incredible, even farcical. How could the governor allow himself to be so grossly deceived? But looked at objectively, this was a spectacular achievement that highlights many of the qualities of this remarkable man. To achieve success in such a daring operation, the leader must first ensure that the intelligence he receives from his supporters on the ground is accurate and up to date. He must have a superb sense of audacity and timing, the absolute loyalty of his followers and conviction of his own invincibility, plus more than his fair share of luck – all qualities which Alexander and Napoleon demanded from their generals. Hasan's coup must count among the most daring and successful feats of military history. He outsmarted the plans of Nezam al-Molk who was a highly intelligent man and fully aware of the dangers which Hasan posed to his government. Above all, Hasan achieved his objective without any bloodshed whatsoever. The qualities that Hasan demonstrated in this operation should make us aware that we are dealing with a totally exceptional man, who was to show the same qualities in the way he directed the Ismaili revolution for the rest of his life.

The early life of Hasan Sabbah

Unfortunately we do not know the precise details of Hasan's early youth and education.[2] The little information that we have comes from the anti-Ismaili Persian historian of the Mongol conquest, Juwayni. He preserved a few fragments from an Ismaili account of Hasan's life called *Sargudhasht-i Sayyidna* (*The Biography of our Master*), which he discovered when Alamut fell to the Mongols in 1256. This informs us that Hasan was born around 1055 to a Twelver Shi'i family in Qomm, a town of considerable antiquity and religious learning in central Iran. His father was apparently of Arab origin and had emigrated from Kufa to Qomm. Some years after Hasan's birth, his family moved to Rayy, an old city a few kilometres to the south of modern Tehran, where he received a traditional Islamic education.

It was in Rayy that Hasan was first exposed to the Ismaili form of Shi'i Islam through the influence of a man called Amira Darrab who cared for him when he was dangerously ill. Thereafter the young man sought out Ismaili *da'is* (missionaries) who convinced him of the truth of their doctrines. After his conversion, Hasan devoted his considerable talents to the Ismaili cause and soon attracted the attention of his superiors. In 1072, when he was about twenty years old, Hasan was introduced to the head of the Ismaili *da'wa* (mission) in Iran, Ibn 'Attash. He was much impressed by the young man's potential and sent him to the Ismaili centre at Isfahan for training as a *da'i*. After a few years of instruction, Hasan was ordered to proceed for further education to Cairo, the capital of the Fatimid empire and headquarters of the Ismaili *da'wa*.

As we have seen in Chapter 1, the politics of the Middle East in the 11th century were dominated by the struggle for supremacy between two rival dynasties: the Sunni Abbasid caliphs of Baghdad and the Shi'i Fatimid caliphs of Cairo. Both dynasties claimed the right to rule over the Muslim community and their armies fought for control over Syria. It was against this background of fierce conflict between the two powers that Hasan Sabbah set out for Cairo in 1076. He followed a long overland route, which took him from Isfahan to Azarbayjan and Kurdistan to the Syrian coast, and then by sea to Alexandria. The northerly route was undoubtedly intended to avoid passing through Iraq and Syria that were under Saljuq control. As the Saljuq authorities were on the lookout for him, Hasan had to be extremely circumspect and travel in disguise as a pilgrim or merchant. He narrowly escaped arrest once in Azarbayjan, where he became embroiled in a religious argument with local Sunni scholars and was expelled from their town.

Upon arriving in Cairo in 1078, Hasan found that the political authority of the Fatimid caliphs was already beginning to crumble. Egypt was just recovering from years of political and economic turmoil, caused by famine and rebellious factions of the army. As we saw in the last chapter, the Fatimid Imam-caliph al-Mustansir had then summoned his Armenian general in Syria, Badr al-Jamali, to quell the unrest and restore peace. This Badr did with ruthless efficiency, but he could not prevent the loss of most of Syria and Palestine to the Saljuqs. Badr's success was rewarded with his appointment as commander-in-chief of the Fatimid armies and as vizier to the caliph. These positions enabled Badr to emerge as the most powerful figure in the Fatimid state. When Hasan Sabbah arrived in Cairo, he found that while al-Mustansir continued to be acknowledged publicly as the head of state and Imam, all political authority was now effectively in the hands of Badr al-Jamali.

We know very little about the three years Hasan stayed in Egypt and whether or not he had the opportunity to meet the Fatimid caliph. Much of his time was likely to have been spent on his studies, probably at the 'sessions of wisdom' organised for Ismaili *da'i*s in the caliph's palace. But Hasan had a highly developed political sense and was fully able to perceive the political realities of the moment and the fact that Badr had accumulated all power in his own hands. It is clear that Hasan did not get on well with Badr and may indeed have clashed with him because of Hasan's support of al-Mustansir's elder son and heir-designate Nizar. The vizier favoured the caliph's younger son, the future Fatimid caliph Musta'li, who was married to his own daughter. When Hasan tried to mobilise support for Nizar in Alexandria, he was arrested and expelled from Egypt. But it so happened that the ship taking Hasan to exile in North Africa sank off the Egyptian coast and he managed to escape with his life. Eventually Hasan found himself in Syria whence he made his way back to his homeland.

Hasan's experience in Egypt and his friction with Badr al-Jamali may well have induced him to believe that the Ismaili cause was under great peril. The very survival of the Ismaili Imamate was under threat from the ambitions of the Armenian general. Hasan's suspicions were confirmed when, following the death

of al-Mustansir in 1094, Badr's protégé, Musta'li, was installed as the new caliph
and Nizar was murdered after leading a brief uprising. This was the reason why
Hasan took the inevitable step of severing all his ties with Fatimid Cairo and set
himself the task of founding a new independent Ismaili movement in Iran, loyal
to Nizar and his descendants – hence the name 'Nizaris' for this branch of the
Ismailis. (Since our book deals mainly with the early Nizaris of Iran and Syria, I
will refer to them in most cases as simply the Ismailis.)

Not long after returning to Iran in 1081, Hasan Sabbah began a series of journeys across the country to assess the conditions of Ismailis in various areas. When
the Saljuqs conquered Iran, the Ismailis were to be found in various parts of the
country. Their largest presence was in the northern and eastern regions, especially
Daylaman, Khorasan and Qohistan. Travelling through these areas over the next
nine years, Hasan would have experienced at first hand the oppressive nature
of Saljuq rule and the lawless behaviour of their Turkish troops. Most Iranians
resented the subjugation of their country and culture to 'the ignorant Turk' – a
term of abuse used by Hasan himself when talking of Malekshah. He shared their
hostility towards the Saljuq ruling class, which had expropriated large areas of
farmland for their own private fiefdoms and imposed extortionate taxes on the
inhabitants. Hasan was outraged by the harsh and repressive policies of the Sunni
rulers towards the Shi'i Muslims, in particular the Ismailis. He realised that his
community was in dire danger unless a resistance movement could be organised
against the Saljuqs. It was in these circumstances that Hasan began to look carefully for a secure base from which to mount his revolt.

By 1090 Hasan appears to have settled in the Daylaman region of northern
Iran and at once set about making his influence felt among the Ismailis in the
area, invigorating the local network of the Ismaili *da'wa* and asserting his own
charismatic personality. As we have seen, he spent the summer of that year living
incognito in Qazvin, from where he directed a number of his men to the highlands
of Rudbar in preparation for the capture of Alamut. Hasan could not have chosen
a better site for his headquarters. Set in the forbidding Alborz mountains, the
castle was remote and inaccessible for his enemies, and yet not too far away for
his agents to slip into the important cities of Qazvin or Rayy. It was strategically
placed, easily defended and a viable, self-sustaining economic area.

Consolidation and expansion

Having assumed control of Alamut in 1090, Hasan Sabbah's first priority was to
establish his authority in the surrounding area of Rudbar. He therefore dispatched
his *da'is* to capture all strategic places near Alamut and win the loyalty of the

local people. Then he set about strengthening the defences of Alamut as much as he could. The narrow base of the summit on which the castle was built gave him little room for major reconstruction. But he certainly buttressed weaker parts of the castle with additional walls and fortifications – archaeological evidence shows this. His workers dug deeply into the rock and constructed large storerooms lined with limestone in which he could keep great quantities of supplies to enable him to withstand a siege of many months. We know that when Alamut fell to the Mongols in 1256, the historian Juwayni was amazed to see the huge storerooms of the castle crammed with provisions that were still perfectly fresh. A thorough examination of these underground chambers, now covered by fallen masonry, would probably reveal many interesting artefacts. Hasan also cut a conduit along the whole length of the rock halfway up the slope and diverted a spring of fresh water into deep cisterns hewn from the rock on which the castle stood.

Hasan's next priority was the development of an extensive irrigation system covering the floor of the valley. The valley is approximately 40 km in length and varies between 10 and 15 km in width. The centre of the valley on both banks of the river is relatively fertile and contains sufficient arable land and water for irrigation to allow the cultivation of dry crops, such as wheat and barley, as well as rice fields. With the willing support of the villagers, Hasan introduced terracing of the slopes to ensure that as much ground as possible was available for cultivation. This terracing still exists today and it is not difficult to determine from the surrounding hills the well-planned agricultural system originally devised by Hasan and his followers. Hasan planted many trees in the Alamut valley, and even today the floor of the valley is green and pleasant, with an abundance of rice fields. It is reasonable to assume, therefore, that in Ismaili times there was never any shortage of food or water, and the great vaults of the castle would have stored sufficient supplies to survive a prolonged siege.

Primarily, however, Hasan relied on the natural geography of the valley for the castle's defence. Its remote position on top of a huge rock rising some 180 metres above the valley floor ensured that it could not be taken by direct assault. The only connecting link with the nearest town, Qazvin, was a dusty mule track, along which any enemy force must advance, betraying its presence as it moved by a cloud of dust. The western entrance to the valley itself is through a narrow defile guarded by sheer cliffs 350 metres high. The gorge, called Shirkuh, lies at the junction of three rivers: the Taleqan, the Shahrud and the swift-flowing Alamut. For most of the year, surging currents of water make it difficult to cross. At its eastern end, the valley is protected by the mountain-knot of Alamkuh, also known as Takht-e Sulayman or 'Throne of Solomon', where the Alamut river itself arises. The centre of the valley on both banks of the river is relatively fertile and contains sufficient arable land and water for irrigation so that dry crops, such as wheat and cattlefeed as well as rice fields, can be grown on flat land or terraced slopes. There are, therefore, abundant sources of food, which could be stored in the great vaults of Alamut and other castles in the valley if, as seemed unlikely, an enemy force should break through the outer natural defences of the valley.

It was probably after Hasan had rebuilt his castle and fortified the whole valley that he established the library of Alamut. In the course of time, the fame of this library spread far and wide, attracting even non-Ismaili scholars to consult its rich collection of books and scientific instruments. There was a steady traffic of Ismaili *da'is*, couriers and other visitors arriving at or leaving Alamut. Some of the travellers undoubtedly came for the purpose of study and would have spent many months or years in the great library. All the visitors would naturally have obtained the necessary permission and security clearance to enter the precincts of the castle itself.

The seizure of Alamut was the first step in Hasan Sabbah's revolt against the Saljuqs. Spurred on by Hasan's success, revolts flared up all over northern and north-eastern parts of Iran. Within three years the Ismailis had gained control of many strongholds in the Rudbar, Qumes and southern Khorasan, such as Sanamkuh to the west of Qazvin, and Tabas, Qa'in, Zuzan, Tun and Dareh in the highlands of Qohistan. We cannot know whether this was a spontaneous uprising or one carefully planned and coordinated by Hasan himself. But we do know that in many places the revolt was led by *da'is* appointed by Hasan and totally loyal to him. The leader of the Qohistani Ismailis, for instance, was Hosayn Qa'ini who had helped Hasan to seize Alamut and was then sent as a *da'i* to Qohistan. At this time Qohistan was the home of a substantial Shi'i community, including many Ismailis, seething with discontent against the Saljuqs. Under Qa'ini's leadership, the Ismailis went on to capture a string of castles and fortresses in Qohistan, making it their most fortified region in the country.

A clear pattern was now beginning to emerge in the uprising. The capture of strongholds was modelled essentially on Hasan's experience at Alamut. His basic strategy was to seize existing castles either by persuasion, subterfuge or force of arms, and from these firm bases to undermine his enemies by further political pressure. As a rule, the Ismaili *da'is* targeted those places where they had operated clandestinely for some time and where local Ismaili populations ready to support the uprising already existed. The majority of these places were in remote and mountainous areas where the garrisons could hold out against Saljuq expeditions sent to subdue them. After taking possession of a stronghold, the Ismaili forces would quickly proceed to reinforce its defences and consolidate their political and military authority in the surrounding areas.

The Saljuq authorities were at first completely taken by surprise by the scale and spread of the insurgency, and fearing that it could engulf the whole of Iran they began to mount a counter-offensive. In 1092, the sultan Malekshah, on the advice of his vizier Nezam al-Molk, sent military expeditions to Rudbar and Qohistan. At one point the Saljuq forces came close to recapturing Alamut when the garrison ran out of supplies, but was rescued with the help of reinforcements from neighbouring valleys. Hasan was so relieved by this outcome that he renamed his castle Baldat al-Eqbal, the 'City of Good Fortune'. Similarly in Qohistan, a large military expedition sent to storm the fortress of Dareh, near Mo'menabad, was forced to withdraw in disarray.

The Saljuq regime was greatly shaken soon afterwards when the vizier Nezam al-Molk was assassinated in his own court by a petitioner dressed as a Sufi. If this act was ordered by Alamut, as some reports suggest, then it must be counted as the first recorded use of assassination as a political weapon by the Ismailis.[3] But according to contemporary Saljuq historians, the vizier's murder was due to internal politics, instigated either by Malekshah himself or one of Nezam al-Molk's rivals, and conveniently blamed on the Ismailis.[4]

Whatever the case, the sensational murder of the vizier gave birth in due course to one of the most enduring legends in medieval Persian literature. It was first introduced to Western readers in 1898 in Edward Fitzgerald's version of 'Omar Khayyam's *Rubbaiyat*. According to this tale, the famous poet, philosopher and astronomer was in his youth a classmate of Nezam al-Molk and Hasan Sabbah at Nishapur in Khorasan. They were the best of friends and promised to assist one another on achieving success in adult life. Nezam al-Molk was the first one to attain high office as vizier to the Saljuq sultan and proceeded to keep his word by offering positions of power and influence to his companions. Khayyam declined the position, preferring instead a pension to help him pursue a life of leisure and writing. Hasan was politically more ambitious and demanded a senior position at the sultan's court, which was duly given to him by the vizier. But they soon found themselves competing for power. Eventually the vizier succeeded in disgracing Hasan who fled the country and found his way to Cairo, where he converted to Ismailism and plotted his revenge upon the Saljuq sultan and his chief minister.[5]

Needless to say, this fascinating story has been disproved by modern scholars on the basis of the simple fact that Hasan was thirty years older than Nezam al-Molk and could not possibly have attended the same school. Nor is there any evidence that Hasan spent his youth in Nishapur or had any contact with 'Omar Khayyam. Nevertheless the tale demonstrates the great fascination that the figure of Hasan Sabbah has exercised in the public imagination of East and West down to the present day.[6]

In any event, a month after Nezam al-Molk's murder, the sultan Malekshah himself died at the age of 37 without leaving a clear successor among his sons, thus plunging the Saljuq dynasty into a major crisis. Several Saljuq princes claimed the throne and a civil war ensued between different Turkish factions that lasted for well over a decade. As a result, all Saljuq attempts to destroy the Ismailis were for the moment abandoned.

Hasan Sabbah used the respite brought about by the Saljuqs' disarray to good advantage. Having made his own castle as impregnable as possible, he set about further fortifying the whole of the Alamut valley and surrounding areas of Rudbar. The inability of the Saljuqs to stem his growing power greatly alarmed the local Turkish *amirs* (governors) and Sunni *ulama* (religious scholars) of Rudbar. In 1093 they assembled a force of 10,000 men in Qazvin which marched against Alamut but were beaten back by the Ismailis in a pitched battle at Taleqan. Having subdued the local chieftains, Hasan now had his sights on capturing the large castle of Lamasar, strategically located about 40 km to the west of Alamut. He appointed one of his leading commanders, Kiya Bozorg-Ommid, to lead an armed assault on the castle, which was duly accomplished in 1096. The possession of Lamasar greatly increased the security of Alamut and the Ismailis, who now controlled the main routes through the Alborz mountains to the Caspian Sea. It also asserted the personal authority of Hasan Sabbah, who now came to be recognised by all parties as the lord of the whole of Rudbar and Daylaman.

Hasan's cause was further advanced with the seizure of the great castle of Gerdkuh, about 15 km north-west of Damghan in the Caspian province of Qumes. The taking of Gerdkuh is another example of Hasan's tactical genius and his readiness to employ diverse means, peaceful or warlike, to achieve his ends. Like Alamut, Gerdkuh was situated on a mountain spur and difficult to take by force of arms. Hasan had previously worked in the Damghan area before he went to Rudbar and made a number of important contacts there among the local leaders. Realising its strategic position along the main east-west routes between Alamut and Qohistan, Hasan devised an ingenious plan to take Gerdkuh. A government officer, Mozaffar (the same Ra'is Mozaffar who had earlier honoured Hasan's draft of 3,000 dinars for the purchase of Alamut) was to encourage his Saljuq superior, the *amir* Habashi, to acquire the castle as his own fief. When Habashi was won over to the idea and obtained Gerdkuh in 1096, Mozaffar moved with him as his deputy and quickly set about making the castle impregnable. It was only four or five years later, after Habashi died in the civil war between the Saljuq princes, that Mozaffar assumed full command of the castle and declared himself openly a follower of Hasan Sabbah. But before doing so, Mozaffar had taken possession of

Habashi's treasury that he had cleverly persuaded the Saljuq authorities to transfer to Gerdkuh. At around the same time, the Ismailis succeeded in capturing other castles near Gerdkuh, such as Mansureh and Ostunavand, thus establishing a strong military presence in Qumes.

Having consolidated his power in Rudbar, Qumes and Qohistan, Hasan Sabbah now turned his attention to the southern and south-western provinces of Kerman, Fars and Khuzistan. Here, too, the Ismailis acting upon Hasan's instructions captured several fortresses. Occasionally, they suffered reversals: some bases were recaptured by the Saljuqs, or they were killed or driven out of towns, as was the case in Isfahan, the Saljuq capital, where hundreds of Ismailis were massacred in 1093. Despite this setback, the Ismailis of Isfahan reorganised themselves quickly under Ahmad, the son of Ibn 'Attash who twenty years earlier had recommended Hasan for higher training as a *da'i* in Cairo. In 1100 Ahmad succeeded in gaining control of the two key military fortresses of Shahdez and Khanlanjan overlooking Isfahan. This he did peacefully, following Hasan's example at Alamut, after converting the garrisons to the Ismaili cause. Around the same time, the Ismailis seized a number of fortresses in the Arrajan area, on the border between Khuzistan and Fars. The capture of these strongholds well illustrates the boldness and resilience of the Ismaili uprising.

Hasan's revolutionary ambitions were not confined to the Saljuq domains in Iran, but reached out to neighbouring Iraq and Syria. He had sent the first Nizari Ismaili *da'is* from Alamut to Syria in the early part of the 12th century. Although they had some initial success in Aleppo and Damascus, they also met formidable difficulties. This was partly because the Syrian Ismailis had to contend with the fierce opposition of multiple forces, including the Crusaders eager to expand their rule into the Syrian interior from the coast (see Chapter 3). As in Iran, the Syrian Ismailis were often able to benefit from the breakdown of the Saljuq state by intervening directly in local politics and striking political deals with Turkish *amirs*. It was by a combination of these methods that in 1095 the Ismailis came to occupy their first stronghold in Iraq at Tikrit, north of Baghdad, which they held for twelve years before being expelled by the Saljuqs.

Insofar as Iran is concerned, by the beginning of the 12th century – that is, within a decade of capturing Alamut – Hasan Sabbah and his followers had succeeded in creating what amounted to an independent state of their own. The four main areas of their activity were Daylaman (including Rudbar and Alamut), Qumes in the north, Khorasan and Qohistan in the north-east, and the south-western regions of Khuzistan and Fars (see Map 2). The remote and mountainous terrain of these regions enabled the Ismailis to hold out in their strongholds for a long time against the Saljuq expeditions sent to subdue them. A distinctive, probably unique, aspect of this Ismaili state was its fragmented nature and lack of territorial continuity. But what is truly impressive is that, in spite of its disparate nature and subjection to regular military assaults, the state maintained its cohesion and singleness of purpose. The Ismailis could not have achieved this success without the strength of their faith and common cause that united them, as well as the dynamic leadership of Hasan Sabbah and his highly effective chain of command, which extended by way of his *da'is* all the way down to the ordinary peasants in the villages.

The great Saljuq offensive

When the Ismailis captured the citadel of Shahdez close to the Saljuq capital of Isfahan in 1100, it became clear to the two warring Saljuq princes, Barqiyaruq and Sanjar, that the greatest danger to their authority was posed by the Ismailis. The insurgents were growing bolder and capturing fortresses all over the country. In some areas the local Turkish *amirs* had become wholly dependent on Ismaili patronage for their survival and could no longer forward tax revenue. Even more troubling was their suspicion that the enemy had infiltrated their armies and government. The Saljuq princes became fearful for their lives, so much so that Barqiyaruk began to wear chain mail under his clothes. It was even rumoured that his brother Sanjar woke up one morning to find a dagger thrust in the floor by his bedside with a message warning him to desist from his attacks on the Ismailis.[7]

In 1106 the two Saljuq warlords decided to join forces and crush their common enemy once and for all. Their offensive – the most sustained assault on the Ismailis since the death of Malekshah – took various forms over the next ten years. First, the Saljuq authorities ordered a thoroughgoing purge of their military and administrative systems in order to eliminate all those suspected of being Ismailis. Several thousand people were killed in this operation, including many falsely accused by their enemies. Then the Saljuqs sanctioned the expulsion of Ismailis from urban areas, a policy that led to widespread killings of civilians, often in mob violence instigated by local Sunni authorities. The largest massacres of this kind took place in the two main centres of Saljuq power, Isfahan and Baghdad. Last but not least, the Saljuqs dispatched a series of military expeditions against the main centres of Ismaili power in Rudbar and Qohistan, retaking some fortified bases and devastating many areas of Ismaili settlement. This was the case, for instance, in the town of Tabas in Qohistan that was completely destroyed and its inhabitants slaughtered.

The most serious setback for the Ismailis came in 1107 when Barkiyaruq's successor, Mohammad Tapar, personally led a powerful force against the strongholds

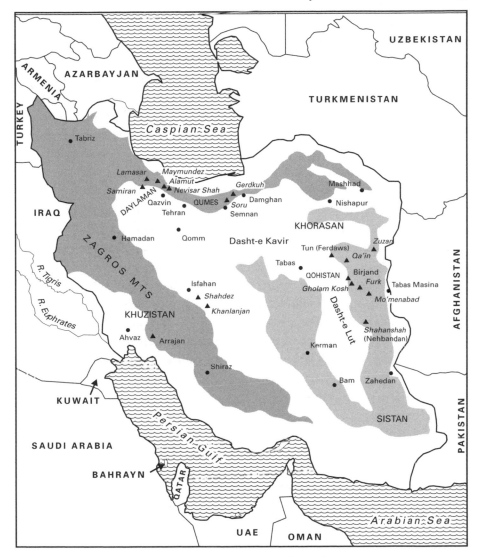

Map 2: Locations of major Ismaili castles in Iran

of Shahdez and Khanlanjan held by Ahmad ibn Attash. After several weeks of siege and negotiations, the Saljuq troops finally stormed the fortress, killing most of its defenders. Ahmad's wife is reported to have put on her best jewellery before leaping to her death from the battlements. Ahmad himself was captured alive and taken to Isfahan, where he was paraded in chains, flayed alive and beheaded in public. Having recaptured Shahdez and Khanlanjan, Mohammad Tapar made full use of his advantage by moving his troops south to Arrajan and retaking several fortresses there. The loss of these strongholds was perhaps the most serious military defeat suffered by the Ismailis, who were never again able to recover their strength in those parts of Iran.[8]

The Saljuq sultan now turned his attention to the main centres of Ismaili power in Rudbar, especially Alamut. From 1108 onwards, the people of Rudbar were subjected to repeated military assaults, which took many lives and caused a great deal of destruction. Juwayni tells us that the Saljuq offensive against Alamut was maintained for eight successive years. During the final siege in 1118, there was a great famine that reduced the people of Alamut to eating grass. The siege was lifted only when news arrived of the death of Mohammad Tapar and the Saljuq forces withdrew to prepare for his succession. Predictably, the ruling Saljuq family fell into yet another dynastic crisis, which offered the Ismailis one more opportunity to recover their losses and rebuild their defences.

Thus ended the last great Saljuq offensive to suppress the growing power of the Persian Ismailis under Hasan Sabbah. Despite their overwhelming forces, the Saljuqs were unable to deliver the final decisive blows against their enemies. The Ismailis continued to hold out in their strongholds with great tenacity and determination. Some of their smaller castles were taken and plundered, but as long as the fortresses in the home valley of Alamut stood firm, their power could not really be shaken. To a large measure, the failure of the Saljuqs was due to their lack of unity, increasing fragmentation of their empire and diminishing resources.[9] The recognition of this reality eventually persuaded Sultan Sanjar to come to terms with Ismaili power. He came to regard the Ismailis with some respect and recognise the advantage of negotiating a truce with them. So he appears to have reached a secret agreement with Hasan Sabbah, allowing the Ismailis to retain their territories, in return for their support in his campaigns against rival princes and other adversaries. In fact Sanjar was so keen to conciliate the Ismailis that he even granted them an annual subsidy from his treasury, permitted them to mint their own currency, and to collect taxes on trade and agriculture in some areas.

The achievements of Hasan Sabbah

Hasan Sabbah died in 518/1124 after a short illness at the age of about seventy and was buried near his beloved castle. Before he died, he appointed his commander at Lamasar, Kiya Bozorg-Ommid, as his successor. The change in leadership at Alamut encouraged the Saljuqs in 1126 to mount one more offensive on the Ismaili strongholds in the Rudbar and Qohistan. Despite all their efforts, the Ismaili garrisons held out in the castles and fortresses they had daringly taken. Sultan Sanjar was finally persuaded to recognise that a complete victory was unattainable and to accept Alamut as an independent power within the increasingly fragmented map of his empire. Accordingly he concluded a tactical alliance with Bozorg-Ommid, recognising each other's power and spheres of influence. As a result, there was a marked decline in military confrontations between the two sides. The truce was maintained after Bozorg-Ommid died in 1138 and was succeeded as Ismaili leader by his son Muhammad. In the following decades, a low level of conflict continued, with occasional cycles of skirmishes, reprisals and massacres, but by and large the Ismailis were able to enjoy a relatively high degree of independence and security. A number of fortresses that had been lost earlier to the Saljuqs were recaptured, additional ones acquired such as Mehrin and Mansureh in Qumes, and new ones constructed at Sa'adatkuh and Maymundez in the Rudbar. The suspension of hostilities has been characterised by Marshall Hodgson as a 'stalemate' between the protagonists,[10] but from the perspective of the Ismailis it amounted to a victory and vindication of their struggle.

By all accounts Hasan Sabbah was a most remarkable man who had outstanding skills as a political leader and military strategist. Possessing a charismatic personality, he was able to command the absolute loyalty of his followers and mobilise them for a life-and-death struggle for survival against the Saljuqs that became a regular feature of their lives. In pursuit of his goals, Hasan was undoubtedly ruthless at times and inspired the fear of his foes and friends alike. But Hasan was much more than a successful commander in the field of battle. Having sent his wife and daughters to reside in the fortress of Gerdkuh for their own safety, he is reported to have seldom come down from his living quarters and to devote much of his time to piety and scholarship. A man of ascetic temperament, Hasan insisted upon strict observance of religious duties and forbade his followers to drink alcohol. Learned in theology, philosophy and astronomy, Hasan's doctrinal works were well known during his lifetime. Unfortunately only a few fragments of his writings have survived to our time, derived mainly from a philosophical treatise on the necessity for a supreme spiritual guide (see Chapter 4).

Hasan Sabbah is one of those rare individuals in history who, on account of their exceptional personality and deeds, acquire a certain notoriety or mystique that is often difficult for historians to explain without falling into conflicting positions. Thus, for the anti-Ismaili historian Juwayni, Hasan was the arch-heretic and evildoer who deceived his followers to wage a war of terror against the entire Muslim world. The same point of view was echoed uncritically by von Hammer and other orientalists, who saw in Hasan a precursor of the modern terrorist, a diabolical schemer who founded a cult of opium-eaters and regicides to serve his own political ambitions. Hasan's detractors had much more success than they deserved, as it is only recently that we can justly assess what sort of people the 'Assassins' were. In modern scholarship, Hasan has come to be seen in a different light as a 'great patriot' and 'staunch nationalist' who fought against foreign occupation of his Persian homeland.[11] Hodgson, while noting Hasan's stern and ruthless character, was impressed by his personal qualities of intensity, rigour and self-denial.[12] For Daftary, 'Hasan Sabbah was an organiser and political strategist of unrivalled capability.'[13]

It is unlikely that Hasan ever envisaged a complete overthrow of the Saljuq empire, for which he neither had the military means nor the support of the majority Sunni population in Iran. Perhaps the closest he came to threatening the heart of Saljuq power was when the Ismailis occupied the citadel of Shahdez near the imperial capital of Isfahan in 1100, but as we have seen this victory was short-lived and resulted in one of their most serious setbacks. Hasan was a master of realpolitik and very capable of calculating the limits of his political and military ambitions. He clearly saw the Saljuq regime as a dangerous and pressing threat to the Persian Ismailis. There can be little doubt that his primary objective was to create a measure of territorial independence and security for his community. To the extent that Hasan succeeded, against overwhelming odds, in founding the Ismaili state in Iran and eventually compelling the Saljuqs to recognise it as a regional power, he may justly be counted among the highly successful revolutionary leaders of history.

Notes

1. Daftary, *The Isma'ilis*, p. 339.

2. Much of the existing material on Hasan's life has been summarised by Farhad Daftary in his 'Hasan-i Sabbah and the Origins of the Nizari Isma'ili Movement,' in F. Daftary, ed., *Mediaeval Isma'ili History and Thought* (Cambridge, 1996), pp. 181–204. See also Hodgson, *The Order*, pp. 41–51.

3. Daftary, *The Isma'ilis*, p. 342.

4. On the murder of Nezam al-Molk see Neguin Yavari, *Nizam al-Mulk Remembered: A Study in Historical Representation* (Ph.D. thesis, Columbia University, 1992).

5. Cf. Hodgson, *The Order*, pp. 137–138.

6. The most recent incarnation of the tale of the three schoolfellows and the myth of the Assassins generally is Amin Maalouf's novel *Samarkand* (London, 1992).

7. Hodgson, *The Order*, p. 101.

8. See Caro Owen Minasian, *Shah Diz of Isma'ili Fame: Its Siege and Destruction* (London, 1971), pp. 15, 62.

9. Carole Hillenbrand, 'The Power Struggle between the Saljuqs and the Isma'ilis of Alamut, 487–518/1094–1124: The Saljuq Perspective,' in Daftary, ed., *Mediaeval Isma'ili History and Thought*, pp. 205–220.

10. Hodgson, *The Order*, p. 145.
11. Minasian, *Shah Diz of Isma'ili Fame*, pp. 13, 62.
12. Hodgson, *The Order*, pp. 50–51.
13. Daftary, *The Isma'ilis*, p. 366.

CHAPTER 3

Rashid al-Din Sinan and the Ismailis of Syria

To most people in the West, Syria is largely associated with either events re-counted in the New and Old Testaments of the Bible or with the Crusaders and their castles. Damascus, principally for its association with St Paul, as well as Aleppo and perhaps Palmyra, are relatively well known, but few other Syrian cities.

Syria is a country that has always been fought over in the course of its long history. Owing to its geographical location, it became one of the great centres of the east-west trade, especially the trade in luxury goods and materials, including spices from India and China. Both Aleppo and Damascus became important junctions of caravan routes, while the port cities of Latakia, Tripoli, Beirut and Acre opened out to the Mediterranean. The old Egyptian kingdoms continually fought to increase their influence in Syria, which at that time was occupied by the Hittites. The Persians made Syria a province of the Achaemenid Empire (539–333 BC) with Damascus as the capital. Then came the Greek occupation with Alexander the Great. The Romans created the province of Syria with their headquarters at Antioch (now Antakya in south-eastern Turkey). Under Roman rule Syria became an important market for wine, grain and luxury goods. In 313 Constantine, whose new capital was then in Asia Minor, declared Christianity as the official religion of the Byzantine empire and Antioch became a major centre of the Eastern Church.

Syria was conquered by Muslim armies a few years after the death of the Proph-et Muhammad in 632, and later Damascus became the capital of the Umayyad caliphate (661–750). The city's magnificent mosque still testifies to the inspired achievements of the early ruling Sunni caliphate. In 750 the Umayyad dynasty was overthrown by the Abbasids, who established their capital at Baghdad which became under their rule the flourishing centre of a new world civilisation. Syria remained under Abbasid rule until 970 when it was occupied by a Fatimid army from Egypt. As we have seen, the Fatimids attempted in the following century to extend their rule into Iraq, but after taking Baghdad briefly in 1058 their forces were routed by the Saljuq Turks and thereafter driven out of almost all Syria and Palestine. The emergence of the Saljuqs as the dominant political and military power in the Near East brought them into open confrontation with the Byzantine emperors of Asia Minor. Their territories in Anatolia were invaded by waves of Turkish conquerors, and it seemed that the overland pilgrimage routes to the Holy Land would be cut. Alexius, the Emperor of Constantinople, tried to put an end to this threat by force of arms and at the same time secure his own dominions. But in 1071, the Saljuq sultan Alp Arslan inflicted a crushing defeat on the Byzantine army at Malazgirt (Manzikert) near Lake Van. The Emperor himself was taken prisoner and the frontier to Constantinople left open to the invaders. By 1080 the whole of Asia Minor was in Turkish hands and the pilgrimage route was permanently lost.

The advent of the Crusaders

In 1088 a new Pope, Urban II, was elected. He decided to call a conference of all the bishops, and among the delegates were ambassadors from the Emperor of Constantinople. At an appropriate point in the conference, they rose and appealed to Western Christendom for armed help against the Turks. The bishops were impressed and the Pope even more so. He at once realised the advantages to the Papacy of a holy war, a crusade against the 'infidels'. In 1095 he made his clarion call for Jerusalem and the Holy Land to be liberated. The first of the great Crusades soon set off and culminated in 1099 with the sack of Jerusalem and the indiscriminate slaughter of its Muslim and Jewish inhabitants.

Western Europe and the Pope, however, were not primarily concerned with the Saljuq threat to Byzantium or even the liberation of the Holy Land. The Pope's real reason was to divert the growing power of the barons and knights who had become a powerful threat to his own position. Probably he also saw in this an opportunity to reunite the churches of Rome and Constantinople under his own leadership. For most of the crusading knights and nobles of Europe who heeded the Pope's call, the prospect of acquiring booty and land was more important than the recovery of the Holy Land. Thus it was that a small number of the most power-hungry and hypocritical rulers of the time were able, in the name of Christianity, to wreak havoc in the Middle East for almost 200 years (1096–1291). Among the leaders of the seven Crusades there were some, such as Frederick II of Germany and King Louis IX of France, who made a serious effort to understand the Muslims and earn their respect. But the lasting historical legacy of the

Crusades has been a tradition of mistrust and deception which has continued to sour Muslim-Christian relations to our day.

When the first Crusaders arrived in northern Syria in 1097, they initially met little resistance from the Syrian citizens and their *amirs* since their activities were confined mainly to the coastal area. It was only much later that the real threat of the Crusaders was clearly perceived. After taking Antioch in 1098 and Jerusalem in the following year, the Crusaders established four Latin states in the conquered area based in Edessa, Antioch, Tripoli and Jerusalem. These principalities were collectively called Outremer, 'the land beyond the sea', and the Crusaders came to be known as the Franks, from the Arabic *al-Faranj*, denoting the French and the Europeans generally.

The Crusader success was largely due to the absence of unity and effective leadership among the Muslims after the death of the sultan Malekshah in 1092. The country was split by civil war and divided into petty states ruled by minor Saljuq princes, who were more concerned with preserving their fiefdoms than confronting the aggression from the Christian West. In her excellent account of the Islamic attitude to the Crusades, Carole Hillenbrand quotes a geographer of northern Syria, Ibn Shaddad (d. 1285), referring to the Muslim defeat as 'ignominious and unnecessary', caused by 'discord between Arabs and Turks' and 'mutual suspicion between the commanders'.[1] There was no one capable of organising real resistance against the European invaders until the rise of Salah al-Din (Saladin), the Sunni military general of Kurdish origin who had deposed the Fatimid dynasty in Egypt and seized power for himself. In 1187 Saladin destroyed the Christian armies at the Battle of Hattin and recaptured Jerusalem. But it was to take another hundred years before the Crusaders were finally driven from the Muslim lands

The Ismailis in Syria

The history of the Ismailis in Syria begins about the middle of the ninth century in the small desert town of Salamiyya. The reader will recall that the early Ismaili Imams had originally emerged in Salamiyya before establishing their Fatimid caliphate in North Africa, Egypt and Syria. Following the Saljuq conquest of Syria and the demise of the Fatimid state in 1171, the Syrian Ismailis found themselves in a highly vulnerable situation. No longer protected by Fatimid governors, the Ismailis lived in small scattered communities in the urban areas, where they were exposed to the hostility of the Saljuq rulers and the Sunni populations of the cities.

As with their Persian counterparts, much of the literature of the early Nizari Ismailis of Syria has been lost, largely because of the turbulent times in which they lived. The works that have survived are mostly from a later period, which contain anecdotal information about their forebears, including a hagiographic biography of their most famous leader, Rashid al-Din Sinan, compiled by Abu Firas who flourished in the 16th century under the Ottomans. In addition to these Ismaili writings, there are scattered references to the Ismailis in Sunni and Crusader writings, which enable us to piece together the early history of the Nizari Ismailis of Syria.

The first Nizari *da'is* arrived in Syria from Alamut in the early years of the 12th century, shortly after the fall of Jerusalem to the Crusaders. But the success of these emissaries dispatched by Hasan Sabbah was relatively slow in Syria for several decades. The Persian Ismailis had been successful largely because they had been able to seize castles in remote and mountainous areas. They had subsequently reinforced and strengthened the castles considerably, so that they became almost invulnerable to attack. Moreover, there was a fairly large number of Ismailis and other Shi'i Muslims in Iran who were strongly antagonistic to the Saljuq rulers and responded readily to Hasan Sabbah's cause.

The situation in Syria was very different. The *da'is* from Alamut were operating in a foreign country with quite different religious traditions and political conditions. The Syrian population consisted then, as it does today, of a mosaic of Muslim and Christian communities. Besides the Sunni majority, there were sizeable numbers of Twelver Shi'is, Druzes, Nusayris and others. The Ismaili presence was small and mostly loyal to the Musta'li Fatimid caliphs of Egypt rather than the Nizaris of Iran. The fragmented nature of Saljuq rule in Syria and the arrival of the Crusaders further complicated the political situation. These conditions could have provided fertile ground for proselytisation by the Nizari *da'is* coming from Alamut. The Syrian Ismailis were certainly ready to follow them, but the old Fatimid regime still commanded considerable support. Moreover, Hasan Sabbah seemed to many a remote figure about whom they knew little, and there was no bold and charismatic local leader who could capture their imaginative support. Thus, it would take the Ismailis several decades more before they were able to acquire and fortify the castles they needed in order to organise themselves on anything like the same footing as in Iran.

For the first thirty years or so of the 12th century, the Nizari Ismaili *da'is* confined their activities to the two principal cities in Syria, Aleppo in the north and Damascus in the south, sometimes with the connivance or willing support of the Saljuq *amirs* of these two cities. Their aim was to convert as many people as possible to their persuasion and then to acquire strongholds for themselves in the adjoining areas. The practice was by no means unusual in Syrian politics of the time. For many local communities and tribal leaders, both Sunni and Shi'a, the establishment of strong fortified positions was their best means of defence against predatory Saljuq or Crusader warlords. To this end, the Syrian Ismailis observed essentially the same tactics of insurgency as their Persian co-religionists, preferring to use peaceful means wherever possible, but not hesitating to take militant action when it suited their purpose.

For their initial phase of activities, the *da'i*s from Alamut selected Aleppo in northern Syria where there was already a large Shi'i population, including some Ismailis. The Ismaili leader Abu Tahir al-Sa'igh had cultivated the goodwill of the Saljuq *amir* of Aleppo, Ridwan, and received his protection. The Saljuq lord allowed the Ismailis to establish a religious centre in Aleppo and to preach their faith openly. As a result, Abu Tahir attracted a large following and was able to exercise some influence in the city's affairs. Ridwan's motivation in collaborating with the Ismailis is unclear. Was he secretly an Ismaili himself or using them as a convenient tool to serve his own political interests? Probably the latter because Ridwan's object was to use the Ismailis against his rival *amir*s in the country, especially Tughtikin of Damascus. Sunni historians attribute several assassinations carried out by the Ismailis to the orders of Ridwan himself, but which were more likely to have been inspired by other local forces.[2] Another factor that may have persuaded Ridwan to support the Ismailis was his fear of the Frankish Prince Tancred of Antioch, who was extending his territories steadily into the mountains south-west of Aleppo, the Jabal al-Summaq, and thus threatening the security of his own city.

These tactical calculations probably explain why Ridwan tolerated, or perhaps even encouraged, the Ismailis of Aleppo to launch their first initiative to capture a stronghold in the Jazr district of the Jabal al-Summaq. This was an audacious but abortive attempt in 1106 to capture the citadel of Afamiya, overlooking the ruins of the ancient city of Apamea first founded by the Seleucids in the third century BC. Afamiya was the ideal choice for Abu Tahir as it was populated mainly by the Ismailis. The castle itself was in the hands of an Egyptian governor appointed by the former Fatimid rulers of Syria. Ridwan had probably thought that the Nizari Ismailis were more likely to fortify the defences of Afamiyya and provide a strong bulwark against further encroachment into the mountains by Prince Tancred. But the Saljuq lord was mistaken in this. Tancred at first besieged the castle, then he permitted the Ismailis to remain in return for an annual tribute. But a few months later he changed his mind and retook the place by force. Abu Tahir was captured and managed to secure his freedom only after paying a large ransom to Tancred. Daftary points out that this was probably the first military encounter between the Ismailis and the Crusaders.[3]

Meanwhile in Aleppo, the Sunni inhabitants were becoming increasingly resentful of Ridwan's alliance with the Ismailis and demanded their expulsion.

The Twelver Shi'a too turned against the Ismailis after a wealthy Iranian merchant passing through the city was attacked by unknown assailants. Ridwan arrested and executed a few Ismailis but was reluctant to take any further action. The inhabitants of Aleppo then took matters into their own hands and massacred a large number of Ismailis, which Ridwan was unable to prevent. Following Ridwan's death in 1113, his son and successor, Alp Arslan, received strict instructions from the Saljuq sultan Muhammad Tapar to eliminate all the remaining Ismailis in Aleppo. The *amir* had no choice but to order the execution of Abu Tahir and over 200 of his followers, which prompted the mobs to resume their assault on the Ismailis. A small number managed to escape from the city and, together with other Ismaili refugees from Afamiya, made a desperate effort to seize the fortress of Shayzar while its owner was away. When the Sunni owner returned, he mobilised the help of local tribesmen and stormed the castle, killing all its occupants.

Following this débacle, the Ismailis transferred their activities to the southern city of Damascus, but here too their experience was very similar to that in Aleppo. The new Ismaili leader Bahram, another Persian *da'i* sent from Alamut, arrived in Damascus in 1126 and soon acquired a measure of influence with the Saljuq *amir* Tughtikin. As in Aleppo, the Saljuq lord allowed the Ismailis to operate in Damascus openly and later gave them the frontier castle of Banyas to guard against the Frankish kingdom of Jerusalem. But the Ismaili presence in Banyas was much resented by the local Bedouin tribes. Their relations deteriorated rapidly, culminating in a pitched battle in which the Ismailis were decisively defeated. Bahram was killed and his head dispatched as a gift to the Fatimid caliph Musta'li of Egypt. This setback for the Ismailis coincided with the death in 1128 of their patron in Damascus, Tughtikin. The Sunni preachers seized the opportunity to exhort their followers to rid their city of the 'heretics'. Contemporary chroniclers have estimated that in the general massacre that followed, as many as 10,000 Ismailis may have lost their lives and a number of them were reportedly crucified on the gates of the city.

It was now becoming clear to the Ismaili *da'is* that their strategy of establishing power bases in the cities was no longer tenable. Their reliance on the goodwill and protection of local *amirs* had seemed to work initially, but this was unacceptable to the Saljuq sultan, nor were the Sunni clerics in the cities prepared to tolerate the growing numbers and influence of the Ismailis in their midst. There was no alternative for them but to withdraw to the mountains of the Jabal Bahra (now called Jabal Ansariyya) in central Syria. The Crusaders had already made some advances in this region, which was part of the county of Tripoli, situated between the Christian kingdom of Jerusalem and the principality of Antioch. In 1132 the

Ismailis were able to purchase their first real stronghold, Qadmus, from the ruler of Kahf, who did not wish the castle to become the possession of a cousin during a succession dispute. The Ismailis then took Khariba from the Franks and in 1140 they captured Masyaf. At about the same time they acquired Khawabi, Rusafa, Maniqa (Maynaqa) and Qulay'a, although we are not sure by what means. Masyaf was often the residence of the chief Ismaili *da'i*, but it seems that Kahf, set in a less exposed position, was probably the real power base of the Syrian Ismailis. The possession of these strongholds enabled them to assert their authority over a large part of the Jabal Bahra and thus for the first time establish an autonomous homeland of their own in Syria (see Map 3).

In spite of this achievement, the security of the nascent Ismaili state remained highly unstable, as it was under constant pressures from the Crusader states on one side and the local Sunni *amir*s on the other. The most serious threat came from the Knights Hospitaller and the Knights Templar. These military orders were immensely powerful and they aggressively sought to expand their territories into the Jabal Bahra. The Hospitallers in particular, based at the citadel of Krak des Chevaliers (Hisn al-Akrad), were a law unto themselves, owing allegiance to none other than the Pope. The Ismailis sometimes retaliated in response to their threats, as in 1152 when Raymond II was struck down at the gates of Tripoli. This provoked the Templars to assault the Ismaili bases and force upon them an annual tribute of 2,000 gold pieces. But on the whole a truce or working agreement seemed to have emerged between the two sides, which permitted the Ismailis to retain control of the southern part of the Jabal Bahra.

The rise of Rashid al-Din Sinan

The castle of Masyaf is, of course, primarily linked with Sinan ibn Salman ibn Muhammad, better known as Rashid al-Din Sinan, and known in medieval European literature as the 'Old Man of the Mountain' (in Arabic Shaykh al-Jabal, a term never used by the Ismailis). Born in Basra around 1133 where he worked as a schoolmaster, Sinan was converted to Nizari Ismailism and then sent to Alamut for training as a *da'i*. Sinan became a close companion to the future Ismaili lord of Alamut and Imam Hasan II (see Chapter 4). In addition to his religious training at Alamut, Sinan also studied at first hand the military tactics and organisation of the Ismaili state in Iran. When Hasan II succeeded to the leadership of Alamut in 1162, he sent Sinan to Syria. Sinan first went to Aleppo and then to Kahf, where he stayed for some years and made himself extremely popular with the local Ismailis. When he was appointed by Hasan II as chief *da'i* of the Syrian Ismailis, he at once set about strengthening his position in the community. Sinan put an end to internal

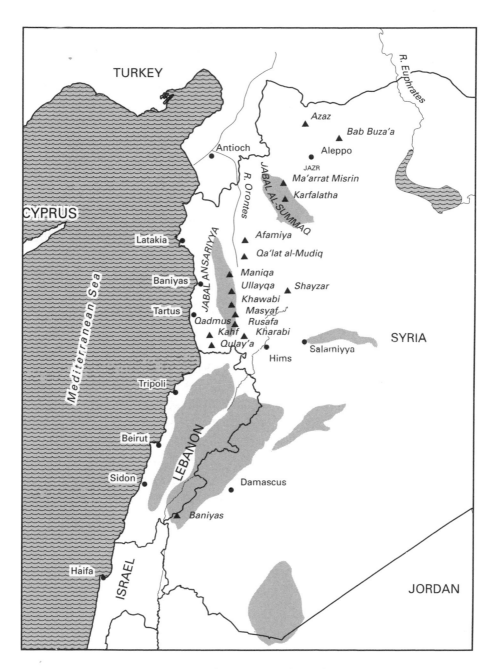

Map 3: Locations of major Ismaili castles in Syria

dissension among the Ismailis and evidently also organised his own élite corps of *fida'i*s. He rebuilt the fortresses of Rusafa and Khawabi, and captured or acquired new bases. Sinan also introduced an elaborate system of communication between the Ismaili strongholds, using pigeons and the exchange of coded messages.[4] Within a few years he was able to establish himself as the head of a united community and gradually began to assert considerable influence in Syrian politics.

Sinan was a shrewd and calculating leader who well understood the realities of the political situation of his country. His basic strategy was to consolidate the power and independence that the Ismailis already held, and to avoid as far as possible confrontations with the local Sunni tribes and the Crusaders. Like other chieftains in this volatile frontier region, Sinan became adept at exploiting the intermittent struggle between the various contending forces, supporting one or the other side as determined by the interest of his own community. By using a combination of diplomacy, threats and armed confrontation, he succeeded ultimately in achieving recognition and even the grudging respect of his enemies in Syria and abroad.

In the early period of Sinan's leadership, the Crusaders were a constant menace to his castles in the Jabal Bahra. The disposition of the rival Ismaili and Crusader strongholds led to frequent skirmishes between the two sides. The main Frankish castles in this area were Margat on the coast, Chastel Blanc and Krak des Chevaliers, all south of the chief Ismaili castles at Masyaf and Kahf. There were no fixed frontlines between the territories controlled by the two sides. The situation must have been constantly fluid, depending on whether an informal truce was in force or not. There certainly were some clashes, for example when the Ismailis captured the castle of Ullayqa from the Hospitallers, and there were frequent skirmishes with the Franks over the possession of Maniqa and other strongholds.

In spite of such frictions, Sinan made a serious effort to negotiate peaceful relations with the Franks. Around 1173, he sent an embassy to King Amalric I of Jerusalem, seeking a suspension of hostilities and the cancellation of his annual tribute to the Templars. Amalric responded favourably and agreed to cancel the tribute, but the Grand Master of the Templars was not pleased and ordered the assassination of the Ismaili emissary on his return journey. The Frankish king was so angered by this act that he personally arrested the murderer and conveyed his apologies to Sinan.[5] In any case, Amalric died in the following year before a proper peace treaty could be concluded. History, unfortunately, does not relate in any detail the negotiations that took place between the Ismailis and the Crusaders. Sinan seems to have had a certain respect for his Christian protagonists, but Daftary totally rejects the allegation of Archbishop William of Tyre that Sinan's ambassador had requested Amalric for Christian missionaries to convert the

Ismailis.[6] In all likelihood, the King of Jerusalem misunderstood Sinan's expression of Muslim reverence for Jesus as evidence of his desire for conversion.[7]

Sinan and Saladin

Perhaps there is no better illustration of Sinan's military and diplomatic genius than his response to the invasion of Syria by Saladin, who ended Fatimid rule in Egypt and was a zealous opponent of the Ismailis. Having established his Ayyubid rule in Egypt, Saladin was now the strongest Muslim leader in the region. He was determined to unite all Muslims under the single faith of Sunni Islam and set about extending his power into Arabia, Syria and Iraq. Standing in his way in Syria were the Crusaders, the Ismailis and the local Zangid rulers of Mosul and Aleppo. After capturing Damascus and Homs, he commenced the siege of Aleppo in 1174. Meanwhile the Zangids and the Ismailis made common cause in the face of the threat posed by Saladin. The regent and ruler of Aleppo, Gumushtigin, sent urgent messages to Sinan offering him many rewards and concessions for eliminating Saladin. Sinan appears to have complied, recognising that Saladin posed a more immediate threat to the Ismailis than the Crusaders. Two attempts were made on Saladin's life in 1175–76. In the first, he escaped unscathed and in the second he only received superficial wounds because of the armour he wore at the time. Bernard Lewis relates that after the second attempt, Saladin took stringent precautions by 'sleeping in a specially constructed wooden tower, and allowing no one whom he did not know personally to approach him.'[8]

Saladin now marched against the Ismaili territories in the Jabal Bahra, determined on revenge. In 1176, after ravaging Ismaili lands, Saladin laid siege to Sinan's headquarters at Masyaf. But astonishingly, for reasons not at all clear to us, within a few days he promptly lifted the siege and withdrew his forces. Several explanations have been offered for this remarkable turn of events. Masyaf was indeed strongly defended, but the strength of its defences cannot have been the sole reason for Saladin's withdrawal. Some sources suggest that Saladin, already unnerved by the previous attempts on his life, was so terrified of finding a dagger planted in his bedroom that he lost heart for the siege. Other sources suggest that Saladin's forces were more urgently needed to fight the Crusaders in Lebanon, or that his uncle, the prince of Hama, only 50 km from Masyaf, fearing for his own life and lands, appealed for a truce. There is also an Ismaili legend, reported by Hodgson, that Sinan used his mystical powers to immobilise Saladin's troops from a distance and to enter his tent without being detected by the guards![9]

Be that as it may, an agreement of some sort was certainly concluded between Sinan and Saladin, and relations between them remained quite cordial thereafter.

Perhaps both of them realised that the expulsion of the foreign invaders was to their mutual advantage and should take priority over all other considerations. As a result, they refrained from attacking each other's forces and in all probability collaborated against their common Crusader enemies. Some Ismaili sources report that in 1187 Sinan dispatched a special contingent of his *fida'is* to support Saladin in his historic victory over the Crusader forces at the Battle of Hattin, about 65 miles north of Jerusalem. A number of Frankish leaders taken prisoner were subsequently held in the Ismaili castles pending negotiations for their ransom.[10]

There are also certain hints of collusion between Sinan and Saladin in the dramatic assassination of the Marquis Conrad of Montferrat on the night before his coronation as King of Jerusalem in 1192. Some Sunni sources say that the act was carried out by Sinan's *fida'is* disguised as Christian monks. But under torture the murderers said that the English King Richard I had been behind the killing. Whether or not this is true we do not know, but Richard was certainly in Palestine at this time at the head of the Third Crusade. The English king was determined to install his protégé, Henry of Champagne, as King of Jerusalem in place of Conrad, which is exactly what transpired. But according to Ibn al-Athir, the famous Arab historian, the real instigator of the plot was Saladin who wanted both kings to be eliminated in order to undermine the Crusader occupation.[11] At any rate, following this event Sinan received many favours from Saladin, and when King Richard signed a truce with Saladin in 1192, Saladin insisted that the Ismaili territories be included in the peace treaty.

The sensational murder of Conrad had an immense impact on the Crusaders and European monarchs alike, and it contributed much to the formation of the Assassin myths in medieval Europe. As Daftary observes, several European kings began to accuse each other of conspiring with the 'Old Man of the Mountain' to carry out political murders on their behalf. It was alleged that the German Emperor Frederick II had used Ismaili *fida'is* to murder Duke Ludwig of Bavaria in 1231. The English King Richard I was similarly accused of plotting with Sinan to eliminate King Augustus of France. Needless to say, there is no basis for these allegations, although there is some documentary evidence to show that Sinan and his successors almost certainly sought to open channels of communication with various European monarchs to earn recognition of their independence.

For Conrad's successor as King of Jerusalem, Henry of Champagne, however, the establishment of peaceful relations with the Ismailis was now a necessity – not least because Henry believed he owed his position to Sinan. In 1194 Henry passed through the Ismaili territories on his way to Antioch and was escorted to the castle of Kahf, where he reportedly met the 'Old Man' himself. The Christian chronicler Arnold of Lübeck records that Sinan entertained the Crusader king lavishly and presented him with handsome gifts. He further reports that, in order to impress his visitors with a demonstration of his power, Sinan ordered a number of his *fida'i*s to leap down from the high battlements of the castle and give up their lives. This legend captured the imagination of medieval Europe and was later recycled by Marco Polo with Hasan Sabbah as the 'Old Man of the Mountains'; in some versions Henry of Champagne is replaced by the German Emperor Frederick II. Many such legends about the so-called Assassins were fabricated, embellished and brought back to Europe by the returning Crusaders. In any event, if Henry did visit the castle of Kahf, the Ismaili leader he met could not have been Sinan, since he died a year or two earlier in 1192 or 1193 and was succeeded by his deputy Abu Mansur.

Like Hasan Sabbah, Rashid al-Din Sinan was certainly a man of outstanding personality who demanded and received complete loyalty from his followers. Despite being lame in one leg, he is said to have moved freely between his castles and mingled with his people without a personal bodyguard. Sinan was well versed in the religious sciences and philosophy, as well as astronomy and alchemy, most of which he probably learnt or mastered at Alamut. In later Syrian Ismaili literature, he is described in almost mythological light as a heroic and saintly figure with supernatural powers, including telepathy, clairvoyance and communing with spirits. The same sources also portray him in very human terms as a kind and honourable man, fond of children, considerate to animals, and among his guests very careful to maintain the traditional Arab norms of propriety and hospitality.[12]

In his early years as leader of the Syrian Ismailis, Sinan had kept in close contact with the headquarters at Alamut, but as the years passed and his own power increased, he began to assert his independence from Alamut. There is no doubt that Sinan's spiritual allegiance always remained with the Nizari Ismailis of Alamut, but by the end of his life the Syrian domain of the Ismaili state had become a virtually autonomous region and there was little, if any, direct intervention from Alamut into Syrian affairs. Apart from Sinan's own character, the great distance between Alamut and Masyaf, as well as the complex and very different political dynamics of Syria, made it quite impossible for the Persians to exercise direct control over the affairs of their Syrian co-religionists. Sinan continues to be greatly honoured by Syrian Ismailis today, and his tomb at Kahf is visited regularly by the faithful as a mark of their respect.

Sinan's lasting achievement was to secure the future of the Syrian Ismailis at a time of great political upheaval and foreign invasions, which presented his community with unpredictable and dangerous challenges. As Daftary has observed, the tactical alliances Sinan struck with his opponents, whether Christian or Muslim, demonstrate his mastery of political strategy and the art of diplomacy.[13]

The cordial relations Sinan established with Saladin continued long after their deaths. The Ayyubid rulers of Syria who succeeded Saladin allowed the Ismailis to retain their castles, and supported them militarily in resisting the Crusaders. This contributed much to their security and there are no further accounts of major conflicts between the Ismailis and the local Sunnis.

Relations between the Ismailis and the Crusaders were also by and large peaceful, although there were occasional conflicts. By virtue of their close proximity to the Crusader states and the need to protect their own interests, the Ismailis were sometimes drawn into feuds between different Latin states. This was the case in particular with the Frankish leader of Antioch, Bohemond IV, who had incurred the enmity of the Templars and Hospitallers, and was also a constant threat to the Ismailis. In 1213 Bohemond's son, Raymond, was assassinated in the cathedral of Tortosa. The murder was probably ordered by the Templars, but Bohemond blamed the Ismailis for it and besieged their castle of Khawabi. It is indicative of the complex shifting politics of the region at this time that the Ismaili garrison was rescued by Sunni forces dispatched by the Ayyubid rulers of Aleppo and Damascus, and the Prince of Antioch was forced to withdraw. In 1230 the Ismailis even joined the Hospitallers, their erstwhile enemies, in a campaign against Bohemond. Pope Gregory IX was so disturbed by this unorthodox alliance that he issued an edict forbidding the military orders from associating with those he called the 'Assassins, the enemies of God, and the Christians'.[14]

Despite the Pope's injunction, it seems that relations between the Syrian Ismailis and the Crusader military orders were far more extensive and complex than has been acknowledged. According to James Wasserman, there is 'a rich tradition of historical suppositions' that maintains that the Knights Templar were greatly influenced by the sophisticated religious doctrines and organisation of the Ismailis. The returning Crusaders brought these ideas to Europe, where they are are believed to have become the basis for the revival of certain esoteric traditions in the late medieval era and which have survived to the present day.[15]

In the early part of the 13th century, the Syrian Ismailis appeared to have enjoyed a great deal of autonomy and they did not hesitate to use their fearsome reputation to demand tribute from both Muslim and Christian rulers. The most astonishing example of this is given by the French chronicler Jean de Joinville, who relates how a group of Ismaili emissaries approached the French King Louis IX after his arrival in Palestine in 1250 at the head of the Seventh Crusade and respectfully demanded an annual tribute. They boasted of receiving similar largesse from the Holy Roman Emperor of Germany, the King of Hungary and the Sultan of Egypt. Although this demand was not met, the French king and the Ismaili leader of the time, Taj al-Din, appeared to have established a cordial relationship.

King Louis sent an envoy, the Arabic-speaking friar Yves le Breton, to meet the Ismaili leader and exchange gifts. Sinan is even reported to have engaged in discussions of religious matters with him. Some of these meetings may well have taken place at Masyaf, where there is an inscription to Taj al-Din dated February or March 1249. Joinville himself collected some information about the Ismailis and remarked that their numbers could not be accurately assessed, 'for they dwelt in the kingdoms of Jerusalem, Egypt and throughout all the lands of the Saracens and Infidels'.[16] But we have a more realistic estimate from Archbishop William of Tyre, the earliest and most reliable of the Crusader historians. He reports that the Syrian Ismailis possessed ten fortresses and 'their number, as we have often heard, is 60,000 or possibly more'[17] – which is more or less the same size of the Ismaili community in Syria today.

Notes

1. Carole Hillenbrand, *The Crusades: The Islamic Perspective* (Edinburgh, 1999), p. 59.
2. Nasseh Ahmad Mirza, *Syrian Ismailism* (London, 1997), pp. 8–9.
3. Daftary, *The Isma'ilis*, p. 359.
4. Mirza, *Syrian Ismailism*, p. 27.
5. James Wasserman, *The Templars and the Assassins: The Militia of Heaven* (Rochester, VT, 2001), pp. 182–183.
6. Daftary, *The Isma'ilis*, p. 398.
7. Mirza, *Syrian Ismailism*, p. 38.
8. Lewis, *The Assassins*, p. 114.
9. Hodgson, *The Order*, p. 196.
10. Mirza, *Syrian Ismailism*, p. 35.
11. Daftary, *The Assassin Legends*, p.73.
12. Hodgson, *The Order*, pp. 193–197.
13. Daftary, 'The Ismailis and the Crusaders,' in *The Crusades and the Military Orders: Expanding the Frontiers of Medieval Latin Christianity*, ed. Z. Hunyadi and J. Laszlovszky (Budapest, 2001), pp. 21–41, at p. 30.
14. Ibid., p. 31.
15. Wasserman, *The Templars and the Assassins*, p. 149.
16. Cited in Daftary, *The Assassin Legends*, p.82.
17. Ibid., p. 70.

CHAPTER 4

Organisation and Ethos of the Ismaili State

Alamut is nowadays a peaceful, sleepy valley and it is difficult to imagine how it must have looked at the time of Hasan Sabbah. Many a traveller making the long journey to Alamut for the first time across the burning deserts of central Iran would have wondered about the castle: would it be imposing, majestic or awe-inspiring? From a distance, the height of the great bluff on which the castle stands would have made it appear smaller than it actually was. But as he came nearer, the weary traveller would soon have sensed the immense power that the castle represented, the abode and power centre of one of the most remarkable men of his time in Iran, revered by his followers and feared by his enemies in equal measure. The great height of the sheer rock crowned by squat powerful walls and towers could not have failed to produce a feeling of awe. The visitor would have marvelled at the strength and power of its fortifications. As he climbed upwards past strong defences at every point on the rock, which could have concealed an attacking force, the impression of impregnability would have increased.

Life inside Alamut

The living quarters of Hasan Sabbah and his men were small, austere and un-pretentious. The food was simple and the drinking of wine was forbidden to the garrison. The more imposing buildings were probably the mosque and the library. There were few, if any, women living in the castle. Hasan had sent his wife and daughters to the fortress of Gerdkuh, which was built at a much lower altitude and afforded more secure accommodation. The wives and children of the garrison would most probably have lived in the village of Gazorkhan at the foot of Alamut or in Shotorkhan, about 5 km away. The castle itself and the defensive walls would be filled with armed soldiers. A maze of passages and stairways would have led to the underground chambers dug deep down inside the rock.

Glancing down at the floor of the valley, the visitor would see a heavily forti-fied and fertile valley with terraced fields of rice, wheat, fruit and other crops on both sides of the river. All the villages in the valley would have had a good water supply for domestic and agricultural use. When I first visited Gazorkhan in 1959, its *hamam* (public bathhouse) was and still is in operation every day for men and two afternoons a week for women, and primitive though it is, almost certainly existed at the time of Hasan Sabbah. At this time the valley was far more wooded than it is today and wood was freely available for building, firing kilns and other purposes. These villages would certainly have played a large part in the running of Alamut, providing for the needs of the garrison, assisting in the building and construction work at the castle, as well as making and washing clothes, furniture, bedding, cooking equipment and everything else that was needed. Some villages had special occupations, such as constructing and working the pottery kilns at Andej or minting the silver *dinar*s used for commercial transactions within the Ismaili areas.

Life inside the castle would have been spartan and uncomfortable at the best of times. In winter the temperatures are always icy, with freezing gales blowing down from the snowy peaks of the Hawdeqan Range, surrounding the valley. In spite of the altitude, the summer months are hot and dusty, requiring the great-est vigilance for attacking forces. The castle itself would have been the centre of continuous activity in all seasons. The water channels and cisterns had to be kept clean, the armourers were busy forging new weapons, the carpenters and masons constructing or maintaining mangonels, or repairing and enlarging the defences. The cooks were busy in the kitchens, replenishing the food stores and keeping them in good order. Study, learning and discussion filled the day for many, espe-cially for those who aspired to become *da'i*s. The basic problem of Alamut castle, however, is one of space. The castle is just too small. Where could all this activity have taken place?

The answer probably is that the main castle area was used almost exclusively by Hasan, his close associates and principal guests. The library would probably have been in this area, as well as the mosque, the mint and a few meeting rooms or classrooms. The onion-shaped eastern edge of the castle was probably used basically for stabling, quarters for the garrison and storage of food and other sup-plies for immediate needs. There was probably a *madrasa* for the education of the garrison's children at the foot of the castle rock, facing the village of Gazorkhan. This area is quite large and now consists of well-watered terraces of fruit trees. Some houses have been constructed recently, looking straight across a narrow valley at the face of the great rock. It would have made good sense to keep the main castle area in times of peace strictly reserved for the Ismaili leadership and their immediate officials, guests of distinction, the mosque, the library and essential supplies, in addition to the underground storage systems. The flat area at the foot of the rock would have provided accommodation for additional guests and officials. The whole village of Gazorkhan would have been fortified as part of the castle complex for, as we have seen, it provided residence for the garrison's families as well as their principal source of food supplies.

Some travellers, especially those from afar needing rest from their arduous journeys, may well have been required to stay two or three days in the village of Gazorkhan before being admitted to the castle. I have been shown, especially on my earlier visits, shards of glazed and unglazed pottery, weapons, rings, coins, even a phial containing some gold which the villagers assured me had been found in the castle. Some genuine artefacts of the Ismaili period are sometimes washed down from the top of the castle by winter rains, but the objects I was shown were probably found in the village itself, where it is still possible to see remnants of broken pottery, probably dating from the 16th century when the site of Alamut was used by the Safavids as a state prison.

Our account of life at Alamut is based on historical data and archaeological evidence of the castle that I have gathered during my own expeditions. The same pattern is likely to have been replicated in the other great fortresses of the Ismailis, such as Maymundez, Gerdkuh and Qa'in. In the Syrian castles, too, the garrisons would have spent much of their time in general maintenance and defensive work. But there is also the alternative account of the Venetian traveller Marco Polo that was accepted by many as fact until recently.

As is well-known, Marco Polo is supposed to have undertaken a long journey to the court of the Mongol ruler Kublai Khan in the years 1271–90. While passing through north-east Iran, he may well have heard from local people the following tale about the 'Old Man of the Mountain' and his fanatical band of devotees who lived in a remote valley hidden in the mountains. The 'Old Man', it is said, had created here the most beautiful garden ever seen, with rivers of wine, honey, milk and water – in imitation of the Garden of Paradise described in the Qur'an. Inside the garden there was a splendid palace into which his aspiring *fida'is* were taken before they were ordered to carry out their special missions of assassination. They were given copious draughts of forbidden wine laced with hashish and entertained for several days by seductive young maidens. After they had awoken from their state of intoxication, the young men were led to believe that they had just experienced a foretaste of Paradise promised to the believers. The 'Old Man' assured them that they would return to the bliss of this same Paradise if they were captured and put to death while attempting to carry out their mission of assassination.

The fictional nature of Marco Polo's account was long suspected by scholars, and its absurdities have been exposed more recently by Farhad Daftary in his *The Assassin Legends*.[1] As he points out, the name 'Old Man of the Mountain' was never used in Persian sources for Hasan Sabbah, but applied in fact to Rashid al-Din Sinan of Syria. The persistent legend that the Ismaili *fida'is* were drugged and received a foretaste of Paradise before being sent out on their mission is clearly as absurd as it is fantastical. There is no contemporary Muslim evidence that this was so. Hashish was in common use at the time in most Middle Eastern countries, as it still is today, and thus it could not have been the secret of the Ismailis' success. No assassin of any political or religious persuasion would in his right mind allow his judgement to be affected by the use of drugs on such a dangerous and demanding mission. Most of the assassinations attributed to the Ismailis would have demanded great patience, skill and dexterity on the part of their *fida'is*. It would have been quite impossible for them to complete their task while under the influence of hashish.

Furthermore, the Ismailis have always interpreted the Qur'anic description of Paradise in an allegorical and spiritual sense, and would have regarded its literal embodiment on earth with a great deal of scepticism. As I have mentioned at the beginning of my Preface, the most recent scholarship on Marco Polo has questioned even whether he ever left Europe for his fabled travels to the East.

We know also that when the anti-Ismaili war-historian Juwayni inspected Alamut after its surrender to the Mongols in 1256, he was greatly impressed by its library, water-cisterns and storage facilities, but he makes no mention of any delectable garden or sumptuous palace inside or outside the castle. I can also confidently assert that there is no place in Alamut or any other Ismaili castle I have visited where such a garden could have been constructed.

It is unfortunate that Juwayni himself, after having examined the original Ismaili documents and finding them full of 'heresy and error,' cast them into the flames. We therefore have little idea how Hasan Sabbah and his followers viewed their mission and the purposes they intended to achieve, apart from the general aim of asserting their political independence of the Saljuqs and promoting the Ismaili way of Islam. So much depends, too, on the personality, ambitions and real aims of Hasan, who was the architect of this revolution and the founder of the Ismaili state which evolved so speedily in the last decade of the 11th century and survived, often against overwhelming military odds, for more than 150 years.

My research over the past forty years has shown that the Ismaili state during the Alamut period did not depend on two or three isolated castles, such as Alamut, Gerdkuh and Lamasar, but it covered a large area including Qohistan and Syria. Alamut always remained the centre until that fortress fell to the Mongols. Although parts of the state were geographically quite widely separated, the Ismailis had organised a sophisticated system of intercommunication between different parts based on subsidiary forts of varying size and watchtowers which also served as beacons.

Although our knowledge of the geographical distribution of the widely separated territories held by the Ismailis is now reasonably complete, we know very little about the origins and evolution of Hasan's remarkable revolutionary movement, let alone an assessment of the reasons for its success. Was it just a natural consequence of an essentially religious dispute in Cairo over the succession to the Fatimid Imam-caliph al-Mustansir and the murder of his heir, Nizar, in 1095? Or was the Ismaili uprising also to some extent an expression of indigenous Persian sentiments against the oppressive and arbitrary rule of the Saljuq Turks? Perhaps both elements were involved.

In the early centuries of Islam, opposition to the Abbasid rule was always present and at times it was particularly strong, especially among the Persians. This opposition was not only political and 'nationalistic' by nature but religious too. By the beginning of the 10th century, Shi'ism was widespread in Iran and the Ismaili *da'wa* had become well established. The rise of the Fatimid caliphate in North Africa offered new hope to the Shi'a, and support for the Ismailis grew in Iran and other parts of the Muslim world. But as we have seen, the expansion of Fatimid rule eastward was checked by the Saljuq occupation of Iran and Iraq in the 11th century. It seemed to the Persians that they had merely exchanged one overlord, an Arab, for another, a Turk. The brutal and boorish behaviour of the Turkish troops, the economic decline of the countryside and unrest in the towns further fuelled this distrust and dislike. All this led to the ready acceptance by the people of any movement promising new hope and a better future. This accounts partly for the extraordinary success of the Ismaili uprising led by Hasan Sabbah.

The aims of Hasan were clear enough. His first priority was to protect his community from being exterminated by the Saljuqs, and secondly to convert as many people as possible to the Ismaili way of Islam under the leadership of the Prophet's descendants. How was this aim to be achieved and his enemy defeated? Hasan relied on a number of pillars: (1) the power of the Ismaili doctrines preached by his Nizari *da'i*s; (2) the unquestioning loyalty of his followers; (3) the lack of resolution among his enemies; (4) the ingenious military tactics he employed against superior forces; and finally, (5) the strength of his fortresses that would ensure the defence of his territories. Hasan's great achievement was to mobilise his followers for the anti-Saljuq struggle and imbue them with a strong sense of unity, vitality and purpose. The glories of the Fatimid empire were over and the momentum had now swung to the successors of the Fatimids, the Nizari Ismailis.

Hasan's supporters flooded to the cause with limitless devotion and zeal. Equally crucial to Hasan's plans were the fortresses, for without them Ismaili resistance would have crumbled very quickly. The geographical division of their state, separated from each other by many kilometres of desert and mountains, could have proved fatal.

The reaction of the Saljuq authorities and their Sunni supporters to the Ismailis was, as we have seen, one of violent denunciation and persecution. In some places, notably Isfahan, Aleppo and Damascus, they joined forces to massacre the Ismailis and drive them from their midst. This reaction was not only based on the charge of heresy directed by a powerful Sunni establishment against a Shi'i minority. Many Sunnis felt that their political and religious institutions were threatened by the Ismaili uprising. A whole spate of horror stories about the Ismailis began to circulate, describing them as dangerous madmen in league with the devil, accusing them of dabbling with magic, indulging in orgies and other perverse practices. It is largely from this era that the black legends about the Assassins became widespread, although some of them had been circulating from a much earlier period. The most prominent Sunni theologian of the time, Abu Hamid al-Ghazali (d. 1111) who taught at the Nizamiyya college in Baghdad founded by the vizier Nezam al-Molk, condemned the Ismailis as apostates and therefore subject to the death penalty.[2] Such was the anathema and rejection heaped upon the Ismailis, which in a certain sense may be regarded as a tribute to the great power and influence once exercised by this numerically small community.

To their Saljuq and Sunni opponents, the Ismailis were known by various names among which the most commonplace was the pejorative *malahida* or 'heretics'. Another abusive term applied to them was *hashishiyya*, meaning persons of lax morality or religious beliefs due to their habitual use of hashish. This was the legend later picked up by Marco Polo and the Crusader chroniclers, transmitted to Europe where the name itself became corrupted to the 'Assassins' and its variants. A third designation for the Ismailis was *batiniyya*, literally meaning the 'esotericists', alluding to their doctrine of the *batin* or esoteric wisdom hidden in the external forms of religion. The term 'Ismaili', however, was seldom used for them, and in their own literature they always referred to themselves as *al-da'wat al-hadiya*, 'the rightly-guiding mission', or simply as *ahl al-haqq*, 'people of the truth'. Today, of course, this community of Shi'i Muslims call themselves the Ismailis (or Shi'a Nizari Ismailis, to be more precise), and this is the term I have maintained throughout this book.

By the time of Hasan Sabbah's death in 1124, the Ismailis of Iran occupied large portions of northern and north-eastern Iran as well as a few other areas in the south-west. The headquarters of this state always remained in the district of

Rudbar at Alamut and its sister castle of Maymundez. A few kilometres to the west lay the castle of Lamasar and still further west on the banks of the Qizinuzun river the castle and city of Samiran. To the east in Qumes, near modern Semnan and Damghan was another strongly fortified Ismaili area dominated by the castles of Gerdkuh and Soru. The largest Ismaili territory was in the modern province of Khorasan, stretching from Tus, near Nishapur in the north, southwards to Qohistan and the border with Sistan, and westwards to the desert town of Tabas. Then there were other areas, which were temporarily under Ismaili control, such as the fortress of Shahdez at Isfahan and others in Khuzistan. I am excluding the cities where there was a sizeable Ismaili presence but no actual occupation.

Altogether there were well over 60 castles and forts in the Alamut valley and the Rudbar area alone, probably 80 in Khorasan, most of them in the Qohistan region, and another 50 in other areas of the country. Additionally, the Syrian Ismailis held 60 castles of various sizes in the Jabal Bahra between Aleppo and Damascus. This makes a probable total of 250 fortifications in Iran and Syria. Of course, only a few were the size of Alamut, Gerdkuh or Soru in Iran, and some were little more than minor forts or outposts. Nevertheless this is a surprising number and gives an indication of the extent and strength of the Ismaili state in the two countries. All the major Ismaili fortresses were built on the same almost indestructible scale and contained similar cisterns of water, hewn out of solid rock and filled by diverted springs, as well as ample supplies of provisions and weapons, stored in huge underground chambers. Their libraries, too, were renowned and the objects of much envy. Each castle was garrisoned by a force of highly trained men, utterly devoted to their cause.

There can be no doubt about the efficiency of the Ismaili administration. This is reflected most impressively in the immense logistical tasks involved in the construction and maintenance of more than 250 castles scattered over vast distances. The construction of new castles required, first of all, detailed survey work and planning of a high order. The execution of the project must have been carried out by a group of supervisors in charge of quarrying the required stonework, and its transportation to the castle site. Under their command would be teams of masons, builders, water engineers, plasterers and other skilled workers. The huge amounts of stone required for keeping the castles and garrisons in good repair for many months and even years demanded what we would call today a quartermaster general and his staff of the highest quality. Finally, the continuous construction and strengthening of these castles would not have been possible without a large and permanent labour force, moving from one site to another as required. We have no information on the composition of these workers, although a good portion of them are certain to have been Ismailis recruited and trained locally.

Military organisation and tactics

Although we have considerable information from Juwayni about the history and beliefs of the Persian Ismailis of his time, he provides few details about their military expertise apart from their fortresses. This lack of knowledge is not really surprising as the chief strategy of the Ismailis was to avoid at all costs being drawn into major battle with their more powerful opponents, whether Saljuq, Crusader, Mongol or any other military force. Their objective was basically defensive, and they showed great skills in the choice of site for their fortresses and defences. The garrisons of the castles must have been organised on very competent military lines and it is reasonable to assume that they came under the direct orders of the governor of each castle.

If we ask ourselves, how the Ismaili military system was organised, I think its structure must have reflected very closely the various grades of the Ismaili *da'wa* itself. At the top was Hasan Sabbah, the lord of Alamut, the chief *da'i* and representative of the hidden Ismaili Imam. Serving him faithfully were his top commanders like Bozorg-Ommid, Hosayn Qa'ini, Ahmad ibn Attash and other *da'i*s appointed by Hasan as his deputies in important regions of the Ismaili state. These men often commanded the most important Ismaili strongholds and their subsidiary bases in the provinces. As we have seen, they were in the first instance highly educated men and religious scholars, some of them having received their training in Fatimid Egypt, as did Hasan himself. There were other *da'i*s of a lower rank, noted for their military acumen as much as their intellectual ability, chosen to command individual castles and fortresses in the Ismaili state. Below them were the garrisons, recruited from local Ismaili men. Known as *rafiq*s or 'comrades', they were trained and equipped to fight on foot and horseback. The most courageous and daring of the *rafiq*s were selected as *fida'i*s, the self-sacrificing devotees assigned to undertake highly special and dangerous operations. We have no precise information on the organisation of these *fida'i*s, but they were probably located at every major Ismaili castle and highly esteemed among the *rafiq*s. Then came the ordinary people: the farmers and peasants who lived in protected villages around the castles, the merchants and tradesmen in the cities, and the manual workers who contributed to the massive building work taking place constantly at the castles. The lives of many of these people must have been humdrum enough, but they too were initiated into the Ismaili *da'wa*, sworn to secrecy and absolute loyalty to the Ismaili leadership at Alamut.

The military equipment needed to sustain the defence of a castle was endless. Bows and arrows, crossbows, explosive canisters and, above all, the ballistas and stones which they hurled were of supreme importance. On my earlier expeditions to Gerdkuh in the 1960s I had come across numerous stone shots of different sizes, all accurately shaped, which had been hurled at the Mongol besiegers by the Ismailis. In my recent expeditions many of these had disappeared. The fortress area doubtless had to be patrolled, and a strike force ready to attack any small body of intruders had to be kept in readiness. Above all, battle defensive tactics and training needed to be maintained at a high level of efficiency. Horses and mules had to be fed and watered. The castle defences had to be constantly maintained and often enlarged.

The Ismaili garrisons probably did not wear armour apart from helmets. They would be armed with spears, lances, swords and sabres, and clearly well trained in hand-to-hand fighting. They must have been superb shots with their bows and skilled in handling their javelins, slings and stones. They were tough and hardy men, able to withstand the severe weather, particularly in winter, of the mountainous areas, and also capable of ascending and descending the steep slippery slopes at great speed. Their diet was much the same as it is today, consisting of bread, rice, honey, cheese, fruit, melons, tomatoes and grapes, supplemented by chicken and sheep meat. They would have grown herbs and probably imported some other delicacies. Most of the state-organised armies of the period relied on regiments of slaves, usually of Turkish or Armenian origin, who themselves sometimes rose to power as did the Mamluks in Egypt. There is no evidence that the Ismailis of Alamut availed themselves of this source of supply, though there were at the time fiercely independent groups of mercenaries, such as the tribal Kurds of the Zagros mountains and the Daylamites from northern Iran, who could well have agreed to serve under them.

We know that the Fatimids too relied on outside sources for their military manpower. The Fatimid army was basically organised along regimental lines based on ethnic identity – that is, groups or tribes coming from one region and owing allegiance to their own commanders. There were thus special regiments of Turks, Armenians, Berbers, Sudanese and others. Detailed records were kept of names of soldiers and where they were stationed. Military parades were considered important and these were usually held on Muslim feast-days. It is very probable that when he was in Egypt, Hasan Sabbah studied the Fatimid military organisation carefully and, after he had established his own powerbase in Iran, he was probably joined by a number of former officers and soldiers from the Fatimid army, perhaps even including some specialists in military architecture and fortification.

Assassination as a method of warfare

The Prussian soldier and military theorist Karl von Clausewitz (d. 1831) wrote in his book *Vom Kriege* that war is 'a continuation of politics with the admixture of other means' (commonly rendered as 'a continuation of politics by other means'). Hasan Sabbah would probably have agreed with this theory. His aims, as we have seen, were twofold: first, to defend his community against the depradations of the hated Saljuqs, and secondly, to advance the cause of Ismaili Islam. Although Hasan was abundantly able to defend the state he had founded, he did not have the human or material resources to wage an all-out military campaign against the Saljuqs. He therefore had to find other means of overcoming his enemies and breaking their power.

One of the means chosen by Hasan to achieve his objective was the careful and selective use of assassination, appropriate to the decentralised nature of Saljuq power structure. Hasan used this weapon as precisely and skilfully as a surgeon uses his scalpel. The target was chosen with great care, often a Saljuq figure of power and influence whose elimination would greatly reduce any imminent threat to the Ismailis. We are not sure who was responsible for killing Nezam al-Molk, but his removal certainly contributed much to relieve the pressure of Saljuq attacks on the Alamut castles. Sometimes the mere fear of assassination was sufficient to demoralise the enemy and dissuade his aggression, as may have been the case when Saladin besieged the Ismaili castle of Masyaf in Syria. It was the skill with which the Ismaili *fida'i* could insinuate himself so closely to the person of his intended victim without arousing the slightest suspicion that was most unnerving for his enemies. Cases are reported of great men finding daggers embedded in their pillows with a note warning them to curb their hostility or face death. As a result, many Saljuq lords, Crusader princes and other prominent dignitaries began to wear armour beneath their ordinary clothes.

Assassination has, of course, been used as a weapon of warfare from the dawn of history and was not invented by the Ismailis. Most rulers of all political and religious persuasions have made deliberate use of assassination as an instrument of policy. In Muslim history, the Umayyad and Abbasid caliphs did not hesitate to order the murder of their leading critics, especially if they happened to be Shi'i leaders. The Saljuq sultans were no less ruthless in disposing of their political rivals, including their nearest kith and kin, when it suited their purpose. Hasan Sabbah and his successors used assassination as a tactical weapon with great precision and calculation. They could not hope to defeat the forces of their more powerful enemies in battle and therefore avoided armed confrontations. In times of siege they preferred to reach accommodation by negotiation and compromise.

According to Hodgson, it was only when all other means of resistance were exhausted that they turned to assassination as 'a weapon of desperation'.[3]

It was inevitable that Hasan Sabbah and his followers should be falsely accused by their enemies of using assassination widely and indiscriminately. They were even charged with hiring out their *fida'is* to do the dirty work of others. Whenever a prominent person was murdered, the Ismailis were inevitably blamed for it. Hodgson mentions an 'epidemic of assassinations' reported during the later Saljuq period for which the Ismailis were held responsible. He discounts most of these reports, observing that since political murder was common enough among their opponents, 'there is no way to be sure (except in rare cases) that any particular assassination was the work of the Ismailis.'[4] As we have seen, even European monarchs fell to accusing each other of hiring assassins from the 'Old Man of the Mountain'. In all probability, the actual number of assassinations carried out by the Ismailis was only a fraction of those attributed to them.

The more spectacular assassinations were inevitably counter-balanced by massacres that followed. After the killing of a prominent figure, the local Sunni population was often roused to frenzied retaliation against the Ismailis. Many non-Ismailis also suffered when they were unjustly suspected or denounced without evidence. Despite all the twists and turns of the Ismaili struggle and putting aside the mindless massacres, if we try to look objectively at the military tactics of Hasan Sabbah and Rashid al-Din Sinan, we must conclude that their use of assassination was ethically no worse or better than any other act of warfare. This weapon appeared to them as the most effective alternative to direct military action against far superior forces. In Hodgson's view, this policy was 'seemingly calculated to avoid bloodshed among ordinary people, whose champions, in the name of justice, the Ismailis felt themselves to be'.[5] Most right-minded people, whatever their faith, would certainly agree with Hodgson when he very properly argues that it was better to kill one powerful adversary than to slaughter thousands of ordinary men on the battlefield.[6]

One other important factor must have influenced Hasan Sabbah and his commanders when deciding how best to defend themselves against their multiple enemies. We must never forget that the underlying military strategy of the Ismailis was of necessity defensive rather than offensive. This policy was imposed by the fact that the Ismailis were everywhere a small persecuted minority and their state lacked territorial contiguity. There were no common frontiers, no hinterland to their castles and positions, with the possible exception of Qohistan, in which reserves of manpower could be stationed, stores assembled and a firm base established. Defence in depth was impossible. Moreover, movement from one part of the state to another was always through hostile territory. The difficulty of communications and the isolation of the Ismaili position could have brought about the collapse of the state at any time. And yet it is remarkable that throughout their protracted struggle over more than a century, the unity and morale of the Ismailis always remained high, and there was little if any dissension within the community.

The spirit of this struggle is well captured in the following lines of a little-known Ismaili poet, Ra'is Hasan, who flourished in the first half of the 13th century. He worked as a scholar and scribe to the Ismaili governor of Qohistan, Shihab al-Din, and composed this poem, with its mixture of courage, bravado, hope and a little pathos, some years before the Mongol conquerors overwhelmed the Ismaili castles:

> O brothers! When the blessed time
> comes and the good fortune of
> both the worlds accompanies us,
> the king who possesses more than
> a hundred thousand horsemen will be
> frightened of a single warrior (from us).
> But it is also possible that when
> our good fortune is on the wane,
> our spring will turn to autumn
> and the autumn into – spring!
> Did you not see rising today
> the sun of the great resurrection
> from the mountains which are the preachings
> of Mustansir and the prayers of Nizar?[7]

Religious and intellectual life

Our account of the rise of the Nizari Ismailis has been confined mostly to their political and military affairs, and little has been said about the religious side of the community. Consequently we may be tempted to believe that their lives were spent mostly in an unrelenting cycle of warfare. It has to be remembered that the Ismailis have always been, first and foremost, a religious community and not a military order. We know that, like their Fatimid forebears in Egypt, the Nizaris of Iran and Syria cultivated an intellectual and spiritual life of a high order in their mountain strongholds. Among the first things Hasan established at Alamut were a mosque and a library, which became the nucleus of a training centre for Ismaili *da'is*. We know that the early Nizari *da'wa* was closely modelled on the Fatimid system and it is likely that the trainee *da'is* at Alamut were exposed to a similar pattern of education. In addition to acquiring familiarity with the Qur'an and Prophetic traditions, they would have learned history, theology, philosophy, languages and the natural sciences. Similar training centres with libraries were later organised in other major Ismaili castles such as Qa'in and Mo'menabad in Qohistan and Masyaf in Syria. In the early decades of the 13th century, these castles gave refuge to a number of Sunni and Twelver Shi'i scholars fleeing from the Mongol invasions of Central Asia.

In his book on the Fatimid traditions of learning, Heinz Halm observes that the ideal Ismaili *da'i* was expected to have an almost encyclopaedic knowledge, 'so that he may be equipped for any discussion among scholars, prepared in any argument, and unbeatable in any field of erudition.'[8] Hasan Sabbah exemplified this ideal in his learning and scholarship. Like so much Ismaili literature of his time, Hasan's works have not survived, but an abridged version of one of his works in Persian has been preserved under the title of *Fusul-i arba'a* or *The Four Chapters*. In this treatise, Hasan proceeds to demonstrate, through a series of logical propositions, the universal human need for a true spiritual guide. The knowledge of God cannot be obtained by reason alone, nor learned from religious scholars or philosophers whose opinions are divided. There must exist in every age, Hasan argues, a single trustworthy teacher who is the wisest and most perfect of all human beings, one who is endowed with superior knowledge and the source of *ta'lim*, authoritative religious guidance. According to Hasan, this person is none other than the Ismaili Imam, who has inherited this function from the Prophet Muhammad and is recognised as such by his followers. He alone interprets the will of God at any particular time, and without his guidance mankind would inevitably fall into error.[9]

Hasan Sabbah's doctrine of *ta'lim* is a rigorous exposition of the original Shi'i belief in the Imamate, with certain important changes in emphasis. It was this doctrine that inspired the early Nizari Ismailis and was their real source of strength. Hasan's teachings provide clear evidence of the paramountcy of a living and accessible Imam for the Ismailis. We have seen in a previous chapter that when Hasan was in Egypt he was well aware of the military commander Badr's intention to deny succession to the caliph al-Mustansir's chosen heir, Nizar. When Hasan championed the cause of Nizar, he was arrested and expelled from the country. Hence, there is every reason to believe that when he returned to Iran, one of Hasan's primary objectives was to establish a secure, fortified sanctuary for Nizar and his successors. When in 1095 Nizar was murdered in Cairo, Hasan led the Persian Ismailis to break away from the Fatimid *da'wa* to found their own independent Nizari movement.

According to later Ismaili tradition, a son or grandson of Nizar was smuggled out of Egypt and brought to Alamut where he and his descendants lived in great secrecy, their identities unknown to all except Hasan and his most trusted confidants. If this was indeed the case, then the descendants of Nizar must have lived under the personal protection of Hasan and other lords of Alamut, presumably as members of their families. It is significant that throughout his thirty years of leadership and despite the absolute power and loyalty that Hasan Sabbah enjoyed among his followers, Hasan never claimed to be the Imam but merely his *hujja*, his 'proof' or 'evidence'. The courage and determination with which the Ismailis defended their castles can only be explained by their conviction in the continuing existence of their Imam who would return one day to reclaim his rightful place at the head of the community. The immense psychological power of this expectation – articulated very clearly in the poem by Ra'is Hasan cited above – has been much underestimated in modern accounts, which have focused largely on the political and military dynamics of the Ismaili struggle.

The history of religious ideas shows abundantly that messianic expectations usually end in disillusion, as the return of the Messiah or the Mahdi is forever postponed and redemption becomes an increasingly unattainable goal for their followers. But this was not apparently the case with the Nizari Ismailis, because forty years after Hasan Sabbah's death, their long-awaited Imam emerged from concealment at a dramatic ceremony at Alamut. His name was also Hasan, but owing to his special status the Ismailis always pronounce his name with the honorific expression '*ala dhikrihi'l-salam*', 'on whose mention be peace'. In order to avoid confusing him with Hasan Sabbah, he is sometimes also referred to by historians as Hasan II.

Born in 1126 and originally presumed to be the son of the third lord of Alamut, Mohammad b. Bozorg-Ommid, Hasan II developed from an early age a deep interest in philosophical and spiritual matters. His eloquence and independence of mind soon brought him a large personal following, including the future leader of the Syrian Ismailis, Rashid al-Din Sinan, who was then at Alamut to complete his studies as a *da'i*. Hasan II assumed leadership of the Ismailis in 1162 at the age of about 35 years. Two years later, on 8 August 1164, which was the 17th day of the month of Ramadan, he ordered a pulpit to be set up on the grounds at the foot of Alamut, flanked by four large banners in red, green, yellow and white. He assembled here his principal *da'is* whom he had previously summoned from Daylaman, Qohistan, Syria and other parts of the Ismaili state. He then mounted the pulpit and after some prayers and a sermon solemnly announced the arrival of the *Qiyama* or Resurrection. Then, according to Juwayni and other Sunni historians, Hasan invited his followers to join him at a table to break the fast and celebrate the Festival of the Resurrection. A similar ceremony was later held at the fortress of Mo'menabad in Qohistan where, in an epistle read on his

Eagle's Nest

behalf, Hasan II declared that he was in reality the Imam himself as well as the *Qa'im-e Qiyamat*, the 'Lord of the Resurrection'. In Syria too, Rashid al-Din Sinan enacted a similar ceremony in the name of Hasan II, announcing the advent of the Resurrection.

The proclamation of *Qiyama* is one of the most obscure and enigmatic events in the history of the Ismailis. The difficulty arises from the fact that there are no contemporary Ismaili accounts of the *Qiyama* ceremony, and the information we possess is derived mostly from Juwayni and other Sunni authors writing nearly a century after the event. These sources, which are naturally hostile, accuse the Ismailis of abrogating the laws of Islam and partaking in licentious activities. But the Ismailis totally reject these charges as absurd and fictitious. They maintain that the *Qiyama* is not to be understood literally as the Last Day or end of history, but in a symbolical and spiritual sense. At one level, it denotes a pivotal moment in their history when the Imam reappears after a long period of concealment. For the Ismailis this signifies the dawn of a new historical era and the emergence of a more pronounced spiritual dispensation for mankind. At another level, the *Qiyama* refers to the resurrection of the soul in its long journey from ignorance and darkness to knowledge and light. At a still higher level the *Qiyama* represents the soul's return to and union with the Light of God. Each human being has the potential of attaining this mystical experience here and now in this world; but it can only be realised through the mediation of the living Imam who represents the path to the spiritual resurrection of every soul.

My intention in introducing the doctrine of *Qiyama* briefly here has been to bring to the reader's attention some idea of the intensity of intellectual and spiritual life at Alamut, which must have occupied the Ismailis almost as much as the harsh daily demands of a life-and-death struggle against their enemies. To some readers, the doctrine must seem bizarre and difficult to grasp, but I trust I have said enough to indicate that this was certainly not the case. As Marshall Hodgson points out, the *Qiyama* was 'a declaration of spiritual maturity', and he draws certain interesting parallels with St. John's Gospel in the New Testament: 'When John defined the life eternal as knowing God – and when he added that he who has seen the man Jesus has seen the Father – he was teaching what must have seemed to the Nizaris undiluted *Qiyama* doctrine.'[10]

Our examination of intellectual life in the Ismaili state would not be complete without some reference to Naser al-Din Tusi, the greatest astronomer and mathematician of his time. Naser al-Din was born in 1201 in the town of Tus, Khorasan. From his early days, he exhibited a precocious talent for learning and was determined to search for truth. In his autobiographical work, *Sayr wa suluk* (*Contemplation and Action*), he gives a brief account of his intellectual growth.[11]

After mastering all the sciences of his day, from theology and philosophy to mathematics and astronomy, Tusi remained dissatisfied, feeling that he was no nearer the truth than before. What frustrated him more than anything else was the great diversity of opinions he encountered on the most basic issues of life and faith. But there was one school of thought that he had not yet explored, and that belonged to the Ismailis. He communicated his inquiries to the Ismaili governor of Qohistan, Shihab al-Din, and later met him briefly near the castle of Gerdkuh. Then he chanced to come across some sermons of the Imam Hasan II, the promulgator of *Qiyama*. This discovery had such a profound impact on Tusi that around 1224 he converted to Ismailism.

In 1224 or shortly afterwards, Tusi joined the service of the new Ismaili governor of Qohistan, Naser al-Din Mohtasham, as a resident scholar at the fortress of Qa'in. The governor was himself a highly learned man and he encouraged Tusi in his philosophical and scientific researches. Among the several works Tusi produced here, the most famous is *Akhlaq-e Naseri* (*The Nasirean Ethics*), a masterly synthesis of Neoplatonic and Islamic ethical philosophy.[12] After ten years of scholarship at Qa'in, Tusi was invited to go to Alamut. He could now avail himself freely of the rich resources of the Alamut library and also work with other scholars under the patronage of the Imam 'Ala al-Din Mohammad. The next twenty years were the most productive of Tusi's life, during which time he produced a large number of books on philosophy, mathematics, astronomy and the applied sciences. Many of these works have survived because of the large readership they attracted beyond Alamut and they are still studied carefully in the seminaries of Iran today. In addition to his scientific works, Tusi composed a number of specifically Ismaili works, including the *Rawda-yi taslim* (*Paradise of Submission*),[13] a comprehensive philosophical exposition of Ismaili doctrines in the age of *Qiyama*.

The life and works of Naser al-Din Tusi well illustrate the significance of Ismaili intellectual and cultural life in the early decades of the 13th century, and the role of Alamut in encouraging the advancement of knowledge. As Marshall Hodgson describes it:

> The Ismaili society was not a typical mountaineer and small-town society ... Each community maintained its own sense of initiative in the framework of the wider cause, and probably a sense of larger strategy was never completely absent ... but what was most distinctive was the high level of intellectual life. The prominent early Ismailis were commonly known as scholars, often as astronomers, and at least some later Ismailis continued the tradition. In Alamut, in Kuhistan, and in Syria, at the main centres at least, were libraries ... which were well known among Sunni scholars. To the end the Ismailis prized sophisticated interpretations of their

own doctrines, and were also interested in every kind of knowledge which the age could offer.[14]

But the dark clouds of war were already gathering menacingly over the mountains of Rudbar and Qohistan. By 1253 the Mongols had overrun several Ismaili fortresses, and in 1256 Hulegu Khan himself arrived in Rudbar and laid siege to Alamut. Just as the Persian Ismailis were beginning a renaissance of their intellectual and spiritual traditions, a new and powerful force burst suddenly upon the Islamic world, destroying both the Shi'a Ismailis and their protagonists the Sunni Saljuqs.

Notes

1. See Daftary, *The Assassin Legends*, pp. 109–12 and 166–168, where several versions of the Paradise legend are translated and analysed in detail.

2. Al-Ghazali's polemics against the Ismailis are analysed by Farouk Mitha in his *Al-Ghazali and the Ismailis: A Debate on Reason and Authority in Medieval Islam* (London, 2001).

3. Hodgson, *The Order*, p. 83.

4. Ibid., p. 111.

5. Hodgson, *The Venture of Islam*, vol. 2, p. 60.

6. Ibid, p. 84.

7. From *Shimmering Light: An Anthology of Ismaili Poetry*, trans. Faquir M. Hunzai (London, 1997). On the Fatimid caliph al-Mustansir and his heir-designate Nizar, see Chapter 1 above.

8. Halm, *The Fatimids and their Traditions of Learning*, p. 64.

9. See Hodgson, *The Order*, Appendix II, for a translation of Hasan Sabbah's *Four Chapters*, and his commentary of the same, pp. 51–61

10. Hodgson, *The Order*, pp. 176–177.

11. Nasir al-Din Tusi, *Contemplation and Action: The Spiritual Autobiography of a Muslim Scholar*, ed. and trans. S.J. Badakhchani (London, 1998).

12. Nasir al-Din Tusi, *The Nasirean Ethics*, trans. G.M. Wickens (London, 1964).

13. Nasir al-Din Tusi, *Rawda yi-taslim*, ed. and trans. S.J. Badakhchani as *Paradise of Submission* (London, 2004).

14. Hodgson, 'The Ismaili State,' p. 456.

CHAPTER 5

The Mongol Conquest

It was the 25th night of November 1256. The garrison of Alamut was on the brink of despair, overwhelmed by a sense of impending doom, which they could do nothing to avert. Every man, whether crouching on the battlements or huddled for warmth in the shelter of the fortifications, was only too aware of the bright fires of the Mongol armies encamped around the great bluff on which the castle stood. There was plenty to eat, but no one had any appetite. Sleep had been fitful for many nights, driven away first by increasing anxiety, then mounting fear, as news of the Mongols' rapid advance reached the castle, and finally a numbing terror all felt as the patrols described the flames and smoke of the still burning castle of Maymundez, captured ten days earlier. From which direction would the attack come, they all wondered? The most likely direction was from the north where a goat track ran round the foot of the cliffs. To the south the broken rock sloped at an angle of 60 degrees and the great water-cistern that ran like a deep gash across the whole front of the castle-rock would well prove a formidable obstacle to the invading army. But the reputation of the Mongols was such that it seemed nothing could stop their hordes from overwhelming them.

Normally a soldier of Islam, especially an Ismaili *fida'i*, had no fear of death in battle for he knew that life in this world was transient and his soul immortal. To give his life in the cause of Almighty Allah and His deputy on earth was his sacred duty, as well as a sure route to Paradise where a rich reward awaited the faithful. Death itself had no terrors and every man was prepared for it. It was barely a month since the first news had reached Alamut that the Mongol forces under Hulegu Khan were advancing rapidly towards the castle, determined on its destruction. At first the garrison was not particularly perturbed. If Hulegu really thought that he could overwhelm the castle defences which had been so cunningly devised by Hasan Sabbah, they were mistaken as Alamut was impregnable and had never been subdued by the Saljuqs or any other enemy of the Ismailis. Every

man in Alamut knew that the castle could withstand a siege by even the mighty
Mongols, equipped with their deadly mangonels, for many months, even years.
But two weeks ago an exhausted messenger had appeared and reported to the
commander of Alamut, Moqaddam al-Din, that the Mongols were already in the
neighbouring valley of Taleqan where they had taken and burnt three castles. The
messenger had seen their victorious footsoldiers, their cavalry, archers and heavy
ballistas. They were then making final preparations to scale the high mountain
barrier between Taleqan and Alamut and plunge with fire and sword into the
central valley towards the fortress of Maymundez, the residence of the Ismaili
Imam Rokn al-Din Khurshah himself.

Ten days ago the Alamut garrison had seen the great swirling clouds of dust
to the east and heard the distant sounds of battle. Their patrols had watched with
growing alarm as the Mongols mercilessly bombarded Maymundez, only 13 kilometres away. The Great Khan had set up his royal tent and flag of war on a hilltop
to the west of the castle, from where he personally directed the siege. The patrols
had heard that Hulegu had already summoned Rokn al-Din to surrender with all
his castles. They reported that the Mongol army, numbering at least 10,000 men,
had put to the sword some of the garrison at the top of the fortress as they offered
a last vain resistance to the invaders.

The patrols had only just managed to return safely to Alamut when a day or
two later the first Mongol troops arrived. The Mongol prince Balaghai led his
army to the foot of the castle and surrounded the rock on all sides. The prince sent
word to the commander that Maymundez had surrendered, and the Imam Rokn
al-Din himself was now in the hands of Hulegu. He now summoned Muqaddam
to join his master in submission and allegiance to the Great Khan. He would wait
until the following day for a reply. If he and his garrison surrendered their lives
would be spared. As the commander made his last tour of the battlements, he
was full of doubts. Had Maymundez really fallen and had his Imam submitted
to the Mongols? Was their promised clemency just a ploy to persuade him and
his garrison to surrender? Should he allow the great castle of Hasan Sabbah to be
destroyed with all its treasures without offering resistance?

As dawn broke on the next day, the commander looked again at the mighty
host surrounding his castle. Already the mangonels were being prepared for the
final bombardment. Then a Mongol herald rode furiously across the steep slopes
of the valley to deliver a message, and when the commander Muqaddam saw the
sacred seal of Rokn al-Din, he kissed it with great reverence. But having broken
the seal he staggered back. Turning to his deputy he said with a trembling voice,
'Our Lord has indeed come down from Maymundez and he orders us to do the
same.' After recovering his composure, the commander hesitated no longer. He

must now leave everything to the will of Allah and none knew His will better than the Imam. He dispatched a messenger to the Mongol prince, saying that he and his men would come down at once from Alamut. This they did with all their weapons and belongings, and were immediately put into chains. For the time being at least, the Mongol prince was as good as his word and the garrison was spared, until he received further instructions from Hulegu as to their fate.

How did this disaster come about? Let me now turn to the Mongols who brought about the defeat of the Nizari Ismailis and their famed armies, which had until then successfully resisted the mightiest powers on earth and earned the respect even of the kings and emperors of Europe.

The rise of Mongol power

There are as many legends and myths about the Mongols as there are about the so-called Assassins. Their traditional homeland is the vast tableland or plateau of inner Mongolia varying from 915 to 1,525 metres in altitude. Their history really begins with Genghis Khan, whose father was the ruler of a few clans or tribes. He was born in the year 1162 with, according to legend, a piece of clotted blood in his veins. The horoscopes foretold a bloody career and seldom has there been a more accurate forecast. After he had established his supremacy over the local nomad tribes, he launched the first of many campaigns against China between 1211 and 1214. As a result he conquered most of China over which his grandson, Kublai Khan, was to reign from 1260 to 1294. Genghis now decided to launch an attack against the west from his capital Karakoram.

In 1218 Genghis Khan launched his first attack on Transoxiana, which was then part of the mighty Khwarazm empire that included eastern Persia and northern India. Genghis was an excellent military strategist who knew how to take every advantage of his enemies. With an army estimated to have numbered between 150,000 and 200,000 men, he subdued the region with his customary ferocity and speed. In 1220 he took Bukhara after a siege which lasted twelve days and massacred the defendants to a man. The same fate befell Samarkand in the following year. He then crossed the Oxus river, captured Balkh, Merv and Nishapur and made himself master of eastern Persia. In 1221 the Mongols sent an expedition to Delhi, which secured him nominal possession of northern India. He then gave permission to his generals to attack southern Russia and his troops crushed the kingdom of Georgia. In 1221 they had reached the basin of the Donetz in southern Russia. Genghis died in 1227 and was succeeded by his son Ogedei. The advance against Europe continued and by 1239 central Russia as far as Moscow was in his hands. Hungary was then defeated and it seemed as though all Europe would fall to the Mongols. But Ogedei died in 1241 and all the Mongol princes returned with their armies to Karakoram so as to secure every advantage they could from the succession. Ogedei was succeeded by Guyuk as Great Khan, though he only reigned for two years and was followed in 1248 by Mongke.

There was now a significant revision of Mongol policy, based on a realistic assessment of the political balance of power at the time. Mongke came to the conclusion that there was little advantage in continuing his attacks on Europe. In 1260 he decided to consolidate and strengthen the Mongol conquests by sending his two brothers Qublai (Kublai Khan) to China and Hulegu to western Asia. Genghis had swept through these vast regions once already but Mongol influence had now diminished and their military presence gradually weakened. Mongke's instructions to Hulegu were to conquer all the central Islamic lands from Persia as far as Syria and the borders of Egypt. He was also to capture Baghdad and put an end to the caliphate. Only then would the Great Khan be truly the 'King of Kings', as one of his titles proclaimed. But standing in Hulegu's way were the powerful Ismailis in their numerous castles. These enemies had first to be eliminated and their castles destroyed. The Mongols were encouraged in this further by a Sunni judge from Qazvin who had appealed to Mongke for help, saying that his people had to wear armour all the time as a protection against the daggers of these dangerous 'heretics'.

A first-hand account of these developments was recorded by the ambassador of King Louis IX of France, the Franciscan friar William of Rubrick, who was sent by the king to Karakoram in 1253 in the hope that the Mongols would support the Crusaders against the Muslims. On his way there he passed close to the Alborz mountains, or as he says the 'mountains of the Hacassins'. William himself is among the first Westerners to have given the Persian Ismailis the name of Hacassin or Assassin, which had up to now been used in Europe only when referring to the Syrian Ismailis. Doubtless William was able to make a connection between the Syrian and Persian Ismailis. When William arrived at Karakoram, he found that strict security measures were in force as forty Hacassins were rumoured to have entered the city under different disguises in order to kill Mongke. The Great Khan had in reprisal ordered his brother Hulegu to proceed as quickly as possible to Persia and put all Ismailis to the sword.[1]

Mongol methods of warfare

The power of the Mongols rested, of course, on their superbly equipped and trained armies. Despite their recent nomadic origins, the Mongol Khans and their generals were far more intelligent strategists than their European or other opponents. The European commanders were out-manoeuvred in every battle they fought. The Mongol army was organised on a decimal basis. The largest unit was a tumen, consisting of 10,000 men. Each tumen was composed of ten regiments of 1,000 men. In addition, of course, they had heavy and light cavalry. The Mongol cavalry normally had five to eight horses to a man as their regular establishment so that their mobility would never be weakened

The Mongol troops wore armour of tanned hide in four pieces, far lighter than the heavy steel mail worn by European knights. Their weapons consisted of a lance, a curved sabre with a sharpened point, which could be used for cutting or thrusting and two bows – a light one for shooting from horseback and their traditional composite bow, made from bamboo and yak horn. It fired arrows at tremendous velocity and was considered the most formidable bow of the Middle Ages.[2] They had three quivers of different arrows, intended for piercing armour or for shooting at unprotected troops. The constant hail of arrows shot by the Mongols in battle from every quarter had a devastating effect on their enemies. One particular Chinese weapon employed by their heavy cavalry was the hooked spear, which enabled a horseman to pull his opponent from his saddle. Lassoes were used as well.

The Mongols had always relied on speed, shock tactics and superiority of firepower to achieve their military aims. Their tactics were based on the strict discipline of their troops under fire, mobility and surprise. These tactics amounted to a tightly-knit battle drill, which worked like clockwork. Their battle formation consisted of five ranks, separated by wide intervals. As the armoured front ranks approached the enemy, the lightly armed rear ranks passed through them discharging a hail of arrows and javelins. They would then withdraw and the front ranks would charge the enemy, who had suffered severe casualties, and deliver the final blow. They had developed a perfect combination of firepower and shock tactics. They constantly lured their enemies into a trap by pretending to flee. Their communications were superb. They had developed a series of signals so that manoeuvres could be carried out instantly. Their chief aim was never to close with an enemy in hand-to-hand combat until he had suffered severe casualties and was demoralised. In this way they were more than a match for the cumbersome, unwieldy forces of their enemies.

During their advance into Europe, the Mongols were not particularly well supplied with siege engines. During Hulegu's advance into Persia, where they knew they would probably have to use siege tactics, especially against the Ismaili castles, they relied on their Chinese or Muslim specialist engineers who had more experience in siege tactics. From the eighth to 11th centuries, Muslim armies

tended to rely on surprise attack, blockade and mining to overcome the resistance of the castle they were besieging. The defenders would at first fight outside
a castle or city to prevent the attackers from setting up siege positions. The early
siege engines were not especially powerful and were principally used to hurl rocks
covered with oil-based nafta into the city in order to set it ablaze. Like most similar
devices these were first employed in China, especially the so-called 'snakes' or
javelins coated with nafta.

The siege engines or ballistas of the Mongol armies were light and mobile,
which the Mongols had adapted from their Chinese prototypes. Unlike the Roman
mangonel which was heavy and cumbersome, the Mongols used a more efficient,
lighter type that could hurl a missile of a kilogram in weight over a distance of 100
metres, and the heavier ballista could fire an 11–kilogram shot over a distance of
150 metres. They made particular use of massed batteries of mangonels and other
siege weapons which would hurl rocks or bolts covered with burning pitch into a
castle at a distance of 2,500 paces. They also used fire weapons, which had been
developed in China including grenades which could be hurled from ballistas.[3]
These weapons would, of course, only be effective if the siege engines could be
set up within range of an Ismaili stronghold.

It is also worth noting that the Mongol army on the march took great reserves
with it, including numerous sheep and cattle to provide a constant food supply,
as well as pack animals such as camels and bullocks. These reserves also meant
that the Mongol armies had no need to live off the land through which they were
passing and so did not run the risk of being halted by their own scorched earth
policy of warfare.

A last but important factor contributing to the success of the Mongol armies, in
addition to their iron discipline, shock battle tactics and mobility, was the terror
they inspired. If their method of warfare was remarkably similar in effect to the
blitzkrieg developed by the German armies of 1939, the Mongols also employed
their own fifth column to strike fear into the hearts of their intended opponents.
When they advanced their effect was that of a hurricane. Juwayni, the war-historian of the Mongols, describes Genghis Khan's first attack on Khorasan, especially
the cities of Balkh, Merv, Herat and Nishapur. After the destruction of Balkh by
the Great Khan in person, he ordered his armies to destroy the other towns in the
vicinity. This was rapidly accomplished and 'with one stroke a world which bil-
lowed with fertility was laid desolate, and the regions thereof became a desert, and
the greater part of the living dead, and their skin and bones crumbling dust; and
the mighty were humbled and immersed in the calamities of perdition.'[4] Juwayni
similarly describes with relish how the Mongols laid an ambush for the 3,000
Turkoman horsemen who were assembled to defend Merv and were defeated by

a mere handful of Mongols. After the city had surrendered the Mongols drove all the inhabitants, nobles and commoners on to the plain. Then:

> The Mongols ordered that, apart from four hundred artisans whom they specified and selected from amongst the men, and some children, girls and boys, whom they bore off into captivity, the whole population, including the women and children should be killed, and no one, whether woman or man, be spared. The people of Merv were then distributed among the soldiers and levies, and in short, to each man was allotted the execution of three or four hundred persons ... So many had been killed by nightfall that the mountains became hillocks, and the plain was soaked with the blood of the mighty.[5]

In a footnote to this account, Professor Boyle, the translator of Juwayni's *History of the World-Conqueror*, explains that the mountains seemed no more than hillocks when surrounded by huge piles of the dead. It is interesting to note that the Mongols spared the lives of some 400 artisans. These men were doubtless needed for the skills they possessed which the nomadic Mongols lacked, though their lives as prisoners would have been no better than slaves.

The siege of Maymundez

Hulegu's instructions were quite clear. He must first destroy the Ismailis and demolish their castles and then proceed west to take Baghdad. The caliph in Baghdad was to be removed and his life spared only if he acknowledged the supremacy of the Great Khan, otherwise he was to be killed.

Hulegu set off for Persia in October 1253 with a force that was even larger than the army which Genghis had commanded. Special preparations were made for this army to move across Central Asia as speedily as possible. Bridges over rivers were built or strengthened if necessary. Land and cattle were requisitioned in advance so that there should be no shortage of provisions. Hulagu's army included Chinese as well as Muslim experts skilled in the use of mangonels and naphtha. At first Hulegu advanced at a leisurely pace. He sent messengers to the Persian rulers telling them that he was coming to destroy the Ismailis and their castles and requesting their aid. Any refusal would risk his severest displeasure. The Mongol lord also dispatched an advanced army of 12,000 men under the command of his Christian general Ket-Buqa to capture any Ismaili castles he could.

The first Mongol attacks on the Ismailis came in April of 1253, when Ket-Buqa captured several of their fortresses in Qohistan. In May he attacked the Ismaili strongholds of Qumes and proceeded to lay siege to the castle of Gerdkuh. The garrison of Gerdkuh refused to submit and in December counter-attacked with an audacious night attack that killed several hundred Mongol troops. The Mongols came close to taking Gerdkuh in the summer of 1254 after an outbreak of cholera in the castle, but the garrison was saved by the arrival of reinforcements from Alamut. In the meanwhile, the Mongols under Ket-Buqa continued their assault on Ismaili strongholds in Qohistan. The towns of Tus and Tun faced the initial brunt of their ferocity and brutality. Both towns had initially attempted to resist the invaders, but surrendered in 1256 and their inhabitants were slaughtered. Juwayni describes the massacre at Tun in these words:

> When they [the Mongols] arrived, the rabble of that place put up some resistance until on the seventh day the army penetrated the inner town and razed its walls to the ground. They drove all the men and women out into the open country and spared no one over ten years of age except the younger women. And returning from thence in triumph to the World-King they proceeded towards Tus.'[6]

According to Persian historians, some 12,000 Ismailis were killed in Tun alone. This was not an exceptional case of Mongol brutality but typical of the Mongol armies throughout their conquest of Iran. The people of Khorasan probably suffered more than any other area from the Mongol invasions. They were the first to be attacked and subjected to the full brute force and merciless barbarity of the invaders. Any hint of resistance was followed by ruthless retribution on all the inhabitants of a city. Whole areas were devastated and were never able to recover. The Mongols imposed draconian laws and many were driven into exile. As a result, the entire population of Khorasan suffered grievously, leaving a once prosperous province with a large population utterly decimated. In fact, many parts of Khorasan have not recovered to this day the level of prosperity they had attained in pre-Mongol times.[7]

It was shortly after the sack of Tun in 1256 that Hulegu entered Qohistan and took direct control of his campaign against the Ismailis. Hulegu and his court stayed for a while at Tus in a splendid tent which had been erected for him on the orders of the Great Khan. Here he summoned the Ismaili governor of Qohistan, Naser al-Din Mohtasham, and demanded the surrender of all his castles at once. Naser al-Din replied that he was unable to comply since only his Imam had the authority to issue such an order. This brief encounter must have convinced the Mongol lord that the surest and quickest way to make the Ismailis submit was to capture their Imam, and he set about this task with grim determination.

The dangerous challenge posed by the Mongols had been clear enough to the Ismaili leaders long before Hulegu left Karakoram for Persia. As early as 1238, the Ismaili Imam of the time 'Ala al-Din Mohammad had recognised that the Mongols posed a serious threat to all Muslims, Sunni and Shi'i, and it was necessary for them to unite before their common enemy. Accordingly he joined the Abbasid caliph of Baghdad, al-Mustansir, in dispatching a special embassy to the kings of England and France calling for a Christian-Muslim alliance against the Mongols. This appeal came to nothing as the European monarchs preferred to see the Muslims vanquished by the Mongols and so preserve the Crusader states in Palestine. The Sunni caliph and the Ismaili Imam collaborated again in 1246 in a joint peace mission to the Great Khan Guyuk in Mongolia on the occasion of his enthronement. But the Mongol overlord refused to receive the Ismaili emissaries and treated them with contempt. The invasion of Qohistan by Hulegu's armies in 1253 and the devastation of Ismaili territories there increased the pressure upon 'Ala al-Din, and there was apparently much dissension among his chief advisers about the right course of action. If there is any truth in the report of William of Rubrick that a group of Ismaili *fida'i*s were rumoured to have arrived in Kara-koram to kill the Great Khan Mongke, it is an indication of their desperation to avert the catastrophe that awaited them.

In 1255 'Ala al-Din Mohammad was found murdered in suspicious circumstances and succeeded as Imam by his 26-year old son Rokn al-Din Khurshah. Like his father, Rokn al-Din was inclined to sue for peace and made a serious effort to enter into negotiations with the Mongols. Although he had little experience in diplomacy and affairs of state, especially with a person like Hulegu, he could not have doubted the seriousness of his situation. In 1256, he sent a number of emissaries to Hulegu declaring his peaceful intentions and offering his submission. But all his messages were rebuffed by Hulegu who demanded that Rokn al-Din appear before him personally to offer his allegiance. This the young Imam was reluctant to do as he feared a trap to take him prisoner and so precipitate the destruction of his people. In another gesture of conciliation, Rokn al-Din sent his brother Shahanshah to assure Hulegu of his submission. Hulegu replied that the Ismaili leader should demonstrate his good will by demolishing his castles. As Rokn al-Din continued to prevaricate, Hulegu prepared for battle and began to move with his army of 10,000 men from Qohistan to Rudbar. He also divided the remaining forces at his disposal into three groups with orders to surround the valley of Alamut in a tight net.

As Hulegu's forces converged on the Alamut valley, Rokn-al Din was still playing for time at the castle of Maymundez where he resided. Traditional judgement has relied too much on Juwayni's vituperative remarks concerning his dilemma as to whether or not he should surrender himself and destroy all his castles. Rokn al-Din was in a hopeless situation from the start. He had to choose between surrender or breaking off negotiations with Hulegu and relying on his well-defended castles to protect himself and his people for the time being. He was above all anxious to preserve his leadership of the Ismailis and at the same time spare them the awful fate they faced at the hands of the Mongols. If he could hang on a bit longer, the snows of winter would prevent the Mongols from continuing their advance. In a further exchange of messages, he told the Mongol lord that he would agree to all his demands, but asked for a year's grace before he left Maymundez. Hulegu insisted again that only Rokn al-Din's immediate submission in person would satisfy him. The Ismaili Imam now promised to send his son as a hostage of his good intention and also to demolish his castles. But Hulegu was not impressed by the removal of a few towers and battlements from Alamut, Maymundez and Lamasar. He also doubted whether the seven-year old boy was Rokn al-Din's son at all and sent him back saying that he was too young to serve as a hostage. Rokn al-Din now sent his brother Shahanshah again, accompanied by a large delegation of the Ismaili hierarchy, to confirm his submission to Hulegu. The Mongol lord suspected that the Ismailis were dragging out the negotiations on purpose, so that his forces would not have time to attack before the winter set in. His patience was exhausted and he immediately set out with his armies to enforce submission. At the same time he sent his final message to Rokn al-Din telling him to destroy his fortress of Maymundez and come down to pay homage before ill fortune inevitably overtook him and his territories were devastated.

On 8 November 1256, Hulegu set up his camp on a hilltop overlooking Maymundez and the castle was now completely encircled by his armies. Hulegu had rightly chosen to attack Maymundez first. As well as being the residence of Rokn al-Din, it was also the only major fortress that could be reduced to submission by mangonels. These great catapults could not have been employed with the same success against the castles of Alamut, Nevisar Shah, Lamasar or Gerdkuh because of their position. All these fortresses were set on top of high peaks, which could not be fully surrounded or overlooked. They could not be effectively reached by mangonels and subjugated only by a prolonged blockade. The Mongols estimated that if they could speedily capture Maymundez, the psychological effect would induce the other castles to surrender. Hulegu now ordered his men to close in while he himself, in a series of forced marches, burst with his troops over the Alamut mountains from the Taleqan valley and suddenly appeared at the foot of Maymundez. The speed of events and the sudden appearance of the Mongol forces in the valley must have been unnerving to the Ismaili garrison, almost catching them by surprise. Strangely enough, there appears to have been no warning of the rapid Mongol advance and consequently no mobilisation of the castle's defence forces.

Hulegu and his staff were immensely impressed by the great strength of the fortifications they saw before them. They surveyed the castle from every angle hoping to find a vulnerable point. Marshall Hodgson contends that the majority of the generals and princes accompanying Hulegu even advised postponing the siege until the spring, given the great strength of the fortress, the approach of winter and the difficulty of obtaining supplies.[8] But Hulegu disagreed and, supported by a minority of his staff, gave the orders for an immediate siege. He may well have concluded that if he gave the Ismaili leader the slightest leeway, all his efforts to destroy his state would be confounded. Perhaps, too, he had a well-justified faith in his mangonels and the ballistas which had a range of 2,500 paces. The area around Maymundez is now totally barren but in 1256 there were many pine trees planted by the Ismailis themselves, which were cut down by the Mongols for their mangonels. In the event, Hulegu's faith in the accuracy and destructive effect of his mangonels in this vital battle were well founded.

The siege of the castle began in earnest the next day. Hulegu set up on a hill the mangonels to bombard the castle. This must have been a formidable operation as we are told that the strongest men were chosen to transport the heavy poles and pillars. This was done and a preliminary bombardment began which lasted three days. Both sides suffered considerable casualties. On the fourth day the Mongols attempted a direct assault, but this was repulsed. The Mongols then brought up even heavier siege-engines which hurled javelins dipped in burning pitch at the castle. At this point Rokn al-Din began to realise that he was losing the battle. It was November and he was evidently hoping that snow would begin to fall at any moment and put a stop to the siege. But when he saw more mangonels being erected round the whole circumference of the castle he decided, in Juwayni's words, 'to knock at the door of peace'. Rokn al-Din sent a message saying that he would surrender if the Mongol lord granted him and his family safe conduct. Hulegu instructed Juwayni to draw up a *yarligh* or royal decree guaranteeing safety, which the historian took personally to Rokn al-Din for his signature. But the Ismaili leader was still hesitant to come down from his fortress for several days, not sure whether he could trust the Mongol lord to keep his word. Hulegu then ordered another, more destructive bombardment which had such frightening effect that at last, on 19th November, Rokn al-Din capitulated and descended from the castle with his entourage.

The evacuation of Maymundez was completed the following day. Some of the garrison refused to surrender and climbing to the top of the castle opened fire with their mangonels on the Mongols, but they were soon hunted down and hacked to death. The whole operation took a fortnight, and although the Mongols were content to spare the lives of the garrison for the moment, they set about destroying the fortress, which Juwayni likens cynically to 'brushing away the dust thereof with the broom of annihilation'.[9]

The fall of Alamut

Hulegu now forced Rokn al-Din to send a message to the other Ismaili castles in the valley ordering them to surrender. As we have seen, the commander at Alamut, Muqaddam al-Din, hesitated at first, unsure if he should comply with his Imam's orders or not, until he saw Hulegu's mighty army surround the castle. The sight of this formidable force struck panic into the defenders and they too sued for quarter and favourable treatment. Three days later at the beginning of December, the garrison surrendered and the Mongol army entered Alamut, set fire to the buildings and began the process of demolition.

It seems to us hardly credible that Alamut, which was in fact a far stronger castle than Maymundez, should have been persuaded to surrender so easily. But if we put ourselves in the position of the garrison commander, we can perhaps understand the intolerable pressures on him. Muqaddam knew that Maymundez had been taken by a sudden overwhelming show of force. He certainly would have heard and probably seen something of the devastating assault by the Mongols. He realised how effective and destructive the mangonels could be, although Alamut would have withstood the effects of bombardment far better than Maymundez. Alamut was a strong stone-built fortress, whereas Maymundez was constructed out of conglomerate rock. The strength of the Alamut garrison was considerably less than that of the Mongol invaders, but nevertheless sufficient to withstand a prolonged siege. Alamut was well provided with stocks of food, supplies of all kinds and had a more than adequate water system. But the castle was small and the massed ranks of the Mongol forces must have seemed frighteningly close once they surrounded the rock on which the castle stands.

The greatest pressure on the Alamut commander must have been the knowledge that Maymundez had offered little resistance and the Imam had been forced to surrender. He had further ordered at Hulegu's behest the surrender and destruction of all Ismaili castles without attempting to resist. The garrisons of some forty castles in the region had already complied with the order, with the exception of Alamut and Lamasar.[10] If Muqaddam had decided to reject the Mongol call for surrender, he would not only have condemned his entire garrison to certain death but also disobeyed the express instruction of his Imam. That would have been totally contrary to his oath of allegiance pledging his absolute obedience to the Imam in all circumstances.

For the Mongols the complete destruction of Alamut and other Ismaili castles was a matter of the highest importance, not so much for religious reasons – although Juwayni makes much of this – as for political and military advantage. The complete subjugation of the Ismailis was essential to the expansion of Mongol power westward into the central Islamic lands. Of course, Juwayni saw the whole Mongol campaign against the Ismailis as a matter of divine punishment visited upon the 'heretics' whom he despised. He calls Alamut 'a nest of satan' and 'a breeding ground of heresy'.[11] The defenders of Maymundez are described as 'purblind, crooked-hearted' unbelievers and 'serpent-like miscreants'.[12] At times Juwayni is sickeningly sanctimonious and this attitude sits oddly with his evident, almost sadistic delight in his description of the brutal and violent deaths meted out to the Ismailis.

We must be thankful at least that Juwayni was of a scholarly disposition and obtained Hulegu's permission to inspect the library of Alamut before its destruction. He examined its treasures carefully and picked out a few Qur'ans as well as a number of rare books and astronomical instruments for his own collection. Then he consigned the rest of the library's precious contents to the flames. He recounts this moment as follows:

> I went to examine the library from which I extracted whatever I found in the way of copies of the Qur'an and other choice books ... I likewise picked out the astronomical instruments such as kursis (part of an astrolabe), armillary spheres, complete and partial astrolabes, and others that were there. As for the remaining books, which related to their heresy and error, and were neither founded on tradition nor supported by reason, I burnt them all. And although the treasuries were copious (with) gold and silver goods without limit, I recited over them the words: '*O yellow, be yellow, and O white, be white,*' and magnanimously shook my sleeve upon them.[13]

There was one book, however, that interested Juwayni immensely. This book contained the 'life and adventures' of the 'accursed Hasan (may God confound him!)'. This is Hasan Sabbah's biography, *Sargozast-e Baba Sayyidna*, which Juwayni claims to have burnt after reading it, although he subsequently quotes extensively from it in his *History*. We must always make allowances for Juwayni's tendency to exaggeration and hyperbole, especially on the political and religious history of the Ismailis. As we have often seen, this historian's primary interest was to celebrate the victories of the Mongols and to denigrate their opponents whatever their persuasion, be they Shi'a or Sunni Muslims.

It is also worthwhile studying carefully Juwayni's description of the strength of Alamut and its destruction on the orders of Hulegu Khan. He relates that all the ascents and approaches to the castle had been so strengthened by plastered walls and lead-covered ramparts that the soldiers who were given the task of destruction found their picks were of no use. The soldiers had to set fire to the buildings and then demolish them almost piece by piece. Juwayni comments on the extensive storage chambers, galleries and deep tanks at Alamut, which were filled with wine, vinegar, honey and all sorts of stores. While the stores were being removed as booty of war, one man waded into a tank of honey without realising how deep it was and was almost drowned. Juwayni comments that although many of the stores had been laid down at the time of Hasan Sabbah, they showed no deterioration even after an interval of over 170 years.[14]

Allowing perhaps for some exaggeration, Juwayni's account is a remarkable illustration of how well stocked Alamut and indeed all Ismaili castles were. This explains how some of them, like Gerdkuh, were able to withstand a siege that lasted for many years. The garrisons of such castles, together with the local Ismailis who had taken refuge in the castle, had a very adequate supply of food and water, while the besieging armies had to live off any food that still grew in the valley around the castles. Many fields would have been destroyed before the siege began in order to deprive the attackers of this food supply. There are many instances, especially among the armies of the Crusaders, when sieges had to be lifted owing to the shortage of provisions among the attackers, while the defenders lived in comparative luxury.

Rokn al-Din's surrender raises many interesting questions. What lay behind the protracted negotiations he had tried to pursue with the Mongols? What sort of an agreement had he tried to obtain? Probably he was prepared to accept some sort of declaration of fealty to the Great Khan if he could not avoid making concessions. But he was not prepared to give up of his own free will any of his castles. This would be a form of submission he could not accept. This must have been a decision over which he agonised considerably. He was probably also deeply influenced by his concept of the sacred nature of his Imamate. The surrender or destruction of his castles would have been tantamount to the abdication of his own authority.

From a military point of view, Rokn al-Din's decision to base the defence of his castles on Maymundez seems odd and difficult to explain. If he had made Alamut the centre of his defence, the outcome might have been very different. It seems, too, that there was no plan for a strategic withdrawal to other Ismaili centres. As mentioned, Rokn al-Din was a young man and inexperienced in warfare, having assumed leadership of his community only a few months earlier. Perhaps he relied too much on the assurance of his advisers that Hulegu would accept his repeated expressions of homage, or that the onset of winter would prevent the Mongols from mounting a concerted assault. The garrison of Alamut almost certainly did not expect the Mongol armies to advance so swiftly and surround their castle. This made it quite impossible for Rokn al-Din to withdraw to Alamut.

What would have happened if Rokn al-Din had based himself on Alamut and refused to surrender? The Mongols would have taken Maymundez anyway, because of their superiority in firepower and the destructive effects of their ballistas. But Alamut and other castles such as Lamasar, Gerdkuh or Soru and especially Nevisar Shah would have been immune to the Mongol bombardment, and he would have been able to hold out for a much longer time, as did indeed the garrison of Gerdkuh which refused to surrender for 17 years until 1270. This is one of the fascinating speculations of history. The prolonged resistance of Gerdkuh gives us some important evidence that the basic strategy behind the construction and location of Ismaili castles was sound, and the Ismailis would have most probably continued to resist the Mongols for many years had it not been for the disaster at Maymundez.

After Rokn-ad-Din had surrendered in person he was at first treated well enough by Hulegu who wanted to use him to secure the fall of the castles that were still holding out. He was taken to Qazvin and there instructed to send messengers to the Ismaili castles in Syria ordering them to surrender. The Syrian Ismailis, however, realised that their Imam was acting under duress and took no notice. Rokn al-Din's position was now intolerable and he asked to be allowed to go to Mongolia to visit the Great Khan, promising that he would endeavour to persuade the outlying Ismaili fortresses like Gerdkuh to surrender. On his arrival at Karakoram, however, Mongke rebuked him for not having handed over Lamasar and Gerdkuh and ordered his return to his homeland. The Great Khan had decided that nothing more could be gained from the Ismaili leader. As Rokn al-Din set out on the long return journey from Mongolia under armed escort, he was led away from the road on the pretext that a feast had been prepared for him. Then he and all his small retinue were one by one put to death. Juwayni finishes his description of this event with almost jubilant glee:

> He and his followers were kicked to a pulp and then put to the sword; and of him and his stock no trace was left, and he and his kindred became but a tale on men's lips and a tradition in the world. So was the world cleansed which had been polluted by their evil.[15]

Meanwhile, orders had been issued that Rokn al-Din's family who had stayed behind in Qazvin should suffer the same fate, including the infants. Despite the promises Hulegu had made to spare the lives of the castle garrisons in Mongol custody, these men were killed too. In Qohistan the Mongol commander summoned all Ismailis to attend a great gathering, where some 12,000 were brutally massacred. Similar atrocities followed in different parts of the country. It is difficult to make a proper estimate of the total number of Ismailis who perished, but the figure could have been as high as 100,000. Some survivors escaped to remote areas of the countryside and others fled to neighbouring countries. The net effect of this policy of extermination was the complete destruction of Ismaili power in Iran and the decimation of the Ismaili population to such small numbers that their existence was barely noticed by Persian historians of later generations. The only things that reminded them of the Ismailis were the legends of Hasan Sabbah and his band of loyal followers who defied the mighty Saljuq sultans from their numerous castles, which now lay ruined and desolate in the remote highlands of Iran.

Enough has already been written to show that the Ismailis were certainly anything but the terrorists and brigands of legend. The influence the early Nizari Ismailis wielded was completely disproportionate to their size and power. Their political and military achievements were far-reaching and effective. They were always considered, even in Europe, to be a power to be reckoned with. Their practical achievements in military architecture, irrigation and agriculture in mountainous terrain exceeded the achievements of many of their contemporaries. Even more astonishing, in many ways, is the fact that despite the totality of their defeat and apparent oblivion of the Ismailis following the Mongol victories of 1256, the eagle – though sorely wounded – was able to fly again. Juwayni's arrogant and brutal boast that 'of him [Rokn al-Din] and his stock no trace was left' was to be proved conclusively false. Of course, the massacres of 1256 were followed by centuries of darkness for the Ismailis, but there were survivors. History has taught us, especially recently, that peoples inspired by a genuine faith can never be completely eliminated as their conquerors hope. Gradually the number of Ismaili survivors grew. Their Imamate was preserved and grew in strength, too, until in the 19th century modern Ismailism emerged under the leadership of the Aga Khans.

When I first started to explore the Ismaili castles way back in 1959 I was, of course, fascinated by the archaeological challenge of the great ruins. Somehow I had to make sense of them, and as I continued my work and learnt more of their history, they began to come alive as the aspirations of a great faith. The castles themselves meant little without the knowledge of why they were built, who were the builders and what was their purpose. Why, too, were they destroyed? These questions became ever more urgent when I was examining the greatest of the castles such as Nevisar Shah, Gerdkuh and Soru. The legends I had read about the 'Assassins' were clearly false. They were totally inadequate to account for the considerable achievements of the Ismailis in art and science. But knowledge of their history and beliefs could provide the answer to my questions. And so, I suggest, it is appropriate in this book to lay firm foundations explaining just how the Nizari Ismaili state came into existence in Iran and Syria, what the state aimed to achieve and why it attracted so many enemies. This I have attempted to do in the first part of this book. We can now look at the castles themselves – the nests of eagles.

Notes

1. Daftary, *The Isma'ilis*, pp. 418–419.

2. Robert Marshall, *Storm from the East: From Gengis Khan to Khubilai Khan* (London, 1993), p. 195.

3. Ibid., p. 95.

4. Juwayni, *History of the World-Conqueror*, vol. 1, p. 132.

5. Ibid., p. 162.

6. Ibid., p. 615–616.

7. I.B. Petrushevsky, 'The Socio-Economic Conditions in Iran under the Il-Khans,' in *The Cambridge History of Iran*: Volume 5, pp. 483–537.

8. Hodgson, 'The Isma'ili State,' in *The Cambridge History of Iran*: Volume 5, p. 344.

9. Juwayni, *History of the World-Conqueror*, vol. 2, p. 635.

10. J.A. Boyle, 'Dynastic and Political History of the Il-Khans,' in *The Cambridge History of Iran*: Volume 5, pp. 303–421.

11. Juwayni, *History of the World Conqueror*, p. 639.

12. Ibid., pp. 635–636.

13. Ibid., p. 719–720.

14. Ibid., p. 721.

15. Ibid., pp. 724–725.

PART TWO

The Castles of the Ismailis

CHAPTER 6

The Strategy of Ismaili Castles

In the first part of this book I have tried to give the reader a brief historical account of the Ismailis from the time of their first Imam 'Ali to the great days of the Fatimid empire. I have also set the momentous events in Fatimid Egypt and elsewhere in their wider historical perspective, discussing the relationship between the Ismailis and other Muslim communities. We have followed the career of Hasan Sabbah from the days of his conversion to the Ismaili cause and his education in Cairo to the time when he gained control of Alamut. From this power base he was able to inspire and direct the Ismaili uprising aimed primarily against the Saljuq occupation. We have seen how the Ismailis were able to create a territorial state of their own based upon a network of fortresses in Iran and Syria, and to defend their independence vigorously for nearly two centuries. Finally, we described in some detail how the Ismailis were eventually overwhelmed by the Mongol invasions that swept across the Muslim world in the mid-13th century.

The backbone of the Ismaili defence system was provided by the chain of formidable castles that defended the borders of their state and without which the state would probably have crumbled. The crucial importance of these castles had not been recognised in the past for the simple reason that many of them had not been located and described until my recent research, especially in Khorasan and the area around Semnan and Damghan in northern Iran. It is undeniable that the Ismaili castles are quite outstanding as examples of military architecture, their strategic position and the skilled use of natural resources which ensured that, despite the difficulties of the terrain, they were well supplied with food and water, and thus able to withstand a prolonged siege of many months, even years. We have also noted the importance of these castles as administrative and especially cultural centres, with their libraries and facilities for advanced studies in science, philosophy, theology and the arts. The successful realisation of all these attributes at once places the Ismaili fortresses in a very different category to the European concept of a castle.

European and Crusader castles

In the West it has always been considered that castle architecture is one of the great and almost exclusively exclusively European achievements, reaching its zenith in the castles of the Crusaders. The spectacular castle of Krak des Chevaliers in Syria is often regarded as the supreme example of this art, but with due deference I maintain that this fortress has been too extravagantly praised by writers such as T.E. Lawrence. For example, Robin Fedden and John Thomson in their *Crusader Castles* describe Krak as 'the most remarkable example of the military architecture of the 12th and 13th centuries, and, in the opinion of Lawrence, "perhaps the best preserved and most wholly admirable castle in the world".'[1]

Ross Burns in his *Monuments of Syria*, starts his description of Krak with the following quotation from *Castles and Churches of the Crusading Kingdom* by T.S.R. Boase: 'As the Parthenon is to Greek temples and Chartres to Gothic cathedrals, so is the Krak des Chevaliers to medieval castles, the supreme example, one of the great buildings of all times.'[2] Such sentiments seem to me to be both excessive and difficult to substantiate.

To an observer like myself, who has studied both Krak and the great Ismaili strongholds in Iran, it is evident that the Crusaders had far fewer problems to overcome in the construction of their castles than did the Ismailis. As we shall see, the Ismailis well understood how to build a defensive structure of great size and strength, capable of resisting long sieges and difficult to attack. The Crusader castles did not often have to withstand long sieges, while the Ismaili fortresses often held out against Saljuq and Mongol offensives for many months, and in the case of Gerdkuh for as long as 17 years. In fact, Alamut and other Ismaili fortresses in Rudbar were so strongly built with enormous provisions of food and weapons that, as Hodgson claims, they could have held out against the Mongols indefinitely and thus should have been able to reach a favourable accommodation short of surrender.[3]

European castles remained fairly simple structures, although adequate for their purposes as military strongpoints, until the Crusading armies encountered first the far stronger Byzantine fortifications and later the Arab fortresses in Syria. The most obvious differences between European and Oriental castles (especially the Ismaili ones) are those of size and method of construction. The early castles in the Western world from the ninth century onwards were of the motte and bailey type. Then came the stone keeps of the Normans, such as the donjon at Falaise, the birthplace of William the Conqueror, the Round Tower at Windsor (built c.1075) and the rectangular White Tower of London (c.1080). Normally the walls of the keep were sunk securely into the soil or built on rock. These castles were of relatively small size and the construction posed no great difficulty. There was no need of a large labour force. Water was readily available from a river or a convenient spring. Accommodation and storerooms were built within the keep on flat ground within the castle walls.

The main subsequent advance of Western military architecture was in the siting of the castle. The Crusaders had learnt that the best location for a castle was on top of a steep, preferably precipitous hill, which could not be approached from heights above. These new castles were built at strategic points to prevent further progress by the invading force. One of the best examples of this type of castle is Chateau Gaillard, near Rouen in France, built by King Richard I in 1196–98, after his return from the Third Crusade. It stands on top of a precipitous cliff 100 metres above the Seine. It was one of the most powerful castles of its day, consisting of three separate baileys in line, each separated by a moat. Great care was taken to give as few opportunities as possible for sapping and mining, another lesson brought back from the Crusades. The reign of Edward I of England (1272–1307) was the most brilliant period of military architecture in that country and in all Europe, when his magnificent series of six castles, including Caernarvon and Conway, was built to control the Welsh. A discussion of these is beyond the scope of this book, but it is worth noting that Edward made extensive use of strong round towers at the corners of each line of defence – a feature that is even more accentuated in the Ismaili castles that had been built some 200 years before Edward came to the throne. Edward I went on a Crusade in 1270 and was clearly very impressed by the military architecture that he saw. It seems likely that he incorporated some of the design features into his own castles. He may have brought a master mason with him , who also built the episcopal palace at Lichfield.

To give the Crusaders due credit, they were not slow to apply to their own architecture the lessons they had learnt from Byzantine and Arab castles. The Crusaders must have marvelled at the defences of Constantinople, especially the city walls. The early defences of Rome (590 BC) consisted of a single wall, 3 metres wide and 8 metres high. The so-called Servian wall which replaced it in the 4th century BC ran for nearly 6 kilometres. Constantinople was surrounded by a moat, an outer terrace and wall, an inner terrace and a massive wall incorporating many round, square and multi-angled towers. This wall was about 18 metres high with the towers spread out at intervals of approximately 55 metres. Wherever they went in the Byzantine empire, the Crusaders found the same powerful, well-planned and overwhelming defence works. This must have come as a considerable shock when they thought of their own relatively puny achievements at home. In Syria the Crusaders found smaller Byzantine castle fortifications, which were normally quadrilateral in form with towers in the centre (a kind of keep) and at the corners of the walls. The Crusaders imitated this pattern when building their own first castles. Byzantine military architecture was undoubtedly of high quality and showed much ingenuity. The fortress of Saone in Syria is a triumph of their architecture, especially the pillar ditch, or moat, some 25–30 metres deep and over 15 metres wide, which had been cut out of the rock surrounding the castle. In the centre of the moat a slender needle of rock was left to support the drawbridge. The castle was captured by Saladin in 1188 and is now a fascinating mixture of Byzantine and Arab architecture.

Once the Crusaders had begun to realise the inadequacy of their castles and to apply the lessons they had learnt from the Byzantines, they did indeed begin to build castles of great strength and beauty such as Margat, Krak des Chevaliers and Chastel-Blanc or Safita in Syria. These castles, built in the Crusader county of Tripoli, are within easy reach of the Ismaili castles; in fact the Ismailis occupied Margat on the coast for a time. But as far as we can tell, the rulers of the Frankish kingdom of Outremer – as the Arab lands occupied by the Crusaders were called – never adopted an overall strategic plan to defend their possessions against the Arabs. This was partly because there never was one firm central authority in Outremer, and also because the militant orders of the Templars and Knights Hospitaller were always jealous of one another and regarded the castles they built as their own property rather than part of a single Christian kingdom.

Oriental and Middle Eastern castles

Turning to India, the building of castles there had started much earlier than in Europe with the fortification of cities around the 5th century BC. Ramparts were made of earth which were at first covered with brick, then solid stone walls. Kausambi, in the centre of the Ganges plain near Aliabad, had most impressive fortifications. The city walls are about 6.5 km long and at some places 50 metres high. The expansion of Muslim power into the Indian subcontinent led to the construction of numerous castles. The Indian medieval and Mughal castles are in a class of their own. Many of them are perched on precipitous hills and, as in Iran, include a city as well as a citadel. They are very large indeed and are surrounded by numerous strong walls and spectacular gatehouses. They are tall enough to accommodate the entry of elephants with their howdahs and mounts. The teak doors are studded with large spikes to prevent them being forced open by the attacking force and their elephants.

In Persia there are even older military sites than in India. At Sangar near Baku on the Turkish border, there is an Urartian fortress of the 8th century BC with a rock-cut chamber and an impressive staircase of thirty steps. The Urartians were a powerful people centred around Lake Van in Turkey, and there seems to have been a close relationship between the Urartians and the Armenians. Ancient Persia has always had a tradition of building on a grand scale – witness Persepolis and the Sassanian site of Takht-e Sulayman with its huge circular mud-brick wall, and the picturesque fortified city of Bam in the Kerman region. During the Safavid period (1501–1722), Bam was a flourishing trading and commercial centre on the famous Silk Road. Measuring 6 square kilometres, the city was dominated by a citadel and surrounded on all sides by a rampart with 38 towers. Bam was almost totally destroyed in a powerful earthquake that struck this historic city in December 2003 with the loss of over 40,000 lives.

When the first generation of Arab Muslims advanced into Syria, Iraq and Palestine in the seventh century, they were content to make minimum alterations to the Christian churches they had occupied to suit the demands of their faith, which generally meant the removal of the Christian altar (and other fittings) and its replacement by a *qibla* wall, realigning it from the direction of Jerusalem to Mecca. The Arabs themselves soon became capable craftsmen, and they also found Byzantine architects and builders who were prepared to help them. A typical example is the Dome of the Rock (the al-Aqsa mosque) in Jerusalem, completed in 691, which is very Byzantine in its architectural concept. The two octagons surmounted by a dome on a circular drum bear a close resemblance to some Byzantine churches such as San Vitale at Ravenna in Italy. The interior decoration could almost belong to any ecclesiastical building in Constantinople.

The 10th and 11th centuries were times of extraordinary Muslim economic expansion and cultural brilliance that was reflected in the buildings of the time. There was almost a frenzy of building and decoration in every part of the Islamic world, a state of affairs that did not occur in Europe. These years were a period of great sophistication in all the arts, sciences and practical craftsmanship. The Muslim rulers built new cities with great palaces and mosques that were exquisitely decorated. People thought on a grand scale, and military architecture was no exception. As a result there was a great demand for architects, masons, craftsmen and specialists in design and decoration. The Yemen, where there had always been a great decorative tradition from pre-Islamic times, was considered to produce the best masons. There was doubtless a constant movement of such people from one construction site to another throughout the vast region that comprised the Islamic world.

The Muslim rulers also invested a great deal in protecting their important cities with walls and fortresses. Whereas the castles of medieval Europe were built by feudal overlords, first for local defence and then to ensure the pacification of a larger area, in the Muslim world defensive structures were generally constructed by the state to protect strategic cities and border towns against armed invasion by hostile powers or incursions of nomadic tribesmen, as well as for the maintenance of internal security.

The extensive use of fortifications in the Middle East was noted by the famous Persian Ismaili poet and philosopher Naser Khosraw in his book of travels, the *Safarnameh* (mentioned in Chapter 1). Naser was writing in the middle of the 11th century, well before the Ismaili opposition to the Saljuqs had built up in Iran. He describes in fascinating detail his seven-year journey from Merv to Nishapur in eastern Iran, then across the Caspian and Caucasian regions, eastern Anatolia, Syria, Palestine and Jerusalem to the Fatimid capital of Cairo. After several years in Egypt, he returned across the Arabian peninsula and through Iran to his hometown of Balkh in Khorasan. Naser's travelogue is relatively short, written in concise prose and with a dry sense of humour. He does not write about religion as such but of the people he met in various regions, their economic and social conditions, and their ways of life. As a former government official in the Saljuq administration, he was especially interested in the administration and defences of the towns and cities he passed through.

Here is Naser's description of the fortified city of Amid in the region of Diyarabakir, south-west of Lake of Van in eastern Turkey, which he visited in November 1046. It is worth quoting the passage in full in order to appreciate the author's meticulous attention to detail in a way that is rarely found in medieval literature:

> The foundation of the city is laid on a monolithic rock. The length of the city is two thousand paces, and the breadth the same. There is a wall all around made of black rock, each slab weighing between a hundred and a thousand maunds [159–1589 kilos]. The facing of these stones is so expert that they fit together exactly, needing no mud or plaster in between. The height of the wall is twenty cubits, and the width ten. Every hundred ells there is a tower, the half circumference of which is eighty ells. The crenellations are also of this same black stone. Inside the city are many stone stairs by means of which one can go up onto the ramparts, and atop every tower is an embrasure. The city has four gates, all of iron with no wood, and each gate faces one of the four cardinal directions. The east gate is called the Tigris Gate, the west gate the Byzantine Gate, the north the Armenian Gate, and the south the Tell Gate. Outside this wall just described is yet another wall, made of that same stone. It is ten ells high, and the top is completely covered with crenellations. Inside the crenellation is a passageway wide enough for a totally armed man to pass and to stop and fight with ease. The outside wall also has iron gates, placed directly opposite the gates in the inside wall so that when one passes from a gate in the first wall one must traverse a space of fifteen ells before reaching the gate in the second wall. Inside the city is a spring that flows from a granite rock about the size of five millstones.

The water is extremely pleasant, but no one knows where the source is. The city has many orchards and trees thanks to that water. The ruling prince of the city is a son of the Nasruddawla who has been mentioned. I have seen many a city and fortress around the world in the lands of the Arabs, Persians, Hindus, and Turks, but never have I seen the likes of Amid on the face of the earth nor have I heard anyone else say that he had seen its equal.[4]

The strong fortifications of Amid were by no means an unusual feature of medieval Arab, Turkish and Persian cities. In fact, most places that Naser Khosraw visited in the course of his journeys appear to have been defended by massive walls, towers and gates. The same was the case in what Naser called the 'forbidden mountains' of Qohistan through which he passed on his return journey. As we have seen, this region of Iran was later to become a major region of the Ismaili revolt under Hasan Sabbah. Naser mentions a number of fortified towns and castles that he had seen at certain strategic points, including Tun with its strong fortress and Qa'in whose outer walls were protected by a trench. Both these cities were to become important Ismaili strongholds within a few decades of Naser's journey and it is quite possible that many of their inhabitants were already Ismailis. This may have been the case of a man Naser reports meeting in Qa'in, who engaged the traveller in a philosophical discussion on whether or not the universe has a limit and what could possibly lie beyond the world of heavenly spheres and fixed stars.[5]

The Ismaili castles

From the earliest days of the Ismaili uprising in Iran, the boundaries of their state had been more or less firmly fixed. These were largely influenced by geographical factors, especially the Alborz mountains in the north and the two great deserts of Dasht-e Kavir and Dasht-e Lut to the south. Alamut was always the headquarters of the Persian Ismailis from the time it was captured by Hasan Sabbah. Although their occupation of some of their castles, such as Shahdez and Khanlanjan in the Isfahan region, may not have lasted very long, the main line of fortresses did not change during the 160 years or so of the Ismaili state. From Alamut this line stretches eastwards to Firuzkuh and then along the road to Mashhad, past the great complex of strongholds in Qumes between Semnan and Damghan. In Khorasan the line runs southward to Qohistan and the border with Sistan, and westward to Tun and Tabas. We shall consider these strongholds in detail in subsequent chapters.

In order to understand the *raison d'être* of Ismaili fortresses – why a particular location was chosen, what were the strategic and tactical considerations behind their choice, as well as the guiding political principles – we must go back to Iran and remember that the same considerations applied to almost all the main areas of the Ismaili state, such as Alamut valley and the Rudbar, Qumes, Qohistan, the smaller areas like Isfahan and Arrajan, and the castles of Syria. These considerations can be defined as follows:

- The Ismailis would only establish a military base in an area that could be viably defended and on a terrain sufficiently remote and difficult to discourage attacks by their more numerous enemies.
- The complex of fortresses within this chosen area must have the ability to support each other in the event of attack and enable an efficient system of communication, whether by beacon or other means, to be established.
- That the chosen area contain enough natural material, especially wood and stone, for the construction or reconstruction of a fortress, to be carried out expeditiously and with the minimum labour force.
- That the terrain be self-sufficient in fresh water and allow the growing of multiple crops to ensure regular and adequate food supplies for the garrison and their dependants.
- And last but not least, the area be inhabited by a significant Ismaili population or other Shi'i Muslims sympathetic to the Ismaili cause, who could be relied upon for support and services.

These are the five cardinal principles that governed the construction of all Ismaili castles. But what of the practical consequences of these principles? From time to time, especially later on in the book, I mention the three greatest dangers facing all fortresses, whether Arab, Crusader, Persian or Turk. These are:

- The danger of forced submission as a result of attrition and no further food or water available to the defender.
- The danger of the breach of strong defences by battering rams, siege towers and particularly mangonels.
- The danger of the undermining of curtain walls or strategic defensive sites by saps and explosive charges placed against the walls.

Apart from the case of Maymundez perhaps, the Ismailis were always very careful to include the necessary counter-measures in their plans of new or enlarged fortifications. The danger of attrition was averted by the numerous storage facilities of food and water. The garrison could not be starved into submission. Gerdkuh survived a siege lasting seventeen years, and when it eventually surrendered

I doubt if the real or primary reason was shortage of food or water. The garrison was probably totally exhausted, ill and disorientated.

The danger from battering rams, mangonels, mines and explosive charges against the walls (which caused the downfall of the crusader castle of Krak) was obviated by the application of the first of the five cardinal principles. It was almost totally impossible (except in the case of Maymundez) for an attacker to set up his mangonels within an effective range, due to the steep angle of the mountainside on which the castle was built and the absence of surrounding hills. It was also impossible to dig tunnels beneath the curtain walls or set charges against them again because of the angle of the slope and the hardness of the rock.

There is one crucial feature, however, that stands out above all else when assessing the Ismaili castles in Iran and Syria. Almost all the castles were built in remote mountainous areas, far away from established sources of skilled labour. This must have greatly increased the difficulty of construction or refortification, especially the problems of obtaining building materials and their transporation. As a result the Ismailis developed considerable experience in building and reinforcing castles in difficult terrain. Their techniques of construction together with associated defensive positions and walls were a considerable engineering achievement.

The Ismaili concept of the design and strategic function of a castle did not rest on the construction of a great citadel either on a natural or man-made prominence. This was basically the Crusader concept, stemming from the original Norman castle. Instead the Ismailis, whenever possible, built upon the crown of a great rock or mountain, dividing the fortifications up into self-contained sections, culminating in the citadel at the top. The best example of this is Qa'in (see chapter 10). This was quite a different approach from that of the Byzantines or that adopted by the Frankish invaders of Outremer. The Ismaili concept was much more sophisticated too as provision had to be made for ample water storage, in the first place, and then for all the needs of the garrison, the defence of the fortress and protection of the local population.

Where and how we may ask did the Ismailis obtain their knowledge and technical ability to build in such difficult mountain areas? Who were their architects, engineers and masons? History is, however, silent as to who actually planned and supervised the construction of these fortresses. We cannot answer these questions in any great detail, just as it is not possible to supply similar information for the Arab and most of the Crusader castles. In any case, as we have seen, most of the Ismaili records were destroyed by the Mongols, and Juwayni has little to say about the complex logistics that must have been deployed by the Ismailis in building their castles. We can nevertheless make reasonably accurate assumptions.

We have already noted the long tradition of building castles and fortified cities among the Arabs, Persians and Turks, as well as the Byzantines. We should not therefore be surprised that the Persian Ismailis were able to draw on this tradition of construction on a large scale with great success. Most of the Ismaili leaders had travelled a great deal and were perfectly familiar with the military architecture of the day. Some of them, like Hasan Sabbah, had been to Egypt and probably obtained first-hand knowledge of military strategy in the Fatimid state. There can be little doubt that Hasan was personally responsible for rebuilding and enlarging Alamut with its subterranean storerooms, and making it as impregnable as possible. The commanders of other Ismaili castles in Rudbar and Qohistan would doubtless have visited Alamut and seen for themselves what could be achieved. Hasan's successor, Bozorg-Ommid, came from Rudbar in the north and so was familiar with mountain conditions and the forts and castles that had already been built there.

The problem for the Ismailis was not the technique of military architecture, but rather the best way of constructing large fortresses in remote areas with limited water resources. The search for water has always been a constant preoccupation of Iranians in mountainous areas and this would have been a crucial task in which natural talent and expertise would have overcome all obstacles. Thus, when Bozorg-Ommid took Lamasar by storm in 1096, he at once set about turning the existing castle into the largest Ismaili stronghold of the time and providing it with a complex water storage system. His success can be measured by the fact that, following Hasan's example at Alamut, he was even able to plant trees inside and outside the castle.

Many of the Ismaili castles in Khorasan and elsewhere in Iran had been built quite a long time before the Ismailis took control of them and we often have no means of knowing who the original builders were. From the surviving evidence, it is clear that these fortresses were at first quite small with limited access to fresh water, probably just a spring or a deep well. All these fortifications needed to be enlarged and strengthened substantially by their Ismaili occupants. Some castles like those at Maymundez, Gerdkuh and Soru were newly built, but whether the Ismailis decided to rebuild existing castles or construct new ones, they set about their task practically and intelligently. The Iranians are by nature a remarkably practical and resourceful people, and there would have been no shortage of competent men in each area capable of planning the new castles within an overall strategy devised by the Ismaili leadership. They knew what they wanted and laboured tirelessly to construct large, strong, solid, highly defensible positions that would be very difficult to overcome by an enemy force.

In addition to building fresh defence works, including sometimes the construction of subsidiary outposts, the Ismailis concentrated on digging deep storage chambers below the main castle area, often connected by a network of passages. There was no shortage of building materials or wood for constructing scaffolding and seasoned timber (mostly willow) for the roofs, floors and walkways. The provision of sufficient labour might have posed some problems, but most Ismaili bases were located in areas where they already had a significant following, and doubtless skilled volunteers would have been mobilised to help in the construction work. We must also remember that the population in Qohistan and other parts of Khorasan was large and the countryside fertile, before the havoc, pillage and systematic slaughter of its inhabitants by the Mongols reduced the region into a wasteland.

The style of military architecture employed by the Ismailis was well in advance of, say, the Normans of this period. The Ismailis well understood how to build a castle of great strength, capable of withstanding long sieges and very difficult to attack. The plan of the castle, the positioning of the towers and the circumference walls is in castles like Soru comparable to a Frankish fortress as outstanding as Krak des Chevaliers. The Ismailis knew the value of two or three curtain-walls and how supporting towers and gateways should be constructed. They also understood the modern military concept of defence in depth and supporting fire.

The great fortress of Masyaf, the centre of Ismaili power in Syria, shows clearly a Byzantine influence, though it is in essence an Ismaili citadel. Masyaf is also interesting in that it provides the link between the castles of Syria and Iran. It is regrettable that T.E. Lawrence was never able to visit Rudbar or Qohistan, as this might have added another perspective to his perception of the function of a castle. There can now be little doubt that the elaborate system of inter-communicating fortresses established by the Ismailis, as the nerve points of their state, was something that the Crusaders never achieved in Outremer. Taken by themselves, most of the individual fortresses were considerably larger and better planned than those of the Crusaders – even though aesthetically the Crusader castles were visually more appealing due to the honey colour of their stone, the lusher surrounding countryside and the Mediterranean background.

The Ismailis understood the need for quick communications between each of their centres, and these were provided by means of smaller forts, watchtowers and beacons. One vital line of communication was always maintained between Alamut and the Ismaili castles in Syria. Despite the vast distance involved, there had to be, and was, a regular interchange of people between these two centres. In addition, as I have constantly stressed, the Ismailis were good agriculturists and water engineers. They placed great importance on regular access to water and food supplies in order to withstand long sieges. They combined their loyalty and intelligence with patience, determination and good management. And the utter conviction of the Ismailis in their mission, combined with their natural skill and complete dedication to their task, must have provided them with the inner strength which enabled them to complete these tasks so successfully. Without such qualities, Hasan Sabbah's vision of independence could never have been accomplished, nor could his followers be able to hold out against their opponents for so long.

Finally, we must always remember that the Ismaili fortresses were not just built for military purposes. They had many other uses that account for the surprisingly great size of some of them like Gerdkuh and Shahdez. These were, in fact, fortified townships, occupying the whole side and top of a great mountain peak. In times of siege they provided sanctuary to villagers from the surrounding countryside. I would not like to suggest that all Ismaili strongholds were as large as these two. In his *History of the World-Conqueror*, Juwayni estimates that there were at least 50 Ismaili castles in Qohistan which the Mongols had still to destroy.[6] From my own observation I would say this figure is very much on the low side. Some are relatively small in area, but this can be deceptive. For instance, at first sight the surface area of Alamut appears surprisingly small, but the storerooms beneath the main castle are numerous and large. Juwayni inspected these storerooms when the castle fell to the Mongols and was particularly amazed at the underground storage chambers:

> And in the cavities of these rocks they had constructed several long, wide and tall galleries and deep tanks, dispensing with the use of stone and mortar ... So too they had dug magazines and tanks for wine, vinegar, honey and all sorts of liquids and solids ... Most of these stores of liquids and solids, which they had been laying down from the time of Hasan Sabbah, that is over a period of more than 170 years, showed no sign of deterioration and this they regarded as a result of Hasan's sanctity. The remainder of the description of the implements of war and stores is more than can be inserted in a book without tedium.[7]

As the seat of Hasan Sabbah and headquarters of the Ismailis, Alamut was probably better supplied than the other castles, but Juwayni's description of the stores and reserves there could be equally applicable to almost all Ismaili castles.

Another feature that impressed Juwayni most was the ingenuity of the water supply. He reports that the Ismailis had brought a conduit to the foot of the castle 'and from thence a conduit was cut in the rock half-way round the castle and ocean-like tanks, also of rock, constructed beneath so that the water would be stored in them by its own impetus and was continually flowing on'.[8] It seems that they could have had as much water as they required, even for a *hamam* or communal bathhouse.

Apart from serving as a garrison for troops, the residence of local commanders, and administrative and religious centres of the Ismaili mission, many of the strongholds provided facilities for higher learning and possessed important libraries. Alamut in particular was sufficiently well endowed with books and scientific instruments to enable Naser al-Din Tusi to produce his great works on mathematics, astronomy and philosophy. As we have seen in the previous chapter, Juwayni was clearly impressed by the quantity of books and scientific equipment he found there. After he had made his choice of the library's treasures and consigned the remainder to the fire, the Mongol warlord Hulegu gave orders for the demolition of the castle. Juwayni relates that a large force of soldiers and levies set about the walls with their picks, chisels and other tools with little effect. Then they set fire to the buildings and began to break the walls piecemeal, a task that occupied them for a long time. He goes on to say that all the entries and exits, as well as the ascents and approaches, had been strengthened by plastered walls and lead-covered ramparts, so that 'when it was demolished it was as though the iron struck its head on a stone'.[9]

The destruction of the other Ismaili castles was no easy matter for the Mongols, who had to spend much time and effort in dismantling them, especially the great citadels of Qa'in and Gerdkuh. This by itself is a great tribute to their builders, which even Juwayni grudgingly admits. Since the Mongols were basically nomadic in character and had no desire to occupy the Ismaili fortresses, they sought to obliterate them as completely as possible so that the Ismailis would not return to them in the future. Mo'menabad, near Birjand in Qohistan, is a typical example of this destructive zeal; but as there were so many Ismaili fortresses large and small, and the work of demolition took up so much time and trouble, the Mongols concentrated their efforts on the more redoubtable strongholds. As a result, they probably succeeded in destroying no more than half of the total number of Ismaili castles and were often content to leave significant parts of the fortifications still standing.

Until my own research in Iran before and after the Revolution of 1979, comparatively little was known about the disposition, size and structure of the Ismaili castles other than Alamut. These castles demonstrate that the Ismailis possessed an accomplished mastery of military architecture and mountain agriculture, together with their ability to ensure ample reserves of food and water. The development of an agricultural policy to feed the inhabitants of the valleys and mountains of Qohistan in time of peace, with sufficient reserves to stock the vast storage vaults in time of war, required organisational skills of a high order. Nor were religious life, intellectual learning or the arts and crafts neglected. In fact, they thrived. Had it not been for the Mongol invasion, there could well have been a period of outstanding intellectual and cultural development comparable to that of the Fatimid Ismailis.

When we consider all this, I think we must conclude that the reality concerning the Ismailis is even more extraordinary that the myths and legends circulating about them for so many centuries. These achievements will become clear in subsequent chapters where I shall describe the major castles of the Persian and Syrian Ismailis in some detail.

Notes

1. Robin Fedden and John Thomson, *Crusader Castles of the Levant* (London, 1957), p. 84.

2. Ross Burns, *The Monuments of Syria: An Historical Guide* (London, 1994); T.S.R. Boase, *The Castles and Churches of the Crusading Kingdom* (Oxford, 1967).

3. See Hodgson, 'The Ismaili State,' pp. 481–482.

4. As translated by Thackston in *Naser Khosraw's Book of Travels (Safarnama)*, pp. 10–11 (quoted with permission of Mazda Publishers, Costa Mesa, CA).

5. Ibid., p.130. For an absorbing study of the life and thought of this Ismaili scholar, see Alice H. Hunsberger's *Nasir Khusraw, the Ruby of Badakhshan: A Portrait of the Persian Poet, Traveller and Philosopher* (London, 2003).

6. Juwayni, *History of the World-Conqueror*, vol. 2, p.637.

7. Ibid., pp. 720–721.

8. Ibid., p. 721.

9. Ibid., p. 720.

CHAPTER 7

Castles of the Alamut Valley – I

The isolation of the Alamut valley was, in effect, the principal reason why Hasan Sabbah decided to establish his powerbase here and was able to maintain it for so long against any attack. Although a mere 120 km from Tehran and 40 km from Qazvin, the region was only accessible by mule-track until very recently. At the time of my first expedition to Alamut in 1959, we had an arduous and difficult walk, carrying a lot of our own baggage over the mountains before we reached the valley. It was only in the succeeding years that a dirt road was built which enabled a bus to get in to the valley of Shahrud at Shahrestan-e Bala, west of Lamasar. Until Captain Roddie Dugmore, seconded to the 1960 expedition by the Royal Engineers, made his excellent map of the 'Valley of the Assassins', which was reproduced in my *Castles of the Assassins*, no reliable survey or map had been published of the quiet and undisturbed Alamut valley.[1]

Nowadays it is a very different story. As we have seen, the new main road from Tehran to Qazvin, which links with a tarmac road into Alamut constructed at the time of the last Shah of Iran, enables the inhabitants of Tehran to drive to the valley, have a picnic lunch and return the same day. Adrianne Woodfine, my research partner, and I were told that this was a common Friday holiday trip, although it is still difficult to get beyond Shahrak by car. The little village of Mo'alem Kelayeh, where we stayed during our exploration of Maymundez in 1960 and other years, is now a provincial administrative and agricultural centre. The road-signs all point towards Alamut and a sign marks the official entry into the valley. After 900 years of isolation, Alamut is now an increasingly popular tourist attraction and is even advertised as such by some British travel agents.

There were two principal reasons why this region was so isolated for many centuries until recent times. Firstly, the relative poverty of the area in natural resources, especially the lack of good arable land adequately provided with water, made the region unattractive commercially and economically. Also, the slow development of the Alamut area may be attributed to the inaccessibility of the valleys, situated between high mountain ranges. The most striking features of the Alborz is the steepness of the slopes, especially in the zone to the south of the Caspian Sea, where the mountain range is both at its narrowest and its highest. The Alborz range at this point, in the midst of which Alamut lies, and which separates the Caspian (10.5 metres below sea-level) from the central Iranian plateau (c.1200 metres above sea-level) is only 80 km wide. Yet within that distance, the mountain ranges frequently reach 3,050 metres, the highest peak being the 5,678 metres extinct volcano of Damavand. The mountain-knot of Alamkuh/Takht-e Sulayman, to the east of the Alamut valley, is also over 4,500 metres, and a neighbouring peak marks the source of the Alamutrud. This stream descends precipitately to the village of Garmarud (c.1500 metres), which marks the end of the main mule track passing through the valley, at the foot of the castle of Nevisar Shah. The Alamut river then flows westward through the valley which is approximately 40 km long and 15 km at its widest, with mountain ranges up to 3,050 metres to the north and south, before joining the Taleqan river in the gorge overlooked by the castles of Shirkuh and Bidelan in the west.

The steepness of the slopes can best be appreciated when travelling along the new tarmac road from Qazvin to Mo'alem Kelayeh. The road itself is a triumph of engineering, rising and falling in a series of startling bends and curves, often at acute angles, and affords a magnificent panorama of the Alborz scenery. It cuts through the mountains 250 metres or so above the turbulent waters of Alamutrud just to the east of the Shirkuh gorge.

The stretch of valley between Garmarud in the east and the Shirkuh gorge in the west is, therefore, bounded by mountain walls to the north, south and east. Furthermore the 350 metres deep Shirkuh gorge itself is impassable for half the year. It becomes filled with floodwaters during the rainy season of winter, and also with the meltwater of spring. The valley of the Alamut river could thus be defended along its whole length, and the fortresses of Shirkuh and Bidelan, guarding the western gorge entrance, and the castle of Nevisar Shah, commanding the eastern approaches through the mountain passes, played an essential role in this defence pattern. In the middle lies the castle of Alamut, in an area which is – unlike much of the region – reasonably fertile and contains sufficient flat land and water for irrigation, so that dry crops such as wheat and cattle feed, as well as rice, can be grown. And herein lay the agricultural basis, protected by castles and mountain walls, of the Ismaili power. Altogether there are 60 or so Ismaili castles, forts and watchtowers in the Alamut valley, including the major fortresses (see Appendix II).

Shirkuh and Bidelan

Before we consider the castle of Alamut itself, let us have a closer look at the fortifications at the western entrance to the valley. The gorge I have mentioned is about a kilometre long and it is possible to wade through it when the river level is low in summer. But it is a treacherous route at the best of times and the traditional approach to the valley has always been along the steep winding path up the formidable Taleqan range that forms the southern rampart of the Alamut valley. During the late Shah's reign a good gravel road, now tarmac, had been built through these mountains that emerged half way above the gorge.

At the time of Ismaili occupation, there were two forts built some 200 metres up either slope, just inside the gorge opening. We were told that the northern fort was called Borjak and the southern one Borj. I have scrambled up to Borj and can confirm that this was indeed a watchtower, although little of it remains today. At the southern headland above Borj is the fort of Shirkuh. This is considerably larger than Borjak and Borj, and until recently one turret remained which could just be spotted from the Taleqan valley below. Shirkuh was clearly intended as an observation post of some size. It has a magnificent view of the main track across the Taleqan and up to the hills above Qazvin.

Some 500 metres to the east of Shirkuh, guarding the entrance to the Alamut valley, is the impressive castle of Bidelan It is sometimes called Badasht (as it stands on the opposite bank of the river to the village of this name) and Gurehdar. It is also referred to as Shirkuh, but as we have seen these are two quite different sites. Bidelan is perched high on the edge of the Taleqan range, some 370 metres above the floor of the Alamutrud to the north and the Taleqanrud to the south. The rock outcrops rise steeply and smoothly to the north and slopes away from the top at about 50 degrees. The south, however, is rubbly and steep. As the slope is very steep, the climb up to the castle from the valley floor is nightmarish and progress is further hindered by a thick tangle of undergrowth.

About 100 metres from the summit on the north side is a large and well-constructed water catchment area, consisting of nine cisterns at intervals of 6 metres from each other, running diagonally down the slope of the hill. The cisterns of Bidelan were clearly part of an overall water system for this part of the valley. The only source of water could have been rain and snow, and the Ismaili engineers certainly made the best use of the catchment area. There are two major groups of cisterns, about 60 metres and 140 metres below the summit, all constructed outside the castle defences. They are grouped on either side of a natural, water-cut gully, and all are interconnected by a system of man-made channels which feeds the water evenly into each cistern. Their size varied between 6 and 15 metres in length, approximately 2 metres wide and probably 6 metres deep. The cisterns are now very nearly filled with rubble and it was impossible to estimate their original depth; the deepest we explored was 2 metres. In 1972 our water survey team estimated that these nine cisterns had a maximum volume of 207 cubic metres, which would give a total capacity of 201,160 litres, sufficient to support 165 men for a year.

Across the top cistern could be traced the foundations of the outer wall of the castle that ran for 200 metres. There are still some remains of a keep and towers on the crest, as well as an outer wall some 60 metres down from the top on the Taleqan side. The most impressive view of the castle is gained from the other side of the Taleqanrud.

We had first investigated Bidelan to see if it would be a contender for the site of Maymundez, as has sometimes been suggested. There is no question of this as it is in quite the wrong geographical location. Bidelan is clearly a fortress of the second rank. It probably did not contain a very large garrison, but it was nevertheless very much in the forefront of the Alamut defences and probably saw more action, especially in the early days of Ismaili rule, than the other castles. It was an important link, too, in the communication system of the Ismailis. It could receive signals from other castles higher up in the Taleqan and would have prevented any hostile force from seeking to enter the valley at the western end. Shirkuh, too, was well situated to send similar signals to Alamut and Maymundez, whence the information could be relayed to Ilan and Nevisar Shah.

Alamut, the 'City of Good Fortune'

As we have seen, the castle of Alamut was both the starting point and the constant power centre of the whole Ismaili movement. In recognition of its crucial strategic importance to his cause, Hasan Sabbah renamed it Baldat al-Iqbal, the 'City of Good Fortune'. It was from here that messengers were sent to the outlying provinces of the disparate Ismaili state, and to which distant commanders referred for instructions and directives. I shall, therefore, start this consideration of Alamut with an examination of what could still be seen at the castle in the 1960s – little, alas, now remains of it – and then consider the other main centres in the east of the Alamut valley: Maymundez, which from its geographical position overlooks many of the neighbouring valleys; Nevisar Shah and the valley of the Taleqan, which runs parallel to the Alamut river; we shall then consider Lambasar and Samiran in the following chapter.

The fortress of Alamut lies about two kilometres north-east of the hamlet of Gazorkhan. When my team visited the village for our first proper examination of the castle in 1960, I wrote that we found the inhabitants friendly, helpful and courteous. They do not claim to be Ismailis but take immense pride in the fame of Alamut. I continued my account in *The Castles of the Assassins* as follows:

> The pattern of their existence has remained unaltered for centuries, and they do not appear to wish for change, even though they might benefit. This is reflected in every external manifestation of their lives: their methods of farming ... their local industries, such as rug-making and wool-weaving; and their dress and customs. Time seems to have passed them by. They live for the moment, and their lives are as unchanging as the mountains around them.[2]

Since I wrote these words, I have visited Alamut many times, the last time with Adrianne Woodfine in 1996, and my description is in general as pertinent now as it was over 40 years ago. Other areas of the Alamut valley have been modernised as a result of the road connecting Qazvin and Mo'alem Kelayeh. But this road peters out near Andej, and Gazorkhan has to be approached by a dirt road making a great détour over the mountains to the west. There is a more direct track, but even in summer it is liable to flooding and subsidence. This détour, however, is valuable as it gives a new perspective of Alamut castle. In my early expeditions we had always approached the castle from the valley floor, which increased the impression of the height of the rock on which the castle stands. The detour enabled me to appreciate fully the strategic position of Alamut in relation to the fortress of Bidelan in the south-west and Maymundez in the north-west. Maymundez overlooks both the northern and western approaches and has a commanding view of the mountains until they slope down towards Qazvin.

The great rock on which Alamut castle was built is a symbol of its immense strength, rising some 185 metres above the village of Shotor Khan. Juwayni likened its appearance to a kneeling camel with its neck stretched out, and other picturesque phrases have been used to describe it. Freya Stark says that it is like a battleship broadside on, but I never considered this description particularly apt. The rock seems to lean to port, so any reference to a battleship would have to imply that the ship is in imminent danger of sinking! (See Plate 1).

From a distance the rock of Alamut looks unimpressive, set against the great peaks of the Hawdeqan range, which towers behind it to a height of some 4,000 metres. It is only when you get nearer the foot of the rock that you appreciate its immensely strong position, guarded by the other two castles of Bidelan and Maymundez. The name Alamut, Eagle's Nest, seems perfectly appropriate for the castle since eagles do, in fact, encircle the rock.

The colour of the rock is reddish-brown and grey, in contrast to the red sandstone of Maymundez. It has its own haunting stark beauty when seen through the slender poplar trees that are such a feature of the valley. The green of the poplars is matched by two bright patches of green near the top of the castle at the south-west end, which are grape vines popularly supposed to have been planted by Hasan Sabbah himself. The rock runs approximately north-west to south-east, consisting of the main fortifications and living quarters, about 140 metres long and varying in width from a very narrow nine to 40 metres, and a shallow south-eastern protrusion consisting of a rounded bluff of sandstone rock joined to the main castle by a saddle of conglomerate rock.

Despite the narrow width of the top, the castle must have been of considerable size. Of the substantial ruins of walls that remained as late as 1961, there is now hardly any trace (Plate 2). The extensive underground storerooms are now all blocked and would warrant proper excavation. During the 25 years since the Islamic Revolution in Iran, much of what remains of the castle has been destroyed – presumably by unauthorised treasure seekers who must have assumed that all the archaeological activity they had seen in previous years was an attempt by myself to unearth Hasan's hidden treasure! The Ministry of Cultural Heritage and Islamic Guidance, which is responsible for the preservation of the ancient monuments of Iran, has recently blocked off the entrance to the underground storerooms, which I had been able to enter in my earlier research, to prevent any further damage, and an officer of the Ministry lives near the site, but these measures have been taken far too late. Without Roddie Dugmore's survey of 1960, and the photographs that were taken then and during my subsequent expeditions, it would be quite impossible to recognise the important features of the castle.

Even in my early expeditions, we encountered considerable difficulties in deciding to which period some of the remains belong. The fortress was used by the Safavid dynasty in the 17th and 18th centuries as a state prison, and remains from this period still exist. The Mongol destruction was more vicious here than elsewhere because for these nomadic conquerors, Alamut with its library, archives and historical associations was the very heart and symbol of Ismaili power for which they had nothing but disdain. The remaining different strata and artefacts at Alamut are, therefore, highly confused and, needless to say, there is little space for Hasan's legendary garden of Paradise!

The topography of the area is important. Immediately to the north stands the magnificent Hawdeqan range, centring around the peak of Siyalan Kuh, which is 3,860 metres high. Beyond this the Alborz mountains slope gradually away towards Ashkavar and the Caspian Sea. This range forms a half-circle round the Alamut rock. Between the Hawdeqan range and the great rock is a smaller hill some 150 metres high, joined to the rock by a narrow neck. It is from this hill that the stone used for building the castle may have been quarried. On the eastern side there is a ravine, up which a very steep and treacherous goat track still runs, giving a somewhat perilous access to the castle. The distance across the ravine is some 140 metres, after which the ground rises again. On the southern side the rock runs steadily down to the foot of the valley, a drop of approximately 250 metres at an angle varying between 60 and 45 degrees. From this side the castle offers a magnificent view over Gazorkhan and Shotorkhan to the main Alamut valley, and beyond the Taleqan range the horizon is closed by the mountains of the Chala Pass. On the eastern side, on which it is thought that the stable and the domestic quarters of the castle were situated, the rock runs fairly steeply down to a ravine, which drops another 15 metres or so. There is no cover from which to launch any direct assault on the castle. The impression of the strategic strength of the castle is overwhelming.

The following description of Alamut castle is based on our research work before its fabric was further damaged in recent times. Looking across the top of the castle from the north-western end, there is first of all a narrow tongue of rock which does not seem to have been used for any building or living accommodation. There are clearly remains of fortifications on each side, and on the northerly side a lookout position is perched precariously on the rock like a swallow's nest. The tongue is about 45.7 metres long and 9 metres wide. Near the western end of the tongue and on the south-westerly face are two external water cisterns. They lie some 15 metres down the steep rock wall and are cut into the side of the rock. In 1961 we risked our necks climbing down to them, and one false step would certainly have sent us hurtling down to the ravine below. The water level inside the cisterns remains high even during the summer, which seems to indicate that they are fed by underground springs rather than accumulated rainwater. In 1996 we were told that various experiments have been carried out to see if the water level varies at any time of the year and it appears not to.

It is on the barren rock face near the cisterns that grow the cluster of vines which can be seen from the bottom of the rock, a sight that is typical of the appearance of the whole valley: few patches of luxuriant green among the grey or reddish-brown rock. A little farther to the east of the cisterns and some 18 metres down is a brick and stone archway in a good state of repair. It is built over a smooth-faced, narrow culvert, which runs straight down the mountainside. This could have been a sally-porte for the garrison. The descent is steep in the extreme, but having seen how quickly and easily the local people move over the most difficult mountain terrain, this theory seems perfectly plausible.

Not far from the cisterns we came across a well-chamber on the lower north-western face. This must originally have had an internal entrance. In 1961 two members of my team scrambled down the slippery rock and over the narrow stone bridge in order to inspect this chamber. The well-chamber is a low vaulted room with three alcoves cut out of the natural rock. The well is in the first alcove and although there is a lot of earth and brick inside, there are still 0.6 metres of deliciously cool water on top. My team could not understand why the roof of the rock seemed to be coated with soot. The answer would seem to be that occasionally the more athletic and foolhardy village lads climb into the well-chamber where they light fires and spend the night.

There is a fairly steep rise from this tongue of land to the main part of the rock, which is on another terrace about 107 metres long and at its widest point some 38 metres across. This part of the rock contains most of what seem to be the principal rooms, and we explored some twenty or so of them. The biggest is in the central part of the castle measuring 12 by 6 metres. The south-east wall of this room is 3 metres high and 0.6 metres thick. Our 1996 expedition found very little other evidence remaining of these rooms, apart from fragments of walls. The plan in Figure 1 gives an indication of the position of the various parts of the Alamut castle.

The most complete part of the castle is the big fortress wall at the eastern end, some of which still remained in 1996, though only in rubble form. Before its recent destruction, it stood about 14 metres high and was approximately 3 metres thick. At each end were two quite well preserved turrets faced with hard stone. Inside were the remains of staircases that wound down inside the rock, but were blocked with fallen masonry and rubble. The entrance to the fortress was through this wall and the remains of a gatehouse could still be traced. The inside of the gatehouse had been covered with white plaster.

The early expeditions investigated carefully the south-eastern protrusion. This natural extension to the main part of the rock is sometimes called Piyaz Qal'eh, as opposed to Pileh Qal'eh or Great Fort, which is the name given to the western half. The picturesque name used by the villagers for the small fort is 'Onion Castle', because of the bulbous top that surmounts the narrow ridge. It has always been thought that Onion Castle was not fortified, but was used for stables and living quarters. At first sight this is a reasonable assumption. Separate enclosures for mules, pack-horses and soldiery are often encountered at other fortresses. But this is scarcely a correct assumption at Alamut. The present ascent to Alamut is very steep indeed and was probably no less steep in Hasan's time. After all, a garrison does not conveniently provide suitable paths along which the pack animals of its enemies as well as its own can proceed. A more likely surmise is that most of the horse transport would have stayed in the villages of Shotorkhan and Gazorkhan, apart from times of direct siege. A few mules would have carried stores into the castle and perhaps been quartered there. The main function of Onion Castle was

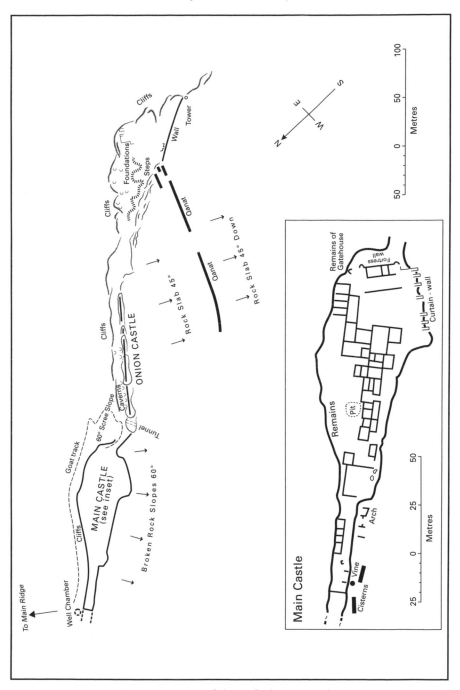

Figure 1: Groundplan of Alamut castle

for keeping stores of all kinds, as there was little room inside the main castle. Near the storerooms an impressive wide, high tunnel opens out through the rock, so that it would have been possible to watch both the northern and southern approaches to the castle.

Onion Castle is very difficult to explore. In a few places the slopes are relatively gentle, but the really interesting parts have slopes of 70 degrees or more. The limestone is covered by a fine layer of pebbles which makes it dangerously slippery. There are clear remains of a tower on top of the 'Onion'. From this tower a wall ran along the entire length of the ridge. Part of this wall ran at right angles down the north-easterly slope to another tower 46 metres below. Here we found the remains of steps cut into the mountainside. An attempt was made, probably by the Mongols, to destroy them, but their general direction can be easily followed. To the east of the tower there is a flattish piece of ground before the slope drops steeply away to the stream below. On this area there was a considerable amount of Ismaili pottery; much less remained in the main castle. Clay waterpipes were also found, but they were so broken that it was difficult to identify the direction in which this channel had run. At the far end of Onion Castle are the ruins of several dwellings and a great number of shards, which suggests that this area may have housed part of the castle garrison.

Moving round to the southern slopes – a difficult and tortuous procedure that demands strong nerves and considerable mountaineering skills – we proceeded to investigate the southern face of the castle in minute detail. Professor Ivanow, in his book *Alamut and Lamasar*, pointed to the possibility of the existence of stairs or paths leading to the lower defences, and suggested that it would be interesting to 'make a careful, detailed and reliable search for them with the help of proper mountaineering equipment and mechanical aids'.[3] This theory was tested by us with the object of investigating any lower fortifications that might exist. We also wished to examine the nature of the great horizontal crack which runs along most of the southern slope of Alamut and which shows up in every photograph taken from the valley floor.

This crack, halfway up the southern slope and actually running along its entire length turned out to be a great water channel or *qanat*. In fact, there are two channels that could be reached either from the Onion Castle or by clambering around the side of the rock. The construction of the *qanat* is, in my opinion, one of the most impressive features of the entire castle. Originally there was probably a faulting in the rock, but the Ismailis succeeded in cutting out a great channel in two parallel sections some 183 metres long, with an almost constant width of 3.6 metres, and a depth that varies between 3.3 and 3.9 metres – an astonishing achievement. We estimated in 1972 that it was capable of holding 2,446,576 litres of water. The channel was intended both for water storage as well as a natural obstacle for any attacking forces. Parts of the channel had been destroyed by the Mongols. Slightly above the giant *qanat* are four cisterns hewn out of the rock, which were also intended for water storage. The *qanat* peters out at the western end. There are no fortifications below the level of the *qanat*. Two flights of steps lead from the *qanat* to the top of the castle and are roughly hewn out of the rock. These stairs provide rapid means of access, although it seems clear that the principal means of approach to the *qanat* was round the eastern side.

My expeditions have explored every inch of the steep, sloping ground and found nothing to suggest any man-made defences. The man-built outer fortifications of Alamut are in fact minimal. Unlike the other great Ismaili castles, there could be no question of two or three perimeter walls. The angle of slope is so steep from the top of the castle to the ground below that there is just no room for them apart from one place near the gatehouse. The only approach to the castle is by the col or depression on the north-west corner where the mule track runs. In time of siege this would doubtless have been dug up, and in any case the besiegers would have had to pass below the garrison lining the walls on top of the castle and be met with a hail of arrows and other missiles. There was no possibility of driving a tunnel underneath the defendants or of establishing a position above them.

On the other hand, the inner defensive walls built on the rock just below the flat summit were substantial. The strongest fortifications were on the south side of the rock and consisted of a well-built curtain-wall faced with dressed stone, set flush against the natural rock and projecting some 4.5 to 6 metres above the top. Semi-circular turrets were built into the wall with an entrance from the castle side. Behind this outer wall stood another defensive wall. Storerooms were also built into the rock. The eastern end of the curtain-wall curved round to join the immensely strong gatehouse, which primarily defended any approach up the mule or goat track. The eastern end of Onion Castle also had its own fortifications and towers leading to the cliff overhang. Other fortifications were built on weak spots on the northern side overlooking the mule or goat track. These were strategically positioned to cover any dead ground or hidden places where an enemy force or patrol could hide, and to prevent the enemy working their way up to the top of the castle along folds in the rock.

Considered as an example of military architecture and combined with its strategic siting, Alamut is quite outstanding. Any European military leader of the time would have considered the extensive fortification of this precipitous rock as out of the question. It is understandable that the Mongols should have razed it almost to the ground, after burning its library and carrying off the valuable treasures it contained, lest it became the centre of future Ismaili activities.

But despite Juwayni's boast that 'in the breeding ground of heresy in the Rudbar of Alamut, the home of the wicked adherents of Hasan Sabbah ... there remains not one stone of foundation upon another,[4] and that the Great Khan had decided 'that none of the people sould be spared, not even the babe in its cradle',[5] there is considerable evidence to show that Ismailism was far from completely destroyed after the disaster of 1256. Nor was the fortress. In fact the castle was occupied again on several occasions by the Ismailis who had survived the Mongol invasions. But they did not have the strength to defend the castle and it was soon reoccupied by the Mongols.[6] During the Safavid period it seems that Alamut became a state prison, particularly for disgraced persons of high rank, and for this reason a part of the castle may have been rebuilt. But from the evidence of what little remains of it today, it is highly unlikely tht the great fortress was ever restored to the glory it attained under Hasan Sabbah.

In search of Maymundez

I have already stressed the importance of Maymundez in the strategic disposition of the castles in the Alamut valley. This great fortress built into the rock is about 13 km north-west of Alamut castle. It is situated high on a cliff face looking directly down a valley and over the Alamutrud, some 1500 metres below. Its excellent position allows it to have a commanding view of all approaches. The garrison on top of Maymundez would have been able to spot very quickly columns of enemy troops moving towards them from Qazvin.

Most historians agree that the construction of Maymundez began in 1126, two years after the death of Hasan Sabbah.[7] By this time the energetic and very capable Kiya Bozorg-Ommid was in power, and in order to consolidate the Ismaili position he captured several Rudbar strongholds and built new ones. He at once saw the importance of the site of Maymundez and set about turning the Gibraltar-type rock into a major fortress. We know little about the history of Maymundez and of what happened there until the Ismailis succumbed to the power of the Mongols under Hulegu Khan. According to Juwayni, however, Maymundez was built in the time of the Ismaili Imam 'Ala al-Din Muhammad (1221–1255), the father of Rokn al-Din Khurshah who was murdered by the Mongols in 1257. It is worthwhile quoting Juwayni's account of the building of Maymundez:

> Now the history of that castle is as follows. At the time when that people [the Ismailis] were at the height of their power, his father 'Ala-ad-Din) ... had instructed his officials and ministers to survey the heights and summits of this mountain for the space of 12 years until they chose that lofty peak which confided secrets to the

star Capella; and on its summit, which had a spring of water on its top and three others on its side, they began to build the castle of Maimun-Diz making the ramparts
out of plaster and gravel. And from a *parsang* [6.5 km] away they brought a stream
like the Juy-e Arziz and caused the water to flow into the castle. And because of the
extreme cold it was impossible for beasts to find a home or live in that place from
the beginning of autumn till the middle of spring. On this account Rokn-ad-Din
thought it impossible for human beings to penetrate to the castle and lay siege to it,
since the mountains intertwined and the very eagles shrank back from the passes
whilst the game animals at the foot sought some other way around. Nay, because
of its great elevation that lofty place applied to itself the words: 'The flood rusheth
down from me, and the birds rise not up to me'.[8]

There is, of course, much hyperbole and considerable poetic licence in Juwayni's
description – sobriety of expression was not his forte – and Juwayni is probably
wrong in ascribing so late a date to the construction of Maymundez.

Although, thanks to Juwayni, we can now appreciate the importance of Maymundez, it was not until 1961 and my subsequent expeditions that I was able to
locate the site of the castle to the complete satisfaction of myself and Professor
Samuel M. Stern, and carry out some excavation. Both W. Ivanow and V. Minorsky
had thought that they had identified the site of Maymundez, the one at Nevisar
Shah and the other at Bidelan,[9] but I felt that I was unable to accept their conclu-
sions, as neither of these sites corresponded to all the details given by Juwayni
when he described the battle for Maymundez.

In order to identify the exact location of Maymundez, I had made a list of the
main points about the castle and its environment as follows. First of all, there
must be prominent hilltops on which the Mongol conqueror could set up his
mangonels and 'parasol of war'. Second, there must be sufficient space around
the foot of the castle for the considerable Mongol armies to encamp and set up
further mangonels. Juwayni mentions that the circumference of the castle was one
parsang, and although we need not literally expect this to be 6.5 km, it must be a
distance of that order. The castle must be set on top of, or built into, a lofty peak.
Its battlements must be made of gravel and plaster, and there must be the remains
of a central tower on which the Ismaili *fida'i*s made their last stand against the
Mongols. In addition and perhaps more importantly, the castle must be well supplied with water and there be evidence of a diverted spring. Finally, Maymundez
must be to the west of the castle of Alamut, as we know from Juwayni that after
Hulegu had captured Maymundez, he stopped at Shahrak in order to rest and
regroup his forces before proceeding to besiege Alamut.

On our first expedition, we had the utmost difficulty gaining access to the
castle. We had walked right round the castle rock and it soon became clear that

we must concentrate on the south-western corner and the central southern section. Just approaching the castle presented many difficulties. The summit of the rock is about 600 metres above the floor of the valley, and to reach its base you have to scramble up 180 metres over steep scree. The top of the rock is about 400 metres long by 80 metres wide, but it broadens out considerably at its base, and with the adjoining foothills it does indeed have a circumference of about a *parsang* (Plate 3).

Our great difficulty was to interpret the outside of the conglomerate rock face and to try and make out any kind of entrance or plaster work. The changing light on the face of the rock did not help, and it took us some time before we discovered a crack in the rock face and above it a plaster archway. We decided that this could be a possible approach. On our way up to the rock face from our base camp in the valley, we passed each morning a small shrine dedicated to some long forgotten holy man. Beside the shrine were two great elm trees, and I asked the headman of the village if we could buy the trees and turn them into a ladder. The headman agreed and the whole village turned to hauling the two great elms up to the foot of the castle slope and making a ladder. It looked as though the ladder would just reach the crevice below the plaster arch and, after strenuous efforts, we placed the ladder in position. Who was to go first? Everyone pointed at me! I think this was the most painful ladder climb I have ever made. The rough nails of the slats seemed to be tearing at my hands and feet as I slowly made my way to the top, but the distance to the crevice was too far and I could not reach out to cover the gap.

We could not stay at Maymundez any longer as the time available for our research was running out. So we decided that we would all return the following year, complete with climbing gear, ropes and film equipment. When we returned the following year, we at once recognised that much more masonry and battlements existed on the southern face than we had previously thought. Practically the whole of the south-west and central sections of the southern face of the rock were covered with well-preserved squares of stone cemented together with plaster and gravel. The stone was covered with a brown plaster that blended very well with the natural reddish colour of the rockface, thus forming a perfect camouflage. The stone facing extended 15 metres up the side of the mountain over a distance of some 300 metres. In the centre of the fortified front were two semi-circular bastions reaching right down to the ground. We could also make out the remains of a considerable area of stonework that had been destroyed by the Mongols, but the tell-tale scarring still remains. We could not understand how we had missed all this the previous year, but there could be no mistake. The southern flank of Maymundez was indeed well fortified. Taking a closer look at this rock we saw that our crevice was about 20 metres high leading to a cave-like opening in the

Figure 2: Possible reconstruction of Maymundez castle

castle walls which formed, so we were told, the entrance to the 'stables', as some manure had been found there a long time ago. We decided that we would force an entrance into the stables the following day. We then walked round the foot of the castle and found three springs leading into the castle. Some 500 metres south of the castle entrance, there is another spring gushing from the spring line at the foot of the cliff. This has been diverted north-west so that it now runs underneath the fortress. This water must have been carried by mules or human chains to the rooms above. We also located the quarry where the stones for the battlements had been cut.

We managed to get into the stable after the village headman had cut some steps for us near the top of our ladder. We were all hauled up by rope and from the stables we found a very narrow external staircase that had been built inside the battlement. It was really a very dangerous catwalk with a sheer drop of 50 metres. Our headman managed to cross the catwalk and rigged up a rope so that the rest of us could follow. This was a nightmarish journey that I and every member of my team dreaded every time we had to make it. But fortunately there were no casualties and at each attempt we were able to penetrate deeper into the fortress, eventually clambering over a huge boulder to reach a gallery that ran for about 200 metres into the rock. Here we came across a series of impressive rooms with high ceilings and plastered walls. These may well have formed part of the apartments of the Imam Rokn al-Din himself. A lot of the plasterwork bore great black scorch marks, reminders that the Mongols had set fire to the castle after Rokn al-Din's submission to Hulegu. We found the usual shards of pottery, but otherwise nothing of significant importance.

Once inside the fortress there was a different menace. Although many of the inner passages and rooms had been carved out of conglomerate rock, the Mongol destruction and the passing of time had loosened the stones in the roofs of rooms and vaults. Evidence of recent rockfalls abounded everywhere and we dared not speak above a whisper. The deeper we penetrated into the fortress, the greater were the chances of falling rock. Our original idea of using controlled explosives to clear some of the blocked galleries certainly could not have been put into operation without suicidal consequences. We would all have been buried under tons of falling rocks. Despite these conditions, it was possible to enter two rooms to the north of the main complex. A well was discovered in one of the rooms which still contained water. The strata dips gently to the south and the well possibly intersects the water table at spring line level. The precarious placing of the well opening made any more detailed investigations quite out of the question. The well was probably no more than 30 metres deep. It is highly likely that other wells had been constructed in other rooms to intersect the same water level and thus provide an adequate source of water.

There was yet another danger. So complex and twisting were some of the passages and rooms that we were often very nearly lost. Frequently we had to struggle through very narrow openings which were very easy to miss on our return journey. The farther we went, the colder it got; water dripped from the walls, and the air was foul. Fortunately none of us suffered from claustrophobia, but there were many occasions when the eerie, oppressive atmosphere was most uncomfortable. Against this must be set our satisfaction when we came across plaster-covered brickwork and the remains of fortifications. We were disappointed at the lack of substantial artefacts, but I imagine that for centuries local villagers must have rummaged through the site and removed everything of value.

We stayed altogether about four weeks at Maymundez, trying to investigate as much of the fortress as we could. In some ways it was a frustrating time because of the dangerous conditions which required us to be extremely careful in our exploration. There were no secure holds for hands or feet, so we were liable to slip and fall. There was also the constant risk of falling stones and rocks – all of which were graphically captured by our cameraman.

In August 1961 I returned to Maymundez at the invitation of Tom Stoppard and Ralph Izzard, two well-known writers and television presenters who were making a series of documentaries on some of the more interesting sites in the Middle East for the BBC. They had also invited the likeable and distinguished mountaineer, Joe Brown, to accompany us, as we wanted to get into Maymundez at the south-west corner, and see if we could link up with the rooms in the southern face. Joe intended to climb into the rock by a chimney that I had noticed two years before, but which was beyond our capabilities to climb. Even this experienced climber found it an extremely difficult task, but it nevertheless made excellent TV footage. Having arrived at the top, Joe let down a light pot-holing ladder so that the rest of the expedition could enter. But even with this aid it was certainly no joyride, especially for myself. After we had recovered from our climb, our party explored another series of tunnels and passages that led from the main gallery. Although we did find evidence of brickwork and plaster, this was far less extensive than in the central section. There was a lot of broken pottery on the ground, most of it plain, but we did find one almost undamaged and very fine cobalt blue ewer, probably dating from the 12th century, and a large slim, grey jug that may well have been used for storing grain. We also found some arrowheads and concluded that this part of the fortress was almost certainly occupied by the garrison.

It may perhaps be appropriate at this point to summarise our findings at Maymundez and compare them with Juwayni's description. We had correctly identified the geographical situation of the castle in relation to Alamut. Roddie Dugmore, our Royal Engineer surveyor, shows in his detailed survey of the area that Juwayni's description of Maymundez matches the topography in the locality of the castle called Shams Kelayeh. This was probably the same as the 'tower of heresy' mentioned by Juwayni later in his account. We had identified the hilltop where Hulegu could have set up his 'parasol of war'. The valleys surrounding the rock were ideal for the Mongol armies to camp and besiege the castle. The total circumference of the rock was about a *parsang*. The rock in which the fortress was built was certainly high and formidable enough to justify Juwayni's description. The battlements were indeed made of gravel and plaster. Some possible remains of the tower on which the Ismaili *fida'is* made their last stand were still there, and we could see where the fortifications had been. We had located, too, the three springs on the side, the water point on the summit explicitly mentioned by Juwayni, and the diverted stream.

The site of Maymundez must have been chosen by Bozorg-Ommid (or 'Ala al-Din according to Juwayni) because of its fine strategic position and the advantage of its natural cave system. To enlarge and develop the caves would have been quite an easy matter. Since the conglomerate at Maymundez is very coarse, the matrix does not bind the pebbles very solidly, and the construction of the tunnels and rooms would have posed no problems. Deeper caves would have provided useful strongrooms, as well as a safe and secure supply of drinking water in time of siege. After the destruction of the fortress by the Mongols, the caves succumbed to natural underground water erosion. Much of the internal layout can no longer be discerned, for streams have cut down through floors and caused the collapse of ceilings. The construction of the external fortifications was quite a different matter and must have necessitated a great deal of engineering ingenuity and hard work. But there was sufficient evidence on the rock surface for my colleague Andrew Garai to attempt an imaginative reconstruction of the original appearance of the fortress (Fig. 2).

On the lowest level, but still 50 metres above ground level were the guardrooms and storerooms (the so-called 'stables'), and these were approached by a track from the south-west corner. There could also have been a similar track from the opposite direction. From the guardrooms two staircases led up to the large staterooms. The main soldiers' quarters were situated in the south-west area that we had explored with Joe Brown. Further internal staircases led to the top of the rock. Compared to Alamut, Maymundez was a much larger fortress, amply provisioned and supplied, a well-fortified garrison and something approaching a royal palace. Its greatest weakness in time of war was the conglomerate rock which could not withstand the weight of the Mongol ballista attacks. When the Ismailis began to construct Maymundez some 150 years before the Mongol invasions, it is reasonable to assume that they had no conception of the awesome power that the mangonels were to develop, especially under the Mongols. The destructive power of these siege machines was in some respects equivalent to the artillery which caused so much damage to European castles.

The grandeur of Nevisar Shah

Let us now have a look at the castle of Nevisar Shah, which Ivanow had thought might be the site of Maymundez. Nevisar Shah is situated almost at the eastern end of Alamut, near the village of Garmarud (there is another village of the same name at the western end of the valley). I had first visited the village in 1961, when I stayed with the local headman, a most forceful character with black hair and fierce burning eyes. On the wall of his main room were the pictures of the rulers of the world in 1939, and it was strange to see portraits of Hitler, Mussolini and King George VI adorning this peasant house. He had five wives, which is more than the number permitted either by his government or the laws of Islam, and how he squared this with his conscience I do not know. At the nearby village of Zavarak, I met Mr Alamuti, a rich and highly educated man who claimed to own the whole of the region. He asked me if I had found the tunnel that was supposed to connect Maymundez and Alamut. When I expressed doubts as to the existence of such a tunnel, he shook his head and begged me to look harder.

Nevisar Shah occupies the most imposing site in the valley (Plate 4). Built at a height of just over 3,100 metres, the castle stands at the easterly tip of the valley of Alamut and commands a magnificent view over the mountains to the east and the whole valley to the west. No finer view of the valley can be obtained. In the morning the scenery was particularly impressive, as the sun climbed over the Taleqan range to the south-east, gradually lighting up the whole of the Alamut valley below, and piercing the grey banks of mist and clouds that covered the entire area like some Wagnerian stage set. To the east the valley is closed in by mountains which form a narrow defile and lead up to the Salambar Pass and the majestic Takht-e Suleyman, which has a height of 4,700 metres according to Freya Stark in her delightful account of her visit.

The gruelling climb from the village of Garmarud to the castle of Nevisar Shah is an exhausting and dangerous climb of over 1,500 metres that took us six hours. The risks entailed are considerable. There are no proper tracks, the steep slope and rocks are covered with loose pebbles and stones, and on all sides there are often sheer drops of several hundred metres. The heat at midday is like an oven, and any water has to be fetched from a tiny spring 300 metres below.

The approach to the high citadel is through two ruined guardhouses at the western end. The general direction of the castle is NW/SE. The high citadel stands about 25 metres above the second gateway and is approximately 50 metres long by 15 metres wide. The building was largely destroyed by the Mongols, but the outline ground plan is clear enough. Below the citadel, the ground falls away in two sweeping arms separated by a steep scree slope that is just long enough to form the middle stroke of an 'E', which characterises the formation of the fortress as a whole. The western arm is about 80 metres long and contains a complex water storage system. The cisterns are lined with plaster and in some cases roofed over. Jubes or channels connect each cistern. The average size of each cistern is 13 metres by 2.5 metres.

The eastern arm slopes down at an angle of about 30 degrees and is protected by a strong curtain-wall on the outside built over a sheer drop of 60 metres. A large number of two or three-storied houses are built into the eastern wall, and the area formed one of the principal living blocks of the castle for the officers and other important notabilities – civil, religious and military – of the garrison. The best view of the principal, southern aspect of the castle can be obtained from the stable areas some 300 metres below. The distance from the outer limit of the stable area to the top of the high citadel is approximately 580 metres. The stables have room for 60 to 80 horses and mules, and are connected to the main castle by a narrow causeway of earth that was once certainly fortified. The causeway drops steeply down to join a small narrow valley running in from the east, and a track then winds up to the foot of the outer defences. The distance from the outer limit of the stable area to the top of the high citadel is approximately 580 metres. The impregnable nature of the site is emphasised by the deep gullies and ravines that surround the castle area. The view from the top is so magnificent that the sight and senses are almost overwhelmed (Plate 5). All around are the very highest peaks of the Alborz mountains. Eagles soar and plunge hundreds of metres below. Breathing is painful and any movement seems to drain you of all energy.

No other fortress, in my opinion, brings home so forcibly the utter determination and sheer genius of Ismaili military architecture. The construction of a Crusader castle, even as splendid a building as Krak des Chevaliers, is child's play compared to Nevisar Shah. Even 500 years after its construction, my companions and I were lost in admiration of what remains of it. It is difficult to gauge the number of men who must have been employed in the back-breaking task of building the castle. Certainly there were enough trees to provide the necessary scaffolding and woodwork, and stone was quarried from the nearby hills. Nevertheless, the number of men engaged in erecting the curtain-walls and the complex range of buildings must have been more than a thousand. It is also difficult to estimate the number of men who formed the garrison. Probably this was no more than 500 or 600, but at the same time the castle could easily have accommodated another thousand or so, especially in times of siege.

Given the imposing and magnificent setting of Nevisar Shah, I can well understand why Ivanow considered that it must be the unidentified site of Maymundez. I found the Russian scholar's name recorded, incidentally, in the visitors' book of the headman at Garmarud. The headman told me that the professor had stayed with him while he investigated the castle area, but found the final ascent too steep to climb, and to his great chagrin was reduced to examining the castle as best as he could through binoculars.

But in any case, as I explained in my *Castles of the Assassins*, for all its impressive qualities, Nevisar Shah could not have been Maymundez. The citadel's height and remoteness corresponded closely to Juwayni's description of the site, but there was no place where the Mongol armies would have camped and there is no real circumference to the mountain (it is quite impossible to measure a circumference in terms of distance, let alone to determine the *parsang* Juwayni mentions explicitly). There is no place where the Mongols could have erected their mangonels, nor is there any trace of the spring inside the castle itself. Juwayni says that the ramparts of Maymundez were built of plaster and gravel, but Nevisar Shah was constructed of dressed stone from the mountain of Boar Kuh, and cemented together with limestone cement of quite high quality.

Apart from the complete absence of space for an attacking force to set up its mangonels (the nearest flat plateau is 1,500 metres below the castle), the climate was the deciding factor in locating Nevisar Shah. We know that the siege of Maymundez took place at the end of November 1256. The Imam Rokn al-Din had hoped that he would be saved from the Mongols by the onset of winter, but the weather was unusually mild that year. There is no possibility of mild weather at the top of the peak of Anarak-Dangaron on which Nevisar Shah is built. Our headman told us that he had never known Anarak-Dangar to be without its mantle of snow during November, and I have seen snow on the adjoining peaks even in summer. Lastly, if we accept Juwayni's account of Hulegu's attack on Alamut, Nevisar Shah is too far to the east. Maymundez must be to the west of Alamut castle as Hulegu stopped at Sharak after he had captured Maymundez in order to rest and regroup before proceeding to Alamut.

Nevisar Shah contains some very good examples of Ismaili pottery in all its considerable range. A guide appropriated one of the best examples of glasswork, a beautiful bottle with a fluted neck. It was clearly of local production and testified to the high degree of local craftsmanship. Freya Stark also found some pottery at Nevisar Shah when she made her way to Garmarud during her travels in Persia in 1931. In Chapter 3 of her *Valleys of the Assassins*, she comments that she hunted among the stones of Nevisar Shah and found quite a large number of shards resembling the pottery she had found earlier at Alamut. She could not resist adding: 'Thirteenth-century pottery in this deserted place, 3,000 feet above the nearest habitation.' She concludes her observations with these words: 'On every side the natural walls fall away in precipices; and from the highest point 10,000 feet at least, for my aneroid could rise no further, one can see the great half-circle of the eastern mountains, covered with snow, nameless on my map.'[10] It is a fascinating thought that Freya Stark and myself, with my team, are perhaps the only Westerners to have visited Nevisar Shah and recorded their impressions.

The main danger to the Ismaili defenders of Alamut of this part of Alamut valley came from armies approaching from the parallel Taleqan valley. This is, in fact, precisely what seems to have happened when the Mongols invaded Alamut in 1256. They came up the Taleqan valley, crossed the mountain range to the east of Bidelan and seem to have aimed for the village of Shahrak, where the valley is at its widest. In this way they outflanked the other castles built by the Ismailis to defend an approach from the Taleqan. It seems probable that the Mongols must have moved at a very fast pace so that the garrisons of the Ismaili castles in Taleqan were either taken off guard or demoralised by the sheer size and rapid advance of the enemy.

There are two further Ismaili castles built with the express purpose of preventing penetration of the Alamut valley from the Taleqan. One is at Kay-Ghrobad, approximately 14.5 km south-west of Nevisar Shah that guards the north-south route along the eastern end of the Taleqan. Its main features are the high citadel, the water cisterns which are situated both at the northern and southern ends of the castle, and the remaining stretch of wall at the southern end. There was also a pottery kiln in the castle, which gives it an added importance. The other castle is called Mansuriyya, where we found particularly impressive water cisterns. The Taleqan, like the Alamut valley, is extremely fertile. The valley is broader than Alamut, the villages richer, and considerably more crops are grown. During Ismaili times the inhabitants of Kay-Ghrobad and Mansuriyya would certainly have used the food crops grown in the Taleqan to supplement their own resources.

Ilan and other fortresses

The reader may well ask what defences there were to the north of Alamut. The mountains here fall gradually away to the Caspian Sea. In 1960 I walked with my team from the Caspian up through the mountains and the very fertile valley of Askavar into Alamut. In all probability, Hasan Sabbah followed this route, too, when he first came to Alamut from Qazvin. The standard of living in these valleys is considerably better, the cattle well fed, the people gentle and kind. From time to time I was told that the rugged inhabitants of Alamut still make raids into Askavar and carry off sheep, cows and goats. The Askavaris are afraid of taking reprisals, and so they tolerate these outrages with considerable patience.

There are a number of small-scale castles and fortresses in this region, such as Ayin in the hills at the west of the valley and Lal which guards the approach road from Qazvin. Some smaller fortresses were used as beacons and watchtowers or as centres for reserve troops. Other castles guard important places like river fords or fertile areas, or the pottery kilns at Andej where there are two further castles. The pleasant and fertile village of Andej still exists and became an important ceramics centre, which I visited on one of my expeditions and found many examples of Ismaili pottery there. There is also an interesting cave complex at Andej which runs for 548 metres into the hills and which probably served as a hiding place for Hasan Sabbah and his men prior to their capture of Alamut. The last village before Alamut is called Dikin and here, too, we found the remains of two Ismaili forts. The most important of these second-rank castles is Ilan, not far from Andej where Freya Stark tasted honey produced by wild bees and thought it sweeter than any honey she had tasted.[11]

Ilan is a few kilometres to the north-west of Nevisar Shah and on the 2,400 metres contour line, some 600 metres lower. Its strategic importance lies in the fact that it guards the back route of the valley at the foot of the mountains. The normal supply route for the valley was along the banks of the Alamutrud, but during times of siege this route would have been impossible. Hence the Ismailis constructed an alternative route running from Ilan to Andej, then to the north of Alamut, Maymundez and westward to Dikin and Garmarud. The three smaller castles at Andej and the larger one at Ilan formed the chief defensive position of this route.

I first investigated the castle of Ilan with two colleagues in 1961. We started from Zavarak on the Alamut river and after four hours we had climbed 900 metres through some of the wildest and most rugged scenery in the whole of the valley. It reminded us of the gorge of Shirkuh, except that it was far steeper and much longer. After climbing up to a plateau covered with fruit trees, we entered a narrow gulley that became even more steep and confined as we advanced. On each side piles of jagged rock lay strewn haphazardly, as if a massive earthquake had thrown them up in one gigantic upheaval. There were great holes in the rocks, which were obviously mouths of caves. We were told that tigers had been seen in the area, and that bears and wolves often came down in winter to prey upon the villagers' flocks of sheep and goats. In fact, during the winter Ilan is completely cut off, and the children do not dare go down to any of the lower villages for fear of being devoured by wild beasts. We were also told that this was outlaw country, and men from the villages lower down in the valley who had committed crimes often took to these hills to live as bandits and outlaws.

When my party arrived at the village of Ilan, my colleagues became ill and I had to investigate the castle myself with a guide provided by the headman. The route was extremely difficult, but eventually we arrived at a small plateau and my guide indicated that a town had been built there. The castle was mostly destroyed and I was informed that the little remaining brickwork had been removed four or five years earlier when the present village decided to build a new bathhouse. I don't think that Ilan had ever been a large castle, but it must have been an important intermediate fort forming one of the links in the chain of castles that stretched all the way down the Alamut valley. The most interesting part of the ruins was what was left of the water systems. At the top of the promontory on which I was standing, there were two water cisterns, 4 metres long and 1.2 metres wide, cut deep into the rock. The first was very deep, but how deep I could not tell. The second had a depth of some 4 metres, and there was still some water in it. The castle commanded a very good view of the central part of the valley. I imagine it probably held reserve forces as well as guarding the back route from Nevisar Shah to Lamasar. There were a large number of fragments of pottery scattered on the ground, most of them glazed in yellow, green and brown.

On the west side of the promontory there were foundations of rooms. I measured what remained of the outer wall, which was 9.1 metres long and 1.5 metres thick. At the southern end there was further evidence of rooms and possibly a well. Right at the edge there was another very deep water-cistern, which was some 6 metres by 1.2 metres, and I estimated its depth to be another 6 metres. Some of the remaining plaster and brickwork looked older than the Ismaili period, suggesting that this castle too probably had a long history dating back well before the Middle Ages. I then returned to the eastern side of the promontory. Much of what remained of the walls had been quarried by the villagers and there were many signs of recent digging, I asked if any treasures or weapons had been found and was told that only one or two rings had been recovered. I was shown one, which appeared to be much later than the Ismaili period, probably somewhere between 1650 and 1750.

I must finally mention one other castle in the Alamut valley that has very little to do with the Ismailis. It is at Shahrak in the centre of the valley. I was told that Sharak was probably the capital of the Daylamite kingdom before the advent of the Ismailis. Built at a very fertile spot on an S-bend of the river, it was supposed to have been a very rich and prosperous township. The castle stands on a mound 137 metres long and 115 metres wide. The four walls still stood in 1961, containing a large hall and several other rooms. It is really rather refreshing to know that there is at least one castle in the valley that can be entered with hardly any exertion at all. I came across one other river castle that defended a fordable part of the river. Apart from the fortresses dominating the Taleqan valley, there are no other castles or forts on the southern side of the river. Most of the fertile ground has been terraced and used for agricultural purposes.

Notes

1. See Willey, *Castles of the Assassins*, facing p. 296.
2. Ibid., pp. 213–214.
3. Ivanow, *Alamut and Lamasar*, p. 51.

4. Juwayni, *History of the World-Conqueror*, vol. 2, p. 639.

5. Ibid., p. 723.

6. Shafique N. Virani, 'The Eagle Returns: Evidence of Continued Isma'ili Activity at Alamut and in the South Caspian Region following the Mongol Conquests,' *Journal of the American Oriental Society*, 123.2 (2003), pp. 351–370.

7. Daftary, *The Isma'ilis*, p. 372.

8. Juwayni, *History of the World-Conqueror*, vol. 2, pp. 627–628.

9. Ivanow, *Alamut and Lamasar*, p. 79.

10. Stark, *The Valleys of the Assassins*, p. 231.

11. Ibid., p. 271.

CHAPTER 8

Castles of the Alamut Valley – II

Just to the west of the Alamut valley is the Shahrud, formed by the confluence of the Alamut and the Taleqan rivers. In this valley lies the castle of Lamasar. The Shahrud valley is quite different from the Alamut. The riverbed is much broader and the hills on either side are far less steep. The ground on the southern bank is relatively fertile and there are numerous small villages. This part of Rudbar is less rugged and awe-inspiring than in Alamut. The people are more prosperous and better clothed, housed and fed. This is probably due to the fact that it is a relatively easy journey to Qazvin, from the western edge of the valley at least, and so there is more contact with the life of the city. When Freya Stark visited Rudbar in 1931, it was unhealthy and malarial; since that time the houses have been extensively sprayed and malaria virtually eliminated.

Lamasar, the shield of Alamut

Lamasar itself lies on a small tributary of the Shahrud, the Na'inarud that flows into the Shahrud at Shahrestan-e Bala, some 5 kilometres from the actual site of Lamasar. The fortress is in a similar geographical situation to Alamut in that it stands on a large, rocky outcrop at the head of a valley with a high range of mountains behind. But in other respects it appears quite different from the other Ismaili castles. Instead of being perched on top of a great peak as at Alamut and Nevisar Shah, or hollowed out of the rock like Maymundez, Lamasar stands no more than 140 metres above the Shahrud.

Lamasar occupies a large area and, at its longest point from the northern walls to the southern defences, it covers almost 550 metres and at its widest 150 metres. It is set on a rounded slope, which is tilted at an angle of 30 degrees. From Shahrestan-e Bala it is easy to get an overall view of the fortress, with the high citadel at the northern end of the slope, and on each side of the tilted table of rock, the ruins of towers, walls and other fortifications. Lamasar appears to have suffered somewhat less than the other castles at the hands of the Mongols (Plate 6).

From a distance Lamasar seems very much like a traditional Norman castle, and it is an imposing sight. Juwayni tells us that there had been a castle at Lamasar for some time before Hasan Sabbah took possession of Alamut and that the lord of Lamasar refused to be converted to the Ismaili cause. Consequently, a small body of troops was sent under Bozorg-Ommid to take the castle. Juwayni relates that these men climbed up by stealth into the castle on the night of 10 September 1102 and overcame the inhabitants. Bozorg-Ommid commanded the Ismaili garrison at Lamasar for many years – Juwayni explicitly states 20 years – until Hasan Sabbah fell ill and nominated him as his successor.

There is no doubt about the strength of Lamasar's strategic position. The castle was well sited to protect the valley of Alamut from attack along the Shahrud. Juwayni relates how the Saljuq sultan Muhammed Tapar had attempted to crush the Ismailis of Alamut and the Rudbar by systematic destruction of their crops in Rudbar. He relates with gusto that this happened for eight successive years from 1109 until there was great famine in the castles and the people were reduced to eating grass, but the castles did not surrender. Finally, in 1117 the Sultan mounted a joint offensive on both Alamut and Lamasar under his commander, the Turkish *atabeg* Anushtagin. Juwayni writes of this encounter:

> Setting up their mangonels they [the Sultan's troops] fought strenuously and by Zul-Hijja of that year (March–April 1118) were on the point of taking the castles and freeing mankind from their machinations, when they received news that Sultan Muhammad had died in Isfahan. The troops then dispersed, and the Heretics were left alive and dragged up into their castles all the stores, arms and implements of war assembled by the Sultan's army.[1]

After the fall of Maymundez and Alamut to the Mongols in 1256, Lamasar continued to hold out for another year. Hulegu Khan stayed for some time in the village of Mansurbagh, hoping that the castle's occupants might soon be persuaded to creep serpent-like out of their holes. But this hope proved to be vain and it was only after a cholera epidemic that took the lives of many defenders of Lamasar that the remainder of its garrison surrendered.

Mansurbagh is the nearest village to Lamasar. From here it is possible to scramble across a series of irregular ditches, cross the Na'inarud and climb to the southern entrance of the castle over steep scree. The principal guardhouse is here, though its main entrance is relatively small, no more than 2 metres high and 1 metre wide, which must have caused considerable difficulties for loaded pack-mules. There are, in fact, two gateways, an inner and an outer one, both built on the same slope, the higher one 6 metres above the lower. They each face a different angle, thus making a bent entrance. Just beside the guardhouse are two towers, part of the defensive system which runs round the whole fortress area (Fig. 3).

The outer walls of the castle, which can be traced quite clearly, rise steeply at the south-western end and skirt a massive stone building with an apsidal projection built on the edge of sheer cliff. Former travellers have suggested that this was probably a residence, and Freya Stark called it on her accompanying plan a 'serai'.[2] Professor Ivanow's suggestion that it is more likely to have been part of the fortifications of the ridge is probably correct.[3]

The rock type at Lamasar is baked conglomerate, cut by acid intrusions. The outcrop is linked to the main mountain mass by a narrow neck of land. The strata here are very much affected by intrusions, and consequently there is not the smooth, steeply dipping slope into the prevailing winds as at Alamut. In building the castle, however, the Ismaili engineers were still able to exploit the up-currents of wind and the relief rain, which falls on the south and south-west faces of the fortress, by constructing water cisterns on the south-facing slope where the general inclination is not nearly as great as at Alamut.

There are altogether 15 cisterns dug into the rock at Lamasar, of which 11 are found on the southern face of the fortress. Seven of these are interconnected with shallow water channels designed to prevent each cistern from overflowing. There are little round holes on their lips that once held posts to support rough shelters, as at Alamut, to prevent evaporation or pollution of the water. Around the great tanks of the cisterns, the marks left by countless picks can still be seen. These tanks are often 5.5 metres deep and sometimes four times as long; the connecting channels are 15–20 centimetres wide. The remaining four cisterns are lined with limestone and vaulted. With one exception, they are situated structurally higher than the other seven and the fourth is placed a distance away from the others. It is possible that these four plaster-lined cisterns were used for storing grain or other foodstuff. There are four more water cisterns to be seen: two on the western side, one on the north and another in the east.

The seven water cisterns at the southern end of the fortress intercept the flow off a catchment area of 9,700 square metres. If one assumes a similar rainfall to Alamut of about 100 centimetres per year, 11 million litres of water would fall on the area annually. The storage capacity of these cisterns is, however, limited and estimated to be around 398,250 litres at any one time. This is far less than at Alamut and there is no sign of underground water cisterns.

The overall water storage system starts on the northern end of the site and runs down channels to two main catchment areas, one described above on the south-western slope and the other on the steep scree slope leading down to the

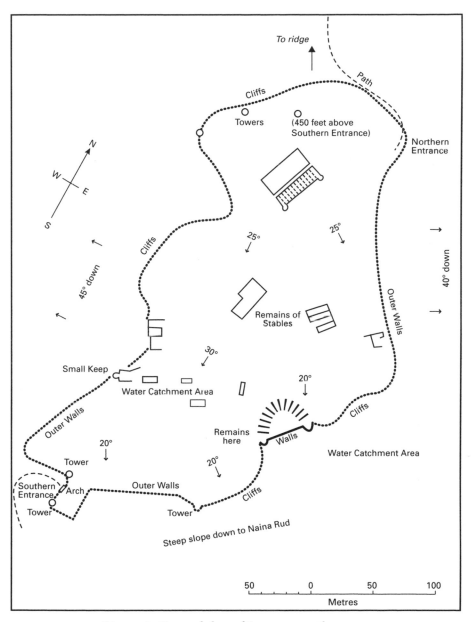

Figure 3: Groundplan of Lamasar castle

Na'inarud on the south-eastern side. Freya Stark has pointed out, in her description of Lamasar, that an open watercourse or leat was also diverted into the northern end of the site, where there are further cisterns within and without the walls.[4] It must be remembered that the northern end of the fortress is 140 metres above the southern entrance, and the Ismailis made the fullest use of the natural drop in elevation to collect as much water as possible.

Careful examination of the rock at Lamasar revealed that there is a man-made *qanat* or water channel passing across the neck of land by which the rock is linked to the main mountain mass. The *qanat* splits, one channel passing around the northern side of the castle and swinging round the eastern edge of the rock. It is not possible to trace the channel very far round the eastern end, but it is possible that it supplied a large cistern situated outside the castle walls, which overflows down a gully into the Na'inarud below. The other branch of the *qanat* passes around the western side of the rock and it may be seen some 20–30 metres below the castle walls from the south-west tower. Inaccessibility made it impossible to trace this completely, but it seems probable that this *qanat* emptied into the cisterns along the western edge of the rock and may even have swung round to supplement the rainwater collected in the cisterns on the southern slopes of the rock.

At Lamasar it seems as if much of the regular water supply came from the *qanat*, rainfall and water from the Na'inarud. In the dry, hot days of summer the garrison relied on the 398,250 litres of water stored in the seven covered cisterns. This amount would be sufficient to keep 500 men and 50 mules and horses for three months. The garrison also drew water from the Na'inarud which runs to the east of the castle, and on the edge of the river they built a small tower 3 metres square guarding a narrow tunnel hewn out of the rock for a length of over 305 metres. It connects with the catchment area on the south-eastern side of the castle. This tower overhangs the river and in winter water could be collected in buckets. All sorts of improbable legends are connected with this tunnel. There is a story that once, when the garrison was besieged and the tower was in the hands of their enemies, sheep were sent down through the tunnel to the river. The sheep had water bags strapped under their bellies and these bags were then filled in the river. A shepherd in the pay of the garrison stood by, unsuspected by the invading forces, and as soon as the water bags were filled, he set a wolf to chase the sheep back up the tunnel. The tunnel is in fact far too steep for this to have happened, but it is a picturesque story.

There appears to have been one other feature of the complex water system at Lamasar. When Bozorg-Ommid refortified the castle, he is said to have ordered the digging of a water channel to the upper reaches of the Na'inarud, a distance of

1. The rock of Alamut.

2. Remains of fortifications on Alamut rock.

3. Tunnels and passages cut into the rock of Maymundez.
4. Below left: The site of the castle of Nevisar Shah.
5. Below right: A view of Alamut valley from Nevisar Shah.

6. Left: The ruined towers and battlements of Lamasar.

7. Above right: Curtain walls of Samiran castle.

8. Below: Artist's impression of Samiran before its destruction.

9. The fortified mountain of Gerdkuh rising above the plains.
10. Below left: Living quarters on the summit of Gerdkuh.
11. Below right: Remains of a water-cistern at Gerdkuh.

12. The main castle at Soru on a high rocky outcrop.
13. Below left: A section of the subsidiary castle at Soru.
14. Below right: A domed entrance at Soru castle.

15. The castle of Qa'in.

16. The castle of Furk, reconstructed in Safavid times.

17. The crumbling walls and towers of Shahanshah.

18. The fortress of Khanlanjan.

19. Above left: A group of villagers dancing at Furk.
20. Above right: Adrianne Woodfine, Ali Moradi (centre) and friends in search of Soru.
21. Below: The author, Peter Willey, with Adrianne Woodfine in Syria.

some 16 km. It is indeed possible that this channel did exist and its construction was certainly not beyond the engineering skills of the Ismailis. The regular supply of water thus obtained would have enabled Bozorg-Ommid to irrigate the many trees and gardens planted by him and of which he was rather proud.[5] However, the water storage system described above would in all probability have been sufficient to meet the needs of the Ismaili garrison, even during the year-long siege after the fall of Alamut.

To the north of the catchment area and the small keep ridge are the stables, which can be seen from practically every point in the castle. The present structure is built on the ruins of the old stables and is a recent one made of mud bricks built on a stone foundation. Even taking into account the greater size of the original building, it could not have accommodated many horses or, more probably, mules.

Some 60 metres to the north is the main keep or high citadel, still in quite a good state of preservation. It is a single-storey building built of stone and the ground is covered with rubble. It occupies a space of about 30 metres by 24.5 metres. The entrance has a rounded arch and inside there are two rooms. The left-hand room has a fine vault 3 metres high, 2 metres wide and 4 metres long. The walls are one metre thick, and the floor was covered with rubble and shards of pottery when we visited it. Behind the building there are ruins of 12 other rooms, possibly storerooms, long and narrow. Freya Stark observed a tower in the south-eastern corner.

To the north of the high citadel the ground rises again to the ruined towers of the northern entrance. The best view of the site can really be obtained from the top of an adjoining steep hill. The inclined plateau on which the castle stands was a natural fortress in itself. Set aside from the surrounding countryside, it arises as a solid rock wall, a tilted slab with three sides that scarcely needed fortifying. The eastern side is perhaps the most vulnerable, and it is easy to trace the line of the continuous defensive wall on this side.

The main importance of Lamasar in Ismaili military strategy was to provide what Ivanow called 'the shield to the rear' of the main Ismaili castles in Alamut.[6] It may also have been used as a base for reserve forces. The size of the fortress – it is considerably larger than Alamut – and the complexity of its water system indicate that a large garrison lived here. The strategic purposes that Lamasar served did not in themselves demand a large force. It is reasonable to assume, therefore, that the fortress had another function, such as the training of Ismail *fida'i*s, although we have no actual evidence of this. But it is equally difficult to believe that Lamasar was no more than a quiet backwater during the long period of Ismaili rule. Three smaller forts protect the eastern approaches to Lamasar from attack.

The lost majesty of Samiran

I always have a special affection for Samiran, as this was the first Ismaili castle I visited during my 1960 expedition, the year after I had located the site of Maymundez. Samiran had not been on my original itinerary. But shortly after my arrival in Tehran I was told by an Iranian friend, who was extremely helpful to me in my pre-Revolution research and whose wife was an interpreter at the British Embassy, that I must visit the site which he called Darband. He had first visited it four years previously and claimed that it was almost as great a city as Persepolis. He said that many monuments were still standing there, as well as the ruins of a large castle, and showed me various artefacts he claimed to have found there.

Although Samiran can bear no comparison with Persepolis, it is certainly a most interesting site. It is built some 20 km to the west of Manjil, on the Qezil-Uzun, a tributary of the Sefidrud, where at the time of my visit a French company was building the great dam which now stands there. As we knew that once the dam was completed the site would be partly flooded, we were anxious to see Samiran before the water affected any of the monuments.

The first person to visit the site (although he did not realise what it was) was the famous English explorer Sir Henry Rawlinson, who travelled down the Sefidrud in 1838. He noted the impressive ruins, and in a paper to the Royal Geographical Society gave the following very brief account of it:

> About three miles below Gīlawan, a ridge of low hills runs across the valley from one range of mountains to the other. The Sefid Rud forces its way, by a narrow gorge, through the ridge, and at this point, on an isolated and most precipitous hill upon the right bank, immediately overhanging the river, are the remains of a large and very strong fort, which, from a distance, have a most imposing appearance. The place is called Derbend, and forms the boundary between Taromi-Khelkhal and Taromi-Payin; the fort is known by the name of Ka'lehi-Kohneh; and strangely enough, is ascribed by the peasantry, to Khaliph Omar; it seems of some antiquity, and would be well worth examining.[7]

The curious thing about this account is not only its paucity but also that Rawlinson locates the main castle ruins on the right or southern bank of the river, whereas in fact they are all situated on the left or northern bank. However, there can be little doubt that this castle described by Rawlinson is Samiran, and we can only conclude that for some odd reason he got mixed up in his directions.

The second visitor was a German delighting in the name of Julius Caesar Häntzsche, who wrote the following description in a letter (my translation):

> Three *fersach* (about 15 miles) west-south-west of Menjil there can be found in the

mountain district of Tarum in north Persia, in the valley of the Kyzel-Uzen, in a gorge between barren mountains covered with pebbles and scree, the remains of an old castle and, apparently, of a somewhat newer town, called in the local dialect Gorkalah or sometimes Schehr-i Berberi. Here are scattered on several hills the remains of an old city and on one in particular those of a fortified castle, which is certainly pre-Islamic, and many octagonal tall towers still partly preserved. In the dips between the hills there are several remains of Muslim baths, etc. The majority of the ruins lie on the left bank of the Kyzyl-Uzen. The general direction of the castle is due south, that of the towers SWS, which indicates the Muslim period. Nearby on a slope in the mountains there is a great heap of stones called Gabr-i Gor on to which muleteers throw fresh stones as they pass by. Immediately adjacent to the ruins on a hill is the Imamzadeh (shrine), and, near the remains of the baths, asbestos can be seen on the sides of the hills.[8]

Besides the fact that Dr Häntzsche does not seem to have heard of Rawlinson, his account is very brief, doing less than justice to the significance of the place. No other travellers had, as far as we knew, visited the castle in the century between Dr Häntzsche's visit and ours.

At Darband (the name literally means 'gorge') the river runs through a narrow gorge a mile long and no more than 100 metres wide. On the southern bank the mountains rise to a height of some 400 metres above the stream, and on the northern bank there is a mile-wide plateau. On the other side the land drops precipitously to a similar gorge formed by another tributary of the Sefidrud. Over this plateau came the caravans from Azarbayjan, making their way northward towards the Caspian Sea or southward to the old Persian capital of Rayy. In all probability the Daylamites were the first to build a castle there and gradually a town grew which certainly became an important centre in the north of the country. That they must have been rich can be seen by the magnificence of the buildings and, in particular, the mausolea. The Daylamites managed to maintain the independence of this particular outpost under their own princes until they were dislodged by the Ismailis.

When the Ismailis decided to extend their power westward from Alamut, they soon came across this fortress. Their intelligence system seems, curiously enough, in this instance to have been faulty. Normally Hasan Sabbah and his successors were supplied with extremely full information about the morale, numbers and movements of potential enemies. We are told that he believed that Samiran was an ordinary castle and he dispatched a relatively small army against it. When his general arrived before the castle, he is reported to have sent a message back to Alamut urgently asking for reinforcements, complaining that he had been told to take a castle and now found that he must besiege a city.

The original buildings of Samiran were almost totally destroyed, but as there are no historical records of the siege of the city or of its destruction by the Mongols, we could only attempt to piece together its subsequent history from our investigations. To the west of the city we noticed some towers and foundations of buildings whose construction was so different from that of the main castle and so similar to the Ismaili fortresses in the Alamut valley that it seemed reasonable to suppose that the Ismailis had been established here for a considerable number of years. Whether they, in their turn, were driven out by the Mongols after the main fortress of Alamut had fallen, or whether they vacated the city of their own free will, must remain a matter for conjecture. Again there are no records, and the only evidence we have are our own plans and photographs (Plate 7).

The site, which covers an area of approximately 1.3 square km, is dominated at the eastern end by the castle (Fig. 4). According to Rawlinson, when he visited the site it had three outer walls. We could trace the remains of two and possibly a third, although it was difficult to be sure about the third one. Rawlinson was certainly an accurate observer, and his record of a triple wall is confirmed in contemporary texts. Although the stone from which the castle is constructed is particularly hard and not liable to erosion by weather, the third wall may have disappeared in this way during the last hundred years, or else it was quarried by the local inhabitants for their own use.

The description of Samiran which follows is based on the site as I saw it in 1960. Very shortly afterwards, the valley was flooded with water as a result of the building of the Manjil dam, and much of what I describe here has been obliterated by the flood waters. But the castle and the mausolea still stand proudly above the greenish debris below them.

The castle is situated on the top of a tilted bluff of sandstone rock covered with a layer of loose stones and gravel, and overlooks the gorge of the Qezel-Uzan, which at this point runs roughly from east to west. This too is the general lay of the castle. The greatest height of the bluff at the eastern end is not more than 45 metres above the valley below. On the northern and eastern sides, from which the most impressive view of the castle can be obtained, it was a fairly uncomfortable scramble for us up the scree-slope with its outcrop of rock in the middle. The ascent would have been far more difficult and hazardous for an attacking force.

At the foot of the bluff there is a narrow, flat piece of ground, along which a track now runs, before the hills rise again, and this depression would also have served as a dry moat. The triple wall must have run along the northern and eastern sides of the castle, and possibly curled round to the western side too. All that remains now is a substantial wall built about 27 metres down the slope

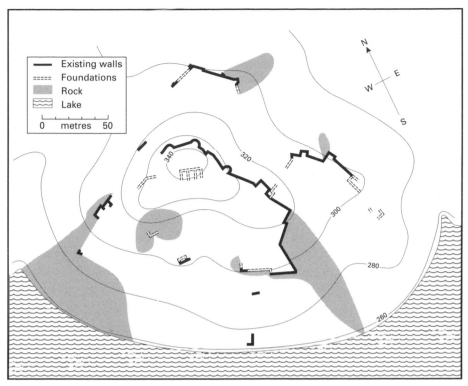

Figure 4: Sketch survey of Samiran castle

from the castle on the north-eastern corner. This wall, constructed of undressed stone, is about 6 metres high and 2.5 metres thick. The remains do not extend for more than 15 metres. At the southern side there is a steep descent of almost sheer rock dropping some 100 metres to the river Qezel-Uzan. About a third of the way down and built on an outcrop of rock, there is a well-preserved tower from which it would have been possible with the aid of a rope to scramble down a chimney in the cliff-face to the river. This tower could have been used as an emergency exit in time of siege or as a means of getting additional water from the river by buckets. On the western side, the ground sinks in a series of terraces, each of which is fortified. The lowest terrace is about a hundred feet above the encircling track or dry moat.

We first examined the main fortifications at the eastern end of the castle. They have been extensively destroyed and virtually only the shell of the outer wall remains. These walls are 9 to 12 metres high and 1.5 to 3 metres thick. From the rather narrow, wedge shaped, eastern neck of the bluff, they run back in a zigzag line along the northern and southern slopes. In effect, the walls form a series of rectangular or square towers interspersed with rounded bastions. This meant that any attacking force would have to break up and disperse, as it would have been impossible to launch a concentrated assault on any one point – there just wasn't room enough for that. Each of the towers could support at least two others, so that a devastating crossfire could be brought to bear upon the enemy by the defenders.

Most of the living quarters seemed to be built into the walls at the eastern end of the castle. Generally, these were three stories high, and wooden joists can still be seen at the different floor-levels. The wood is extremely hard and looks like olivewood, in spite of the fact that there are no olive trees in this part of the country. We noticed that the stone and mud-brick at the bottom of the walls had been reinforced with beams of the same wood. Some of the windows puzzled us, as they were far bigger than we expected, with considerable decoration in the form of ornamental tracery in the stonework. There were probably more rooms below ground level, as we saw the remains of staircases, but we had neither the time nor the equipment to excavate. At the southern end of the castle the bluff drops by a series of terraces, each of which contains the remains of a large number of rooms. Here the destruction is even more complete, and it was very difficult to trace the original groundplan. It was in this part of the castle that we found the greatest number of shards of pottery, mostly small, brown, glazed fragments. In addition, we came across some examples of Caspian grey ware, which must have survived from the most primitive period of the potter's art. We were lucky enough to find an almost complete bowl. This was a large conical bowl standing on a foot-ring with inscribed decoration and splashes of coloured glaze in brown, yellow and green (see Appendix III). Its date is certainly in the Ismaili period and is another indication that the Ismailis had settled in Samiran after they had taken it.

Having completed our tour of the castle, we next turned our attention to the surrounding site. The gorge and the river respectively formed the natural eastern and southern boundaries, so we decided to find the northern limits first. About 700 metres from the castle bluff, we found the remains of a stone wall on top of a hill and traced its course for about 5 km. This was presumably the outer wall of the site and could conceivably be the third wall mentioned by Rawlinson, although it was some distance away from the castle. From here we walked about half a kilometre down to the western end of the area where our attention was at once attracted by a graceful and slender tower which could have been a minaret of a mosque, but at the same time showed unmistakable signs of having once been fortified. It was built on a slight rise about 15 metres above the river, and from the top there was a fine view to the north-west over the plain to Kurdistan. It was about 10 metres high and inside there was a double spiral staircase, still quite well preserved. At the foot of the tower there was a small guardroom, 2.5 metres high by 2 metres wide, the walls of which were pierced with arrow-slits. Below the tower and to the west were the remains of a remarkably fine stone bridge. The river here is quite wide and the length of the bridge must have been considerable. The bridge as such no longer exists, but some complete arches still stand on both banks, and in the middle of the river can be seen the base of one of the piers. Unfortunately, we could fine no traces of the foundations of houses or any other buildings by the bridge, but the ground is marshy here and they may well have disappeared; and it seems unlikely that a second bridge would have been built here unless there was a considerable community nearby.

Three other buildings stand out prominently upon the rocky hills. The most prominent is a mausoleum on a hill about 150 metres to the north-west of the castle. It is octagonal in shape and its windows generally face east. It is about 15 metres high, made of brick and surmounted by the remains of a brick dome, which had probably been about 5 metres high. The mausoleum is in an exceptionally fine state of preservation and is an imposing building. A few steps lead up to the fine arch of the main entrance. Inside it is severely plain and there are no friezes on the wall. The ground was covered in rubble from the collapsed dome, and after digging down about one metre we found the original floor but, to our disappointment, no signs of mosaics. We walked round the outside, which was decorated with rounded columns, and on the northern wall we came to the remains of an external staircase that led up to the roof. We began to climb up the stairs, but it was clearly unsafe and we abandoned the attempt half-way.

Almost due north from the mausoleum and standing on another rise 80 metres away is a mosque. This consists of a central rectangular building 18 by 21 metres. We were told that it contained the tomb of a saint who had died about the year 1410, and the whole building had been converted into a shrine in his honour. The mosque is surmounted by two circular domes which were, according to our informants, a sign of royal dignity. Much of the building seemed very old and of the same date as the castle and the mausoleum. The walls are solidly made of stone and plaster, and there is a brick roof that looks as though it was restored about a hundred years ago. Inside there are two main rooms, 6 to 7 metres high. One contains the now-empty tomb of the saint, crudely painted and hung with tawdry and tattered trimmings. The second was likewise empty and its blackened walls indicated that it may have been used by the local population as a field kitchen. To the east of the building there is a graveyard littered with recent tombstones and, as if standing apart from the plebs, the ruins of two or three older and more sumptuous tombs.

Between the mosque and the castle are the ruins of two collapsed towers, and it is reasonable to assume that this was the site of many more houses. The last building of note is the eastern mausoleum, which stands on a rise some 300 metres to the north-east of the castle. It is not so large or impressive as the main western one, but scenically it stands out well. It has been badly damaged and only three walls are left standing. Round the top runs a frieze, which presumably stated the name of the prince buried there. Unfortunately, only the first two letters can be read. This is a great pity, as otherwise we might have been able to date both the mausoleum and the castle with greater accuracy. All that we can say is that Samiran was certainly built well before Ismaili times and that it was taken by the Ismaili followers of Hasan Sabbah who used it as a military base.

In 1963 I returned with Ralph Pinder-Wilson, who was working in the Department of Oriental Antiquities at the British Museum, and a small team to carry out further research on this obviously important site. We had managed to obtain quite a lot of sponsorship and the promise of considerable publicity, but when we arrived in Tehran we learnt to our utter chagrin that the whole site had been flooded as a result of the completion of the Menjil dam – and no one had told us! We were able to do a little work, but the floodwater had, of course, shifted the artefacts below ground and accurate measurements were impossible. The castle and the minarets were still standing proudly on their elevated ground, but instead of the dry sand everywhere, there were large patches of greenery. Fortunately we had been able to make a film of Samiran during our original expedition, so all was not lost.

Before the flooding, Samiran with its great castle was a remarkably picturesque, even dramatic site, but now it is no more than a shell of crumbling tomb-towers and mausolea. The castle so impressed our artist, Tony Garnett, that he painted a possible reconstruction of how it may have originally appeared, with a certain artistic license (Plate 8). Although many of its features, especially the towers, walls and water catchment area, are typical of many Ismaili castles, Samiran is built on relatively low ground and so lacks the boldness of construction of fortresses like Gerdkuh, Nevisar Shah or Soru. Nevertheless, it still has a haunting quality of past greatness and splendour, enhanced by its magnificent setting – a photographer's dream, especially in the morning light. Samiran, like the glorious ruins of so many other medieval castles or mosques, reminded me forcefully of the following verse from Omar Khayyam:

> Think in this batter'd caravanserai,
> Whose frontals are alternate Night and Day,

How sultan after sultan with his pomp
Abode his destin'd hour and went his way.[9]

Space does not permit me to describe in detail all the castles in the Alamut and
Taleqan valleys, but the reader will find in Appendix II a list of all the important
castles, forts and watchtowers that I have located, together with a brief description.
The prime importance of these valleys was their ability to increase considerably
the production of food available for storage at times of siege in the main castles
and sites (i.e., Alamut, Maymundez, Nevisar Shah, Lamasar, Andej, and the forts
of Shirkuh, Bidelan and Garmarud at the entrance to the Alamut valley). Although
some parts of the Alamut valley, especially in the centre, could have provided
sufficient foodstuffs for the day-to-day requirements of the castle garrisons and
their dependent villages, the soil was insufficiently fertile, even with the benefit
of the new irrigation system constructed by the Ismailis, to fill the huge reserves
that were kept in the castles. Hence, we can assume that a good proportion of these
reserves were actually grown in the Taleqan and Shahrud valleys.

From the military point of view, the castles in the Taleqan and Shahrud valleys
were intended to delay for as long as possible, or halt the advance of, enemy troops
towards Alamut. Doubtless these defences would have been sufficient to stop any
Saljuq military offensives. Once the initial Saljuq attacks were called off following
the assassination of the vizier Nezam al-Molk and the sudden death of Sultan
Malekshah in 1092, the Ismailis would doubtless have seized this opportunity to
energetically strengthen their castles and defensive positions in these valleys. But
they were ultimately powerless to resist the greater numbers, speed and ferocity
of the Mongol armies.

We must, therefore, always be careful not to regard Alamut as a unit in itself.
Strictly speaking, we should refer to the Alamut complex, which includes the
Taleqan and the Shahrud valleys of the Rudbar.

The pottery kilns of Andej

As mentioned previously, our early expeditions had been able to discover a few
fragments of lustre painted ware from Alamut, as well as an almost complete
bowl at Samiran. A great deal of ordinary unglazed domestic pottery was also
found and no doubt some of this was locally made. Our attention was particularly
drawn to the village of Andej, situated between the strongholds of Maymundez
and Nevisar Shah, where we found a large number of pottery shards and kiln
material. It seems to me that Andej could have been the main kiln-site built by
the Ismailis for pottery-making.

In 1972 I asked our archaeological team, led by Tony Garnett, to investigate Andej and the kilns we suspected to be there, and to identify and classify other pottery types recovered from the castles. In his excellent report Tony Garnett writes as follows:

> On the eastern slope of the hill, the broken edge of a circular clay structure was partially exposed in the side of a small gulley. This turned out to be the damaged remains of a circular fired clay cylinder, between 25 cm and 28 cm high where complete, 64 cm in diameter and its orange coloured wall 5 cm thick. This cylinder had neither top nor bottom and rested on four flat stones. Surrounding it was a 5 cm layer of whitish ashy soil, while inside the kiln layers of charred earth and dark ashy material were frequently encountered. At the base, a circular shape which extended round one side contained a burnt red clayey earth surrounded by a more compacted white and grey ash. Outside the kiln structure a group of large flattish stones lay at a level just below the kiln base and may have supported air ducts. Adjoining it was a hard packed rectangular step 20 cm by 25 cm. This kiln resembles others found in Nishapur and Siraf, both in size and construction, and of a probably similar period, and would have been fired by inserting wood or scrub into a chamber below the perforated kiln floor so that flames passed through the setting and out through holes in the domed roof.[10]

Tony Garnett also makes the following observations in the report: Several other kiln-sites were located on or around the edge of the small plateau, their positions hinted at by the pieces of kiln fabric and heavily sintered kiln material lying in gullies on the steep hillside. The fact that the largest deposits of kiln-wasters were found around the edge of this field suggests that the centre of pottery-making was inside it, and that evidence of other kilns and waste-pits is buried under the thick top-soil and cultivation at present covering it.

The pottery shards found in the kiln were typical of all types found on the site and, indeed, on the castle sites of the area visited by members of the expedition. The most common were lead glazed over a white slip, embellished with brush marks of copper green and manganese purple, and cut through with a *sgraffiato* design. The ware comprised mainly bowls and dishes of many differing profiles and with well-turned foot-rings. Many of these were lightly and delicately thrown, though only distorted wasters and broken fragments (as was expected) were found, but perhaps the greater part were heavily potted and summarily decorated. Other glazed items included small oil lamps and ointment bowls.

Also found in the kiln and in very large quantities all over the site were un-glazed waterpot fragments. The necks and bases and handles were often found intact but the wider bellies were always in fragments. The fabric of the pottery was usually of a fairly fine-textured buff coloured body, mostly light in colour and well oxidised in the firing. However, some of the glazed bowl fragments were of a much darker colour, indicating a reducing atmosphere in the kiln and many showed distortion through over firing.

Cooking-pot fragments were found occasionally, always heavily reinforced with sand or shelly inclusions, and since these were exclusively hand-formed it was concluded that these additions must have made the body too non-plastic to throw with. To support the glazed pots in the kilns, many tripod stilts were found, some still fused to the base of glazed bowl fragments. Lastly, several finger-imprinted clay plugs appeared during excavations. These were arbitrary in shape and were too irregular to have been the plugs used to control the kiln's ventilation. It was decided that these may have been casually manipulated by the potters and perhaps fired unintentionally.

Evidence that Andej was an extensively used site was provided by the many hundred-weights of shards scattered all over the hill-slopes and buried thickly round the banks at the top, and also by the fused and sintered kiln fabric found in several places. This suggested that there may have been a dozen or so kilns in different parts of the hilltop and quite possibly very many more during the period of the site's occupation. There was no local knowledge or legends connected with the site, which indicated that it must have been abandoned for several centuries. Kilns were also found at two castles in the Taleqan valley.

Stylistically, the Ismaili pottery relates to the lead-glazed ware of northwest Persia of the 10th and 11th centuries. This has been agreed by both Ralph Pinder-Wilson, formerly a Curator at the Department of Oriental Antiquities at the British Museum, and by James Allan of the Ashmolean Museum at Oxford, though this is clearly a local and crude variant. That it is found on an Ismaili castle sacked by the Mongols and not since reoccupied confirms a date before the mid-13th century.[11]

In my *Castles of the Assassins*, Ralph Pinder-Wilson pointed out, in his Appendix on Persian pottery at the time of the Ismailis, that during the Saljuq period there was a revival of commerce and industry, accompanied by new developments in architecture and the arts. New religious institutions required new types of buildings and the great school mosque or madrasa for the teaching of theology and law came into its own. Prosperity in the great cities created wealthy patrons for the products of artists and craftsmen. In the course of the 12th century the decorative arts, in particular pottery, textiles and metal-ware, reached full maturity, and the style of decoration developed in this period directed the subsequent course of Persian art.

The Persians do not appear to have made lustre-decorated pottery before the second half of the 12th century. The Mesopotamians had been the first to paint in lustre in the 9th century, a tradition that was preserved in Egypt and later refined by the potters of the Fatimid era. It is probable that after the fall of the Fatimid dynasty in 1171, some of the Ismaili potters of Cairo found asylum in Persia. In Persia there is evidence of two centres producing lustre pottery: at Rayy, a few miles outside Tehran and an important city in the Seljuq period, and at Kashan, south of Tehran. These two cities are close to the Alamut valley and it is highly likely that some potters, converted to Ismailism, would have found their way to the Alamut valley and found work at Andej.[12]

Our archaeological group also collected and assessed shards from the many castle and fortress sites visited by other members of the expedition. Several Rayy and Kashan lustre-ware were found which may have been used by the cultured elite of the Ismailis. Chinese celadon-ware fragments provided evidence of trade with China. Many shards of the finely thrown and elegantly decorated alkaline glazed wares of Kashan and Gorgan were collected. But by far the predominant pottery types were the Andej glazed wares and the unglazed waterpot fragments, clearly showing that Andej was the main pottery centre for the Ismaili state in the Alamut and Taleqan valleys.

When Adrianne Woodfine and I visited the Andej site in 1996, the kilns and pits had all disappeared. There were still quite a few shards lying on the ground but far fewer than in 1972.

Water storage and agriculture

As already outlined, there is plenty of evidence that the castles of the Alamut valley and Rudbar were never short of water, thanks to the complex storage system of water-cisterns and channels constructed by the Ismailis. Let us assume that the average daily requirements per person was 3 to 3.5 litres a day. Each man would, therefore, require approximately 1,270 litres of water per year. Of course there must have been many other requirements for water, the most important being the watering of mules and horses. Each horse or mule would consume approximately 36 litres of water daily, much of which would come from rivers and streams.

In 1972 I led a very large expedition of over 50 people to Alamut consisting of 30 pupils from Wellington College where I was teaching, my colleagues and two officers of the Royal Engineers. We enjoyed the patronage of the Minister of Court who had approved the loan to us of Iranian army officers, Tehran University students and a considerable amount of transport. The expedition was split into six main groups: a castle exploration group, a water and agriculture exploration group, a survey group, an archaeological and photographic group, and finally a base team and medical group which treated both the members of the expedition and any villager who asked for assistance. The expedition stayed in the valley for a month and a great deal of useful work was accomplished. Just before we left we gave a party for all the village headmen which was attended by the British ambassador. Needless to say the expedition caused a considerable stir, not only in the valley but in all the surrounding district.

The water survey group of the 1972 expedition made a thorough examination of how the garrisons of the fortresses, all situated high above the valley floor, obtained the necessary water. The following notes are taken from the report of N.R. Jones who led this group:

> We estimated that the annual rainfall at Alamut (Gazor Khan) was in the region of 100 centimetres. Air currents as winds blow directly on the west face of the rock as they rise rapidly over the Hawdeqan range. This natural phenomenon was undoubtedly exploited by the Ismailis as several million litres of water fall on this face each year. Much of this was directed into the cisterns or the man-made channels. The total capacity of the channels and the cisterns is seven million litres, but the two main channels possibly conducted water to large underground cisterns hewn out of the rock itself. The main evidence for this was a widening of the channels at the southern end and, immediately beneath the centre, a man-made brick-lined opening which contained water. When this was drained, the water was replaced within hours in the absence of rain, indicating a seepage of water from a hidden source. This group summarised its report as follows:

>> Our results enabled us to estimate the minimum number of men and livestock that could have been accommodated at each fortress. These calculations are based on the assumption that at the beginning of the year the cisterns were full and that there was no rain to replenish the dwindling stocks. This, of course, was not the case and so the number could very well have been higher.

>> - Alamut – 8000 men and 900 horses and mules.
>> - Bidelan – 150 men and only a few mules inside the castle perimeter.
>> - Lamasar – 500 men and 50 horses and mules.

>> Of course, Alamut would never have had as large a garrison as its water supplies would have permitted. It is very difficult to assess the number of people living at Maymundez, but 600–800 would be a reasonable assumption.

Agriculture today in Alamut is limited to the valley floor where there is water and shelter, but in Ismaili times the extent of cultivation was very much greater. Evidence of terracing and irrigation ditches was found and the areas which were cultivated in the 11th–13th centuries were assessed as follows:

- Alamut – 349 acres
- Bidelan – none
- Maymundez – 319 acres
- Lamasar – 150 acres

These acreages appear insufficient to feed the inhabitants of the castles in the Alamut valley, the supporting villages and the livestock, and there certainly was not sufficient arable land to grow enough to store in the event of siege. Hence the vital importance of the fertile Taleqan valley, which must have supplied the castles and fortresses in the Alamut valley with sufficient food for their immediate use and for storage in their great underground chambers. Lamasar, on the other hand, was close enough to the fertile valley of the Shahrud, which probably also provided food for Alamut. While the castles were on the whole self-sufficient in water, thanks to their sophisticated system of *qanats* and cisterns, they had to rely on the surrounding area, particularly the Taleqan and Shahrud for their food. But as far as we know, except in times of prolonged siege, there was never any shortage of food and the Ismaili fortresses were always well provisioned. The resilience of the Ismailis in defending their mountain strongholds over such a long period of time could not have been possible without their remarkable skills in harnessing the natural resources of the mountains and valleys to the maximum advantage.

Notes

1. Juwayni, *History of the World-Conqueror*, vol. 2, p. 681.
2. Stark, *Valleys of the Assassins*, p. 243.
3. Ivanow, *Alamut and Lamasar*, p. 68.
4. Stark, *Valleys of the Assassins*, p. 247–248.
5. Hodgson, *The Order*, p. 78.
6. Ivanow, *Alamut and Lamasar*, p. 63.
7. H.C. Rawlinson, 'Notes on a journey from Tabriz, through Persian Kurdistan, to the ruins of Yakhti-Soleiman, and from there by Zenjan and Tarom, to Gilan, in October and November, 1838,' *Journal of the Royal Geographical Society*, 10 (1840) pp. 1–64.
8. Quoted by H. Brugsch, in his *Reise der k. Preussischen Gesandschaft Nach Persien* (Leipzig, 1860–1861).
9. E. Fitzgerald, *The Rubbaiyat of Omar Khayyam* (London, 1955), stanza 16.
10. The Archaeological Report of the Wellington College expedition to the Valley of the Assassins, Iran (unpublished). In Appendix III, Rosalind A. Wade Haddon uses material from another similar report published in the *Bulletin of the Experimental Firing Group*, which she acknowledges in her note no. 12.
11. Here ends Tony Garnett's report on the Andej kilns.
12. Ralph Pinder-Wilson, 'Persian Pottery at the time of the Assassins,' in Willey, *Castles of the Assassins*, Appendix C, pp. 32–38.

CHAPTER 9

The Mountain Fortresses of Qumes

There is considerable historical evidence of Ismaili activities in many Iranian cities from the 9th century onwards, but in general it had been assumed that apart from the Alamut and Rudbar fortresses, the castle of Gerdkuh and one or two other sites, there were few substantial traces remaining of Ismaili monuments, especially their castles. I, too, had assumed that Gerdkuh had always stood on its own as an important but isolated Ismaili outpost in the south Caspian region (called Qumes in medieval times). I first visited Gerdkuh in 1966 on the advice of Dr Lockhart of Cambridge and have examined this great castle several times since. But it was not until 1997 when Adrianne Woodfine and I located one of the largest Ismaili castles, Soru, near Semnan, together with a complex of other castles in the neighbourhood, that we realised that the whole of this mountainous area of northern Iran, south of the Caspian sea, had once been fortified by the Ismailis. The area around Semnan and Damghan, in particular, appears to have been far more heavily fortified than was previously thought, and should be regarded as one of the main centres of the Ismaili state in Iran. This fact has not been appreciated until now and, of course, it alters our perspective of the history of the early Nizari Ismailis.

Gerdkuh, a fortified mountain

The story of the acquisition of Gerdkuh by the Ismailis is well known. A fortress had already existed there for some time, though its origins are uncertain. The site of Gerdkuh has always been strategically important, as it controlled part of the main trade route – the great Silk Road –which, starting from the Mediterranean, passed through western Iran, then Damghan where Gerdkuh is situated, and on to Khorasan and eventually China. It will also be recalled that Gerdkuh fell into Ismaili hands when the local governor, Ra'is Mozaffar, in the service of the Saljuqs and well connected amongst the officers at Isfahan, the Saljuq capital, persuaded the amir Habashi, to acquire Gerdkuh and make him, Mozaffar, its guardian. The amir agreed, forcing the luckless incumbent of the castle to surrender it in 1096. Subsequently, Mozaffar also persuaded the amir to deposit his treasures in the castle under his protection. Unbeknown to Habashi, however, Mozaffar was secretly an Ismaili and receiving his instructions from Hasan Sabbah. Upon arriving at the castle, he immediately began to strengthen its fortifications and defences. When he felt sufficiently secure to withstand a prolonged siege, he openly declared his allegiance to Hasan Sabbah.

Mozaffar lived at Gerdkuh for many years until his death, during which time he made it into the strongest of all the Ismaili castles. The fortress itself is the greatest tribute to the ingenuity and expertise of Mozaffar and his architects. The sheer audacity of their achievement in transforming what must originally have been a relatively small castle into an impregnable fortress is remarkable. The strategic position of Gerdkuh, dominating the central section of the east-west trade route, made it in some respects the most important Ismaili stronghold after Alamut. Its impregnability also made Gerdkuh the safest castle within a relatively short distance from Alamut. In times of danger, Hasan Sabbah and other Ismaili leaders, sent their wives and families to Gerdkuh as a sure place of refuge. The history of Gerdkuh clearly illustrates that it could have provided the Ismaili leadership with an alternative, more secure and defensible headquarters than the castles of Alamut and Maymundez whose garrisons surrendered within days of being besieged by the Mongols.

Gerdkuh certainly deserves to be called a fortified mountain. It is perhaps one of the most dramatic Ismaili castle sites to be found. It lies some 15 km west of Damghan off the main Semnan road. It is best approached through the village of Aliabad (or Hajiabad), which is still surrounded by Mongol walls. Beyond the village there is a fairly flat plain stretching for about 2 km to the foot of Gerdkuh. The distinctive shape of the great conical peak is visible from a long way off. It rises graphically some 300 metres above the steep scree slopes surrounding it on every side (Plate 9). Apart from the east, the slopes are so precipitous that no defensive fortifications are necessary – in fact, it is quite impossible to scale them. The rounded top is prominent amongst the lower foothills of the eastern Alborz mountains, which form an impressive backdrop to the castle. The height of the plain on which the fortress is built is 1,230 metres and the height at the top of the fortress is 1,525 metres.

At the southern foot of the mountain is a rectangular outer gatehouse that gives the false impression of being the main entrance to the castle (Fig. 5). It was, in fact, little more than an observation post and a reception point for visiting

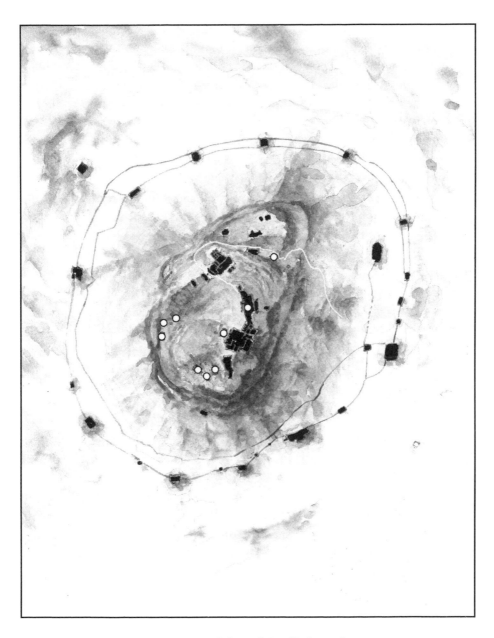

Figure 5: Groundplan of Gerdkuh castle

dignitaries. The proper entrance leading to the ascent of the mountain is much further round to the east. It was certainly possible for the agile members of the garrison to scramble over the rocks from the outer to the main gatehouse. Above the outer gatehouse, a line of mostly ruined walls and fortifications runs round to the east about a third of the way up the eastern side. The main gatehouse is 10.5–12 metres wide and 7.5 metres high. It is an immensely strong and well-constructed blockhouse that dominates all approaches over the plain from the direction of Aliabad. Inside are two vaulted rooms with low arches set behind each other. Two smaller rooms lead off to the eastern side. The main front guardroom overlooks the approaches across the plain through fairly large windows let into the centre wall. The right hand room has a small sally-port. Steps lead down from the western side of the gatehouse to the steep scree slope and on the eastern side steps lead up to the main fortifications. There are two round turrets on each side of the gatehouse made of smooth dressed stone. There is evidence of an upper storey and crenellated battlements. There is a spring just above the gatehouse, but no evidence of water storage here. This gatehouse was used as the main entrance and exit, except in times of siege.

The main perimeter defences of Gerdkuh are the remarkable rings of 35 forts that surround the castle. The total circumference of the rings is about 6 km. In 1997 we were able to drive across the plain to examine these forts in some detail. There are pleasant springs on the plain from which water is channelled to nearby farms. Outside the shade of the occasional tuti tree (the fruit of which is a delicious white mulberry), the sun is blisteringly hot in the summer, and in the evening a sharp wind blows up the dust of the plain that whips stingingly against the faces of anyone in its path. The majority of the forts are situated on the eastern side, where there are three rings. The outer ring is 300 metres from the castle, a second ring at 200 metres and a third ring at the foot of the castle. There is an inner defensive ring a third of the way up to the castle. These were all substantial buildings. A typical one investigated by Adrianne was 200 metres long and 9 metres in width. The outside walls were built of well dressed stone, 2 metres thick and with a rubble infill. Inside there were a considerable number of rooms.

There is some discussion as to whether these forts were originally built by the Ismailis or, as some commentators say, by the Mongols during their long siege of the castle. The architectural style of the main fortress and the surrounding forts, however, is convincingly Ismaili. It would have been natural for Mozaffar and his architects to construct the whole complex of forts at the same time. He would not have intended to remain in splendid isolation at the top of the mountain or to make repeated ascents and descents. He would need somewhere more convenient to keep his horses and mules as well as some stores. The Ismailis certainly cultivated the fertile ground at the foot of the mountain, and the forts would protect this enterprise. The forts would also serve as useful bases from which to collect taxes from passing caravans on the main east-west highway.

There are many buildings in the vicinity of Gerdkuh, some of them quite significant which were undoubtedly erected by the Mongols during their long siege of the fortress. But unlike the Ismaili forts, which are built of stone and intended to withstand a large-scale attack, these are mostly mud and brick constructions. There is no doubt that the Mongols built the steep scree slope leading to the outer gatehouse at the foot of the mountain. This slope or ramp is constructed of desert soil and stone dug from the surrounding plain. The Ismaili forts are much more solidly built and seem to me to form an integral part of a strategic defence plan. There are other remains of Mongol buildings at Aliabad and nearby villages. These are relatively intact and better preserved than the former Mongol palace at Tun, or the Mongol castle at Nehbandan, south of Shahanshah at Neh. They seem to have been in continuous occupation and are adapted now, of course, for domestic use. There is no doubt, however, that they were originally military buildings. One of the main walls encircling Aliabad is crenellated. Probably they were used as a permanent base during the siege of Gerdkuh. Now these buildings are largely deserted, except for wild dogs which wander through the ruins. There are also remains of Mongol siege works on the flat plain between Aliabad and Gerdkuh.

The mountain fortifications at Gerdkuh are well defended with double walls built between towers every 200 metres or so (Plate 10). Perpendicular drops were used to increase the effectiveness of the defence. On the north side of the castle, there is a drop of 27 metres from the top. There are two outer rings of forts beyond the drop. The same pattern is followed wherever necessary. The combination of natural and well-planned blockhouses, towers and defensive walls makes the mountain impossible to assault directly. Every possible approach, apart from the east had been blocked off. The original access was probably from the main gatehouse via a series of steps to the first line of defences on a natural ledge, which leads round to a second entrance in the eastern face. This is now the only way up to the main castle and originally it was strongly defended. Here there are two wells protected by a fort. The eastern well has been half excavated. Its diameter is 1 metre and the unexcavated infill is 3 metres below the surface. On my first visit in 1966, I noticed bones and an intact skull by the tip of one of the wells, but on my next visit two years later these were found to be broken.

From the well there is a steep scramble to the first of the inner defences. From here there is a magnificent view over the plain and the eastern wadi at the foot of the hill that was covered with mangonel shots. The altimeter reading is 1,410. Here there is a heavily fortified tongue of land to the north. The tongue or spur is about 30 metres long and little remains on it. The access path continues upwards over almost sheer rock and passes through two block-houses until it emerges on to a rocky platform. Here there is a citadel 30.5 metres long and 24 metres wide, containing two large rooms and two smaller ones. The base of the citadel is made from square well-dressed blocks of stone, with a well dug in the middle. From here there is a good view of the western side of the castle and the remains of the two lines of fortifications at the top, extending 45 metres down to the slope. This is below the top of the mountain, and it is very difficult to climb down to it.

The view from the top of the mountain is spectacular. To the south there is a wide vista over the nearby village to the Great Salt Desert shimmering in the background. To the east you can see Damghan and, on a clear day, as far as Shahrud. After a heavy rainfall the agricultural area on the south-east slope inside the outer defence walls is very clear, and there even seems to be evidence of recent strip farming. To the west stretches the road to Semnan and the chain of the Alborz mountains. From the top of the mountain there is a vertical drop on all sides after 15 metres or so, apart from the west where the ground slopes gently away at an angle of 15 degrees for 60.5 metres before it, too, becomes vertical. The only possible ascent for an attacking force is on the eastern side.

The peak of the mountain itself is very narrow, the widest part being no more than 15 metres and the narrowest 6 metres. The top has its own fortifications. On the north-east side are the remains of a mud wall of a much later period, and little is left of the few buildings that were originally there. The main inhabited areas are on the south-eastern slope of the hilltop. Unlike the more northerly set of buildings which is squat and probably only one storey high, the complex on the south-eastern slope is much bigger and grander. There are two rows of buildings here, all of them at least two or three storeys high and still quite well preserved. They probably constituted the main residential area of the castle and their ruins can be clearly seen from the plain below. On the south-western side are the remains of a tower with arrow-slits and next to it a water cistern. As the top edge of the slope here is no more than 10 metres long, there is no space for further buildings.

Although it is related that Mozaffar attempted in vain to dig a deep well in the fortress, and was only successful after an earthquake allowed the ground level of the water to rise, the water storage system built by him at the top of the mountain is remarkable. At the southern tip of the mountain, the ground drops steeply for about 60.5 metres and runs down to the main water catchment area. This consists of three magnificent cisterns to collect the precipitation from the clouds that constantly spill over the Alborz mountains from the Caspian Sea (Plate 11). The first cistern measures 15.75 metres in length, 4.2 metres wide and 4.5 metres deep, the second cistern is 13.5 m x 5.75m x 7m, and the third cistern is 16m x 4.2m x 3.5m. As the bottom of all the cisterns are filled with the rubble from the collapsed stone roofs, it would be reasonable to double their depth. The outer walls of the cisterns are 3 metres thick and buttressed with three turrets. Mud brick was applied to the stone and then a layer of plaster. All had vaulted roofs and steps leading down to the tanks. At the end of the water catchment area, there were no signs of fortifications, but as the hill drops perpendicularly for 121 metres or so, it would have been impossible for us to scale it at this point.

In addition to the cisterns I have mentioned, there are other cisterns at different levels in the fortress. Wells had also been dug, but they are now filled with debris and it is difficult to know how far down they extended. As was usual in Ismaili castles, the quarters or barracks for the soldiers were on the lowest level and the high citadel area was kept for the lord and his notables. The residential part of the high citadel must have been quite substantial to house the various distinguished visitors who came to Gerdkuh for safety. A very large number of people could be, and most probably were, quartered in the fortress. The provision of sufficient food could have been a problem, but there is every likelihood that the Ismailis cultivated the land at the foot of the mountain and stored the crops. There was plenty of natural water even in the hot summers.

When the Mongols first arrived at Gerdkuh in 1253, they must have taken possession of the outer rings of forts at once. The Ismaili defenders had in all probability withdrawn up the mountain by then, as there was little point in waiting like sitting ducks to be defeated piecemeal. After the failure of their first attempt to storm the castle, the Mongols had no alternative but to surround the fortress and to starve its garrison into submission. There was no possibility of mining or sapping or using their much-feared mangonels – the range and the height were too great. The mountainsides were too sheer to be scaled in force, and although the mangonels might have caused some damage to the lower fortifications, they could not possibly have reached the areas where the bulk of the defenders were grouped in force.

After the fall of Alamut in 1256, the Ismailis were required to surrender all their castles to the Mongols. Most of the garrisons in Rudbar, Qumes, Khorasan and Qohistan are reported to have complied, albeit unwillingly, to this demand. Lamasar submitted one or two years after Alamut, but the troops at Gerdkuh held out for 17 long years from 1253 to 1270. The fact that this garrison, probably in the region of 1,000 or more and their dependants, could survive a siege for so long and repel all attempts to dislodge them, is truly remarkable. This must have been one of the longest castle sieges in medieval history. When at last the survivors descended from the towers, their numbers decimated by an outbreak of cholera and their clothes worn to rags, they were all put to the sword by the Mongols.

The fortress itself was not destroyed by the Mongols who continued to make use of it for some time, although they may well have dismantled parts of it when they left eventually. Doubtless, some parts were later used by local lords despite their inconvenient position, but the possibility of preying on passing caravans may have been sufficient reward for them. There seems to be little mention of Gerdkuh in the following centuries until the time of Naser al-Din Shah (1848–96) of the Qajar dynasty, who showed an interest in the site and encouraged Shaykh Mohammad Mehdi Abdol Rab-Abadi to investigate it. The Shaykh's report, though somewhat brief, provides surprisingly accurate measurements;[1] otherwise very little has been written about the castle.

During our visit to Gerdkuh in 1967, a number of stone mangonel shots still lay on the ground, and it is difficult to know whether these were unused Mongol ammunition or if they had been hurled down from the fortress. There was some evidence of local digging, but clearly without great results. The lower slopes and top of the castle was covered with shards and artefacts. When we examined the area again in the following year, only a few shards remained. In 1997 we were told of a secret tunnel between Gerdkuh and Soru, the second major Ismaili castle in Qumes about 80 km away, but as yet we have no evidence of this. If ever such a tunnel existed, its construction would have required an extraordinary feat of engineering and supply of resources.

Gerdkuh, even more than Alamut, is a marvel of Ismaili architecture, enterprise and administrative planning. The complete fortification of a mountain – for Gerdkuh is a small mountain – is an astonishing accomplishment by any standard. When Alamut castle was destroyed by Hulegu's army, they found it almost an impossible task, so strongly was it built, and they left some of its underground storage chambers almost untouched. The fortification of Gerdkuh was on an even greater scale, demanding infinitely more resources and energy. The construction of the main buildings and the water cisterns on the summit must have demanded extraordinary effort, skill and endurance by the builders as they carried the necessary materials up the mountainside. Ismaili castles were built to be completely self-sufficient and sustain sieges indefinitely. The men who built them and lived in them, enduring considerable hardship, especially during times of siege, must have had supreme self-confidence in their cause. If any further refutation of the old legend that the 'Assassins' were merely a bunch of rough and ready brigands were needed, the answer lies in their construction of immensely strong and complex fortresses, such as Gerdkuh and, as we shall see below, Soru.

The mystery of Soru

It is strange that, to the best of my knowledge, there is little written reference in our historical sources to the castle of Soru, and Juwayni is inexplicably silent about it. I was first informed of its existence by an American traveller called Jim Whittaker who had visited Soru before the 1979 Revolution with an Iranian friend, Mehdi Shalforushan. Jim knew of my research work and he subsequently sent me a letter saying that he was surprised that I had not investigated a 'huge castle, deep in the mountains, north of Semnan'. He enclosed some photographs he had taken on a recent visit. The castle indeed looked very impressive. But owing to the Revolution, I was unable to see it for myself until 1997. We had looked for it in 1996 when Adrianne and I were accompanied by an Ismaili friend, Dr 'Abbas Badakhshani. He took us on a tour of various Ismaili sites between Mashhad and Semnan. When we arrived at Semnan, we attempted to find this castle. We followed a number of tracks into the mountains north of the city and asked the few local people we met for information, but they knew little of it and we were unable to find any trace of a castle. The heat was so intense that we had to give up the search, but we were determined to find the castle if we possibly could when we returned the following year. So in 1997 we made the location of Soru one of the main aims of our research programme. We were fortunate in obtaining from our Ismaili friend in Tehran, Mr Isa Mirshahi, an introduction to another friend in Semnan. This gentleman told us that, indeed, he knew the castle and would take us to it. After one mistake when we found ourselves outside an 18th-century semi-fortified domestic dwelling, we drove through a narrow mountain gully and, rounding a corner, saw in the distance the towers of a very large castle that seemed to be in a good state of preservation. The track on which we were travelling led past it to a second castle built at the foot of the hills at the northern end of the valley. These two castles were distinguished by the names Greater and Lesser Soru.

Soru is also the name given to the valley in which the two castles have been built. The centre of this valley is 13.5 km north of Semnan. The surrounding mountains form a huge shield all round them, as though the mountains themselves were protecting the two castles in the valley beneath them. The valley must once have been very fertile. There is still a pleasant and productive farm in the middle. This is part of the estate, including the castles, owned at the time of our visit by an Iranian businessman. Unfortunately he was then in Switzerland, and we were unable to ask him for further information on the castle. The farm is surrounded by fruit trees and vegetables of all kinds. There is plenty of water, including drinking troughs for animals and goldfish ponds. We were told that in winter the riverbed, dry in summer, becomes a rushing stream. This information was important, of course, as an indication of a very adequate food supply and water for the garrisons of the two castles, as well as the inhabitants of the valley.

Greater and Lesser Soru castles are probably among the best preserved Ismaili castles in existence (see Plates 12–13 and front cover illustration). Greater Soru is visually the most impressive castle I have seen, perhaps on account of its position, planted solidly and grandly on a great rocky outcrop. It is the quintessential castle, powerful and dominant over the surrounding countryside. From the valley floor you can see that the great outer defensive walls have suffered considerable damage. But the massive bulk of the main castle and especially the huge towers of the high citadel, which seems to rise up in defiance, seem relatively unscathed. When we had absorbed the great size of the fortress and visited the castle of Lesser Soru a kilometre away at the end of the valley, we were quite amazed that so few people had known about or visited this site. The name may, of course, have changed down the centuries as is often the case with towns and villages.

After Adrianne, our driver 'Ali Moradi, and I had been shown the site of Soru, we decided to return the next day, as it was by then getting late and very hot. We returned to the government tourist hotel in Semnan where we were staying. Later, over a meal we were told by an Iranian academic that the castle was certainly attributed to the Ismailis; he also believed that it had never been taken by the Mongols or anyone else. The castle was supposed to be amply provisioned and had its own supply of water. Our Iranian friend, who had shown us the castle, had to return to Tehran the next day, but he said that he would arrange for a four-wheel drive vehicle to pick us up at 6:00 a.m. and take us to Soru. At precisely six, a young man arrived with a four-wheel drive pick-up truck. We followed the same route as the day before which leads to the township of Payghamberan. We were told that there had been a Zoroastrian fire-temple on this spot, which was considered particularly sacred. It had also been used as a burial site for holy men.

We travelled through the stark, barren mountains and on the way noticed a watchtower from which warning could have been given to the main fortress of any attacking force. When we arrived below Greater Soru, we stopped and saw to our dismay a chain across the dirt track. The chain had not been there the previous day and must have been put up by the owner's steward. It meant, however, that we had to alter our plans and leave our vehicle. We realised at once that it would be impossible for me with my crutches to climb up the steep scree slopes to Greater Soru. The size and extent of Greater Soru also meant that no useful exploration of the site could be achieved by Adrianne with just the help of 'Ali. So after 'Ali had made breakfast, we took many photographs of the castle and described it as fully as we could in our notebooks and then set off walking down the track to the farm and Lesser Soru. We arrived there about 11:00 a.m. (the sun was already getting very hot) and rested in the orchards around the farm. We then set out on foot to examine Lesser Soru, which seemed tantalisingly close. Our driver was our guide and he took us by the direct route from the farm to the castle, up what seemed to me to be a steep and incredibly rough slope covered with camel thorn. I had one crutch to help me, but this proved more of a hindrance than a help. 'Ali was determined that I would make it and more-or-less man-handled me to the top of the slope. From here it was possible to look at Lesser Soru which was built on an adjoining slope and look back at Greater Soru. Our taxi-driver told us that gold had been found here but, of course, there was no proof of this. I was in no fit state for the final scramble to Lesser Soru and so contented myself with taking photographs of it, while 'Ali and Adrianne examined the castle. I wearily made my way by a gentler path back to the farm. Then we all plodded back to the spot where we had left the truck and drove back to Semnan.

We were pleased with our day's work, but disappointed that we had not been able to get into Greater Soru. We realised realistically that it would take three or four days to examine this castle thoroughly and we had a strenuous programme in front of us. In any case, due to my physical disability I would probably never be able to make it to the top. So we decided to wait until we could ask someone to do this work for us. After my return to England, I asked our Ismaili friend Isa Mirshahi if he would go to Semnan and take photographs of the interior of Soru. He very kindly made two visits, one with Ali, and sent me some very helpful photographs and a map taken from a local publication. But Isa, for all his many qualities, is not an archaeologist or surveyor and he was unable to give me all the information I needed. Then luck came to our aid. *The Times* published an account of my research findings in Iran including a photograph of Soru.[2] This article was spotted by Mehdi Shalforushan, the friend of Jim Whittaker who had originally written to me about Soru many years before. Mehdi and Jim at once got in touch with me and when Mehdi heard about my problem, he said he was sure that his brother-in-law, Amin Dara, who lives in Tehran and is an artist and surveyor, would be delighted to go to Soru and make a thorough survey of the castle. This Dara did and he paid several visits to Soru, producing an excellent report, fully illustrated with photographs and plans.

In a letter at the beginning of his report, Amin Dara said that although he had requested assistance from civil and military cartographical officials in Tehran and Semnan, it was clearly indicated to him that such information was restricted. The only aerial photographs of the area had been taken by the American Air Force some forty years ago and these were also restricted. He, like our Iranian Ismaili friend Isa Mirshahi, was unable to find any reference to Greater and Lesser Soru in the libraries he consulted, except for a short reference in *The History of Qumes*.[3]

The author of this history published in 1950 is Professor Abu'l-Rafi Haqiqat, who states that Soru must be considered as one of the most important castles in eastern Iran, although access to it is now very difficult. He comments that the main castle has three floors, of which the first was used for horses and other animals, the second as accommodation for 'farmers and other ordinary people and their families', and the third floor contained a 'prayer-hall, bath-house and kitchen'. Professor Haqiqat also comments on the way the Ismailis were able to bring water from Lesser Soru to the main castle, despite the fact that Greater Soru is 100 metres higher than the springs at Lesser Soru.

No one was able to explain satisfactorily the origin or meaning of the name Soru. In the standard Persian dictionary by Dehkhoda, a work comparable to the *Oxford English Dictionary*, Soru is described as a prefix to names of places such as Soru-Je and Soru Khani, or to people such as Soru 'Ali. This was particularly the case in Safavid times (1502–1730). More to our purpose, it transpires that Soru is also the name of an area in Semnan, which is well known for its coal mining. We did in fact pass a mining area on our way to the castles. There was also a suggestion, discounted by Amin Dara, that in the Armenian language Soru means mountain. The word is also used as a boy's name. Soru has no particular meaning in the Semnan dialect, and it is highly likely that in previous centuries the fortress was known by one or more other names associated with a ruling dynasty. As time went by, Soru became the accepted name, as the castle is in the middle of a mining area. For us, in any case, the elusiveness of the name, and the fact that so little was known of the castle, added to its mystery and made our investigation even more worthwhile.

It is generally assumed that Soru was in Ismaili hands for some time and that it was built on the site of much earlier fortifications. There can be little doubt that this is a correct conclusion. The valley of Soru is almost a fortification in itself. Greater Soru reminded Amin Dara of the Sasanid castle of Firuzabad in Fars. In pre-Islamic times, the Sasanids (226–642 CE) ruled over a vast empire with their capital at Ctesiphon, and like the Ismaili Iranians, they were highly accomplished military architects. Professor Haqiqat asserts that there was probably a hidden access road from Gerdkuh to Soru, a distance of about 80 km, or if a 'by-pass road' were used this could reduce the distance to 60 km. He also contends that the Ismailis held this castle for 200 years. Despite the local legend of a tunnel connecting the two fortresses, it is unlikely that such a hidden road existed.

It is now time to describe the castles themselves, and I acknowledge with grateful thanks the details given to me by Amin Dara and Isa Mirshahi. I am particularly grateful to Dara's detailed and carefully constructed plans of Soru, illustrated with a large number of photographs, which give full justice to this remarkable site. His contribution supplements significantly the work of Isa Mirshahi and the observations made by Adrianne Woodfine and myself. I must also thank sincerely our guide and driver, 'Ali Moradi, who enabled me to see as much as possible of the castles despite the physical difficulties of the terrain. Space, however, compels me to restrict my account to the salient details.

As we have seen, the strategic position of Soru makes it highly likely that the site had been fortified quite early and that the valley may have been home to a considerable number of people from pre-Islamic times. The Sasanids may well have enlarged or rebuilt the original fortification. Amin Dara points to the use of heavy dressed stonework in the structure as well as the shape of the ceilings and the crescents above the doorways as evidence of this. We do not know when and how the Ismailis took possession of the main southern castle of Greater Soru. Dara suggests that they may have added another floor to the building in the citadel area. There can be little doubt, however, that the Ismailis were responsible for the construction of the outer defence works, which are highly sophisticated and complex. The Ismailis were also most probably the architects of the ingenious water system which runs from Lesser Soru to the main castle area. It is likely, too, that they built Lesser Soru after they had already occupied and rebuilt the main castle, with the view precisely of defending their water supply, as well as preventing any attack on the valley from the north. The construction of Lesser Soru is typically Ismaili.

Greater Soru is built in the form of a polygon or a very rough rectangle on the upper slopes of a steep rock bluff about 200–230 metres high (Fig. 6). The whole structure fills half the jagged and precipitous slope, and the Ismailis ensured that every possible approach route was guarded by high walls or other defences which would provide insuperable obstacles to the attackers. The southern and highest side of the polygon is approximately 165 metres across and 75 metres above the lowest part of the outside curtain wall. The northern or lowest part of the outer curtain-wall is another 75 metres above the valley floor, 1,700 metres above sea level.

The inner core of the citadel is built near the top of this very rugged and steep bluff. The inner western wall is 80 metres long, the southern 62 metres and the eastern approximately 65 metres. The citadel thus forms a kind of triangle on its side. The construction of the walls, particularly in the south-west is most impressive. The walls are higher as the castle slopes to the valley floor. In some places the walls follow the twisting sinuous course of the natural rock, where towers and turrets have been built to provide extra strength, especially at acute angles. The thickness of the walls vary; in some places they are quite thin. The angle of slope also varies considerably, but is roughly 45 degrees. Any approach from the valley is difficult, the steep sides of the castles are covered with loose scree, and there are many hidden gullies and dips in the rocks. When the castle was occupied there must have been reasonable mule tracks, though the approach from the southern side is easier. Nowhere does there seem to be any flat piece of ground on which mangonels or trebuchets could have been mounted. The axis of the castle is roughly north-east/south-west. The curtain-wall of the fortress has two entrances on the south-west side. These led into the inner area which is naturally much more extensive on the southern and eastern side.

The distance from the main entrance in the south-western curtain wall to the imposing main gate-house is some 60 metres. The great gatehouse block, 45 metres above the lower curtain-wall, is an imposing sight and very strongly built. The tower is 7 metres high and 1.5 metres wide allowing horses to enter comfortably. It is built at right angles to the lower part of the citadel, thus forming a bent entrance. There is an outer and inner entrance to the gatehouse, which is impressively vaulted with brick. A semi-circular buttress adjoins the gatehouse and there is at least one fortified storey above it. These walls are so designed that even if the enemy forced a passage through the main gatehouse, his troops would have be trapped in a great impasse surrounded by high walls as they advanced. The walls of the main citadel are particularly strong, as are the great towers that can be seen from a distance. The thickness of the walls varies from 75–130 cm, and they are made of well-dressed stone anchored into the living rock. The defensive walls on the top of the slope and descending into the southern side are also strongly built and dramatic in appearance. Beyond these walls are the remains of a small external guardhouse acting as a kind of barbican. Some of the rooms inside the citadel are remarkably well preserved (Plate 14).

There are two main water catchment areas. The first is at the foot of the outer mud-brick defence wall in the south-west corner below the main entrance to the castle. The cisterns are built into the outer perimeter wall and were filled by rainwater running down the slope. There are at least three, built of stone and brick and lined with limestone cement. There are more cisterns inside the castle, but the main water supply came from the springs at Lesser Soru. The water at Lesser Soru is particularly sweet and good, as it comes directly from the mountain behind the castle. It was conveyed to the larger castle through pipes, some of which still survive. The Ismailis, as we have seen elsewhere, had an advanced knowledge of hydraulic technology which they used to good effect at Soru. A stream runs through the centre of the valley and, although mostly dry in summer, it must be quite a turbulent river at other times of the year.

I would suspect that Greater Soru was capable of containing a very large garrison indeed, who needed to be fed and the valley was cultivated for this purpose. The site is probably the best example I have seen of an exceptionally fertile valley protected by two castles.

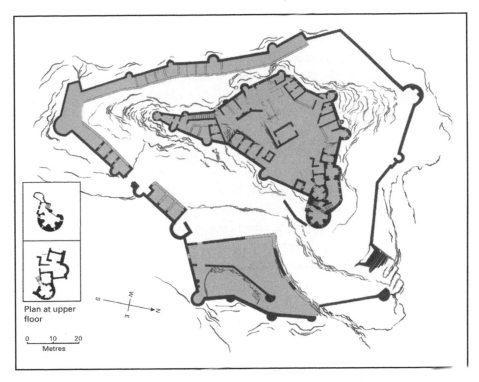

Figure 6: Groundplan of the main Soru castle

In the course of his explorations, Amin Dara found shards of the typical blue pottery of the Islamic period with black scroll decorations. He also found some Mongol shards. We found few shards at Lesser Soru, probably because this castle is more easily accessible and certainly attracts the curious and the treasure-seekers who may have taken all they could find. Dara noted evidence of illicit excavations in the north tower of Greater Soru. The damage to Greater Soru is nowhere as extensive as in other castles taken by the Mongols. Apart from some damage to the roofs of the outer cisterns and perimeter walls as well as in the high citadel, why this formidable Ismaili castle was left relatively intact is a mystery.

Lesser Soru has been much more damaged than Greater Soru, though a good deal remains of it (Plate 14). Although not as large as the main Soru castle, Lesser Soru was certainly a significant fortress in its own right with a surprisingly complex construction, belying its initial simplicity when first sighted. It was well able to ensure the defence of this fertile valley from the east. The fort was deliberately sited at the northern end of the valley in order to prevent any attack on the main castle from behind and to protect the water supply from here to Greater Soru. There was, of course, complete visibility between the two castles.

Built on a slope behind the farm in the middle of the valley, Lesser Soru is much more accessible than Greater Soru. The castle is rectangular in shape, covering an area of approximately 6,500 square metres, divided into two sections. In some ways it is reminiscent of the forts around Gerdkuh. The interior of the front section, which occupies about half the total area, is in ruins apart from its outer walls flanked by towers. This area was probably the soldiers' quarters, which corresponds to the plans of other Ismaili castles. There are few signs of additional buildings. The castle itself really consists of a series of quadrilateral boxes, the whole protected by an outside perimeter wall with strong towers at the corners. There is evidence of a further perimeter wall which has been destroyed. The inner castle beyond the soldiers' quarters is defended by a stout wall leading to an open space. Another gateway leads to the core of the castle. Although not extensive, this core probably housed the residential quarters of the castle's commander and his staff. The walls are solidly built. The dressed stone work and limestone cement are reinforced with timber, some of which is visible at breaks in the wall. The central rooms certainly had two storeys, perhaps more, and the walls are covered with plaster. The arches of the gateways are particularly fine, and the towers must have provided the sentries with a comprehensive view of the valley and the mountains beyond. A visiting party of Ismailis from Mashhad had left their names and greetings on the walls. I wonder how they had come to find the castle.

Firuzkuh and other castles

Having identified the site of Soru, we naturally enquired what other Ismaili castles there were in the area and were told that there were several including a 'Soldiers' Castle'. We had originally intended to proceed directly to Gerdkuh, but now we decided to investigate the other fortresses in the area. Some 20 km from Semnan we stopped at Cheshmeh, noted for its sweet, cool water. Here we saw a small castle situated on a hill above the spring. The remains of the walls, two turrets and some rooms were clearly visible. We were told that there was another 'Hasan Sabbah castle' at Vehel immediately behind this one, but it was not visible from the road.

Before I go on to describe the other castles we visited, I feel I ought to tell the reader that I do not intend to give a chronological account of our journeys. We often had to twist, turn and retrace our route as fresh sites came to our notice. This could be confusing and I feel it better to give a broader description of our studies than to describe the route we took.

The first castle we visited was near a deserted village called Mansurehkuh. We were able to drive to the foot of the hill on which the castle was situated. My altimeter showed a height of 1,720 metres. We climbed up to the castle from the northern side and could see at once that this was a big castle, though not as large as Soru. It was badly destroyed but the ruins of the towers, walls and high citadel were impressive. We examined the construction of the walls closely. These followed the typical Ismaili pattern. The outside walls were built of dressed stone, with rubble infill, then more stone covered with plaster. Shards were difficult to find, but we picked up some fragments of 12th-century pottery. We drove round the south of the site and were again impressed by the strength of the position and the square high citadel. Our driver 'Ali Moradi seemed to make light work of helping me up the slopes. Using one crutch, with his help, I was able to get as near the top as possible. Adrianne had little difficulty in nimbly scaling the rocky heights despite being clad in manteau and headscarf.

We then turned our attention to another fortification which the locals called a Soldiers' Castle. This was a puzzle. The castle was relatively small and was certainly not the residence of a notable. It was strictly functional and could have been used as a barracks, housing perhaps 300 men. It could have been used as a reserve for Gerdkuh or another castle nearby, called Mehrin (or Mehr Negar) which is about 20 km from Damghan. The Soldiers' Castle is situated on the top of a steep hill at a slope-angle of about 90 degrees. It has been badly destroyed, but the remains of the curtain-wall half way up the slope were still visible as were some of the buildings on top (200 metres or so) with a tower leaning at a perilous angle.

We were also told of four other castles in this area, which we did not have time to visit, and there is strong evidence of interconnecting watchtowers. I must mention, however, the whole complex of castles in the Firuzkuh area, which we were able to inspect. The Firuzkuh road skirts the extinct volcano of Damavand and the landscape here is really magnificent. Firuzkuh itself is strategically placed at the entrance to a narrow gorge and the mountain peaks around are topped with many forts. Some of them were built in Daylamite times and were later taken over and enlarged by the Ismailis. One guards the entrance to the gorge. Firuzkuh was always an important stronghold because of its strategic position. The castle goes back to Sasanid times. We know that it was taken by the Mongols in 1227 and later the Ismailis of Alamut obtained possession of it. It fell again to the Mongols in 1256, and Juwayni gives a brief but dramatic account of its fall and the fate of its commander, Sultan Rokn al-Din:

> The Mongols laid siege to it (Firuzkuh) and after five or six months forced him (the sultan) to come down with all the people of the castle. For all their pressure, he refused to kneel on the ground in fealty; and finally they put him to death with all his followers and the garrison of the castle.[4]

Juwayni adds a sanctimonious exhortation to those who may be tempted to stray from the one true path: 'Plant thy foot firmly in the centre of resignation and trust in God that thou fall not. And step not forward lest thy foot be caught.'

At first sight the castle seems small and the only part visible from the opposite track is a half-destroyed wall and the ruins of a bastion on the eastern side. But the building is, in fact, very large. The entrance from the east is protected by a triple outer wall and a strong gatehouse. The line of the outer wall is now confused and difficult to reconstruct. Behind the outer defences is a large residential or garrison area, stretching to halfway up the hills on which the castle is situated. A little above this is a rock-hewn cistern, which is part of a catchment area, which is 7 metres deep, 4 metres long and 2 metres wide. Rock steps are cut down into the cistern. This cistern was originally vaulted and the rubble of the roof lies at the bottom of the cistern.

The high citadel, which is invisible from the track on the eastern side, is reached by steps cut into the rock. The wooden beams of the strong gatehouse were still visible in 1969. The lower slopes of the high citadel are protected by another wall, beyond which is a second residential area. The keep inside the citadel area is defended by another two walls and towers. The high citadel is also defended by walls running down the slope at right angles. There are the remains of several rooms clustered around the great tower, of which 12 metres remain. This is a fine example of rugged military craftsmanship. The defence walls and turrets were the most impressive feature of the castle. In some ways the fortress reminded me of Gerdkuh, standing high across two hills in a fine strategic position guarding three valleys. It has excellent all-round visibility. We picked up some good shards of pottery belonging to different periods. In the distance we could see the snow-covered slopes of Mount Damavand and we were told that in the nearby hills, near Jellehjhan, is to be found another Ismaili castle called Nadrkuh.

Apart from Firuzkuh itself, we visited two or three other castles, and our attention was particularly drawn to Lajevardi and Kelar Khan. Other Ismaili castles which were pointed out to me included two at Shahmirzad, near a popular tourist site famous for its healing waters at Cheshmeh, Sara Anzar and Jironsefid. We were also told of two castles closer to Mashhad in the east known as Zaydar and Qa'leh Biar at Biajarmand. All this means that the area of Semnan and Damghan was much more heavily fortified by the Ismailis than had previously been thought. Gerdkuh was probably the most important castle, but Soru came very close to it. It seemed to us that a large portion of the area on both sides of the road to Mashhad in the east was once firmly in Ismaili hands. Although with the exception of Gerdkuh, history has little to say about the Ismaili presence in this part of

Qumes, we can certainly assume that it was an important semi-autonomous part of the Ismaili state as a whole.

Wherever we went in the Qumes region, we were struck by the outstanding quality of the Ismaili castles. The strong stone walls were exceptionally well built, demonstrating an architectural expertise that is not so evident in the Alamut area. The process of building these elaborate fortresses demanded a huge supply of manpower, stone, equipment and material. The process of quarrying the good quality stone required was a considerable feat. All this labour force had to be fed and accommodated. Where did the labour come from? Who were the architects? All these questions point to a competent, imaginative and far-sighted group of people who could achieve technical, economic and organisational results of a very high order.

Summarising, then, the castles we were able to locate in the south Caspian region of Qumes were Gerdkuh, Greater Soru and Lesser Soru, two castles at Shahmirzad near Cheshmeh, Mansurehkuh, Mehrin (Mehr Negar) and Firuzkuh, as well Sara Anza, Lajevardi and Kelar Khan which are in the mountains overlooking the road to Firuzkuh. We were also told of additional forts and watchtowers to be found in the area, but unfortunately we did not have the time to investigate them.

I must again stress that we would not have had success in our research work without the help of our Ismaili taxi-driver, 'Ali Moradi, and we owe him much. We were originally introduced to him by our mutual friend, Isa Mirshahi, in 1996 and we got on very well together. A helicopter pilot before the Revolution, 'Ali was a superb driver and we felt perfectly safe in his hands – which we certainly could not say about the other taxi drivers we employed in Tehran or their vehicles. Some of them had only one handle to open the four windows, which then had to be passed round as required!

When we suggested to 'Ali in 1997 that he become our sole driver, he enthusiastically agreed. We had thought of hiring a four-wheel drive vehicle with a driver, but this would have been far too expensive. 'Ali was worth his weight in gold. He entered into the spirit of our research work with much dedication. He was beyond praise in helping us set up camp, preparing our camp food and sorting out any difficulties we had with the local gendarmerie or revolutionary guards. He was the complete master of every situation. He understood at once my own physical disabilities, helping Adrianne to lower me on to a camp bed at night and hoisting me up in the morning. He realised that I wanted to see for myself the castles that we visited, and whenever at all possible he would manhandle me up or down a difficult slope. He became completely involved in the research work we were doing and was invaluable in providing us with information from every possible source. 'Ali was a mine of information about modern Iran and the Ismailis. He was determined to help me find as many Ismaili castles as possible and took a positive pride in our discoveries. He continually asked local people we met if they knew of any castles in the area. 'Ali was tough and strong but sensitive too. He could not have come across a Western woman like Adrianne before, but he adapted himself perfectly to the very unusual situation with which he was confronted.

I suppose that one of the most uncomfortable occasions we experienced was when 'Ali took us to a spot on a hill above a town called Shahrud where we could camp for the night. It was a deserted cul-de-sac with a spring running by the road. But to our dismay, it turned out to be the favourite picnic spot for the inhabitants of Shahrud, and this was Friday evening, their day of relaxation. We had set up our camp beds and were preparing to settle down for the night when dozens of cars and motorbikes began to arrive. As night fell they started to unload their rugs, cooking pots, etc., and started to prepare their evening meal in large extended family groups. Those not cooking strolled around chatting within inches of us, so that we had to abandon all ideas of sleep. They eventually started to pack up their belongings and leave between 2:00 and 3:00 am. We had a long drive over a very hot desert next day and so were very keen to have an early start. We were rather weary when we set off at 6:00 am, but 'Ali was able to drive quite happily even after such a short night.

It was with genuine regret that we had to say goodbye to him at the end of our stay. We are glad we can still exchange letters. He gets a friend to translate his letters into English, and he is clearly as fond of us as we are of him, and looks back on our time together with happy memories.

Notes

1. Cited by Abu'l-e Rafi Haqiqat in his *Tarikh-e Qumes (The History of Qumes)*, (Tehran, 1370/1950), pp. 322–324.
2. *The Times* (2 August, 1998).
3. See note 1 above.
4. Juwayni, *History of the World-Conqueror*, vol. 2, pp. 475–476.

CHAPTER 10

Castles of the Qa'inat

The nature and extent of the eastern part of the Ismaili state in Iran, particularly the location and description of the fortresses in various regions, has remained until recently vague and imprecise. This is not really surprising, as even the modern province of Khorasan, which includes most of the eastern part of Iran from Mashhad in the north – the present provincial capital – as far south as Nehbandan, a distance of some 700 km, is a huge area. (The length of France from north to south is a little over a thousand kilometres.) Most of the area is mountainous and inhospitable, bordered to the west by the Dasht-e Kavir or the Great Salt Desert, to the east by Afghanistan, and to the south by the flat sandy terrain of Sistan which leads to the southern province of Baluchistan and the border with Pakistan. There has always been only one main highway, running parallel to the Afghan border. There are, of course, mule tracks leading to villages in the hills, but until very recently communications within this region have been tenuous and uncertain. Whereas the northern part of Khorasan is comparatively flat, the southern part, known as Qohistan, is hilly and mountainous, and it was this area that became the centre of Ismaili power in eastern Iran.

As we have seen, shortly after Hasan Sabbah seized the castle of Alamut, there was a spontaneous uprising of the Ismailis against Saljuq rule in towns and villages across northern and eastern Iran. In this vast region – a great crescent spanning from the Alborz and Zagros mountains in the north to the borders of Afghanistan in the south-east – the Ismailis embarked upon a bold and determined strategy of capturing and building as many castles as possible. But perhaps nowhere was this revolution as widespread and popularly supported as it was in Qohistan, where the bulk of the Ismaili population lived in medieval times. It is possible that Hasan Sabbah may have visited Qohistan before he made Alamut his headquarters. The leader of the Qohistani Ismailis was Hosayn Qa'ini who had helped Hasan to seize Alamut. In 1091–92 he returned to Qohistan as a *da'i* to lead the Ismaili resistance against the Saljuqs. This he did with considerable success, turning Qohistan into the most heavily fortified province of the Ismaili state.

In 1101 the Saljuq sultan Sanjar resolved to do all he could to destroy the Ismaili rebels, and sent his amir, Bazghash, to subdue Qohistan. Three years later another Saljuq expedition was sent to Tabas in the east of Qohistan at the edge of the Great Salt Desert. These offensives caused much destruction and loss of life to the Ismailis, but they were able to regroup and set about reinforcing and enlarging their castles with great skill and energy. Before long Qohistan became the most heavily defended part of the Ismaili state, and by the time of Hasan Sabbah's death in 1124, it became virtually an autonomous Ismaili state, although always owing allegiance to Alamut.

It should come as no surprise, therefore, that Qohistan has the highest concentration of Ismaili castles surviving today in varying conditions of ruin and decay. The two chief towns of Qohistan are Qa'in and Birjand, and the area between – known as the Qa'inat – contains some exceptionally fine examples of Ismaili military architecture. Apart from the great fortresses, there are a very large number of smaller forts and military outposts, as Adrianne and I discovered in our 1997 expedition. For instance, there are at least eight smaller castles within easy distance of the central Ismaili stronghold of Qa'in. In Ismaili times the whole area came under the authority of a single *muhtasham* or governor who was appointed from Alamut and usually resided in Tun (modern Ferdaws), Birjand or Qa'in.

The great distances involved (Mashhad is 924 km from Tehran) and the rugged nature of the terrain has inevitably been a formidable obstacle to research in the region. Professor E. Herzfeld (1879–1948), in an article written for the *Zeitschrift der Deutschen Morgenländischen Gesellschaft* of 1926, states that he had visited several villages in Qohistan where he was received with great hospitality.[1] In Sedeh, the headman informed him of three Ismaili castles in the neighbourhood. He also paid a fleeting visit to the great castle of Qa'in, and was astonished at its immense proportions. Some additional work has been done recently in this area by Professors Robert Hillenbrand and Chahriyar Adle, but on the whole, little was known about the exact location of the Ismaili castles until I began my own work.

Samuel Stern had always stressed the importance of Qohistan and its castles and had urged me to start work there as soon as I had finished my research in Alamut and the Rudbar. I made my first visit to Qa'in in 1961, followed by two further expeditions in 1966 and 1967. In 1968, as a result of a research grant I had received from the Winston Churchill Trust, I was able to make a prolonged visit to the area and also do some important work in Afghanistan, Pakistan and

Central Asia. We received considerable help from a prominent and enlightened landowner, Mr Alam, who had a large family estate in the area. He asked his nephew, who administered the estate while his uncle was in Tehran, to see that we received all the help that we needed. As a result we were able to do a lot of useful and original research. I returned again in 1978, but it was clear that political trouble was brewing in the country and we were advised to return to Tehran without completing our programme.

It was not until 1996 that I was able to return to Iran again with Adrianne Woodfine. We were fortunate on this visit to meet Dr 'Abbas Badakhshani, who was then chief engineer of the Khorasan electricity company, and his family. An Ismaili himself, Dr Badakhshani was keenly interested in all aspects of Ismaili history, especially the castles, most of which he had visited, and agreed to assist us as much as possible. When I asked 'Abbas how the Ismailis came to be settled in Qohistan, he replied that the Caliph 'Ali, the first Shi'i Imam, foreseeing the inevitability of his assassination, had urged his followers to go to the mountains of Iran and build themselves fortresses. Although there is an Ismaili tradition to this effect,[2] the conversion of the local population to Ismaili Shi'ism in large numbers almost certainly took place in the 12th century, after the arrival in Qohistan of the *da'i* Hosayn Qa'ini from Alamut in 1091–92.

The castle ruins of Tus

Before exploring the main castles in Qohistan in 1996, Adrianne and I with Dr Badakhshani visited Tus, the most northerly Ismaili site in Khorasan. It is only 26 km from Mashhad, the capital of the province, but Tus was an important city long before Mashhad came into existence. Nearby is a modern mausoleum, believed to be the tomb of the great Persian poet Ferdawsi. He was born at Tus around 935 and probably wrote the 60,000 verses of his great epic, the *Shahnama* (*Book of Kings*) there. His mausoleum is considered a national shrine. Tus is also the birthplace of the famous astronomer, mathematician and philosopher Naser al-Din Tusi. I have referred previously (in Chapter 4) to Tusi's close association with the Ismailis over nearly thirty years and the many works he produced under their patronage at the castles of Qa'in and Alamut.

Tus was the first town in Khorasan to be taken by the Mongols under Hulegu Khan after his generals had slaughtered most of the Ismaili population in Tun. The existing ruins of the citadel of Tus are extensive. They seem largely Mongol in character, resembling the Mongol castle we examined later at Sedeh. It would be reasonable to assume that the Mongols had destroyed the original fortifications and then rebuilt their own defensive position. The fortress itself is on a flat plain and surrounded by a perimeter wall some 2 km in diameter. Most of the walls are baked brick and it seems as though they were once surrounded by a moat. The remains of the castle were in two definite parts. Lying on the ground we found many lumps of marble as well as bricks covered with a light blue glaze. The site was littered with shards of pottery, some of which were certainly of pre-Mongol origin. But there were few indications that would enable us to determine whether the Ismailis had occupied the fortress for a sustained period.

Before we left Mashhad we went with Dr 'Abbas Badakhshani and his family to Qal'at, some 16 km away, close to the border with Kazakhstan. 'Abbas thought that this might be the Ismaili castle of Zuzan, as it was a garden city surrounded by high and, until recently, inaccessible mountains. The road had been constructed under the last Shah as a military road leading to the Soviet border. When we arrived at Qal'at we realised that this was no Ismaili castle, but a lovely little palace built by the Afsharid king Nader Shah (1736–1747) for his own delight. Nader Shah was a brilliant commander and general who founded the Afsharid dynasty and extended his empire as far as the Indus valley. All that remains of his palace in Tus is a central octagonal building, set on a large rectangular stone platform. The main building is surmounted by a drum 34 metres in diameter. Around the drum are 36 ribs or flutes divided by four windows. Some of the original plaster carving is still intact. The colours are remarkably vivid reds and blues. Fortunately, this little gem of a building is now being restored by the Ministry for Cultural Heritage.

It was only when I returned home and was able to go over my past diaries and those of my team that I realised that my memory had played me fasle. We had visited Zuzan in 1966 and 1967. The castle was called Qal'eh Dokhtar and was 30 km or so south-west of Khargerd and may well have been part of the northern defence of Khorasan. It would be reasonable to assume that Khargerd also played a similar role. The entry for Zuzan records that the walls were in adequate repair and there were also walls of a considerably older period. The castle had probably been occupied and partially restored much later than the Ismaili period, but the water cisterns appeared to be of Ismaili origin.

After our excursion to Qal'at, we set off for Qohistan, the southern part of Khorasan, on the next day. I was much impressed by the good tarmacked road which led to the town of Torbat-e Haydarieh, a great contrast to the rough un-graded track along which I had to bump in my pre-Revolutionary expeditions. At that time the town was far from pleasant. It was dirty and unkempt and, on one occasion at least, was the centre of a cholera epidemic. In the intervening years it has undergone a facelift and now appears to be a thriving community. It is only 100 km from the Afghan border and there were large numbers of Afghans wearing their long shirts, baggy trousers and turbans. Most of them were probably refugees. In my early expeditions we had noticed and visited a large watchtower there, which was probably part of an Ismaili castle guarding the approach to Qohistan, but we could see no sign of it in 1997.

Our first visit was to Khaf, a prosperous village of some 5,000 people. The population is all Twelver Shi'i, although in the Alamut period its inhabitants were mostly Ismaili. We could see no evidence of fortification at Khaf itself, but in the next village of Khargerd, there were substantial remains of a fairly large castle. Khargerd is famous for its great *madrasa* or college completed in 1444–45. This is an early Timurid building and the decorated tilework is magnificent. The *madrasa* was locked when we were there as it was being repaired. Fortunately, Adrianne and I were able to visit it again in 1996 and inspect the interior. The building is 100 metres long and 80 metres wide, with two minarets and two domes. The decorative pattern is simple and very effective in its geometric designs of turquoise and lapis tiles. Some of the brickwork has been renewed, but there is still much more work to be done to restore this jewel of the desert to its former glory.[3] A few metres from Khargerd on top of an adjoining hill are the ruins of a fortress which, like the one at Tus, may well have been used by the Ismailis, captured by the Mongols and then rebuilt in the Mongol style. Later it was evidently used as a caravanserai, probably for pilgrims who came to pray at the local mosque.

Qa'in, castle of the *Mohtasham*

One of the largest and most impressive Ismaili fortresses in Qohistan is located at Qa'in (Plate 15). Although the castle was extensively destroyed by the Mongols, it still retains much of its original plan. Qa'in had been described by travellers in medieval times as a dirty little town, and they complained that the inhabitants spoke with a barbaric accent. Dirty it may have been, and still was at the time of my first visit in 1966, but it was, and continues to be, the chief town of the Qa'inat with its huge and impressive fortress.

In 1966 I talked with the oldest inhabitant of Qa'in, Mr Mohammad 'Ali, as I have always found local accounts helpful in piecing together the history of a relatively unknown site. He told me through an interpreter that he had lived under five Shahs and spent all his life in the town apart from two pilgrimages he made to Mashhad on foot. According to the story he told us, the castle had been built by a local governer of Qohistan to rival one built near Herat (now in Afghanistan) which was then part of Khorasan. The Herat governor had often tried to take the Qa'in castle by storm, but had failed every time. Eventually he smuggled some men into the fortress concealed inside boxes strapped to camels and so was able to overcome the garrison. This variation of the legend of the

Trojan horse amused us greatly. He also told us that Qa'in used to be the capital of the Qa'inat rather than Birjand. He estimated that the population of Qa'in was 80,000.

Geographically, Qa'in is the first great castle of the Qa'inat proper, although Tun to the west is even more strongly defended. Originally it was probably quite small and intended to be a conventional stronghold, but its role must have been altered very soon after it was captured by the Ismailis. Qa'in developed into the administrative capital of Ismaili Qohistan and seat of the Ismaili governor (*muhtashem*), as well as a fitting residence for distinguished visitors and scholars. As we have seen, the eminent Ismaili thinker Naser al-Din Tusi stayed for many years at Qa'in as resident scholar before moving on to Alamut. Qa'in is now an important administrative town and the seat of local government. The changing character of the fortress is illustrated by the somewhat architecturally disjointed nature of the interior. If it had originally been conceived as an organic whole, the plan would probably have been somewhat different.

We know little about the fall of Qa'in to the Mongols, but we do know that after capturing Alamut and taking the Ismaili Imam into their custody, the Mongol troops were ordered to kill all Ismailis, and Juwayni assures us that this was done with ruthless efficiency. Hodgson quotes one particularly appalling atrocity.[4] The Mongol commander is said to have rounded up 80,000 Ismailis in Qohistan, pretending that he wished to address them. Most were massacred; some, of course, must have escaped. The women and children were sold into captivity as slaves. The devastation, especially in Khorasan, which followed the Mongol invasion was quite appalling. The province was noted for its agricultural fertility and prosperity before the Mongols arrived. Ilya P. Petrushevsky, in the *Cambridge History of Iran*, quotes Juwayni as saying 'where there had been a hundred thousand people, there remained not a hundred souls alive' after the invasion.[5] He also quotes Sayfi, writing about 1321, who cites eye-witnesses of the massacre to report that 'from the frontier of Balkh as far as Damghan people ate only human flesh, dogs and cats for a whole year, because the warriors of Chengiz Khan had burnt down all the granaries.'[6]

I had visited Qa'in four times before the Islamic Revolution and on each occasion we camped in the gardens of the electricity generating station. My last visit was in 1997 with Adrianne Woodfine and I was glad to see that the castle had not suffered at the hands of vandals. It stands on a promontory of rock 246.8 metres above a broad sandy plain 3.2 kilometres south of the town. There is a rough track at the foot of a small hill to the west of the fortress that contains a tomb-shrine to a local holy man called Abarzah. The shrine is undistinguished, built about 250 years or so ago, although I was told by local Qa'inis that it was older. Outside the shrine is a pleasant, shady courtyard that also houses a water reservoir. Herzfeld called the fortress Qal'eh Kuh-e Abarzah, but the locals call it quite simply Qal'eh Kuh.

From the shrine you can obtain a good overall view of the western side of the castle. A track runs along the south-western side of the castle from below the shrine for 2.4 km. This is particularly steep and treacherous scree, but at the time of the Ismailis it must have been a reasonable mule track, as it leads directly to the stables, which are outside the main fortifications. A double row of six (twelve in all) stone stables can still be seen. Beyond the stables is a fortified triangle of sloping ground that was doubtless used for unloading supplies.

The fortress proper is about 300 metres long (Fig. 7). It is divided into three main areas which we called Lower Fort, Central Fort and High Citadel. In addition there is a strong outer fort called Chehel Dokhtar that guards the southern flank. The hill on which the fortress stands is steep and rocky. The width varies from a few metres at the central 'waist' of the fortress, to some 40 metres at its widest. Each section is a self-contained unit with is own complete fortifications. It seemed to us that the fortress could well have been built at different periods, starting with the strongly fortified high citadel. The Ismailis could have decided after seizing the castle to fortify the rest of the ridge and build the outer fort.

The triangle of ground beyond the stables is now a mass of confused rock. The entrance to the lower fort is quite clear and the walls enclosing it are strong. Inside is a complex of shattered buildings, but it would be reasonable to suppose that there were at least a hundred small rooms, probably quarters for the garrison. In 1966 an Italian construction company was building the new main road to the south, and one of their engineers, Mr V. Fiorani, had amused himself in his spare time by making a survey of the fortress. Although the survey was unfinished, he gave us a copy on which he had plotted some of the buildings, particularly in the lower section. At the extreme northern tip of this section we found at least four large water cisterns and there were probably many more. There was a tall rock outcrop a few metres above the cisterns, from which the precipitation was directed into further cisterns.

The top of the lower section narrowed to a ridge that led to the central section, which measured 40 metres long and widened out to 28 metres. The entrance to this section was through a strong bent gatehouse, standing 30.5 metres or so above the lower section, which it completely dominated. On the northern edge of this central section was a huge semi-circular tower and several rooms were built into the strong walls on the eastern and western flanks of the fortress. This central section came to an abrupt end after 30 metres. The curtain-wall continued, and there were at least two sally-ports in the eastern side leading to the desolate narrow valley 91.5 metres below. The height of the walls at this juncture was 12 metres. They were very strongly built of stone with semi-circular towers at intervals of 4 metres.

The whole high citadel running for 60 metres still has its strong outer walls. Again, at its southern end overlooking the central and lower sections of the fortress are great round towers. Rooms are built into the external walls, some of them are of considerable size. The hill on which the citadel is built turns midway slightly to the south-east, and the upper part of the high citadel contains a rectangle of confused rubble and broken stones. This could well have been a tower, the governor's residence, a library or a combination of all three. The high citadel ends in a fortified crescent. There is only one weak spot in the natural defences from a direct attack and that is from the mountains to the south-east. It was here that the Ismailis built the fort of Chehel Dokhtar.

The rock on which Chehel Dokhtar stands is higher than the fortress proper and gives a superb view over the fortress and the Qa'in plain. Its primary object was to block any enemy approaching along a narrow defile at this point. The fort of Chehel Dokhtar is of quite large proportions and most of the castle is built on the forward (northern) slope of the hill opposite the main fortress. There are remains of the high citadel (or keep), a largish structure at the top of the hill and part of the curtain-wall runs round the northern slope. The ground slopes steeply down from the castle, except on the western side where a narrow spur acts as a bridge to the main fortress. Outposts have been constructed at this point. The castle occupies an area some 300 metres long by 50 metres in width. There are remnants of storage chambers above and below ground, but unfortunately we did not have the time or equipment to investigate them further.

We spent a considerable amount of time examining the water storage systems of the main castle at Qa'in. There are indications that the plain surrounding the castle had been very fertile in Ismaili times. This was particularly evident in the evenings when the plain was illuminated by the setting sun. The outlines of fields and the *qanat* systems leading almost up to the foot of the high citadel were very visible, as was also a green patch near the citadel with a line of *qanat*s running down from it. We had already noted the spring at the nearby shrine, which would certainly have formed part of the castle's water supply, and I have mentioned the water systems that we had found. These were numerous and large: a typical medium-sized cistern was 4.5 metres deep, 2.4 metres wide and 3.5 metres long, and plastered with limestone cement. Some water cisterns were considerably larger. We also found other cisterns as well as storage chambers built into the castle walls, so that the defenders of Qa'in were never short of food or drinking water.

Of course, like all Ismaili castles, Qa'in had to be strong enough to withstand

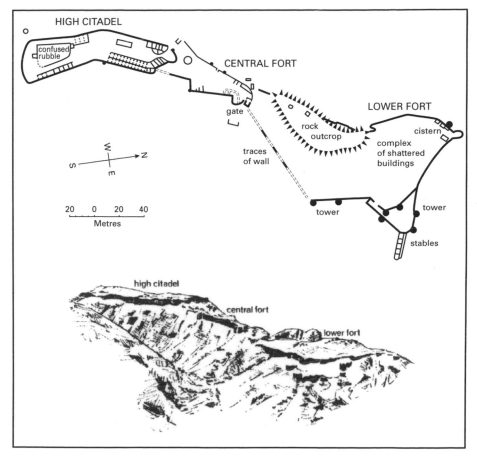

Figure 7: Groundplan of Qa'in castle

an attack or siege for a considerable period of time, which it was certainly able to do. The storage system of food and water, if not as comprehensive and ingenious as that of Alamut, was perfectly adequate. The defences at Qa'in are as strong and substantial as any other Ismaili castle. The walls themselves are massive and exceptionally well built. The division of the castle into three independent sections would have required an attacking force in effect to storm three separate castles with very little cover. As one section was captured the attackers would come under renewed fire from the higher walls of the next section. Each section was, of course, fully independent as far as provisions, stores and water were concerned.

Nonetheless, Qa'in illustrates a different kind of fortress from Alamut, Soru or Gerdkuh. The hills around Qa'in are not as high and the fortress does not occupy a commanding strategic position. It is neither situated in an isolated position nor in a narrow valley where every line of approach has to be fortified. The valley at Qa'in is broad and there are major castles along its entire length. There is no evidence of external defensive walls below the castle like the ones found at Soru. On the other hand, there is a spaciousness about the fortress, a far greater emphasis on living quarters and a certain magnificence, which indicates that this fortress was primarily regarded more as an administrative and research centre than a major military facility.

Although we were told that we would discover a lot of pottery shards, all we came across at Qa'in and Chehel Dokhtar were a few crudely decorated examples of earthenware and none of glazed pottery. We were a little disappointed with our meagre find, but this was scarcely surprising as the castle was constantly visited by villagers looking for whatever they could find. Fortunately, they did not seem to have made any attempt to dig for any buried treasure, which could have resulted in further structural damage to what remains of the castle.

Abbas Badakhshani, who had made a study of all the Ismaili castles he came across while travelling around Iran, gave us his opinion that the Ismaili population in the Qa'inat at the time of the uprising may have been around 60,000. He considered that the garrison of Qa'in probably consisted of 1,000 men, a figure with which I agree. A mullah friend of his suggested that there were about 150 Ismaili castles in Qohistan, which he defined as the region between Torbat-e Haydarieh and Zabol.

One of the most interesting sites in Qa'in is an old and highly venerated mosque. When we first visited it in the 1960s it was very dilapidated. We were told that it was one of the oldest mosques in Iran and had been restored by the Safavid king Shah Abbas I (1587–1629). Somewhat surprisingly, the local community had allowed it to fall into serious decay. But on our 1997 visit, it was quite a different story. Abbas Badakhshani and a group of local men were clearly proud to show us the completely refurbished building. Abbas told us that the mosque had been built by the first Muslim settlers on the site of an old Zoroastrian fire-temple.

The Qa'in mosque is one of very few having two *mihrabs*. The *mihrab* is a niche in the wall indicating the *qibla*, the direction towards Mecca. The original *mihrab* in the Qa'in mosque points towards Jerusalem and a smaller one, surmounted by an arrow and pointing towards Mecca, was added a hundred years or so later. There are two possible explanations for the original direction of the *mihrab* towards Jerusalem. The first is that the Muslims have had from the beginning a great reverence for the holy city associated with Abraham, Moses and other biblical prophets. Hence the Prophet Muhammad and his followers initially prayed towards Jerusalem but subsequently received a divine revelation changing the direction of prayer to Mecca, thus endowing Islam with its own central shrine. Another reason, perhaps, is the story of the Prophet's *mi'raj* or heavenly ascension. Briefly, the story tells us that Muhammad was woken one night by the angel Gabriel who took him on his winged horse, Buraq, to the Temple in Jerusalem. From there he ascended through the seven heavens, meeting all the prophets from Adam to Jesus who greeted and honoured him as one of them, the elect apostles of God.

The newly renovated mosque at Qa'in is regarded with great affection by the local inhabitants. In 1997 we were able to walk all round the mosque, even climbing to the top of the dome where we were shown the magnificent view. We visited the underground ablution chamber with its stream running through it. The stone and plasterwork had been beautifully restored together with the tilework. I was much taken by the following inscription on a memorial there in honour of an anoymous woman referred to as the 'handmaid of Zahra'. The name Zahra, meaning 'the illuminated one', was one of the epithets of the Prophet's beloved daughter Fatima and the wife of Imam 'Ali. According to the inscription, the woman died in 1931 and her family were probably the principal sponsors of the newly refurbished mosque. The inscription was translated for me by the late Reverend Norman Sharp, a much-respected scholar of Persian, who spent many years ministering to the Christian community in Isfahan:

> He [God] is the Living, the Immortal One. The handmaid of Zahra – who will intercede for her on the Day of Judgement, the second Bilqis [Queen of Sheba], the second Mary, the second Hagar [Abraham's consort] – after a full life, took her departure from the passing world to the world of certainty. The bird of her spirit flew away to perch on the branches of the trees of Paradise, at the break of day, with tranquillity, on the fifteenth day of the month of Safar, with the aid of the illustrious Seyyed 'Ali. There was a helper of noble rank to mourn her. He was like a relation, the true friend of this husband, an inheritance derived from the Lion of God [Imam 'Ali] who lamented the death of the daughter of the Prophet and sought consolation from the cupbearer of the water of the river Kawthar in Paradise. The woman's name should not be made known. The title of that resplendent moon was Light of the World [Fatima]. May God, in honour of Zahra, show mercy, and place her beside Fatima. In the year 1350 [1931], after the Prophet's flight [migration to Medina], that blessed traveller departed.

The castles of Tun

I have considerable affection for the town of Qa'in, as my expeditions there had received warm hospitality in 1966 and 1967. The mayor of Qa'in, too, was very helpful and made arrangements for us to be well looked after later in Tun (now called Ferdaws). It was from Qa'in that we were able to carry out a great deal of research in the neighbourhood knowing that, however hot it was during the day, we would always return to a relatively cool and friendly base. We concentrated particularly on the western route that took us through Afriz, Dastabad, Sarayan, 'Ayaz and then Ferdaws. We also made diversions from time to time into the mountainous area to the north, where we passed a considerable number of small forts and watchtowers, which were part of the old Ismaili communication network. There could be no doubt that this part of Qohistan, although considerably more rugged than the area around Khoshk and Afin, was equally well defended. Some of the fortifications had been rebuilt, probably during the Safavid period. Dastabad had been destroyed in an earthquake 10 years previously, but in 1967 it seemed to have recovered and again become a prosperous village with large herds of sheep and goats.

Sarayan was interesting as 12 km away we located the castle of Qal'eh Gholam. We were warned that the track stopped 6 km away and that we would have to cover the remaining distance on foot. In the event, we found a *wadi* that the landrovers were just able to negotiate as far as the village of Yanbu, situated below the castle. The castle turned out to be quite a small, round structure 70–75 metres in diameter. There were two distinct rings of walls (we had been told there were seven) around a circular peak and there were good natural defences on all sides. The lower defensive wall was built 21.5 metres below the summit and the inner wall 10 metres below. The keep on the summit was a square well-constructed building, though extensively ruined, with excellent visibility towards the west and Ferdaws.

This small castle was a typical example of the forts built primarily for warning and communication purposes. The garrison at Qal'ch Gholam was probably no more than 50 men, but it was easy to defend for a short while until reinforcements arrived, summoned by beacons. All such castles are normally approached by a mule track behind the castle and there is always an outpost guarding an exposed flank. There were, of course, a number of water cisterns, now filled with rubble. We visited this castle at Qal'eh Gholam on a swelteringly hot day when the temperature rose to 45 degrees. We asked our guides to fetch us more drinking water from the village, but when they returned they said with genuine regret that they had drunk much of it themselves on the way up!

As we approached Ferdaws the land became more fertile. At Ayask we saw the first of the Ismaili forts guarding the approach to the mountain route. We also saw a new deep (75 metres) water pump which had recently been built by a local landowner. Good clear water flowed from it and irrigated the fields. The name Ferdaws (meaning 'paradise') for Tun is of very recent origin. The last Shah allowed the town to change its name at the request of its citizens. I was told that Naser Khosraw, the Ismaili poet, philosopher and traveller of the 11th century, had spent some time teaching in Tun before he fled to Badakhshan. In the 13th century, Tun seems to have had a substantial Ismaili population. Its castles, together with those at Tabas 190 km to the west, must have provided a formidable defence complex to any invader rash enough to attack Qohistan from this direction. Daftary tells us that after Hulegu entered Khorasan in 1256 he selected Tun as his first target.[7] In the event Hulegu was not able to lead the assault personally as he had wished, and the town was taken by one of his generals after a siege of two weeks. The Mongols slaughtered all the inhabitants of Tun, except for the younger women according to Juwayni, or the artisans according to other sources.[8]

In Ismaili times, Tun was guarded by two formidably strong fortresses which still survive today, Qal'eh Dokhtar to the south of modern Ferdaws and Qal'eh Hasanabad to the north-west. Qal'eh Dokhtar is considerably larger than Qal'eh Hasanabad, and to distinguish the two fortresses in our own minds we gave Qal'eh Dokhtar, which is also called Qal'eh Kuh, the sobriquet of Big Ferdaws, and Qal'eh Hasanabad therefore became Little Ferdaws.

Qal'eh Dokhtar is about 13 km south of Ferdaws and the approach route is very difficult. On our visit there in 1967, we had with us two guides and a representative from the Museum of Iran Bastan who also acted as our interpreter. The landrovers were heavily loaded and made slow progress until we found a *wadi* along which we were able to bump along until the ground became too rough for our vehicles. We were now faced with a climb of an hour and a half, but Qal'eh Dokhtar, when we eventually reached it was certainly worth all the sweat and trouble it caused. The castle stands at an altitude of 2,020 metres and is very large and impressive. The highest part of the fortress is built on a spur of rock over 100 metres long. The general direction of the castle is NW/SE. There is a large spur on the south-west side that is heavily defended by five and in certain places six outer walls.

We found it very difficult to survey the castle because of the continually sloping ground, which made an overall view difficult to obtain. Although the main buildings have been largely destroyed we came across an interesting piece of wall containing an arched window two metres high and almost a metre thick, through which we had an excellent view of Ferdaws. There were five courses of brick above the arch, and the roof was made of yellowish green and red bricks, all of the same standard size.

The defensive walls were strongly built and strengthened by towers. The construction of the walls and other buildings must have required a vast amount of stonework. We were told that the stones were passed up to the masons by a human chain after they had been cut to shape by other masons working at the nearby quarry from which they came. There are more than ten large water cisterns at Qal'eh Dokhtar: a typical size was 13 x 4 metres and 5 metres deep. During our work on the castle, one of my team saw an eagle soaring above the towers. It seems that Qal'eh Dokhtar too, like Alamut, deserves the title of Eagle's Nest.

Our surveyor, Andrew Dobson, described the high citadel of Qal'eh Dokhtar as follows:

> The high citadel is protected by its own walls. There are two further rows of walls to the north-east and a 30.5 metre sheer cliff defends the north-west. To the south-west there is a nine-metre cliff and several layers of intercommunicating fortifications. The south-east end of the spine contains a complex of two-storied long narrow galleries. The slope of the cliff here is fairly gentle and two lines of fortifications have strengthened the defence of this somewhat weak spot. The top of the spine is very narrow, not much more than four metres, and the citadel is built on both sides of this spine. The spine runs roughly east-west. The southern side is the principal fortified side, consisting of five walls in addition to the main buildings. The central section of the high citadel contains three water cisterns roofed over with brick. A flight of steps leads down to them. Some of the main buildings are still quite well preserved. A typical building in the citadel is about 10 metres long and six metres wide.[9]

The second castle, Qal'eh Hasanabad, is considerably smaller. It is built on a chain of lava hills some 4 km from the village of Hasanabad, 18 km north-west of Ferdaws. Between the castle and the village are two dried up riverbeds that converge just beyond the castle. These riverbeds provide the most convenient but by no means easy approach to the castle, and doubtless the rivers played an important role in its defence for part of the year. The castle itself is built on a small promontory of a lava hill, which is no more than 110 metres high. The surrounding plain is dry and salty, but there is a valley nearby in which sheep and goats graze. From the castle there is an excellent view towards Ferdaws and the Great Salt Desert to the west.

Much of the main castle of Hasanabad is still standing. The outer walls, built of dressed stone on the outside and a rubble core, are about 1.5 metres thick. There are three defensive walls and a well built gatehouse leads into an inner courtyard, much of which is now ruined. But some of the turrets are quite well preserved, especially those near the high citadel at the top of the lava hill. This area consists of three-storied buildings and galleries with high vaulted roofs. The length of the high citadel is 36.5 metres and the width 40 metres. The ground drops steeply away at the edge of the area.

The water systems of Hasanabad come up to the usual high standard we have met in all Ismaili castles. There were three main catchment areas. One reservoir was semi-circular in shape, measuring 10 by 7 metres, and built of brick, probably vaulted. We could not estimate its depth as it was filled with camel-thorn. Another cistern measuring 8 by 7 metres near the high citadel and also vaulted was a fine example of the durability of the usual amalgam of stone, brick and plaster. The cistern had been cut out of the solid rock and was probably very deep. A third cistern, somewhat bigger and much ruined, was situated at the junction of the south-western and western walls.

The most striking features of both these castles near Ferdaws are the strength and sophistication of their fortifications. Qal'eh Dokhtar must have been able to accommodate a large garrison, while Hasanabad, though smaller, could still have held a significant force. In both castles the natural features of the physical environment had been exploited fully and to the best strategic advantage. Set against the desert background, both castles gave an impression of great strength, combined with an aesthetically satisfying beauty too, in the way that the darker stone of the castle walls supplemented and harmonised with the lighter hues of the rock and the desert. The exploration of the Ferdaws castles was, all in all, a deeply satisfying experience.

It is certainly a tribute to the Ismailis who built these castles that even after they had been partially destroyed and ransacked by the Mongols, many of the walls and bastions still stand proudly today. We do not have any details of the Mongol assault upon these castles, but it seems that, unlike Gerdkuh and Soru, they were well within range of the devastating Mongol mangonels, and their resistance must inevitably have been short.

Many years after the capture of Tun, the Mongols rebuilt the town with a palace of some grandeur, leaving intact the famous mosque and *madrasa*. With the establishment of their Il-Khanid dynasty (1256–1353), the Mongols turned their attention to more positive achievements in architecture, the arts and government. In 1967 we had occasion to admire greatly the mud-brick walls of their palace at Ferdaws, which appeared to be almost indestructible. The great gateway and tower were particularly impressive. The whole area was surrounded by a moat 4 metres wide and 2 metres deep. A causeway linked the palace with the city outside. Despite the appalling barbarity and utter ruthlessness of the Mongols, this palace is one of their great achievements. But they showed no pity in its construction, for I was told that any worker thought to be slacking was immured in the walls he was helping to build.

When Adrianne and I revisited Ferdaws thirty years later, we were shocked to see the devastation caused by the earthquake of 1968. The great Mongol palace had almost completely disappeared. The main mosque and the old *madrasa* were still standing, though badly damaged. To our surprise, we saw at this mosque – called

the Habibeh and thought to be 800 years old – a repetition of the two *mihrabs* that
we had seen at the Qa'in mosque, the central one pointing towards Jerusalem and
the other to Mecca. The old *madrasa* is a very attractive building and its original
water system is still in use. The Ministry of Cultural Heritage was restoring this
school, but we were somewhat shocked to see that some original tiles and brickwork had been carelessly discarded and thrown onto a rubbish heap.

Other castles of the Qa'inat

The most westerly Ismaili site in Qohistan was at Tabas, some 80 km south-west
of Ferdaws. There are two towns of the same name in Khorasan: the second is
on the eastern border not far from Furk and Asadabad. It is called Tabas Masina.
This town was one of the main centres of the smuggling trade between Iran and
Afghanistan before the 1979 Revolution. When I asked some of the men there why
they needed to wear such a large number of European manufactured watches, they
replied that it was essential for them to know the exact time so that they could
be sure that they enjoyed the full quota of water rights that had been assigned
to them!

I have visited Tabas twice, in 1966 and with Adrianne in 1997. It is a pleasant
enough town, but indescribably hot in summer. It has always been an important
centre on one of the ancient caravan routes that cross the Dasht-e Kavir, the
Great Salt Desert. It was known as the 'Queen of the Desert' and the gateway to
Khorasan. Marshall Hodgson relates that it was one of the first towns in Qohistan,
together with Qa'in and Tun, to respond to Hasan Sabbah's summons to rise up
against the Saljuqs.[10] In 1101, Sultan Sanjar determined to root out Ismailis in
the region, but his *amir* Bazghash was bribed to spare Tabas. The reprieve was,
however, only temporary, as three years later the Saljuqs returned and destroyed
Tabas and a number of strongholds. They killed the garrison, enslaved much of
the population and left after extracting from the survivors a promise not to arm
themselves nor to practise their religion.[11] Juwayni does not mention Tabas in
any detail. Hodgson records another raid against Tabas in 1160 by the Saljuqs,
but concludes that this was more likely to have been against Tabas Masina in the
mountainous east.[12] There are indeed ruins of fortifications at Tabas, but there is
not enough evidence to date them precisely, and in all probability several castles
were built on the same site.

Adrianne and I were now on our return journey to Torbat-e Haydarieh, but
we intended first to investigate another group of Ismaili castles in the Qa'in area
and then turn eastward to Esfedan. The first town at which we stopped was
Sedeh, which I had visited several times during my early expeditions. There was

originally an Ismaili castle there, probably on the site of a rather fine Mongol castle situated behind the small town. This was the typical rectangular Mongol castle, 200 metres long and 50 metres wide. The high walls still stood firm but there was otherwise little to see. The interior was filled with rusting agricultural machinery. About 5 km away we thought we saw a dome of a mosque, which on investigation turned out to be an interesting Ismaili watchtower about 20 metres high. There were two other small castles in the area including one that was almost entirely underground.

We next turned out attention to a cluster of villages to the north-east of Se-deh called Khoshk, Esfedan and Afin. Esfedan was the centre of the disastrous earthquake that had resulted in a great loss of life a few weeks before we were there in 1997. We had heard news of this before we left home and were informed incorrectly on television that the centre of the earthquake was at Qa'in. Khoshk was the native village of our driver 'Ali Moradi and naturally we were all looking forward to visiting it. I had visited both places before as well as the old mosque at Afin and wanted to refresh my memory. 'Ali had left Khoshk as a boy of seventeen, but he returns whenever he can to see his numerous relatives there. The population of the village is 5,000 of whom four-fifths are Ismailis. Many of its sons have, like 'Ali, moved to the cities to find work, but they regard Khoshk as their real home. Khoshk, like Dezbad near Mashhad, is one of the centres of the Ismaili community in Iran. Ismaili Shi'ism continues to have a following in the countryside, in the small villages rather than in the towns.

The countryside around Khoshk is very fertile. There are two buses a day to Tehran and the village was full of activity when we arrived as two marriages were due to take place that day. We were warmly greeted and having viewed the Ismaili watchtower we were invited to visit the *jama'atkhana*, the Ismaili gathering place. We were told that this *jama'atkhana* was built a hundred years previously, although the facade and courtyard looked fairly modern. The interior was divided into three bays: the right-hand and central bay were reserved for men and the left bay for women. Five square pillars supported the low vaulted roof. The floor was covered with lovely carpets and the atmosphere was welcoming and peaceful. We met the *mukhi* or minister, who kissed me on each cheek in welcome and told me that the *jama'atkhana* was used every day for services. We were offered tea and as we talked, more and more local men of distinction arrived. As we left the *jama'atkhana*, we noticed that the courtyard was full of huge cooking pots, which would be used for cooking the food for the wedding. Five hundred guests were expected. We saw a party of women escorting the bride to the baths for the washing ceremony. They waved cheerfully and we waved back.

From Khoshk we drove for about 50 km to Esfedan through a hot dusty

desert. Naturally we looked for the first signs of damage caused by the earthquake, but we could see none. Instead we travelled through a sultry, heavy, barren landscape, passing occasionally a cluster of new houses built in the middle
of nowhere. After more than an hour of desert travelling we suddenly arrived
at Esfedan. It was an appalling sight, of complete horror. The entire town,
including its modern buildings made of reinforced concrete, had been flattened
by the earthquake. Apart from the gendarmerie building at the entrance to the
town, we passed street after street of utter devastation. Out of a population of
10,000, about 2,500 had been crushed to death by falling masonry when the
quake struck. The precision with which the earthquake struck was frightening.
The fault line here is called the Nehbandan fault and it was only exactly above
this fault-line that any damage occurred. One or two other villages suffered
minor damage, but Esfedan bore the full brunt. There were tents everywhere
providing temporary shelter for the survivors, but we saw very few people moving about. Those that remained were there to guard the few possessions they had
left, and apart from the tents we could see little sign of relief work or rebuilding.
We approached two helicopter landing sites where we expected to see a buzz of
activity, but there was none. The horror and tragedy were so great that we felt
it would be profane to take photographs. Tears were streaming down 'Ali's face
and we all remained silent until we reached Afin. The horror of Esfedan will
remain with us for a long time.

On our way to Afin we passed two Ismaili watchtowers. The mosque at Afin,
which I had first visited in 1967, had suffered some damage from the earthquake.
But it still stood firm. At first sight it seemed more of a fort than a mosque, as it
appeared to be built on a platform of stonework and the external walls are thick
and compact. The building is quadrilateral in shape, some 20 metres in length
and 10 metres across. The outer courtyard, which is enclosed within thick walls,
occupies well over a third of the site. We saw the remains of badly damaged tiles
on the floor. A well-preserved archway leads into the mosque proper, corresponding to the sanctuary in a Christian church. Somewhat to our amazement we saw
that this enclosed sanctuary had a second storey of arched arcades, rather like a
triforium in a cathedral, supported by stout columns. The roof had collapsed but
a shallow dome over the *qibla* wall was still intact, as were the two metres high
remains of the two minarets on either side of the wall. A stone *mimbar* or pulpit
still stood against a wall. The *qibla* wall is set 4.5 metres behind a stone screen
and the *mihrab* was relatively undamaged. In fact, the small space behind the
stone screen had preserved a remarkably quiet and serene atmosphere. This is a
remarkable building and poses all sorts of fascinating questions. Who had built
this apparently very untypical mosque and when? Unfortunately the villagers

could not provide us with any information about it.

Esfedan and Afin lie in the centre of a whole series of Ismaili villages and castles. There are two castles at Abiz, and other castles at Khoshk, Zordu, Ahangaran and Uniq. Space prevents me from describing all of them. There can be little doubt that the strength of the fortifictions of the Qa'inat was to the east of the Qa'in-Birjand road. On the west side of this road lay the castles of Bihud and Sarab defending the approaches over the mountains to Ferdaws and Tabas.

In 1997 our visit to Afin almost landed Adrianne and myself in some difficulty. As we were leaving Afin to return to Qa'in a policeman stopped our taxi. The police car had broken down and the officer asked us if we would give a lift to his passengers to Qa'in. We soon realised that one of the passengers was an important regional official and he naturally became curious about our reasons for being in this out of the way area. He also asked me many questions about life in England, and poor 'Ali had to translate both his questions and our answers with his very minimal knowledge of the English language. When we arrived at Qa'in the official told us to report to government headquarters. We had our passports, but no other documents authorising our journey, apart from some out-of-date papers given to us by the Iranian Foreign Ministry the previous year. We were locked in a carpeted room until an official of the state police arrived, who said that we would have to see the governor of the province. When I said that we were entitled to come to this area as tourists, his manner seemed threatening and he started to ask me detailed questions about whom I had seen, where I had been and what I had done. This was a very unpleasant moment for both of us and we were beginning to feel alarmed. Eventually after questioning by more local officials, a schoolteacher was summoned who spoke some English. Having looked at our passports he confirmed that we had every right to be in Qa'in as tourists, and was able to persuade the officials that we should be allowed to leave, which we thankfully did some four hours after our arrival.

That night we decided to camp in the open, as we felt that we needed to keep out of sight of officialdom for a bit. We had possibly been pushing our luck too hard by visiting so many out of the way places and arousing the suspicions of the authorities. We could only surmise the exact nature of these misgivings: espionage perhaps, as we were so close to the Afghan border or, as someone suggested, the possibility that we had something to do with the narcotics trade. The suspicions probably arose because it was so unusual at the time for two Westerners, a man and a woman, to be travelling around the remote countryside locating, examining and photographing castles. It was unlikely that we could be in any serious danger, but we were very concerned that 'Ali could suffer because of his association with us. We decided that we would return to Tehran by way of Ferdaws visiting the castle at Bihud on the way. We had achieved a great deal and were now beginning to feel somewhat tired.

On our way to Bihud we passed numerous water points at intervals of 2 kilometres built beside the road. They are basically water cisterns 6 metres deep dug into the ground and into which rainwater and water from the mountains is directed. They are covered over with a domed brick shelter and have steps down to the water. They reminded me of the ablution chamber at the mosque at Qa'in. For some villages such as Khoshk, these are the only water supplies for the people and the animals, and I feel that a similar system must have been employed by the Ismailis in pre-Mongol times when the population of Qohistan was much bigger than it is now. Harvesting was in full swing and everywhere we saw the winnowing of grain, sacks of corn and sheaves of straw. The fields were bright with cornflowers, but we missed the poppies of the European fields.

Bihud is a large but impoverished village of 6,500 people. As soon as we stopped, we were surrounded by the usual group of welcoming and curious villagers who pointed out to us the remains of a Mongol castle in the middle of the village. We were told that it was only half its original size, as the other half had been demolished to make way for new houses. We were invited to be the guests of Mr Mohammad 'Ali Mikmameh, who was the local medical officer responsible for the care of a group of villages. Both he and his son spoke some English and his son's wife taught English in a primary school at Mashhad. She showed us some textbooks and we were amused by the illustrations of English girls all wearing headscarves. The book itself was good, clearly and intelligently written.

Mr Mikmameh said that there were no Ismailis in Bihud now, though it had originally been an Ismaili village. He offered to take us to the castle at once and we all bundled into his landrover. When we arrived at the foot of the steep rocky crag on which the castle was built, it was clear that I could not climb it because of my disability and so Adrianne set off with 'Ali, Mr Mikmameh and two of his sons. I watched in some anxiety as the small party made their way slowly to the top. There seemed to be a terrible wait while they were out of sight exploring the castle remains. In fact it was only about 45 minutes, then they started the descent. Adrianne was obviously finding the going quite difficult as some of it was extremely steep and other parts covered with loose scree, and I was highly relieved when she reached *terra firma* in the valley. Discussing the climb with Adrianne afterwards, she made the point that although Mr Mikmameh had been very helpful in pointing out footholds he, like many conservative Muslims in Iran, was forbidden to make physical contact with a woman who is not a relative.

Adrianne had wondered what would have happened on these climbs if she had fallen. Later, when she mentioned this to a Muslim in England, he explained that a man would always give assistance to a woman who requested it, but must never put himself forward unasked. If a woman required help because she was hurt, help would naturally be given. Adrianne had made a point of not asking for help as she thought that she must not put a man in this position.

I had watched Adrianne's descent anxiously through my binoculars and when I hurried to meet her I put my binoculars on the ground. I forgot all about them until later that day after we had left Bihud. When we returned to Tehran, 'Ali telephoned Mr Mikmameh who at once went to look for them and found them intact. Considering the poverty of the villagers, this showed the scrupulous honesty of the people. The binoculars were sent back to us in Tehran on the local bus.

The castle of Bihud stands impressively on a hill 213 metres above the valley floor. Adrianne described the castle as being somewhat similar to Alamut, about 200 metres long and 50 metres wide. The only standing walls were those that can be seen from the valley. A high turret overlooks the valley, but in general the castle was a jumble of stones and the remains of walls. The villagers reckoned that there were about a hundred rooms in the castle. Adrianne said that there appeared to be three levels of fortifications, but the ledge on which the castle was built was very narrow, before it terminated in a steep vertical drop. There were three water cisterns built into the outside walls, and another in the main castle area. Mr Mikmameh had observed at least three watchtowers in the vicinity.

On our return to the village, we were invited back to Mr Mikmameh's house, given tea and pressed to stay for lunch. The boundless hospitality of the Iranians was sometimes the cause of embarrassment. If we had accepted every invitation, we would never have got any work done. But to decline could cause great offence, and unfortunately it did on this occasion. But it was still only mid-morning and lunch would have involved us staying there for most of the day, achieving very little.

From Bihud we returned to the main road and drove to Gonabad where, after lunching at the local hotel, we watched on television the installation of the new Iranian President, Mr Khatami. Gonabad is a very old city, which had once been strongly fortified by the Ismailis with three castles. It has a mosque said to go back to the 11th century and a *madrasa* 400 years old. The college is a charming place with a lovely rose garden in the centre of the main courtyard. Each student had a pleasant room in the surrounding arcade. Gonabad is famous for its *qanat*s or water systems, a series of ever deeper shafts dug at intervals of 50–100 metres. The deepest shaft was 400 metres, and the longest *qanat* stretched for a kilometre.

According to the Ismaili traveller Naser Khosraw, the *qanats* of Gonabad were originally built under the Sassanian king Kay Khosraw or Chrosroes I (531–79) in the pre-Islamic era.[13]

Gonabad is a pleasant town and we regretted that we could not prolong our stay. The day had been very hot and it was delicious to rest a while in the cool arcades of the *madrasa*. But to my surprise our rest was cut short when I was told that a young man wanted to see me. He was a journalist and 'Ali had told him about our work. He was naturally curious to know my impressions of Iran and asked if we had received all the help we needed. Strangely enough, I think this was the only encounter we had with the press in post-Revolutionary Iran. Before 1979 we were constantly badgered and asked for our comments. However, we knew that our public relations were in good hands with 'Ali, who rather enjoyed telling everyone what we were doing and always presented us in a favourable light.

Notes

1. E. Herzfeld, 'Reisebericht,' *Zeitschrift der Deutschen Morgenländischen Gesellschaft* (1926), p. 273.

2. Reported by Nasir al-Din Tusi in his *Paradise of Submission*, pp. 156–157.

3. For a description of he interior of Khargerd, see Arthur Upham Pope, *Persian Architecture* (London, 1964), pp. 159, 197 and colour plate VIII.

4. Hodgson, *The Order*, p. 270.

5. Petrushevsky, 'The Socio-Economic Conditions of Iran under Il-Khans,' p. 481.

6. Ibid., p. 486.

7. Daftary, *The Isma'ilis*, p. 423.

8. Hodgson, *The Order*, p. 266 and note 2.

9. Personal communication.

10. Hodgson, *The Order*, p. 74.

11. Ibid., p. 88.

12. Ibid., pp. 115–116, note 46.

13. Naser Khosraw, *Book of Travels*, p. 129.

CHAPTER 11

The Fortified Province of Qohistan

As we have already noted, Qohistan is the name given to the southern part of Khorasan which in Ismaili times consisted of a considerable network of castles and fortresses, extending from Tun and Qa'in in the north to Nehbandan on the borders of Sistan to the south. The area around Birjand, in particular, contains a great many Ismaili fortifications which have been barely investigated. I had visited Birjand at least four times before the Islamic Revolution and in 1967 had carried out a detailed investigation of the district. After the Mongol invasion of Qohistan in 1256, Birjand became just a small village, but it grew again in importance and size during Safavid times. Nowadays it is a thriving town and one of the main administrative centres of Khorasan. The town has an impressive old mosque. The Russian scholar of Persian Ismailism, Wladimir Ivanow, was unable to establish its age when he visited it, but considered that the mosque incorporated some pre-Islamic elements.[1]

When Adrianne and I first arrived in Birjand in 1997, we were taken by Abbas Badakhshani to see the director of the local office of the Ministry of Cultural Heritage. Despite my worries that this visit could result in a hostile reception, the director turned out to be a pleasant young man who went out of his way to help us. He seemed overawed by our presence and did not even ask us to produce any papers as proof of our identity. We were delighted to learn that he was drawing up a map of Ismaili castles in Qohistan and trying to gather as many details about them as he could. He had no hesitation in sharing his knowledge with us and showing us his draft maps. His list unfortunately was far from complete and some of his descriptions inaccurate, but it was a pleasure to find an Iranian doing original archaeological and historical research. He had taken photographs of the sites that he had visited and showed them to us. I was able to give him details of other Ismaili castles that he had not yet visited. We visited his library which, though small, was at least a start.

In 1997 Birjand seemed a large city compared to what it had been thirty years previously. There is a largish mudbrick citadel in the centre of Birjand which Adrianne and I visited. Most of the local inhabitants think this is the main Ismaili castle. The Ismailis probably had a fortification on this site, but most of the present structure is of later construction. Inside, there is now very little to see. It is a rectangular empty shell about 152 metres by 91.5 metres. It has a large water cistern lined with limestone cement and with built-in steps leading down to the base. The young man who showed us this castle also pointed to the mountains in the south in the direction of Gholam Kosh. He told us there was another castle there, but said it was far too difficult to visit, though he gave us to understand that he had been there. I felt a little proud that I could say that I had indeed visited the castle myself thirty years ago.

Gholam Kosh, the castle of Dareh

I have mentioned that the chief sponsor of many of my Iranian expeditions before the 1979 Revolution was Dr Bagher Mostofi. On our visit to Birjand, he had kindly arranged for me and my team to stay at the home of Mr Alam, a distinguished and much respected landowner who held an important position in the government. A man of considerable wealth, Mr. Alam made it his duty to ensure that all his servants and tenants were well treated, housed and fed. In 1968 Mr Alam had given orders to his kindly and efficient steward, Mr Jambaz, that we should be treated as distinguished guests in his impressive house, which had belonged to his family for 400 years. It had been restored twenty years previously in the somewhat flamboyant Persian 19th-century manner and the carpets were truly magnificent. When our somewhat scruffily dressed expedition arrived at the house, all the servants were lined up formally to welcome us. I was given the main guest room, complete with bathroom and two lavatories, one Western and the other Persian, and was told that the Empress herself had once slept in my room. Needless to say, our meals, served in considerable state, were delicious.

In addition to looking after our bodily needs so well, Mr Jambaz was an excellent guide. On our first day he took us all, including our museum representative, to the castle of Dareh also called Gholam Kosh, which lies in the mountains about 16 km south-east of Birjand, north of Sar-e Pol, just to the east of Chahar Kesht. The name of the mountain is Bagheran. We left our landrovers at a spot where our altimeter registered 1,580 metres and after a very steep climb lasting 50 minutes we reached the foot of the castle with the altimeter reading 1,855 metres. Here we found the remains of the outer walls, towers and storage cisterns for grain and water. From here we made our way up to the high citadel that overlooks the town, its airport and the plain around Birjand. The main axis of the castle is east-west. Juwayni reports that Dareh was besieged by the Saljuqs in 1092 shortly after the Ismaili uprising in Qohestan, but on the news of Sultan Malekshah's death the siege was lifted.

The central tower of the high citadel is protected with double walls on two sides. On the other two sides there are sheer drops of 90 metres. A water-cistern has been built into the eastern outside wall measuring 11 metres by 14 metres and 4.5 metres deep. It was lined with limestone cement and had originally been arched over. Little is left of the high citadel, apart from the remains of a round bastion and a few other ruins. A little village called Band-e Darren nestles below the southern drop.

On the western side the high citadel slopes away to the middle section of the castle, which too has been extensively destroyed. We came across further large water cisterns and an area some 12 metres long on which were built six rooms, each two metres across and 7.5 metres long connected by an arched gallery. There is also evidence of underground cisterns and storage chambers. A lot of bricks littered the ground, as well as pottery shards typical of the period.

At the north-western end of the castle, overlooking the city of Birjand, we came across a remarkable building constructed as part of the massive defensive walls. The height of the walls here is 8 metres and they are about 3 metres thick. The building measures 20.5 metres in length and is 22 metres wide. Inside there are 10 square columns, built of brick and reaching to the height of the existing walls. At the extreme north-western corner of the structure a hole or tunnel has been made in the outer wall, measuring 0.5 metres wide and 0.6 metres high at the beginning, then broadening out to a width of one metre and a height of 1.2 metres. At the end of the tunnel there is a drop of 60 metres. We had, in fact, noticed this tunnel earlier from the village below. We found a similar hole along the northern wall.

We could not make out the purpose of this structure. The walls have four layers of plaster, and are made of dressed stone. The pillars have a rubble core and are faced with two courses of brick. On the external plaster, family names have been scrawled, all apparently of a fairly recent origin. There are four rows of three pillars and the tallest seems to support a three-way arch. They are arranged in a rough circle, but it seems unlikely they supported a dome. Perhaps the eastern and western ends of the structures were arched over, leaving an open space in the middle. The building could, I suppose, have been a very large water cistern, but I have never seen so large a cistern, or one whose roof is supported by so many pillars. Most of the larger cisterns I have seen were arched over without supporting pillars. All we could do was to take measurements and photographs. We could not get any satisfactory explanation from our museum guide or anyone else. On mature reflection I tend to think that the building, or at least a part of it, was a large water reservoir and that the tunnels had been made after the capture of the castle to ensure that it could never be used again for water storage. But this is surmise and I have no direct evidence of it.

The citadel of Dareh or Gholam Kosh was clearly a strong one that occupied an important strategic position overlooking Birjand and the surrounding countryside. It formed part of the chain of fortresses running from Qa'in southwards to Nehbandan. When we descended from the castle in the afternoon, we found Mr Jambaz waiting for us with rugs and refreshing cool drinks. He told us that the second name of the castle, Gholam Kosh, means the place where Gholam was killed. Legend has it that when the water cistern was constructed, the unlucky Gholam was drowned in it, either by design or by accident. The castle is almost inaccessible now, though doubtless originally there were better tracks leading to it. When Adrianne and I returned to Birjand in 1997, people pointed out the direction of the castle to us. It was clear that no one had visited it recently, although a mullah claimed to have been there for some obscure reason.

We were then driven to another of Mr Alam's houses, where we found his nephew, Mr Monsef, who had been delegated to be our official host, waiting to give us a delicious lunch. Mr Monsef suggested that we would be interested to see some rock tombs at Chenesht that contained skeletons of great height and size. Professor Ivanow had mentioned these to me when I had met him at Tehran University in 1963. Although they were clearly not Ismaili tombs, we thought that we should look at them. Chenesht was two and a half hour's drive from Mr. Alam's house and when we got to the end of a very rutted, bumpy track, we found that we had another 6 km to walk before we arrived at the attractive village.

We were told that thirty years before there had been an earthquake in the surrounding hills (2,195 metres high) and the villagers had then noticed fresh cave-like openings, explored them, and found the tombs. Accompanied by three villagers with lamps, we scrambled down a slope inside the hill for about 75 metres and found ourselves at the entrance to a subterranean gallery 200 metres long. There seemed to be three separate levels of tomb galleries superimposed on each other. On the first level we found the broken remains of a box or coffin containing human bones. There were also animal bones at this level. On the second level there was an interesting plastered tomb, but no bones. On the bottom level we found a great number of skeletons, wrapped in partly decayed shrouds. The atmosphere was very dry and some tissue was still clinging to the bones. The macabre element was the absence of any skulls. What had happened to them? We were told that the bodies had originally been buried upright as was then the normal custom. The skeletons did seem to be unusually tall. Some unglazed pottery lay on the ground, but there were no other funerary remains. There were clearly further galleries, all forming part of a complex of caves. We stayed below ground for about three hours before being persuaded by the villagers, who were clearly frightened and kept up their spirits by singing, to leave and return to the village. By this time we too were tiring of the spooky atmosphere and the weird headless skeletons fitfully illuminated by our flickering lamps. Some of the bones were indeed of exceptional size, but we were unable to obtain any positive information, apart from the fact that this was an important necropolis.

Another example of similar tomb-caves has been cited by Sylvia Matheson in her book, *Persia: An Archaeological Guide*.[2] She reports that in 1949 Dr Carlton S. Coon had excavated a prehistoric cave in the same area near Khunik. His findings showed that new converts to Islam had settled there around 700 CE and threw their debris into a rock shelter. Higher up the mountainside, an earthquake had opened up a much earlier cave used by hunters in the last glacial period. The contents of the two caves had been thrown together to the puzzlement of the investigating archaeologists. But for some obscure reason, the galleries we entered at Chenesht had not been damaged and their contents lay in good order.

A network of castles

There are a large number of smaller Ismaili castles in Qohistan which Adrianne and I visited in 1997 with 'Ali, our driver. One of the most attractive is called Mud, about 30 km south of Birjand and situated on a low hill overlooking the main road to Zahedan. The castle is rectangular in shape about 300 metres wide and 260 metres long. There are six formidable towers on each side built of mudbrick and complete with arrow slits and small lancet windows. The castle was originally an Ismaili one but was later 'mongolised', to use Adrianne's picturesque expression. The walls are three metres thick and rooms have been built into them.

To our great surprise and delight we found that the inside of the castle was now partly farm and partly orchard. Cows were feeding inside the area originally occupied by the gatehouse and rows of pistachio trees filled the central area. The farmer came to greet us and he led us to his house at one end of the site. There we met his wife who invited us to have tea sitting on the steps of the veranda. She told us that the site had belonged to the Alam family and that in Qajar times they had built the house as a hunting lodge and laid out the gardens with a lovely central avenue and a fountain. After the Revolution the farmer had taken over the site that was now his home. His wife told me that she recognised me from thirty years ago, but unfortunately we were unable to chat for very long, as the farmer and his wife were going to have a meal at a friend's house. We gave them some of the presents we had brought with us and reluctantly took our leave of this pleasant, peaceful pistachio orchard and pavilion, which had once been an Ismaili castle.

After we left Mud we decided to drive to a village called Khunik (a different Khunik from the daughter castle near Nehbandan in the south), and as we drove along we realised how heavily fortified this area of Qohistan had been. We passed castle after castle and were told of others, many of which were presumably once held by the Ismailis. As it was not possible to investigate this complex network of castles, we took photographs of the sites whenever we could. When we reached our destination, Khunik, we found the ruins of Ismaili defensive walls. The central area of the old castle had become an orchard and some of the bricks and stone-work had been used to construct a new village nestling at the foot of the slope on which the castle had stood.

The next Ismaili castle Adrianne and I intended to visit was Sarbisheh 80 km south of Birjand. It is situated on a hilltop near a village of the same name. The track leading to the castle had been blocked since my last pre-Revolutionary visit, but we were assured that we could approach it from the side. We threaded our way through the narrow streets and were examining some fortifications, both Mongol and Ismaili, near the village I had not seen before. As I was hurrying forward my foot slipped and I crashed heavily to the ground which was covered with refuse and broken glass. Adrianne had been dreading this happening and feared that I had really hurt my leg, but fortunately I was only badly shaken, although we could not continue with our plans to visit the castle.

The castle of Sarbisheh occupies a commanding position over the road and from the top there are excellent all round views. It stands in an almost impregnable position, with no weak spots discernible in its natural defences such as an adjoining neck of land or a *col* as at Qa'in. It is divided into three main sections: a high citadel, a middle section and a water catchment area. The construction is of stone and red and yellow brick. Little remains of the high citadel; the walls have been almost completely destroyed. In our earlier expedition it was clear that a great deal of amateur digging had taken place and the area was covered with rubble, fragments of reddish pottery and earthenware pipes. Names, dates and other graffiti were scrawled on the limestone cement remains of some rooms, especially in the middle section, which is the largest. We also found some quite good pottery shards, including gold lustreware. The remains of the water cisterns were almost totally filled with rubble. The best-preserved remains are on the eastern side. The walls here are very thick and large rectangular water cisterns are built into them.

From Sarbisheh the mountains give way to a much flatter plateau, though still bordered by hills, which gradually merges into the desert countryside of Sistan. Sarbisheh was built to protect the route north to Birjand and Qa'in and, equally important, to prevent any hostile force attempting to outflank the fortresses of Furk, Tabas and especially Mo'menabad, 30 km or so to the east.

The castles of both Furk and Mo'menabad are to the east of Qa'in in the district of Sunnikhaneh (literally, 'district of the Sunnis'), containing about twenty villages, with Fayzabad as the centre. Mr Jambaz told us that Arabs had settled there shortly after the Islamic conquest and were quickly absorbed into the community.

I first visited the site of Furk in 1967 and was struck by its size and very picturesque position (Plate 16). In 1968 Mr Jambaz took us on a complete tour of the fortress. He said that although it was originally an Ismaili castle, probably intended to defend Mo'menabad 16 km or so away, it had been reconstructed during the Safavid period and had then during the reign of Shah Abbas (1587–1629) come into the possession of the Alam family: this was later confirmed by Mr Alam's nephew, Mr Monsef.

The village of Furk, or Darmiyan as it is sometimes known, lies to the west of Asadabad, the nearest sizeable town, at a height of 1,760 metres. The top of the castle is only 90 metres higher but it guards the north-western end of the hills on which Mo'menabad is situated. Two valleys cut into the hills at this point and Furk is built on the spine astride the two valleys. The original castle was built on the top of this spur: it was probably semi-circular in shape and held a garrison of at least 300 men. It has the usual massive walls and its own water cisterns lined with limestone cement. From the top of the castle there is an excellent view of Mo'menabad and the plain stretching beyond Asadabad. The high citadel is still in good condition and there is a maze of little corridors and arched rooms.

When the castle was repaired and enlarged by the Alam family in the 17th century, a much more grandiose Safavid style of architecture was employed, and it was most interesting to compare the two styles corresponding to the English Norman and Tudor periods. The Safavid builders used a certain amount of Ismaili stonework, so it is at times difficult to distinguish the two. As a result of the reconstruction, the fortress of Furk appears far more domestic in character than the usual Ismaili castles. There are many living quarters and high crenellated walls. The most interesting feature is the huge water storage cistern 27.5 metres long and 18 metres wide at the foot of the castle. It was probably constructed in Ismaili times and then considerably enlarged. It was in use until quite recently and restored as the principal water supply for the village by the Alam family.

The overall impression of the castle of Furk is the comparative simplicity of its construction (Fig. 8). Although it is quite clear that the original castle was built

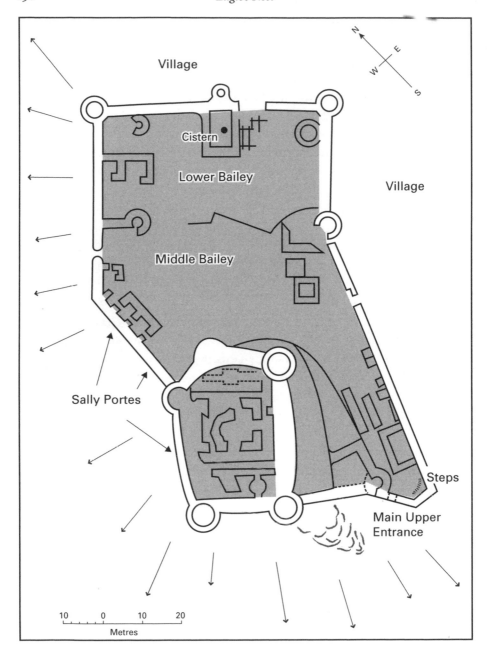

Figure 8: Groundplan of Furk castle

on top of the spur, it is also possible that the middle and lower baileys were added by the Ismailis and then rebuilt in the Safavid period in a more sophisticated and grandiose style. The huge water-cistern, too, may have been of Ismaili construction, although there were at least six considerably smaller cisterns in the upper castle. I have seen similar examples in other fortresses, including Gerdkuh and Gholam Kosh.

In my 1968 expedition to Furk we had found pottery of both Ismaili and Safavid periods. We were also shown two underground tunnels that led from the interior of the castle to the outside. The one on the south side led to the riverbed and is now blocked. The northern tunnel, which was probably built at the time of the Ismaili occupation, ran for 107 metres and was arched with stone vaulting about 1.7 metres high. These 'secret' tunnels were a novel feature, as I have not come across them elsewhere, although we know that a much longer tunnel had been constructed in Rudbar from the castle of Lamasar down to the Na'inarud below.

It was our last evening at Furk in 1968 when I and my team were treated to a captivating display of dancing by the men of the village organised specially in our honour. As we sat below the castle, a group of some twenty men clad in elaborately embroidered tightfitting waistcoats and white silk shirts and skirts performed a wonderful sequence of dances to the rhythm of flute and goatskin drums (Plate 19). I think this will always remain as one of those rare, memorable moments which gave me the greatest pleasure during my wanderings in Iran. I had met many of the performers during the daytime, when they had struck me as men who were tough, hard as nails and ruthless into the bargain. Many of them were undoubtedly smugglers. I have never before seen men wearing so many Rolex watches (five or six per man) and sporting numerous Parker pens. But here they were under the starlight, performing an exquisitely sensitive and beautiful dance. This was a moment of complete magic, comparable only to sleeping under the star-spangled sky, while our guides sang age-old songs of love, parting and heroic deeds.

When the men had finished dancing the women showed how well they could dance too. We were then offered delicious dishes of meat, yoghurt, fruit, sweet-smelling herbs and other delicacies. Vodka and wine were brought and toasts were proposed to various distinguished persons including, to my great embarrassment, myself – '*le petit professeur*'. This, of course, could never happen under the present regime in Iran, but it remains a very happy memory.

When Adrianne and I visited Furk again in 1997, the village seemed at first to be empty, but our taxi-driver, 'Ali, told us that many people were working in the fields at harvest-time and the villagers were now sleeping out in the open because of recent earthquakes in the area. Fortunately there had been no earthquake damage at Furk and the population of the village seemed to have increased, numbering now some 1,500 souls. The desert around Furk was full of the green plant called *zereshk* that grows in this desolate soil.

I was delighted, too, to see that nothing serious had happened structurally to the fortress since my last visit thirty years previously. As I looked closer at the buildings I realised that I had previously underestimated its Ismaili character and that much more of the castle was of the Alamut period than I had at first thought. This meant that I had to revise my estimate of the probable Ismaili garrison, especially when told by the local expert that he considered that 600–800 people could have lived in the castle. Furk is one of the most photogenic of the Ismaili castles, largely due to the additions made by the Alam family. Some of the stonework has been used to build the houses in the adjoining village.

We were, of course, invited to take tea by a very pleasant village family, consisting of grandfather, his sons and their children. The women, naturally, did not appear. This family also took us to see a carpet being made. Two men were knotting the carpet, which was quite large and very beautiful, in a tiny room with very little light. We were told that the carpet would take the men three months to complete and bring the family a great deal of money when it was sold.

The palace-fortress of Mo'menabad

One of the most important Ismaili sites in Qohistan about which little is known is Mo'menabad. Its chief claim to fame lies in its connection to one of the most seminal events in early Nizari Ismaili history, the proclamation of the *Qiyama*, the Day of Resurrection, by the lord of Alamut, Hasan II, on the day of his emergence from concealment as the long-awaited Ismaili Imam. As we have seen (in Chapter 4), the *Qiyama* was announced in two solemn ceremonies, the first at Alamut on 17 August 1164 and two months later in October at Mo'menabad. The fact that Mo'menabad was chosen for the second part of the proclamation indicates the importance it held at that time, second only to Alamut, within the Ismaili state in Iran.

In 1997, Adrianne and I wished to visit Mo'menabad from Furk, but we were told that it was now impossible to reach the village even in a four-wheel drive vehicle. I doubt whether this was strictly true, but as I had visited Mo'menabad in 1967 and again with Mr Jambaz in 1968 when we were able to make a sketch-plan of the fortress and city, we did not insist.

In 1967 we left our vehicle in the village of Karandik and then walked for two hours in the sweltering heat through Shamsabad to Nasrabad, the village at the

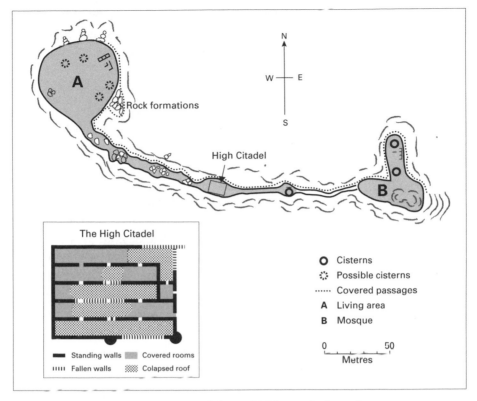

Figure 9: Groundplan of Mo'menabad castle

foot of the hills on which Mo'menabad stands. The villagers, who constantly referred to the castle as Qal'eh Hasan Sabbah, told us that they had recovered coins which they were wearing on their wrists, weapons and amber necklaces from the castle site. The castle stands proudly on top of a high table-rock some 400 metres above the village at a height of 2,470 metres. The climb over the steep rough scree leading to the castle entrance is an exhausting one, which even taxed the strength of our local guide. Until you actually reach the main gateway, flanked by its two great stone-dressed towers, it is very difficult to see the extent of the castle walls and the city.

The groundplan of the castle site (Fig. 9) shows that Mo'menabad occupies an enormous site spread out in a great U-shaped curve along the top of three adjoining hills. The length of the site is quite spectacular, giving the impression of a great palace demolished by a massive earthquake. Almost all the buildings, with the exception of the high citadel, have been destroyed and the whole area is covered with the arched remains of underground storage chambers at frequent intervals. The main entrance with its two tall towers has probably been rebuilt, perhaps by smugglers or bandits who may have used Mo'menabad as their base. There is a remarkable series of parallel underground passages and rooms near the entrance, presumably all that remains of the original high citadel buildings apart from the two towers.

The connecting spur of land joining the inhabited areas at the bottom of the U-formation is quite narrow: only three metres wide at its narrowest and 15 metres at its widest. The remains of the external curtain-wall still stand at a height of 5–10 metres. Just below the high citadel there is a large well-preserved water cistern, lined with gypsum compound. We estimated that it was 12 metres deep. Two underground tunnels lead to fresh springs in a little valley to the north of the castle some 2 km away. The area marked 'A' in the plan seemed to be the main living area and contains a tangled area of ruins, before the rock slopes sharply down to the south. From the top of the castle there is a magnificent view of the plain towards Tabas. The most likely area for a mosque to have been built is the protuding tongue of the land on the right of the diagram marked 'B'. We came to this conclusion because the area was reasonably flat and more open than anywhere else in the castle. Unfortunately, we could not find any positive evidence to identify its site, although our guide agreed with us.

We were, of course, struck by the peculiar U-shape of the site, which must have made living and moving difficult. Mo'menabad is, in fact, the fortified top of three interconnecting high hills. But the slope on all sides is relatively easy to defend and there is no record of any attack on Mo'menabad until the final onslaught of the Mongols. The valley beneath the castle is very fertile and food supplies would have been no problem. Doubtless, the underground storage chambers would also have been kept well stocked

After the capture of Mo'menabad by the Mongols, the castle was thoroughly and meticulously demolished. The scale of the Mongol destruction here, as at Shahanshah further to the south, is quite astonishing. Although Juwayni does not give us any details of the destruction, he refers to Mo'menabad with typical disparagement as 'the castle that was the fountainhead of their infidelity and heresy'.[3]

It is most unfortunate that we were unable to visit Mo'menabad for further investigations in 1997, as the castle is of great interest both historically and from an archaeological point of view. It would certainly repay closer investigation, although given the extraordinary scale of the site this would require considerable resources of manpower and almost limitless time.

The castle-city of Shahanshah

I have now described the major Ismaili fortresses of Qohistan, including Qa'in, Sarbisheh, Furk and Mo'menabad. We must now move to the southern end of the province, with modern Afghanistan in the east and Sistan in the south. This is a most interesting area, especially for the Nehbandan complex at Neh. The main Qohistan line of Ismaili castles beginning from Ferdaws (Tun) ends at Nehbandan. It is here that the hills give way to the flat plains and desert of Sistan. It was, therefore, natural that the area should be heavily defended. Nehbandan is a flourishing small city and 'Abbas Badakhshani often visited it on his official tours for the provincial electricity company. Shortly after reaching Nehbandan from Sarbisheh, he insisted that Adrianne and I should look at the castle at Neh, called Shahanshah, as soon as possible. Also called Shahdez by the local people, it is not to be confused with the equally great Ismaili castle of the same name near Isfahan.

By the time we arrived at Neh, it was evening and we only had a short time of daylight left. I was still very much shaken by my fall and waited by the vehicle near the bottom while Adrianne climbed to the top with 'Abbas, 'Ali and two local villagers. It was a very steep climb over loose rocks with the added hazard of very high winds. Adrianne found this climb very difficult, partly owing to the stresses of the day and also because, due to the late hour, she was feeling tired before they started. The climb was very rushed, Abbas setting a fast pace, and then doing a rapid tour of the main features of the castle while Adrianne tried to make notes and take photographs.

Shahanshah (meaning 'king of kings') is by any standards a very large and complex structure, and cetainly the most massive and capacious Ismaili fortress I have seen (Plate 17). It is now mostly in ruins, but once contained literally hundreds of rooms. Abbas, who knew the castle well, estimated that there were approximately 1,200 rooms and that the garrison consisted of 2,500 men. He said that the soldiers were allowed to have their wives and children there, and that there were special quarters for the governor. The hill on which the fortress stands is 150 metres high, although the site rises another 50 metres to the top. The view from the bottom of the hill is deceptive as it is only possible to see a small part of the curtain-wall.

During her brief visit to Shahanshah with 'Abbas, Adrianne saw five water cisterns, and 'Abbas said that he had discovered more than twelve. The average size of a cistern was 8 x 11 metres with a depth of 6 metres. The most interesting water system was built into the wall of the high citadel, which was in reality a brick *qanat* or aqueduct 40 metres in length and 3 metres deep. The slope was covered with a huge expanse of destroyed buildings. They were mostly the remains of small rooms and there appeared to be little trace of external defences, but Adrianne and 'Abbas only had time to visit a small part of the fortress on this occasion.

When I returned home from our 1997 expedition, I found that I had made exactly the same comments about the extent and complexity of the Shahanshah water systems in my 1968 diaries. I had described the fortress in my notes as consisting of at least six main complexes, each of which had its own independent defensive system as well as its own water supply. Most of the site was ringed by massive walls, which constituted a chain of forts. There were rectangular block-houses, roughly 100 metres x 10 metres with towers, now ruined, at each corner. Each complex had three or four water cisterns 10 metres long by 6 metres wide and 5 metres deep. Below these fortifications, the ground slopes steeply down for another 200 metres and is covered with the remains of individual dwellings, mostly built of stone. Although the ruins are now piles of masonry jumbled together, there was clearly a highly organised scheme in the construction of the castle. Shahanshah is a most astonishing site and I ended my diary notes by writing: 'It is impossible to give an adequate picture of the vast size of this castle-city. Ruins cover the whole mountainside. Perhaps 2,000 or more people lived here.'

Shahanshah intrigued me greatly. I am not sure that the castle had been properly located before. I have certainly not come across any description of it. The tactical position of Shahanshah also gave me problems. The castle site is joined to another higher hill by a col. The castle could presumably have come under attack by mangonels from there, and there were no signs of a ring of protective forts as at Gerdkuh. This raised some questions in our minds: What precisely was the strategic importance of this fortress? Why should so many men have lived there? Adrianne thought it could have been a strategic reserve or even a centre for training Ismaili soldiers. This is possible. More likely is the assumption that the Ismailis felt that the relatively open southern end of Qohistan must be massively protected against attacking forces coming across the plain of Sistan; otherwise the whole defensive system of Qohistan could have been imperilled. This was also the thinking behind the castles at Ferdaws, which protected the western flank of Qohistan, facing the Great Salt Desert.

In 1968 I had recorded the position of other Ismaili castles that formed part of the Nehbandan complex. The first site was at Shusf, some 60 km north of Nehbandan on the road to Birjand, where we saw two small castles and a watchtower. We had also stopped at a charming village called Hosaynabad a little further south down the road. This was then the last petrol station before Zahedan, and it was a little oasis in the desert landscape which we had now reached. While having tea the inhabitants told us that there were more Ismaili castles at Khoshareh, 24 km further south, and others near Birjand at Shahkuh near the village of Mayhan, another at Bandan, near Zabol on the Afghan border, and yet others at Khayrabad, near Ahangaran. Finally, we visited an Ismaili stone castle at Khunik, south of Nehbandan. The whole border area was, therefore, heavily fortified by the Ismailis.

When we visited Nehbandan in 1997, we were astonished to see the substantial remains of another large castle there. It was probably built by the Ismailis and re-fortified by the Mongols during their siege of Shahanshah, as the whole ruin now appears typically Mongol. The extended walls, the large archway and keep, and a series of lofty rooms testify to the importance of this building. We were told that Nehbandan was originally part of an Ismaili complex of castles in the area and we were referred to three daughter castles nearby. This was additional evidence that the Nehbandan complex of fortresses, including Shahanshah and the neighbouring fortifications, formed the southern defence line of Qohistan. This area, where the mountains give way to the plains of Sistan, was particularly vulnerable. The daughter castle of Khunik would have taken the brunt of any offensive from the south, supported by the much larger garrison at Shahanshah. No further proof was needed of the ability of the Ismailis to develop an overall strategic defensive system in which each component part had its own role to play.

Notes

1. Personal communication.
2. Sylvia Matheson, *Persia: An Archaeological Guide* (London, 1972), p. 205.
3. Juwayni, *The History of the World-Conqueror*, p. 691.
4. Lewis, *The Assassins*, p. 69.

CHAPTER 12

Castles of Isfahan and Arrajan

In this chapter I would like to describe some other Ismaili sites I have researched in Iran. I will begin with a journey I made in my landrover as long ago as 1968, which took me from Shahanshah, the site of the great ruins of Nehbandan, which I described in the last chapter. This still seems in my experience an epic journey mainly over desert and vast empty spaces. I had one companion, as the rest of my team on this occasion was carrying out research work elsewhere. It was quite a hazardous journey too. Although there were reasonable tracks in some places, it was all too easy to lose your way in the sun-baked desert. We were travelling in August, the heat was intense and our water supply was limited. If we had broken down we would have been in real trouble, as for long stretches of our route we met very few other vehicles. Fortunately the landrover that Dr Mostofi had lent us was well serviced, tough and reliable.

The road from Nehbandan to Zahedan runs between the lower foothills bounding the Kavir-e Lut and the desert area around Zabol on the Afghan border. This is the province of Sistan, where the Ismailis once had a strong following. The Ismaili mission was first introduced in Sistan in the 10th century by one of its leading Iranian exponents, the *da'i* Muhammad b. Ahmad al-Nasafi. One of the most original Ismaili thinkers and writers, al-Nasafi later extended his mission-ary activities to Bukhara in Central Asia, where he was arrested and executed in 943. The Ismailis of Sistan collaborated closely with their brethren in Qohistan and sought their assistance in military and political affairs. In 1226, for instance, a combined force of Ismailis from Qohistan and Sistan defeated the local military ruler in a pitched battle that forced him to conclude a peace treaty.[1] Following the Mongol invasions, the Ismaili population in Sistan dwindled to small numbers.

My plan was to drive across Sistan to Bam, Kerman, Sirjan and Estabhanat to Shiraz and Persepolis in Fars province, and then on to the city of Isfahan, the capital of the Safavids in central Iran. In 1968 I particularly wanted to visit the existing Ismaili communities in this part of Iran as well as the Ismaili castles at Arrajan in the border region between Khuzistan and Fars provinces, with the hope of finding more fortifications that were as yet unlocated.

Zahedan, my starting point where I had the landrover checked, especially the tyres, is a town with modern amenities and a good hospital from which my research teams have benefited on more than one occasion. Our first stop was to be Bam and the road that took us past Nasratabad was quite good. Nasratabad was at one time the capital of Sistan. It is a small pleasant town, consisting of low houses with high chimney-like structures, which are in fact excellent ventilators. We passed two ruined forts and were delighted to see, as our *Guide Bleu* had informed us, the tower of Mil-e Naderi, which was built in 1078 as one of a series of towers to guide travellers crossing the Great Salt Desert, a vast depression covered with sand-dunes with very salty deposits.

The name of Bam now evokes the horror of the appalling loss of life in the earthquake of December 2003. It is a pleasant town, famous for its dates, as well as the high crenellated walls and citadel dating from Safavid times. In 642 Bam was occupied by the Arabs, and in the 10th century the historian Ibn Hawqal described the town as possessing a citadel reputed to be impregnable and containing three mosques. In 1968 Bam was very much on the tourist route. An English student told us that there was an Ismaili castle nearby. Unfortunately we failed to find it, if it really did exist.

In Kerman we had some interesting conversations with the Ismaili owner of a sugar factory at Bardsir. He told us that there were about 500 Ismaili families living in the Kerman area, most of them settled on their own land. Additionally there were groups he called nomadic Ismailis. In fact, he referred to them as Ismaili tribes, explaining that until very recently they were as nomadic as the Bakhtiari. Originally they were wealthy, owning camels and sheep as well as land at Bandar 'Abbas and Sirjan, but as time passed they became poor and now lived in their black goatskin tents, cultivating barley, wheat and sugar beet, and making carpets. They recognised the present Aga Khan as their Imam, but in daily affairs they followed the biddings of their own local leaders. Our host said that the Ismailis were favourably regarded in the Kerman area, although the population of Sistan and neighbouring Baluchistan province was overwhelmingly Sunni.

At Sirjan we received a warm welcome from the local Ismailis. Their leader, a Mr Valliolah, stated there was a fairly large number of Ismailis in the district and gave us the name of 17 villages and towns where they lived. The main centre was Eskureh. He said that the Ismaili community in Sirjan was the oldest in Iran and had originally come from Egypt in the days of the Fatimid empire. He told us that there were several *jama'atkhaneh*s in the district, including one that was built 700 years ago. He took us to visit the one at Babak and regretted that we had not time to visit the one at Arak. Mr Valliolah was a mine of information about conditions in Sirjan and expatiated freely on the political and social problems of Iran as a whole.

Shortly after we had started our journey again on the indescribably bad and dusty road, where we were always in danger of losing ourselves in the heat and haze, we passed an Ismaili nomadic encampment. It consisted of about twenty families, who lived in tents made of bamboo and goatskins. They had found water in a deep well and were trying to grow their own crops. They had some sheep and goats, but no camels. They assured us that they were indeed Ismaili followers of the Aga Khan.

In answer to our inquiries about the way to Shiraz, they insisted that we were on the right track and that it would shortly improve. Nevertheless, we managed to lose our way and it was very late at night that we arrived at Shiraz totally exhausted. We had hoped to visit two or three Ismaili fortresses at Arrajan, which had been seized early in the Ismaili rising against the Saljuqs by a *da'i*, Abu Hamza, who was formerly a shoemaker by profession. We needed official permission from Tehran to visit the site and unfortunately the telephone links with Tehran, which had been out of order for three weeks, were still not repaired and to our regret we had to postpone this visit for the time being. We intended to try again when we reached Isfahan. So after admiring the splendour of Persepolis – what great architects and craftsmen the Iranians have always been! – we drove the 550 km to Isfahan on a very good tarmac road. We were glad to have left the desert behind us, but our long journey had been well worth while as it had given us the opportunity of talking with some of the Ismaili communities in the south of Iran.

Shahdez, the 'King's Castle'

The main purpose of our visit to Isfahan on this occasion was to inspect Shahdez, the great royal castle built on a mountain about 8 km south of Isfahan. The story of Shahdez is a fascinating one. It is the centre of one of the more remarkable episodes in the Saljuq period, especially when occupied by the Ismailis in the early part of the 12th century. There can be little doubt that there has always been a fortress on the mountain almost since the dawn of Persian history, and it is probable that the Sasanid kings built their own castle there. It has also been generally accepted that the present citadel, which is now much ruined, was built in the 11th century by the Saljuq sultan Malekshah to defend his capital, Isfahan, on the advice of his vizier, Nezam al-Molk. But after the Ismailis gained control of the castle in 1100 by converting its garrison, they could only be dislodged with the greatest difficulty by Malekshah's successor, Muhammad Tapar. The sultan then destroyed it in 1107 with as much vigour as that shown later by the Mongols in their demolition of the Ismaili castles in Rudbar and Qohistan.

Caro O. Minasian, an acknowledged expert on Shahdez, with whom I stayed for a week during my own research in 1968, disputes the theory that Malekshah ordered the construction of the castle. In his book, *Shah Dez of Isma'ili Fame*, he says that history shows that the sultan certainly did not have the necessary time at the end of his reign to build such a large castle, and he contends that a fortress called Dezkuh already existed on the site long before the reign of Malekshah.[2] The sultan had merely enlarged and rebuilt the existing castle, bestowing on it the royal title of Shahdez or 'King's Castle'. It is difficult to resolve this problem as very few artefacts of an earlier period have been discovered on the castle site, apart from some Sassanian relics. Certainly I did not come across any in 1968. If there had been an earlier castle, historians would almost certainly have mentioned it and there would have been greater archaeological evidence. When I was working on the castle, I noted a distinct homogeneity of architectural style and construction, apart from a few exceptions, which points to the fact that the castle was built in quite a short period of time.

Both Minasian and Daftary describe in detail the part played by the castle in the Ismaili uprising. We have seen that once Hasan Sabbah had established himself in Alamut, there was almost a spontaneous uprising against the Saljuqs in other parts of the country, whose rulers acknowledged Hasan as their lord. Despite an energetic Saljuq attempt to put down the insurgency, the Ismailis held their own, especially in Qohistan, and even as far away as Kurdistan in northern Iraq they gained control of the city of Tikrit and held it for 12 years. The Saljuq sultan sent an expedition to retake the town, but it ended in failure despite a siege lasting several months. The Saljuqs were now having to fight hard to maintain their hold on the country. As Farhad Daftary says, 'Not only were the Nizaris seizing strongholds and consolidating their position in Rudbar, Qumes and Qohistan, as well as in many other mountainous areas, but they were spreading the *da'wa* in numerous towns and had begun to intervene directly in Saljuq affairs.'[3]

The Ismaili *da'wa* had, of course, been secretly at work in Isfahan for several decades before the Ismaili uprising. There appears to have been a sizeable Ismaili minority in the city that was often persecuted by the Sunni majority. In 1093 a large number of Ismailis were rounded up and thrown into a bonfire in the centre of the city. The chief of the Ismaili mission in western Iran and Iraq was 'Abd al-Malek b. 'Attash, who resided in Isfahan. He had played a significant role in the recruitment and training of Hasan Sabbah. It is quite probable that Abd al-Malek encouraged Hasan Sabbah's subsequent activities, including the capture of

Alamut in 1090. We do not know when 'Abd al-Malek died, but at some point the overall leadership of the Ismaili *da'wa* in Iran, now independent of the Fatimids of Egypt, passed into the hands of Hasan Sabbah. Although the headquarters of the *da'wa* was transferred to Alamut, the movement continued to be active in Isfahan under the leadership of Abd al-Malik's energetic son, Ahmad b. 'Attash. He is reported to have converted some 30,000 people to the Ismaili cause in the Isfahan area. Ahmad now conceived an elaborate and ingenious plan for taking the fortress of Shahdez.

The whole story of Ahmad's capture of Shahdez is in many respects reminiscent of the way Hasan Sabbah was able to take over Alamut. But whereas Hasan targeted Alamut for its remoteness and inaccessibility from the major centres of Saljuq power, Shahdez lay on the mountains very close to Isfahan, guarding the very heart of the Saljuq empire in Iran. Daftary relates that according to Saljuq chronicles Ahmad played the role of a schoolmaster for the children of the garrison at Shahdez. The garrison was composed mostly of soldiers from Daylaman with Shi'i sympathies. Ahmad was gradually able to convert the entire garrison and by the year 1100 gain complete control of the fortress. Whether he made any payment to the governor for the castle as Hasan did at Alamut we do not know. But there is a remarkable similarity in the events at Alamut and Shahdez and the reader may wonder why both garrisons were so easily converted. They indicate not only the attractions of the Ismaili cause to ordinary Iranians, especially the Shi'a Muslims, but also their dislike of the Saljuq Turks who were regarded as foreign occupiers of their country. Adding insult to injury, the Ismailis seized a second fortress, Khanlanjan, some 30 km south of Isfahan and began to collect taxes in the area under their control.

The outrageous impudence of the capture of these two fortresses overlooking the Saljuq capital was, of course, as great a boost to the morale of the Ismailis as much as it was a bitter blow to the prestige of their enemies. The Ismaili possession of these two castles was not only a direct threat to the capital but to the whole Saljuq empire. Malekshah's successor, Muhammad Tapar, determined that it was time to launch a counter-attack in force to end the Ismaili threat. In 1107 he personally led the assault against Shahdez. In Chapter 3 we referred briefly to the sultan's assault on Shahdez and it would be worthwhile to explain the event in more detail here. As the Saljuq forces prepared to besiege the castle, the Ismaili leader Ahmad ibn Attash had the audacity to delay the attack by engaging the Sunni sultan in a theological debate. The Sunni sultan, argued Ahmad, had no legitimate ground for acting against their fellow-Muslims who differed from the Sunnis only on the question of Imamate, that is, spiritual leadership. He maintained that the Ismailis were quite willing to recognise and obey the sultan in temporal matters. A number of Sunni jurists and scholars in the Saljuq camp were inclined to accept the Ismaili argument, but a leading Sunni cleric bitterly denounced the Ismailis and accused them of having gone far beyond the pale of Islam. The debate was broken off and the siege renewed. Now came a fresh debate over the terms of surrender which the Ismailis would accept. These appear to have been very generous. Part of the Shahdez garrison would be given safe passage to other Ismaili strongholds in Arrajan and Qohistan. The remainder would remain in one wing of the fortress until news arrived of the safe arrival of their colleagues at their destination, when the rest of the garrison would come down from Shahdez and be allowed to proceed to Alamut.

When news was received confirming that the first part of the garrison had reached its destination safely, Ahmad suspected the Saljuqs of reneging on their agreement to give him and the remaining garrison of 80 men safe conduct. He therefore declined to surrender and decided to fight to the death. His men put up a strong resistance, but most of them were killed, though a few managed to escape. Just as the resistance was ending Ahmad's wife adorned herself in her best clothes and jewellery and, thus regally clad, leapt to her death from the castle battlements. Ahmad himself was taken prisoner, forced to walk in ignominy through the streets of Isfahan, cruelly tortured and executed. His son was beheaded. With their deaths, Ismaili influence in Isfahan virtually came to an end.

Caro Minasian strongly refutes the legend that a traitor among the Ismailis had informed the Saljuqs that the garrison at Shahdez had become so weak that they had resorted to the stratagem of making as many weapons as they possessed visible to the Saljuqs so that they might over-estimate the number of defenders.[4] Minasian's view is perfectly acceptable as the Saljuq sultan must anyway have gained a pretty good insight into the real strength of his enemies during the protracted negotiations with Ahmad that preceded the final assault.

As mentioned before, my team and I spent a week in 1968 with Caro Minasian and his assistants as we examined the castle for ourselves. The fortress is breathtaking in the grandeur of its scale, especially the great wall, which varies between 2 and 4 metres in width, over 5 metres in height in some places and about a kilometre in length. It is beautifully dressed on both sides with faced stone. The way it soars and sweeps over the hills is intensely dramatic and I consider it one of the finest castle walls I have seen. The whole fortress was conceived on a massive scale, taking full advantage of the natural contours to ensure that every approach is defended. The main water supply is in the form of a large dam 20 metres square. There are other water tanks too, measuring on average 5 x 4 metres.

The ground-plan of the castle inside the front and back covers of Minasian's book shows the citadel situated at the eastern part of the northern ridge of Kuh-e

Sofa. It was probably from this spot that Ahmad's wife threw herself to her death rather than surrender to the Saljuq sultan. The citadel occupies an area of about 100 metres long and 20 metres wide. To one side and below it are, in Minasian's words, the 'quarters of the grandees'. They cover an area of 160 metres in length with an average width of over 30 metres. The whole area is now a mass of rubble, but Minasian imagines the original building as a series of rising terraces with the citadel at the top, 'highly reminiscent of a ziggurat'. His plan shows three sets of barracks for the garrison, each containing a large number of rooms, as well as the site of the water dam and the stores.

Minasian's observations are very close to mine with some minor differences. We were very impressed with the citadel, the fortified gatehouses, the turrets and block houses. My diary shows that we noticed certain differences in style in some parts of the fortress, which could either have been part of the castle before the main construction by Malekshah or additions by the Saljuqs. When I was examining the castle I thought I had detected some Ismaili alterations, but on mature reflection I would not like to press these. After all, the Ismailis occupied the castle for only seven years and I doubt if Ahmad b. 'Attash and his men had the time to carry out any great building work apart from minor additions. The water cisterns are probably of Ismaili origin, since they have a similarity with those found in the Ismaili castles of Qohistan, especially at Furk. Shahdez was an easier castle to build compared with some of the castles we have been examining. Its height is considerably less than the Qohistan castles. The stone was quarried on the spot and the Ismailis of Isfahan must have been capable of providing a large labour force, unlike small towns like Qa'in or Sarbisheh.

I have not gone into any greater detail about the construction of Shahdez as it was built by the Saljuqs and not the Ismailis. Moreover, Dr Minasian's book contains the essential details for those who are interested. I think that Shahdez illustrates very well the ability of Iranian planners and craftsmen of the medieval period to build highly complex castles on a large scale complete with the necessary water supplies and storage chambers. My constant theme in this book is that the Iranian castles of the 12th and 13th century are, in many important respects, superior to those of the Crusaders. Shahdez belongs to this category. In medieval Europe, large castles were relatively few and far between. In Iran many more castles were built and cities fortified because of the constant threat of invasion by nomadic tribesmen from Central Asia or local warlords. The mountains of Iran, whether large or small, invited fortification, and it was not difficult to quarry stone. I imagine that, as in Europe, specialist builders and masons moved from place to place whenever a major new construction was in progress. I wonder whether any of them had worked in the Ismaili castles. But given the anti-Saljuq character of the Ismaili struggle and the hostility of the Sunni Muslims towards them, I think it highly probable that the Ismailis preferred to employ builders from their own community and other Shiʿa sympathetic to their cause.

The citadel of Khanlanjan

No more than 10.5 km to the south of Shahdez lies the isolated castle of Khanlanjan or Kanlanjan, sometimes called Kuh-e Boz, the 'Goat Castle', perhaps a reference to the difficulty of scaling it. We know little about the history of Khanlanjan. The castle was taken by the Ismailis soon after they gained control of Shahdez, and this double blow to the Saljuqs so close to their capital doubtless increased their fear and anxiety alarmingly. It is clear that the castle played an important part in the Ismaili occupation of the area around Isfahan, though we have yet to establish its precise relationship with Shahdez. The fortress of Khanlanjan was destroyed by the Saljuq sultan Muhammad Tapar soon after he had retaken Shahdez from the Ismailis.

In 1965 I had intended to do research work in Khorasan, but as there was a severe cholera epidemic in the area where I intended to go, Elizabeth Beazley, Mary Burkett and I decided to lead a team to survey Khanlanjan. Subsequently, Elizabeth together with Dr S.M. Stern and Andrew Dobson, wrote an excellent report on the site which was published in *Iran*, the journal of the British Institute of Persian Studies.[5] The following account is based, with minor amendments, on an article I wrote for *Asian Affairs*, the journal of the Royal Central Asian Society in 1969, after I had lectured to the Society on my more recent work in Iran.[6]

The castle crowns the top of a long mountain ridge round which the Zayandehrud flows on its way to the city of Isfahan (Plate 18). It thus dominates the bend in the river and the broad fertile valley it irrigates, a pattern we were to find constantly repeated in our discoveries in Khorasan in 1966. The fortified area is 445 metres long and 347 metres above the floor of the valley at its highest point. At the narrowest neck the ridge does not exceed three metres in width and at its tip it drops away to a relatively accessible lower fortress. The pottery we recovered on the site confirms that the most important occupation period of the castle was about 1100, when the Ismailis were known to be in possession of Shahdez. The earliest recovered pottery is 9th and 10th centuries, which again fits into the known pattern whereby the Ismailis took over an already existing castle and rebuilt or enlarged it. Some of the buildings were probably used quite recently.

The fortress consists of a high citadel, the central fortifications and the lower fortress. The high citadel comprises the area of the summit ridge, here running north-west–south-east, and measuring 88.5 metres along its axis and 16 metres across its greatest width. The cliffs to the north-east and the south-east are almost a sheer drop of between 152 and 213 metres. The main building is a keep in the form of a rectangular tower 9 metres by 5.5 metres overall, with walls 1.5 metres thick, plastered externally with mud and internally with a gypsum type plaster.

The citadel's main use was probably that of a lookout post, for it commands views of up to 16 km to the south and 9.5 km in other directions except to the north-west where the mountain ridge blinds it. The high citadel may have been used as a final defensive position where the desperate Ismaili *fida'is* would have had to make their last stand after the fall of Shahdez to the Saljuqs, but there are few traces of other supporting buildings in the vicinity.

The central fortifications guard the main approach to the high citadel and provide the garrison buildings. Those consist of substantial blockhouses, a great cistern which may have also carried a gatehouse above, two redoubts and further garrison buildings. These are all enclosed by curtain-walls and turrets. The lower fortress forms an entity in itself, with stone walls built round the perimeter so that the whole forms a bailey. The main building is the keep, probably the residence of the ruling governor, which commands a splendid view of the valley, and there are the remains of numerous other buildings which served either as barrack blocks or residential quarters. The whole complex is built on a much larger and more magnificent scale than the castles in the Alamut valley, with the possible exception of Nevisar Shah, and great attention was paid to solving the problems of internal communications.

The site of Khanlanjan has been known for two or three years and the lower fortress has been visited, notably by Dr Minasian who has done a great deal of work on Shahdez, the more famous sister fortress at Isfahan, and Dr Samuel M. Stern. But our expedition was able to make the first fairly complete surface record of the castle under the patient and skilled direction of Elizabeth Beazley, who was our architect with Mary Burkett, and in particular we were able to explore the central fortifications and high citadel, which demanded of the team no mean skill and courage.

Castles of the Arrajan

When I was in Isfahan in 1968, I made two more attempts to get to Arrajan, but each time the telephone system let me down. We always had a tight schedule and could not spare the time to go to Arrajan without some assurance that we could visit the Ismaili castles. In 1997 Adrianne and I had thought of making another attempt, but we were put off by the suspicious attitude of the authorities whenever we started to examine any fortified remains. 'Where are your papers?' was the constant question we had to face and this naturally had a depressing, almost intimidating effect upon us, especially as in 1997 we had very few official papers.

Arrajan is the name of a medieval city and province in south-western Iran on the Zagros mountains between Khuzistan and Fars. The city is said to have been founded in the 5th century by the Sasanids, and in the 11th century it ranked among the leading centres of Fars. We do not know when the Ismaili mission was first introduced here, but in the early years of the 12th century it was headed by the *daʿi* Abu Hamza. Not much is known about his background other than that he was formerly a shoemaker and had received training in Fatimid Egypt. His missionary activities in Arrajan appeared to have been highly successful as it enabled him to seize a number of castles in the vicinity of the town.

Since my return from our last expedition in 1997, I have tried unsuccessfully to find out more about these castles, which I think were not very large. An article by H. Graube in *The Encyclopaedia Iranica* identifies them as Qalʿat al-Jess, about 15 km north-east of Arrajan in the mountains, Qalʿat Haladan/Dez Kelet 50 km north of Arrajan, and Qalʿat al-Nizar 30 km north of the city.[7] In my reckoning, the ruins of these fortresses lie between 7.5 and 11 km north-east of modern Behbahan in an area now known as Argun. According to Daftary, these Ismaili strongholds, too, were besieged and destroyed by the Saljuqs shortly after their capture of Shahdez and Khanlanjan.[8]

About 300 km to the north of Isfahan is the town of Mahallat, which is regarded as the ancestral home of the Aga Khans. The honorific title of Aga Khan was first bestowed on the Nizari Ismaili Imam Hasan ʿAli Shah (d. 1881), by the Qajar ruler of Iran, Fath ʿAli Shah. Although not an Ismaili himself, the Shah held the Imam in high regard, gave him one of his daughters in marriage and appointed him governor of Qomm. He also gave the new Aga Khan additional land in the Mahallat area. Since then the title of Aga Khan has remained hereditary among his successors. When I visited Mahallat in 1968, I was warmly received and taken to see the tombs of Ismaili Imams at Anjudan and Kahak, many of them dating back to medieval times. I also visited an Ismaili village nearby and talked to the children in the school. Quite a few 'nomadic' Ismailis had moved into the area and were busy cultivating new plots of ground or setting up as merchants or traders.

I cannot leave my account of the Ismailis in Isfahan without some personal reflections on this great city. It used to be said that an Englishman always regarded two cities as his capital, London and Paris. This does not really apply to myself, because although I love Paris and her splendid monuments, I feel that I am in many ways an honorary citizen of Persia, and Isfahan especially is close to my heart. When Naser Khosraw visited Isfahan in 1052, he was most impressed by its bracing climate and prosperity: 'Of all the Persian-speaking cities,' he wrote in his travelogue, 'I never saw a finer, more commodious, or more flourishing city than Isfahan.'⁹ The city's most glorious epoch was, of course, during the reign of the Safavids who made it their capital city. The architect of many of its glories was Shah Abbas I, also known as Shah Abbas the Great (1587–1629), and his legacy is still powerful. Isfahan is famed also for one of the finest products not only of Persian but probably all architecture: the city's Friday mosque, the Masjed-e Jomeh, constructed in 1088. Fortunately, Isfahan has not suffered such destruction over the centuries as other Iranian cities, and this city must stand high among the great architectural jewels of the world.

Although I have concentrated in these chapters largely on the Ismaili castles and their remains in Iran, we must not underrate the part played by the ordinary Ismaili citizens who for generations went about their ordinary lives under the protection of their castles. It is difficult to give an estimate of the number of Ismailis in the Alamut period. By far the larger number lived in Qohistan, but there were considerable enclaves elsewhere, notably in Alamut and the Rudbar and Qumes areas, in cities such as Isfahan, the nomadic tribes of Sistan and other pockets like Arrajan and the Zagros mountains. I would suggest the figure of 150,000–250,000 as reasonable.

Our study shows that there were very many talented and capable architects and craftsmen among the Ismailis. Their advanced agricultural systems, dependent on a good water supply and the acquisition of fertile or potentially fertile ground, testify to their creative ingenuity and good husbandry, as well as intelligent administration. We know that the larger castles had impressive libraries and were the centres of intellectual life and thought, including philosophy and the physical sciences. But we sometimes tend to forget in our discussion of political and military issues that the Ismaili state primarily consisted of quite ordinary citizens. Despite the unremitting hostility of the Saljuq rulers and the difficult terrain they chose to inhabit, the Persian Ismailis were able to live their lives in peace and security for the most part. Even in the anti-Ismaili accounts left to us by Juwayni, there is never a hint of dissatisfaction, let alone rebellion, with their leaders, which must be proof that they were loyal and happy enough with their lot. Nor is there any evidence of Ismailis leaving their faith in large numbers to join their Sunni opponents. And when threatened with defeat and possible extinction, either by the Saljuqs at the beginning of the Ismaili state or the Mongols at the end, they were ready to lay down their lives for their beliefs. This fact alone proves the falsity of the legends that the so-called Assassins were little more than bloodthirsty terrorists stimulated by hashish or visions of a false paradise.

I think that it is clear to the reader that much of the research work I have been describing, especially the location of the castles and other sites, could not have been carried out without the help of the Iranians themselves. This is true of all the expeditions both before and after 1979. In contrast to the suspicion and unhelpful attitude of government officials that we often encountered, Adrianne and I marvelled at the helpful and friendly way in which we were received and helped by the vast majority of the ordinary people we met, even in the humblest village. I was particularly glad to talk to the older folk. One man who claimed to be 120 years old and his wife ten years younger, who lived in Sarab, were a mine of information about past events, the sites of castles, the names of villages where Ismailis lived, the geography of Iran and a host of other matters. To them all I express my deepest gratitude.

Notes

1. Daftary, *The Isma'ilis*, p. 414.

2. Minasian, *Shah Diz of Isma'ili Fame*, pp. 20, 61–62.

3. Daftary, *The Isma'ilis*, p. 354.

4. Minasian, *Shah Diz of Isma'ili Fame*, pp. 59–61.

5. S.M. Stern, E. Beazley and A. Dobson, 'The Fortress of Khan Lanjan', *Iran*, 11 (1971), pp. 45–57. Dr Stern passed away in 1969 prior to this publication.

6. Peter Willey, 'Further Expeditions to the Valley of the Assasins', *Royal Central Asian Society Journal*, 54 (1969), pp. 156–162.

7. H. Gaube, 'Arrajan,' in *The Encyclopaedia Iranica*, ed. E. Yarshater (London-New York, 1987), vol. 2, p. 519–520.

8. Daftary, *The Isma'ilis*, p. 362.

9. Naser Khosraw, *Book of Travels*, p. 126.

CHAPTER 13

Citadels of the Syrian Mountains – I

In Chapter 3 on the Syrian part of the Ismaili state, we first looked in broad detail at the background history of Syria, the advent of the Crusaders and the rise of Ismaili influence from the small town of Salamiyya in the middle of the ninth century. We then made a closer study of the relationship between the Ismailis and the Crusaders, based on the reality of power politics rather than the difference of their respective religious faiths. Undoubtedly the two most fascinating characters of the 12th and 13th centuries are the Ismaili leader Rashid al-Din Sinan, the so-called 'Old Man of the Mountain', and the Sunni general Saladin who crushed the Crusader armies at Hattin and finally absorbed the Ismaili possessions into his own domains.

I have visited Damascus on a number of occasions, sometimes on a stopover in a flight from Tehran to London. Each time I was immediately struck by the difference in atmosphere between Iran and Syria. This was not only political or geographical. In my early visits to Damascus there always seemed to be a revolution in process or in the offing, whereas Tehran was outwardly a model of tranquility. The ambience, the feel of the country was quite different. Damascus is after all a thousand miles from Tehran, and inevitably there is a change of rhythm. So, I must ask the reader to put aside for the moment his impressions of the great Iranian fortresses like Nevisar Shah, Gerdkuh and Soru, as we now turn to the Ismaili castles of Syria.

Although reference is often made to the political history of the Ismailis in Syria, very little attention has been given so far to their castles, except in short articles such as 'Assassin Castles in Syria' published many years ago in *The Connoisseur*.[1] At the beginning of his article the author, John Phillips, observed that apart from Masyaf these castles are rarely visited by the modern traveller because of their remoteness and inaccessibility. This statement is certainly true and is reinforced by Ross Burns in his historical guide, *The Monuments of Syria*. In his entry on the castle of Kahf, to which he gives two stars (indicating a 'well worthwhile' visit) he writes: 'Finding al-Kahf can be a major exercise and the Ismailis did well in searching out a location deeply hidden in the folds of the Jabal Ansariyya.'[2] I can certainly testify to this as a result of my expedition with Adrianne to Kahf in 1998, but this should really cause no surprise since almost all Ismaili fortresses in Syria were built in relatively inaccessible parts of the Jabal Ansariyya, the mountainous region called the Jabal Bahra in medieval times.

Such considerations assumed an even greater importance in Syria than Iran because of the greater vulnerability of the Ismaili strongholds. However well they chose their positions in the hills of the Jabal Bahra, the Syrian Ismailis were never very far from their enemies, whether Christian or Muslim. The Ismaili castles in Syria are not normally as large as those in Iran, nor did they have the great advantage of space and distance that existed in Iran. They were hemmed in by the Mediterranean to the east and the great fertile plains of Syria to the south. The hills of the Jabal Bahra, 920 metres high, are puny compared with the Alborz mountains or the highlands of Qohistan at around 2,140 metres. There was little room for manoeuvre. These natural obstacles could only be overcome by using geography and human ingenuity to the full – in other words, by taking maximum advantage of the inaccessibility of their castles and increasing the strength of their defences.

Though smaller than their Iranian counterparts, the Ismaili castles in Syria are generally bigger in area and extent than the famous Crusader castle of Krak des Chevaliers The Syrians had already obtained much experience in building and reinforcing castles from their co-religionists in Iran, but their architects had to adapt their techniques to local conditions in the Jabal Bahra, which they did admirably. In order to gain more storage space for water and other supplies they dug deeper. The Syrian castles lack the grandeur that is a feature of some of the Iranian Ismaili castles, such as Soru. The courses of stone are not as fine and have been even more extensively destroyed. Apart from Kahf and Masyaf despite its previous ruinous state, it is sometimes difficult to picture them as they were, but they must have been imposing enough. However, Qadmus on its hilltop and the great length of Khawabi, with many towers and stretches of wall still standing, enable us to have some idea of how they once looked.

It was, of course, in the Masyaf/Kahf area that the Ismailis came closest to the areas controlled by the Crusaders. The proximity of Masyaf to Krak des Chevaliers was of considerable importance: the distance between them is only about three days' march. I know the area well, since I first visited it in 1970 and again with Adrianne Woodfine in 1998. Below Krak there is a charming valley called the 'Valley of the Christians', an important centre of Greek Orthodox Christianity since the early Christian period. The Monastery of St George, founded in the sixth century by the Emperor Justinian, still flourishes in the valley. There are now two chapels in the monastery, the earlier one dating from the 13th century. The lower court also includes remains of the Byzantine monastery. This monastery in the valley would have made an ideal meeting place for conversations between representatives of Sinan, the Ismaili leader, and the Knights Hospitallers for their secret discussions on tributes and other matters of joint interest.

Although both Christians and Muslims borrowed architectural concepts from each other there is no evidence of this at Krak and Masyaf. The Hospitallers wanted their fortress at Krak to be symbolic of the grandeur and might of their order as well as being the strongest Crusader castle. They certainly succeeded in their project. Indeed, Ross Burns too has considerable justification in calling Krak 'the supreme example of castle building',[3] if he is referring to castles constructed by the Europeans or Arabs. Krak is indeed an exceptional castle. As Hugh Kennedy points out in his *Crusader Castles*: 'It owed its glories to the wealth the knights acquired from their own rich lands, from exacting tribute from the neighbouring Muslims and from the generosity of visiting Crusaders.'[4]

But the glory days of Krak were not to last that long. The castle was probably reconstructed in something approaching its final form after an earthquake in 1170. In 1202 there was another earthquake which led to further reconstruction. But after King Louis IX of France had left the Levant, where he had spent much time and energy strengthening the Crusader fortifications, Krak met with a series of misfortunes culminating in the surrender of the castle to the Mamluk sultan Baybars I of Egypt in 1271. Hugh Kennedy relates that in 1252 a horde of Turkmans, estimated as 10,000 in number, ravaged the fertile lands around the castle.[5] He also quotes Deschamps as saying that Baybars allowed his horses to graze on 'the meadows and crops of Krak, and this was one of the reasons why it was captured since its only provisions came from its crops and these were all used up by the Muslim troops at the time.'[6] All this is in stark contrast to the siege of Gerdkuh in Iran which held out, as we have seen, against the Mongols for 17 years.

Baybars launched his attack against the south-west front of Krak, having already isolated the castle, by using his heavy siege engines, the trébuchets, to break the Crusader defence, which, ironically, had been specially constructed to prevent such a move. He also used mining (sapping) to good effect. The whole process took a mere 26 days before the walls were sufficiently destroyed to allow the Muslim troops to pour into the castle. The garrison retreated to the inner defences and opened negotiations for surrender. The knights were then allowed to leave the castle and go in safety to Tripoli. They also had to promise that they would not stay in Arab lands. Baybars immediately rebuilt the walls that he had shattered and constructed a massive new square tower to cover this potentially weak spot.[7]

It would be idle to deny that the Ismaili castles cannot boast the visual architectural harmony and grace so evident in Krak, splendidly illumined by the mellow honey-coloured stone. Nor should we underestimate the strength and expertise of the massive structure and the precision of the masonry which bind together the courses of ashlar that form the glacis and walls of the inner and outer enclosures.

But the weakness of Krak was also evident. It could be approached without difficulty by a large attacking force. It did not possess the great storage capacity of food and water of the Ismaili castles. It could not withstand assault by powerful trébuchets and was susceptible to the dangers of mining. Once a breach in the walls had been made the castle could no longer be defended and the garrison had no choice but to surrender. As we have seen, the castle of Qa'in in Qohistan was composed of three independent parts, each sited above one another, to prevent this eventuality. The Ismailis did not possess the almost limitless resources in money and manpower available to the knights of Krak and had to concentrate on strategic necessities. Finally, of course, the actual construction of Krak and other Crusader castles did not pose the same difficulty as those experienced by the Ismailis. Most of the Crusader and Arab castles were built on relatively flat ground of no great height, which made the process of construction relatively easy. The castle of Nevisar Shah in the Alamut valley, which we have considered in Chapter 7, was infinitely more difficult to build and was considerably larger in area. This is also true of Gerdkuh, Mo'menabad and other Ismaili castles in Qohistan. But the existence of these castles was hardly known in the West, let alone appreciated, until my research expeditions, and it is only now that we can make a valid comparison between Ismaili and Crusader castles.

Historians differ in their lists of the chief Syrian Ismaili castles, that is to say, those which remained in Ismaili possession for a considerable period of time. We must also not forget that one or two castles are situated in modern Lebanon. Present-day Syrian Ismailis are sometimes apt to suggest that almost every castle in the area of the Jabal Bahra had been occupied by their ancestors at some stage or the other. But I would suggest that the main complex of Ismaili castles was centred at Masyaf and Kahf, and included Rusafa, Qadmus, Khawabi, Khariba, Ullayqa, Maniqa and some smaller castles. A little further away, but belonging to this central core were the castles in the Jabal al-Summaq near Aleppo, including strongholds at Azaz, Bab Buza'a, Sarmin, Kafarlatha and Inab.

It is worth mentioning that when Adrianne and I visited the great Crusader castle of Margat or Marqab, we were categorically assured that the Ismailis had occupied the castle for a short time in the middle of the 12th century before it was sold to the Knights Hospitaller in 1186. But there is no reference to this event by Daftary or other historians. T.E. Lawrence praises it as 'the best of the Latin fortifications of the Middle Ages in the East ... informed with the spirit of the architects of central and southern France.'[8] But like Krak, the great south tower of Margat was undermined by Qalaun, the successor of Baybars in 1285. The fortress surrendered a month later after a succession of bombardments.[9] I write the above as a further illustration of the differences between French and Iranian architects, and to illustrate that the Ismaili castles, particularly in Qohistan, were specifically constructed in places where mining was impossible.

The medieval castle of Masyaf

The best-known Ismaili castle in Syria is without doubt Masyaf, though Daftary points out that the first Ismaili stronghold in the country was Qadmus, which the Ismailis had purchased from the Sunni ruler of Kahf in 1132–33.[10] Shortly afterwards they were able to purchase Kahf itself from the owner who did not wish the castle to become the possession of a cousin during a succession dispute. The Ismailis then took Khariba from the Franks and in 1140–41 they occupied Masyaf. At about the same time they captured Khawabi, Rusafa, Maniqa and Qulay'a.

Masyaf owes its importance primarily to its geographical position. The town and castle stand on the main road approximately midway between Banyas on the Mediterranean and Hama to the east. It is also a nodal point on the road running north from Homs (Hims) to Latakia and Aleppo. These roads are most probably ancient caravan routes and Masyaf was almost certainly a town of some importance during the Seleucid, Roman and Byzantine times. Inside the citadel is evidence of earlier occupation in the form of columns, stonework and a possible tomb-chamber worked into the rock. The town stands at the foot of the great forested hills of the Jabal Bahra, through which two important roads run across the mountains to the west. The citadel dominates the extensive fertile agricultural plains to the east.

The best view of the town and citadel can be obtained from the south-east. Here, the Masyaf road joins the modern highway leading to Tortosa. The commanding position of the citadel, partly obscuring the town behind it, is at once apparent (Plate 22). Masyaf is an obvious place to build a castle and the first fortification was probably an Arab one built around the 10th-11th centuries, much influenced by Byzantine models. Raymond de Saint-Gilles conquered the site during his march to Tripoli in 1103. Sinan acquired it for the Ismailis in 1140–41. The Mongols occupied Masyaf briefly in 1260 but the Ismailis recovered it in the same year after the crushing defeat of the Mongols by the Mamluk armies of Egypt at Ayn Jalut in Palestine. In 1271 the Ismailis were forced to surrender the castle to Sultan Baybars after he suspected them of plotting against him. They regained Masyaf under the Ottomans and it became the residence of Ismaili *amirs*, such as one called Mustafa who had an inscription to himself carved in the castle dated 1793–94. In the 19th century some limited restoration work was carried out by local Ismailis, but it fell increasingly into ruins. The citadel is now a national monument under the protection of the Department of Antiquities in Damascus. It receives quite a few visitors who in 1998 were free to wander at will through the castle.

I first visited Masyaf in 1970 and encountered considerable difficulties with the local police as an army camp had been established nearby. I was eventually allowed to photograph under strict supervision with the help of a local Syrian who was studying English attached to my party. At that time there was considerable hostility to the French who, I was told, had severely damaged the citadel during the Mandate (which I found difficult to believe). The castle itself was in a ruinous state. Many of the outer perimeter walls were in danger of collapsing completely. The stonework of the castle walls had lost most of its mortar and the interior seemed a hopeless jumble of ruins which were dangerous to investigate.

In sharp contrast to our previous visit, in 1998 Adrianne and I were warmly greeted and shown round by the chief guide, Mr Nizar Ullakeh. I was much impressed by the restoration work that had been carried out during the 30 years since my last visit, which, if stylistically not always very happy, had at least preserved the castle from further decay. The restorers had also tried to make as much sense of the shattered interior as possible. More recently the Aga Khan Trust for Culture has commenced a systematic programme of restoration which will hopefully make the citadel of Maysaf more accessible to local people and tourists alike (see Chapter 14).

The first view of the citadel as seen from the approach road is impressive by any standard. It stands proudly on a rocky prominence some 20 metres above the plain and makes a superb picture set against the green hills of the Jabal Bahra. The walls at first sight appear remarkably complete due to the restoration work, and the honey-coloured stone in the evening sun gives it something of the romantic aura that is associated with Krak des Chevaliers. The photogenic quality of the castle is similar from whichever angle you approach the castle. It has the air of a medieval castle *par excellence*.

Ross Burns does the citadel scant justice when he writes in his otherwise excellent *Monuments of Syria*: 'An hour and a half should be sufficient for an inspection of the castle (and a quick circuit of the central part of the town where some buildings of the Ottoman and French periods retain a certain faded charm).[11] This is a cursory and inadequate overview indeed. The castle is a complex structure and difficult to read because of the many different periods of architecture it incorporates and which are now jumbled together; but it is nevertheless an important building of considerable distinction.

The population of the town of Masyaf is estimated at about 15,000. In my 1970 expedition most of the town was still contained within the old walls, but in 1998 I noticed that there had been a considerable expansion of the population and that virtually a new town had sprung up outside the walls. The original walls can still be traced without too much difficulty, though houses and gardens are often built right up against the castle walls or the walls are incorporated into domestic buildings. The walls themselves are about 6.5 metres high and some arrow slits are still visible. The date normally ascribed to them is 1248/9 because this date appears on various inscriptions. Three 13th-century towers still exist as well as a centrally placed mosque dating back to the 12th century and which the local people associate with Saladin.

Originally the town had four main gates, three of which can be dated by the inscriptions upon them. The east gate is the most complete. It is about six metres wide and five metres high, though the top part is missing. The tower has two inscriptions stating that it was erected in the year 646 AH (1243 CE), which corresponds to similar dating on the other towers.

The castle stands on an oval rocky promontory about 150 metres long with a maximum width of 70 metres. From a distance it reminds you of a ship with a narrow bow and stern. The castle buildings form a compact mass, often divided into rectangular blocks. The height is probably an impressive 50 metres. There are certainly six levels of buildings and in some places an additional two or three. Although the castle has been described by John Phillips as 'one of the best preserved castles in Syria',[12] the interior is difficult to decipher because of the damage caused by landslides and earthquakes during the centuries, as well as attempts to shore up and preserve the structure. The outside walls had been repaired in a very haphazard way with stone and material taken from other parts of the building. At the beginning of the 20th century, a part of the castle was used to house the poor and doubtless the citadel has been used for all sorts of similar purposes.

The castle lies on the open eastern side of the town with houses clustering round its western base. On the plain side of the castle an outer wall encircled the castle 150 metres or so away from the rock. The base of the rock is 30 metres above the plain. A path runs from the open eastern side through a well-preserved archway to a reconstructed flight of steps leading to the main entrance in the south-western corner of the castle. The same approach is also defended by a barbican, now in ruins. This is an excellent spot to study how the castle walls are anchored into the stone prominence on which it is built and to appreciate the sharply angled towers defending the main entrance, thus giving a maximum arc of defensive fire from the arrow-slits in the walls and casements. The walls at this point (mostly early 13th century) are particularly strong and well preserved (Plate 23). The main door is made of cedar studded with iron bands. Above is a row of splendid machicolations. This gateway opens into a narrow room, which is only the width of the two sides of the door. Beyond this is a further room, trapezoid in shape. The entrance arch rests on two pillars whose capitals probably date from the 6th century. From this room a short cobbled corridor leads to two others to the right and left. The room in front is barred by a portcullis, so that an attacker can be brought under fire from three sides. The square room beyond is dark like the other, which must also have been a disadvantage to an attacker, and there are 'murder holes' in the roof.

A mass attack upon the castle would have been virtually impossible owing to the steep external staircase that is strongly defended by well-placed arrow slits. Attackers who may penetrate these defences are held up by the narrow dark passages they encounter, where they are exposed at every angle to the fire of the defenders. As John Phillips points out, this is a classic and very early example of the bent entrance, designed to break up the momentum of the enemy attack and to limit his room for manoeuvre once he had penetrated inside the castle. It is a concept that can only be used in castles that are reasonably compact in form. I have occasionally seen examples of this in Iran, where military architecture normally follows different principles. Once the attackers succeed in penetrating the initial defences they have two choices. A cobbled passage to the left will eventually take them back to the southern fortifications by the main gateway, but they would then be easy targets for the defenders. Alternatively they would become lost in a maze of passages, barred by iron gates. We were amazed in 1998 by the excellent ventilation system. Wherever we went, through casements or along steep dark mural galleries, sometimes as long as 75 metres on the western side of the castle, there was plenty of air, however dark the narrow passage through which we had to crawl.

Another major difference between the Iranian and Syrian castles of the Ismailis becomes clear at Masyaf. This is the principle of the concentric castle, which denotes an inner castle or high citadel protected by an encircling wall. As John Phillips observed, the plan of Masyaf is completely concentric and was greatly influenced in this by the configuration of the site.[13] The perimeter wall is overlooked by the high citadel, from which fire can be brought to bear on an attacker. This again can only be used in castles of the same format as Masyaf.

The ground floor level of the castle is given over entirely to defence, storage and water cisterns. As the castle was built into solid rock, the danger of mining or sapping was minimal. The defence of the castle rested on the immensely strong, rectangular outer walls around the entrance, which were provided with a large number of arrow-slits. These walls belong probably to the earliest part of the castle, though strengthened considerably in the 13th century. The bent entranceway belongs to this period, too. In the second level of the castle, more space is given to residential accommodation. The walls are thinner and the rooms somewhat larger. The third level represents the topmost level of the perimeter wall and the platform on which the three levels (or possibly more) of the high citadel are built. Some of the buildings are evidently considerably later, possibly 18th century, but the most interesting building is without doubt on the fourth level, which is reached by a stone staircase. This is a series of four rooms, which are traditionally claimed to be the private quarters of the 'Old Man of the Mountain', the redoubtable Sinan Rashid al-Din himself. There is no firm evidence that this was the case, of course, since in many Syrian castles special rooms are designated as the dwelling places of the local *amirs*.

In addition to the ventilation, great ingenuity was shown in the water system. There are wells on the lower levels, four or more we were told. The water cisterns deep inside the castle are quite remarkable. They are filled from pipes, many of them still in existence, which conduct the rainwater from the upper levels. In 1970 we estimated that the main lower water cistern had three bays, measuring 50 metres in width and 10 metres high. It was large enough for the local Masyaf boys even to swim in it. We were told that on the eastern side of the castle there were two bathhouses.

The masonry used in the outside walls varies greatly. The largest block measures about 80 centimetres in length, the smaller 40–60 centimetres. Gaps are filled with small stones, some 20 centimetres long. Sometimes stones are placed upright or at an angle or wedged through the walls to give greater strength. A considerable amount of mortar must have been employed and much of this has worked away and has not yet been renewed. On closer inspection, the outer courses of stone are not as well cut or placed as in the Iranian castles, although from a distance the general impression is even enough. During later repairs, all sorts of stones taken from different parts of the castle have been used, among which we were surprised to see one stone incised with the Crusader Maryan cross. The overall thickness of the walls is 1.80 metres though the thickest measure five metres.

Our general impression of Masyaf is that of a very fine example of Arab castle architecture in the 12th and 13th centuries. Its historical association adds considerable piquancy. From any vantage point on the eastern side of the castle,

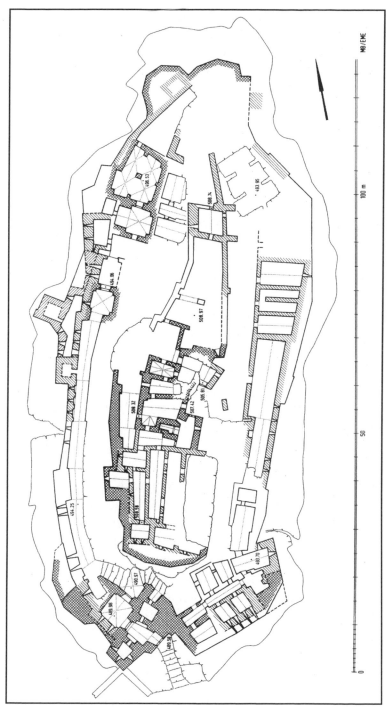

Figure 10: Groundplan of the citadel of Masyaf

you can see a large stone slab on the plain below, which is supposed to mark the spot on which stood a tent in which the two great Muslim leaders of the time in Syria, the Sunni Saladin and the Ismaili Sinan, negotiated their extraordinary truce. Like Krak des Chevaliers, Masyaf is a fortress that represents power and dominion, and in this respect it seemed to me very symbolic of Sinan's personality. The citadel has a very European feel about it, and the great temptation is to compare it with Krak des Chevaliers. It can certainly stand such comparison both on aesthetic and architectural grounds, though this has not been recognised up to now.

In 1983–84, a very detailed study of Masyaf was undertaken by Dr Michael Braune and his wife from Hanover, as part of a research project of the German Archaeological Institute in Damascus on the mediaeval fortresses of north-west Syria.[14] In his excellent description of Masyaf, Dr Braune distinguishes three main building periods (Fig. 10). Apart from earlier fortifications that must have existed, he dates the first building period as the 9th and 10th centuries. But these additions were probably fairly elementary with narrow simple walls and a keep. There were few if any rectangular towers to strengthen the defences. Shortly afterwards there was a second building period in which the main curtain-wall was strengthened, particularly on the western side and towers were added. Dr Braune does not accept the thesis that the main fortifications were built by the Byzantines. He argues that Byzantine castles always contained a large garrison, which was ready at any moment to launch an attack on any hostile force. But this tactic demanded a large number of sally-ports and Dr Braune failed to find any evidence of such openings. Moreover, the lack of Maryan crosses (apart from the single one I spotted) is very unusual for a Byzantine castle. There is also no evidence of any Byzantine name or inscription for a fortress of this size and importance.

After the Muslim conquest of Syria in 634, many fortresses were rebuilt and enlarged by local Muslim rulers, but this was not the case with Masyaf, even after the castle was taken over by the Crusaders in 1103. It came into Ismaili hands in 1140. In Dr Braune's opinion, the third and greatest building period of Masyaf was in the first quarter of the 13th century while still under Ismaili occupation. The date 620 AH (1223) appears on an architrave at the entrance to the citadel. The defensive positions were immensely strengthened, especially to withstand the impact of huge blocks of stone, sometimes weighing half a ton, hurled by mangonels. The towers were built or reinforced and the whole fortress brought to the highest standard of defence. The town walls were also similarly strengthened. Masyaf is certainly one of the outstanding castles in existence and reflects the genius of Ismaili military architecture.

Dr Braune concludes by saying that a fourth building period might have been expected after the Ismailis surrendered Masyaf to Sultan Baybars in 1271, but there is little evidence for this, although Baybars rebuilt the nearby castle of Shayzar in 1261. Dr Braune gives two possible explanations. Perhaps Masyaf did not need any further fortification or restoration after the Ismailis had occupied it for 130 years, or that the strategic and political situation had so altered that the castle had lost its military significance. In an appendix to his work, Dr Braune gives the German translation of thirteen inscriptions he found, most of them dating from the 13th century.

In 1970 my Syrian guide insisted that I must visit Sinan's tomb and palace at Masyaf. This was situated on a hill 890 metres higher than the castle. We were told that the palace was originally built by 'Ali Mahmet some 200 years before Sinan as a *madrasa* and he so liked the site that he converted it into his private residence. It is an interesting building that has undergone many alterations since then. We were shown to a room, which we were told was Sinan's mosque. Adjoining it was another room containing two tombs of early Ismaili personalities. We were also taken to a collection of single-story rooms, the last of which contained Sinan's tomb. A pleasant Ismaili guide gave us tea and took us into the tomb chamber. This contained a rough stone sarcophagus under a wooden frame covered with a green cloth. Other visitors came in, kissed the sarcophagus and walked out backwards. It was clear that they were very proud of Sinan whom they regarded as a great hero and saint. An adjoining chamber contained the tombs of 'Ali Mahmet, Sulayman Zinzar and 'Ali Naharwani. The latter were two of Sinan's senior commanders. There is another tomb alleged to be of Sinan located at the castle of Kahf, which I visited in 1970, and equally honoured by the local Ismailis as his final resting place (see Chapter 14). This discrepancy did not seem to trouble Ahmad and other Ismailis who joined us as we chatted, enjoying the magnificent view over Masyaf and the delicious scent of aloes drifting over to us from the houses below the walls.

Rusafa and other castles of the Masyaf complex

Before we consider Qadmus, Kahf and the other Ismaili castles in Syria, we must look at the subsidiary or daughter castles of the Masyaf complex, especially Ba'arin and Rusafa. I visited Ba'arin in my 1970 expedition. It is on the main road from Hims to Masyaf on a rocky outcrop above the village of Lok. There is little left of the castle although it must have been a substantial building. There are also one or two other watchtowers on the Hama-Masyaf road. In the same year we also visited the castle of al-Qaher north-west of Sinan's palace, and one of the main supporting or daughter castles of Masyaf. We were told that it is also called 'The

Conqueror's Castle' or 'The Old Citadel', that it was built originally by the Romans and was an important Ismaili stronghold. The castle is built round the top of a hill and there is not a great deal left apart from some walls and storage chambers above and below ground. The undergrowth is very thick and we were told that snakes were plentiful.

A more important site is Rusafa, about 10 km from Masyaf. I visited it in 1970 and we returned to it in 1998. The castle is set on a high promontory 60 metres above the village of the same name just off the Shaykh Bader road (no.34) from Masyaf to Tartus (Plate 25). The castle is roughly oval in shape about 75 metres in length and 30 metres wide. Although not large it is much bigger than at first appears. It is built on three levels from good local stone. Although Sinan is credited with its construction, there may have been a castle here before the time of the Ismailis. The remains of a double wall can be found at the foot of the castle. The entrance to the castle is from the north-west, protected by a tower. The ruins of the outer walls follow the contours of the prominence, and numerous galleries and chambers are built against the walls which act as battlements. Some of the storerooms are built deep into the rock and extend to a depth of 20 metres. Their construction reminded me very much of the storerooms at Alamut, which could be accounted for by Sinan's personal knowledge of the Iranian castles. The casements are built on top of the storerooms and also buttress internally the walls. The stone is good quality and well dressed. The central section of the castle contains many vaulted rooms. The towers are still quite high and indicate that there were at least three levels to the central block. The villagers assured us that there was ample water and that, during times of siege, it could have been fetched from the passage built to the river, as at Lamasar in Iran. Despite the dense undergrowth and trees that cover the site, substantial ruins still remain pointing to the strength and size of the castle.

On the opposite side of the road, more or less at the same height as Rusafa, are the ruins of another castle. Much of the stone work of the village houses must have come either from this castle or Rusafa. Whether this was the older castle mentioned before Sinan built Rusafa or not, we do not know. It is much more likely that both castles were operational and garrisoned in Sinan's time, as between them they command completely the road through the mountains.

The citadel of Qadmus

Qadmus occupies a central position in the network of Ismaili castles in the Jabal Bahra. It lies west of Masyaf on the road to Banyas at a height of 1,170 metres. The road from Masyaf rises through the superb high, rocky countryside with

22. The citadel of Masyaf in Syria, overlooking the old town.
23. Below left: Main entrance to the citadel of Masyaf.
24. Below right: Gateway at the castle of Qadmus.

25. The castle of Rusafah, as seen from a nearby village.

26. The castle of Kahf, set in a green lush valley.

27. Building housing the tomb of Sinan near al-Kahf.

28. Remains of the central citadel at Khawabi castle.

29. Shrine of Naser Khosraw in Badakhshan, Afghanistan.

30. The renovated fort of Baltit in Hunza, northern Pakistan.

31. Pottery fragments from Alamut castle.

32. Agate beads and fine moulded wares from Andej.

33. A blue-glazed water pot, possibly from Hanarak.

34. Fragments of glazed pottery, possibly from Nevisar Shah.

35. Alamut region *sgraffiato*, possibly from Andej.

36. Selection of *sgraffiatto* sherds from al-Kahf, Syria

37. Exterior view of Samiran bowl.

38. Interior view of Samiran bowl.

39. Exterior view of Ayiz bowl.

40. Interior view of Ayiz bowl.

wide vistas of great ravines and narrow valleys. The area is very fertile despite the numerous boulders that lie as though scattered from the heights by a giant's hand. In particular, tobacco plants seem to flourish, as well as grain and cotton. In 1998 the road was being widened and we were held up from time to time as controlled dynamite charges blasted open the rock face.

The town of Qadmus is visible from a considerable distance and lies on top of a high peak in the hills. Scattered in an almost complete circle are the castles of Khawabi, Kahf, Ullayqa, Maniqa, Khariba and, of course, Masyaf. Shayzar is not very far away to the north-east. To reach most of these castles nowadays, you have to take the road to Qadmus and then branch off. The Crusaders had already made an unsuccessful attempt to gain control of this area. In 1132–33 they were driven out of Qadmus when the local Muslim ruler sold the castle to the Ismailis. This was a key purchase. Before then, as noted in chapter 3, the Ismailis had tried in vain to gain a permanent foothold further north in the Aleppo area and in the south around Damascus. Now for the first time they had their own independent castle, and working from Qadmus they were able to gain control during the next seven or eight years of the castles I have mentioned above. We know little of how some of these castles were acquired and, until the emergence of Sinan on the scene, the Ismailis spent the intervening years consolidating their power.

In the 12th century when the Ismailis occupied the castle, Qadmus must have been a bustling and thriving town with messengers arriving from other fortresses nearby. The hill on which the castle stands must have acted as a kind of beacon to all travellers in this part of the Jabal Bahra. It stands out clearly against the folds and ravines of the encircling hills and is a natural centre of communication. Qadmus thus occupied a strategic position in the Ismaili state. The castle continued to be in Ismaili hands under the Ottomans, although it was much damaged in 1838 by the Ottoman general Ibrahim Pasha, and again in 1919–20 when it was attacked by the Nusayris, a rival Shi'a sect with a strong presence in the area. Today Qadmus is a fairly sleepy and peaceful market-town, famed for its vegetables, especially the succulent runner beans.

As in Masyaf, the citadel of Qadmus has now been largely absorbed into the modern township that lies around the steep hill on which it is built. From a distance (we approached it from the north) it is far easier to discern the oval shape of the citadel than it is close at hand, when buildings cover all but the steepest part of the slope. There are really only two paths that lead up to the top and one is private property. The owners were not keen to let us through in 1998. We tried another route at the southern end and were successful. After a fairly steep climb we came to the original gateway built against the rock. It was a square building with two arches, and, incongruously a large modern arc-lamp was fitted on to the second arch. The path continued upwards to the main castle some 70 metres above the village. Here it was difficult to reconstruct the original plan as the whole area at the top was covered with houses, many built since my first visit in 1970 when the summit was reasonably clear. It was then possible to see clearly the original base of the high citadel on which some of the buildings were erected. Nevertheless here and there we could still see traces of walls, arches, doorways, columns and machicolations, which were clearly parts of the original castle (Plate 24). It was also possible to see the entrance to some of the underground storage chambers. The hillside on which the castle is built is terraced for agricultural purposes and fertile enough to feed a medium-sized garrison.

It was at Qadmus that we had one of the delightful incidents which enliven a dreary day. Having been initially turned back from the castle by not very friendly people, we met a charming elderly man living in a house inside the castle wall, who made us feel most welcome. He had been alerted to our presence by the barking of his dog, but when our guide Ahmed explained who we were he at once became a model of gracious courtesy. He could not have been more attentive to Adrianne and gallantly presented her with a posy of roses and other flowers growing in his garden.

Ullayqa and Maniqa

Ullayqa is a comparatively short distance north-west of Qadmus. In 1970 we had tried to find a way up to the castle, which we could see through binoculars, but there seemed no passable track. Now the main road to Banyas runs past the foot of the castle and we had no difficulty in finding it. The landscape from Qadmus to Ullayqa was typical of this region: great vistas over rocky, stony hills cut by dry ravines. The area is believed to have once been part of the seabed and fossils have been found in the rocks. The soil is fertile, planted mostly with tobacco crops. Olive trees abound and we passed flocks of sheep and isolated cows, wandering peacefully along the roads, all looking very healthy and well cared for. The height is 830 metres.

Ullayqa is built on a limestone cliff 760 metres high. The main gateway, a strong stone archway still stood firmly at the top of a steep stone approach track until quite recently. The great wooden gate was still in use and closed at night, as people were living inside the castle area. But later it fell down and was removed, causing the inhabitants to move elsewhere.

The castle site is divided into two areas. About 100 metres inside the main gateway are four interlocking arches of considerable size. We were somewhat astonished to see a group of village lads sitting on purple plastic chairs under the archway. They had rigged up a loud speaker for music and were making tea. We assumed that the building had originally been a mosque and we were later pleased to find our surmise reinforced by Dr Zakieh Hanna, a local historian.[15] The roof of the mosque is half cylindrical and vaulted. The walls have fallen down, but the arches remained. Beside the mosque there are two wells. Dr Hanna also mentions that near the mosque a *hammam* or bathhouse had been built into the castle walls on the western side, measuring 8.45 metres long and 6 metres wide. The mosque is very difficult to enter now and the steps leading down into it are broken.

The remains of the main citadel buildings lie another 40 metres away on top of the conical hill, and although they are now only ruins and very overgrown they must have been once quite substantial. The arched inner wall gate is particularly impressive. The width of the triangular site which the castle of Ullayqa occupies is about 120 metres and from the citadel the site tapers a length of 200 metres to the end of the rock on which the site is built. Most of the perimeter walls can still be traced and in some places they are obviously strong. There are four storerooms on the eastern side and a well fortified gateway complete with machicolations on the western side. On the northern end of the main citadel are the substantial remains of buildings and storerooms.

On the northern side of the entrance way (to the right of the entrance path) there is a large cultivated field of 20 by 30 metres, which at first sight seemed totally empty. On closer examination, however, we realised that it formed part of the castle and ended in a sheer drop. We could distinguish the remains of the encircling wall. We also found at least two ventilation shafts, which point to the fact that there are storage rooms underneath. If this field is included in the total area of the castle, as it must be, Ullayqa was a castle of considerable size and certainly larger than Qadmus.

Not far from Ullayqa and about 25 km north-west is the castle of Maniqa or Maynaqa, which I visited in 1970. This site is also not very easy to find. The history of this castle shows how frequently such fortresses changed hands. It was probably first constructed by Arabs in the early 11th century and then fell to the Byzantines. It passed to the Franks in the early 12th century and a few decades later, around 1140–41, it was taken and later re-fortified by Sinan. Then it became the property of the Hospitallers who may have allowed the Ismailis to remain as tenants in the castle, paying a rent or tribute. As we have seen, such accommodations were not unusual, especially between the Ismailis and the Hospitallers. At any rate, Maniqa was in Ismaili hands again when the Mamluk sultan Baybars dispossessed the Ismailis of their castles in the Jabal Bahra in the years 1270–73.

I visited Maniqa in 1970. It is rectangular in plan, strongly built on a ridge and surrounded by very impressive basalt walls. The castle is some 300 metres long and some of the defences and towers are relatively intact. It is instructive to see how the Ismailis made the best use of the natural defensive position by building strong walls of basalt and cutting ditches in rocks. Like Qadmus and so many other Ismaili strongholds in this area, Maniqa commands a magnificent view over the surrounding mountains and ravines.

Notes

1. John Phillips, 'Assassin Castles in Syria,' *The Connoisseur*, no. 770 (1976), pp. 287–289.

2. Burns, *The Monuments of Syria*, p. 176.

3. Ibid., p. 138.

4. Hugh Kennedy, *Crusader Castles* (Cambridge, 1994), p. 148.

5. Ibid.

6. P. Deschamps, *Les Châteaux des criosés en Terre Sainte, I. Le crac des chevaliers* (Paris, 1994), pp. 129–132.

7. Kennedy, *Crusader Castles*, p. 150.

8. Cited by Ross Burns, *The Monuments of Syria*, p. 179.

9. Ibid.

10. Daftary, *The Isma'ilis*, p. 377.

11. Burns, *The Monuments of Syria*, p. 153.

12. Phillips, 'Assassin Castles in Syria,' p. 287.

13. Ibid.

14. Michael Braune, *Untersuchungen zur mittelalterlichen Befestigung in Nordwest-Syrien: Die Assassinenburg Masyaf* (Damascus, 1985), pp. 318–321.

15. Zakieh Hanna, *The Castles and Archaelogical Sites in Syria*, trans. B. Khoutry and R. Botrus (Damascus, 1994), pp. 101–105.

CHAPTER 14

Citadels of the Syrian Mountains – II

In 1970 I wrote in my diary that although Masyaf is the best preserved Ismaili castle in the Jabal Bahra, it was potentially the most vulnerable to attack and, therefore, unlikely to have been the headquarters of the Ismaili state under Sinan. At the time I thought that this must have been Qadmus, principally because it occupies the most prominent topographical position inside the area controlled by the Ismailis and, like Krak des Chevaliers, it dominates the region psychologically as well as physically. It is also the nodal point for communications, being surrounded by a ring of fortresses to the east, north and west. I had further assumed that the main importance of Kahf was that it could prevent any attack on Ismaili territory from the south-west, a view that is shared by John Phillips in his article in *The Connoisseur* cited earlier.

But as a result of my 1998 research, I think I had come to an incorrect conclusion. Qadmus is too open to attack, its defences are not particularly strong and the space it occupies is relatively small, in fact much smaller than Ullayqa. From all that history tells us about Sinan, we can be sure that he would have chosen a much more remote and impregnable site, where messengers could come and go without his enemies being aware of their movements, where he could keep a strong garrison of troops, and which would serve as an imposing and powerful venue for his secret meetings with his own supporters and with the emissaries of his opponents, Crusader or Muslim. Where better than Kahf which he knew intimately?

Kahf, the 'Castle of the Cave'

Even today Kahf is the most difficult site to find. To quote Ross Burns again: 'Finding al-Kahf can be a major exercise and the Ismailis did well in searching out a location deeply hidden in the folds of the Jabal Ansariyya.'[1] In 1998 we had the utmost difficulty in locating it, despite asking directions from all and sundry. Eventually we succeeded and even found some road signs in English pointing to al-Kahf. But the directions were unreliable and it was only by sheer luck that eventually we found a small road that led to the eastern end. In 1970 I had approached the site from the western direction led by a guide from the village of Juwaei. I had noted in my diary that the track we had come along in my landrover was most appallingly bumpy and we feared for the springs of our vehicle. Fortunately, there is now an adequate tarmac road which approaches the castle from the south-west. A village called Esrakeh is about 2 km due south. Kahf, in my opinion, is quite the most interesting and exciting Ismaili castle in Syria and fully repays the difficulties and problems of finding it.

It is perhaps worthwhile to summarise once again the history of Kahf. As far as we know, it was built around 1120 and purchased by the Ismailis probably in 1138 during the time when they were establishing their foothold in the Jabal Bahra from 1132–40. We know that when Sinan assumed the leadership of his community in Syria, he based himself initially at Kahf and it was also in this castle that he died in 1193. Legend has it that in 1197 the Regent of Jerusalem sought an alliance with Sinan's successor in order to gain Ismaili support or at least neutrality in order to preserve his kingdom from extinction. We are told that Sinan invited the Regent to visit him at Kahf where, in order to demonstrate the complete fidelity of his followers, he ordered two of them to jump to their death from the battlements. This implausible story, sometimes also attributed to Hasan Sabbah, is rejected by Daftary as another of the medieval myths of the Assassins. He cites the German scholar Leopold Helmut, who has argued convincingly that the 'death-leap legend' is most probably derived from the ancient Alexander romance. According to a later version of the romance, Alexander the Great commands some of his soldiers to leap into a ravine in order to terrify the emissaries of the Jews.[2] Be that as it may, the French king Louis IX, who led the disastrous Sixth Crusade, also attempted to make an alliance with the Ismailis. Despite Sinan's hostility to the Crusader king, the king sent the friar Yves le Breton to Kahf and an alliance was concluded.

Kahf held out against the Mamluks until 1273, but then capitulated, one of the last of the Syrian Ismaili castles to do so. It remained a military outpost and at times served as a prison for important personages during the Ottoman rule. Ross Burns remarks that 'Of all the mountain sites this is probably the one most marked by a raw and untamed beauty, the environs unsoftened by the cultivation of crops and orchards.'[3] I have a somewhat different point of view. The castle of Kahf is certainly most difficult to access, but apart from the added physical difficulty caused by the dense undergrowth, I fell very much under the charm of this almost virgin site. In 1970 I wrote in my diary: 'The castle is set in surroundings that are majestic in scale, but utterly natural. The red and green hills rise steeply all round. Green luxuriates and at times it is just like walking down a densely wooded English country lane.' Untamed yes, but raw no (Plate 26).

The castle is set on a rocky promontory at the confluence of three deep river valleys. The cliffs are almost sheer and provide their own natural defence. I have now visited it twice from different angles, each of which gives a slightly different impression. But of one military fact there can be little doubt: the complete isolation of this heart of the Ismaili state in Syria and the almost insuperable difficulty of reaching it and taking it by storm. The only way to do this was through a prolonged siege, perhaps taking years, until the provisions ran out. There would never be any shortage of water as it was brought into the castle through canals made of clay, using the same technique as we had observed at Soru in Iran, utilising the many natural springs in the thick woodlands that surround the castle.

The general direction of the castle is east-west, running along the spur of rock on which it is built. This spur is up to 500 metres long and 40 metres wide, rising on three sides from the steep ravines. In contour, it is reminiscent of Alamut. The castle is divided into three, or possibly four, main sections. At the western end of the castle there is a long flat section about 170 metres long, clear of any buildings except for the outside walls and a bastion at the extreme western end. Here are a number of water cisterns. The three sides are sheer, with a drop to the valley floor of about 22 metres. In winter the rivers would have formed a natural moat. From this outer bailey the ground rises up towards a central citadel and fortifications, which must have occupied almost two-thirds of the castle length. These buildings probably contained living quarters and storerooms. This is also the main water storage area. John Phillips noticed seven cisterns. In 1970 I pinpointed four, one of which was 2 metres wide and 6 metres deep. The rocks here are porous and the water would filter down into the main bathhouse on the north-eastern side. Traces of post holes and runnels connecting the cisterns were still evident.

From this middle section the ground continues to rise until it terminates in a sharp point about 10 metres wide. Here the walls are massive. The top of the castle is now completely overgrown, and in 1970 I noted that even then it was covered in aloes, walnut and oaks as well as dense undergrowth. The workmen who had destroyed the castle had done their work well. There is a drop of 10 metres to a fortified platform and then another drop of 20 metres or so to ground level. This is the most vulnerable point of the castle. But the site is surrounded by another massive wall running half-way down its northern flank.

The most unusual parts of the castle are the main entrance gate and the *hammam* or bathhouse. There is only one entrance to the castle, which runs along a narrow path, now severely overgrown, half-way down the steep northern slope.

This leads to a guardhouse, with an inscription, hollowed out of the rock like a tunnel. Those who manage to find it have the impression that they are entering a cave. In fact, the name al-Kahf means Qaha't, the Castle of the Cave. This cave or guardhouse, situated two-thirds along the northern side of the castle, had double doors at each end with double gates and doors bolted and barred and from it access to the top of the castle is gained. But this steep path among the rocks had two or three sharp bends, further grilles and a defensive tower where it emerged on to the castle. The bathhouse is some 30 metres inside and below the main entrance to the castle. I had seen it in 1970 but had not explored it. In 1998 when my small party approached the citadel from the eastern end, we at first despaired of getting into the castle at all. Adrianne and Ahmed, our excellent guide, made their way along the traditional entrance way, now very much overgrown, and spotted a hole in the ground and the arched entrances to what appeared to be two water cisterns. When I arrived, Ahmed pointed out to me an inscription over a doorway which he translated as 'Ismail Alajameh, died Ramdhan 635 AH' (1237 CE). Above this inscription were three lines which Dr Zakieh Hanna transcribes as follows:

> In the name of God, the Most Gracious, the Most Merciful. Enter ye here in peace and security, and on God let the believers put their trust. The building of this blessed bath has been ordered by the just patron, the able patron Serajeddin and the victorious star, Muzaffar ibn al-Husayn. God bless al-Amerah, in the reign of the slave of God, the needy to the mercy of God and to the mediation of his masters, the chaste Imams. God's blessing and peace be unto them all. Hasan ibn Isma'il al-Ajmi al-Alamuti. Ramadan 572. (Lma Ad Kho).

The Muslim year 572 corresponds to the year 1176 of the Common or Christian Era Dr. Hanna cannot explain the meaning of the last mysterious message in brackets and surmises that it must have an esoteric meaning. He also quotes an inscription of the famous Throne-verse from the Qur'an (2:255) carved on a stone near the guardhouse:

> In the name of God, the Most Gracious, the Most Merciful. There is no God but He, the Living, the Self-subsisting, the Eternal. No slumber can seize Him nor sleep. His are all things in the heavens and on the earth. Who is there can intercede in His presence except as He permits? He knows what (is) before or after or behind them. Nor shall they compass aught of His knowledge except as He wills. His Throne doth extend over the heavens and the earth, and He feels no fatigue in guarding and preserving them, for He is the Most High, the Supreme.

The inscription ends with the date: 'The last ten days of Ramadan, 791 AH,' which is 1388 of the Common Era calendar.

The entrance into the *hammam* is now half sunk into the ground so that we had to crawl through on all fours and fight our way through a sloping tangle of bushes and trees. A little further down the slope are the remains of what must have been quite a distinguished room. The walls are five metres high and over one metre thick. On the northern side is a window through which a sheer drop to the ravine below can be seen. Carved mouldings of good quality run around the upper area of the room. On the eastern wall a doorway in a very low arch leads to a corridor with two domes. This corridor gives access to a remarkable ablution or bath chamber, which is octagonal in shape. There are four doorways and four distinct alcoves the same height as the doorway (one metre). Each contains a single pipe opening about two-thirds of the way up the alcove. Around the base of what would have been a domed roof are clusters of four or more pipes.

To the right of the bath chamber is another large rectangular room, which was probably used as a water storage chamber – the water probably being supplied from an aqueduct. This was lined with limestone cement and there were V-shaped patterns of pipes in the walls. To the east and west of the ablution chamber are rectangular rooms with arched doorways leading to the ablution chamber and rectangular doors leading to the large water storage chamber. At the western end of the water storage chamber was a window which appeared to give on to the two arched chambers we had first seen.

The size and design of this *hammam* demonstrates the sophisticated water system of the castle and underlines the fact that Kahf was no ordinary castle, but a residence of considerable importance. It is fortunate that this bathhouse was not destroyed at the same time as the castle; perhaps it was overlooked, or already covered with dense vegetation. It is an archaeological feature of the greatest importance.

When we first arrived near the eastern end of the castle, we noticed a domed tomb chamber of uncertain date which reminded us of the fact that Sinan is supposed to have been buried near here. In 1970 we were told that the local villagers indeed believed that this was the tomb of Sinan and regularly offered prayers there (Plate 27). They insisted that Sinan was buried here and not at the palace above Masyaf. There were also stone arches and considerable remains of buildings which seemed to be connected with the castle. If in fact they were, and there was no reason to doubt this, then the total length of the fortified site could have been about two to three kilometres. It was quite clear that in its heyday this was a castle of great size and strength, and considerably more formidable than Masyaf. Under Sinan, Kahf must have been one of the most imposing castles that existed in the whole of Syria.

Khawabi, the 'Castle of the Ewes'

The site of the castle of Khawabi, like Kahf, is set in the midst of magnificent scenery, but is not, fortunately, quite so difficult to find. I first visited it in 1970 and again in 1998 with Adrianne and Ahmed. It is about 20 km from Tortosa (Tartus) and the nearest village is Albatteye. From here the road continues to wind over a series of hills and ravines for another 3 km and the castle is easily spotted. It is built on a narrow ridge above a river and is surrounded on all sides by encircling hills.

The name Khawabi means the 'Castle of the Ewes', and as far as we know it was never taken by the Crusaders, though they called it Coible and were well aware of it as a potential menace to their own position. It was acquired by the Ismailis probably at the same time as Masyaf, Rusafa and Maniqa, that is around 1140–41, and Sinan rebuilt it as a formidable stronghold after 1160. Geographically and strategically, it is important as it affords an important additional defence for the cluster of Ismaili castles in the Jabal Bahra against attack from the north-east. In 1213 it was besieged with great determination by Bohemond IV of Tripoli after his son Raymond was killed by unknown assassins in the cathedral of Tortosa. The Ismailis had to call for Sunni reinforcements from Aleppo and Damascus, and eventually the siege was raised. Little is known of its history after Baybars I had consolidated his control of the Jabal Bahra around 1273. The castle site and many of the original buildings were later destroyed or adapted for domestic or agricultural use.

Khawabi is at the moment home to a small village community. At the time of my first visit in 1970, much more remained of the original fortifications, especially the immensely strong citadel area at the northern end (Plate 28). The still formidable ruins show clearly why the Crusaders were unable to take the fortress despite their superior numbers. In 1970 and 1998, we approached the castle from the southern side through rows of neatly terraced olive groves. A track leads to the main approach to the castle, which consists of two flights of shallow steps, suitable for horsemen. The first flight has twenty steps, then it makes a turn to the right where the second flight of forty steps leads to the main gatehouse. The walls on the southern side are still well preserved and provided with arrow-slits at suitable intervals. Some of the upper rows of arrow-slits have been enlarged to provide more light for the farm outhouses which have now been built inside the ramparts.

The main gatehouse is at the northern end of the castle walls protected by a barbican protruding beyond the main castle walls. The gatehouse is well-preserved and still retains its original height, although the windows in the upper rooms have been enlarged. The gatehouse has a bent entrance, the second at right angles to the first. Both entrances are very strongly protected with strong archways and substantial walls. The doors of the archway were probably studded with iron bosses and held shut by great bars. The postholes are still visible beside the doors. From the gatehouse complex a path leads to the foot of the main citadel. Here there are strong double walls; the space between them is now roofed over and used as stables and storerooms. Although Ross Burns is somewhat contemptuous of the quality of the stonework, this was not our impression. There is still some fine solid masonry in the perimeter walls.

As at Masyaf, the fortifications at Khawabi are built on the concentric principle, allowing an attacking force that has penetrated the outer defence to come under a hail of fire from the high citadel. The fortress is about 350 metres in length and 200 metres in width. The rock on which it is built is some 80 metres high with a sheer drop on all sides, apart from the entrance at the east. The main defences are on the eastern side, but the northern end of the spur is also well fortified. The high citadel is in the centre of the site, constructed on another rocky promontory. Some of the buildings have been made into very comfortable residences for the present occupants of Khawabi. The northern end also contains water storage chambers. A narrow cobbled street now runs along the centre of the site from which alleyways branch off to the walls on the east and west. We noted a house near the northern water cistern, on which a plaque gave the date as 1310 AH (1892 CE). The former ramparts are now outhouses for sheep, goats and cattle.

We were invited to enter a house near the high citadel and were entertained to tea by the owner, who had nine daughters and four sons. The owner told us that the castle was re-inhabited about 100 years ago and now contained eight families, all descending from the original settlers. All the families living at Khawabi owned their own houses. This seemed to be a very self-sufficient community. They had electricity and hoped that the telephone would soon arrive. Our host added that at some time during their Mandate, the French authorities had burnt the high citadel in reprisal for disobedience by the villagers. This gentleman took us to a fine house built on part of the site of the high citadel, which now belonged to the head of the community. Behind the house of the headman on the western side of the spur are to be found some very substantial ruins underground, which no one has attempted to explore. There are also two small forts or watchtowers on the surrounding hills.

Other Ismaili castles in Syria

Three other important Ismaili castles in Syria must be mentioned. The first is the citadel of Afamiya (Apamiya), also called Qal'at al-Mudiq, the famous Seleucid castle founded at the beginning of the 3rd century CE. Apamea was taken by the Romans and ambitiously rebuilt in the imperial style. A fortified outpost in northern Syria, the citadel of Afamiya guarded the approaches to Aleppo and played an important role in the Arab defence against the Crusaders.

As will be recalled from Chapter 3, Afamiya was the very first castle that the Ismailis of Aleppo captured in 1106 under the leadership of Abu Tahir. Within a few months, however, they were driven out by Tancred, the Frankish prince of Antioch. According to Daftary, this was probably the first military encounter between the Ismailis and the Crusaders in Syria.[4] The Ismailis of Aleppo received an even greater reversal in 1113 when they lost the support of the city's Saljuq governor Ridwan and the local Sunni population turned against them in bloody massacre.

I visited the site of Afamiya in 1970 when I stayed in the vast Ottoman cara-vanserai, built to lodge pilgrims on their route from Istanbul to Mecca. There is little trace left now of the Crusader or Ismaili occupation, apart perhaps from parts of the walls which have been reconstructed from stonework of many different periods.

The second castle is Shayzarin in central Syria on the Orontes river. Like Afamiya, Shayzar was very much a key centre in the Arab defence against the Crusaders. In the spring of 1114 a small group of about a hundred Ismailis, mostly survivors from Afamiya and other places, made a surprise attack on the castle of Shayzar, while its *amir* and garrison were away, and took it. The governor im-mediately mobilised the local tribe for a counter-attack and after a fierce battle recaptured his castle.

The third castle is Abu Qubais, located north of Khariba in the Jabal Bahra. This castle too had originally been built by the Arabs and further fortified by the Byzantines. The Ismailis acquired it around the same time they purchased Qadmus and Kahf in the 1130s. Abu Qubais is a small round castle that also has a superb view over the Orontes plain.

The history of these three Syrian castles illustrate very well their complex and colourful past. They demonstrate the determination of the Syrian Ismailis to establish their own powerbase, as well as the constantly shifting relations and alliances between the Ismailis, the Crusaders, the Saljuks, the Mamluks and other local rulers. This pattern of struggle was to continue for nearly 200 years until the end of the 13th century, by which time the Mamluk sultan Baybars I had succeeded in expelling the Crusaders from Syria and asserting his authority over the entire country. The Ismailis agreed to pay an annual tribute to the sultan, who in return permitted them to retain their fortresses in the Jabal Bahra.

A comparison of the different styles and techniques of military architecture between Byzantine, Arab and Mamluk castles and those of the Syrian Ismailis would make a fascinating study, but it is not really within the scope of this book. I have already written about the strategic and military thinking that lay behind the Ismaili strongholds (see Chapter 6). These considerations had, however, to be modified in the Jabal Bahra to suit the local topography. Only Kahf can truly be regarded as an example of classical Ismaili military architecture. The other castles, which were largely designed by Sinan, had to be scaled down in size and extent. There are certain features which are, of course, common to all types of military architecture in Syria, such as the multi-angled entrance towers, the concentric design of many (excluding Kahf), the water storage systems, and the design and position of the keep or donjon and the high citadel.

The Crusader castle of Saone

There is one Crusader castle, however, that is very similar to the typical Ismaili castle, and that is Saone (Sahyun) near Latakia. It would have been interesting to compare this with Kahf, were it not for the destruction visited upon the latter during the Ottoman period. Sahyun was officially renamed Qal'at Salah al-Din in 1957 to commemorate Saladin's capture of the fortress in 1186. This, of course, gives the impression that Saladin founded or had part of the castle built, which is not the case.

The site of Saone is an ancient one. The Phoenicians had probably built the first castle there. The Byzantines fortified and garrisoned the site in 975. The Franks seized it at the beginning of the 12th century, and it was assigned as a fief to Robert of Saone. It must have been Robert and his successors who enlarged the castle and undertook the building of what Hugh Kennedy calls 'the greatest of all the 12th-century castles in the principality and one of the most impressive in the entire corpus of Crusader buildings in this period'.[5] The remains of the Byzantine castle are still large and impressive, especially the water storage chambers and the citadel. Robert practically doubled the size of the castle, which (unlike Krak des Chevaliers) was never the property of the Knights Hospitaller. In 1187 Saladin won his great victory over the Crusaders at Hattin and recovered Jerusalem. He then moved north to Syria to test the Crusader defences. In July 1188 Latakia surrendered and Saladin moved on to Saone. The Crusaders were only able to resist the fierce bombardment by mangonels for two days. The walls of the lower area of the castle were breached and the garrison was overwhelmed and surrendered.

In all probability the Frankish garrison was far too small to defend such a large castle. Many men who served in the original garrison must have perished at the Battle of Hattin the year before, and it is likely that the fortress was only held by a skeleton force which, despite their bravery, were no match for Saladin's troops.

I personally have great admiration for the castle which is certainly one of the finest early Crusader fortifications. Every visitor would be amazed and enthralled, as were Adrianne and myself, by the large man-made channel, cut out of the living rock, which acts as an immense dry moat, 156 metres long, 28 metres deep and 14 to 20 metres wide, on the eastern side. This channel separates the castle area from the main mountain spur on which there seem to be no fortifications at all. It would have been impossible to build a drawbridge over such a distance and the Crusaders, therefore, left a needle of solid stone to support the drawbridge in the middle. Robin Fedden and John Thomson estimate that 170,000 tons of solid rock must have been removed to make this channel.[6] The postern gate which formed the entry and exit over the moat is still very much in evidence in the middle of the great walls that tower above the moat. The bossed masonry and round towers near the keep are still in excellent condition. The stone keep consists of two storeys and the vaulting is carried on a large central pier. A staircase leads to the roof parapets, where there is a splendid panoramic view of the whole area.

The main gatehouse and entrance is on the southern side. It is now reached after a climb of 142 steps, and when I got to the top, somewhat breathlessly, the wife of the gatekeeper told me that Saladin had said that if your wife is out of breath at the top, get another one! The main gate-house is an early example of a bent entrance and is strongly fortified. Saone or Saliyun was the last castle which Adrianne and I visited on our research in Syria.

The Crusaders never regained the castle. For almost a hundred years after its capture, Saone was under the control of a local *amir*, whose family gave it to Sultan Baybar. A number of additions were made to the castle during the Mamluk time, including a bathhouse and a mosque. The lower enclosure had quite a few houses on it for a time, but gradually the inhabitants moved away to more convenient places higher up the ravines.

Although never occupied by the Ismailis, Saone resembles a typical Iranian Ismaili castle in shape and structure. It has a long triangular site, wider in the centre, containing the three essential elements of an Ismaili castle: the area for soldiers and civilians taking refuge, the water catchment areas and the high citadel. But Saone has three great weaknesses that distinguish it from the Ismaili castles. First, Robert of Saone built his keep or donjon in the middle of the castle wall, disregarding the Byzantine citadel at the highest point of the site, which should have been strengthened as a high citadel. Thus, once the walls had been breached there was no second line of defence, nor a higher citadel or keep. The second weakness was that the surrounding walls were too thin and far-flung to withstand the fierce mangonel fire. And finally, Robert's cardinal mistake was his failure to appreciate that the entire site was well within mangonel range from positions across the ravine on both sides of the castle. Robert had instead relied on the narrow ditch, 28 metres deep and 15 metres wide, which had been dug on the east side of the castle as the principal defence. This is one of the main features of the castle and may have been completed before Crusader times, probably by the Byzantines. It was after the loss of Saone that Crusader military architecture was radically improved, although by this time the Crusader cause was almost lost.

I have discussed previously that there can be little doubt that Ismaili military architecture and planning was, in certain important respects and contrary to popular judgement, considerably superior to that of the Crusaders. The Ismailis already had a long experience of building castles in remote places, especially in Iran, whereas for the Franks the castle served mainly as a strong garrison and powerbase, dating back to the Norman keep. The Ismailis had always had to consider carefully the topography of the land and the strength of their defensive position, as well as problems of water storage and food supply. Their castles may not have the grandeur of Krak or Margat, but as mountain fortresses they are of the finest quality, in addition to their function as places of refuge and centres of Ismaili learning.

It would have been interesting, too, to see what the Syrian Ismailis would have made of the citadel of Aleppo – that is, if they had ever succeeded in gaining control of the city. I agree with Ross Burns when he describes the entrance bridge to the citadel and the stupendous guardhouse as 'a masterpiece of Arab military architecture which combines the practical with the flamboyant,'[7] although I would replace 'flamboyant' with 'monumental'. The 55 metres high stone-faced glacis, on which the citadel stands, was constructed around 1211 by al-Malik al-Zahir Ghazi, a son of Saladin – hence its name, 'Saladin's Castle'. The citadel was twice destroyed by the Mongols and rebuilt each time.

The answer to my historical hypothesis is that the Ismailis would probably never have built a citadel of this monumental style. There is no case to my knowledge of an Ismaili fortress inside a city. The Ismailis were always a minority in the urban areas of Iran and Syria, and they regarded the remoteness of their strongholds and difficulty of approach as the key to successful military defence. They were always aware of the danger of sapping, the need to survive long sieges and the havoc that mangonels could cause. This principle, of course, increased enormously the problems of construction, the provision of adequate storage space and especially the requirement of a reliable water supply. And it was in the way that the Ismailis solved these critical problems that their true genius in military architecture was demonstrated.

Our visit to the Ismaili castles in Syria was immensely helped by the Ismaili community at Salamiyya, their centre in the country. Here we first met Mr Sayf al-Din Kassir, who was at the time the headteacher of a mixed secondary school catering for pupils aged 13 to 18. He told us that the first Ismailis settled at Salamiyya in the 9th century. It soon became the centre of an influential and powerful community and as such incensed the wrath of the Saljuq authorities who razed the town to the ground. During the Ottoman occupation of Syria, the Ismailis kept together in their old villages around the famous castles such as Qadmus and Kahf. The Ottomans grouped them for tax purposes and called them 'castles of the mission'. In the 19th century some villagers began to rebuild the castle sites as new habitations, for instance at Khawabi and Qadmus.

The new Salamiyya began in 1849 with the arrival of a local *amir*, who obtained permission from the Ottoman authorities allowing the Ismailis to settle in the area. The soil is fertile and the sultan wanted Salamiyya to provide a buffer zone against the marauding Bedouins. The Ismailis were exempted from military service and encouraged to become farmers. A considerable group came together to rebuild the town which had almost been swallowed by the desert. Salamiyya is now a dusty but fairly prosperous town of about 50,000 inhabitants and a place of some importance in modern Syria. The Ismaili community has established good relations with the present government and no particular restrictions are placed on it. Mr Kassir told us that women play a large role in Syrian society, adding that the majority of teachers in the country are women.

Mr Kassir said he could not actually help us with our research, but at once gave his approval when a member of his teaching staff, Mr Ahmed, said he would willingly come with us to the various castles we wished to visit. Mr Ahmed was responsible for the religious education department of the school and spoke excellent English. We could not have had a more friendly and helpful adviser. He arranged all the necessary transport for us at very reasonable terms and was very enthusiastic himself about our research. We could not have done without him – he was especially helpful when we were examining Kahf – and we owe him a considerable debt of gratitude.

Throughout our research in Syria, Adrianne and I were rather shocked at the lack of conservation or repair work by the Syrian and other authorities on the great monuments belonging to the Islamic and Christian faiths. This was particularly evident at Masyaf, which I have described in some detail, and also at the Crusader castle of Margat. The chapel at Margat is a perfect example of a medieval castle chapel, with its apse, vestries and frescoes still almost miraculously preserved, though there is little time left if they are to be saved for posterity. As noted in the previous chapter, I have been particularly pleased to learn about the recent work of the Aga Khan Trust for Culture. The Historic Cities Support Programme of the Trust was established in 1992 with the object of actively promoting the conservation of buildings in the Islamic world. To date the programme has assisted projects in widely dispersed areas, such as the Northern Areas of Pakistan, Zanzibar, Samarkand, Bosnia, Cairo and Syria.[8]

The Syrian initiative stems from a request from the Syrian Antiquities Department to provide technical assistance in the conservation of a number of historic citadels in the country, particularly those of Masyaf and Saladin's Castle at Aleppo. The Masyaf project began in 2000 CE. Its aim is to arrest the process of deterioration of the citadel and where necessary to carry out reconstruction to avert the threat of a collapse. Visitors will also be provided with information about the citadels, so that they can understand the history of each castle. I have also visited the castle of Baltit in northern Pakistan since its reconstruction by the Aga Khan Trust for Culture and can personally testify to the excellent and imaginative work of restoration (see Chapter 15). It is to be fervently hoped that similar projects will be established to help restore the real gems which both Islamic and Christian buildings represent.

Notes

1. Burns, *The Monuments of Syria*, p. 176.
2. Daftary, *The Assassin Legends*, pp. 106–107.
3. Burns, *The Monuments of Syria*, p. 176.
4. Daftary, *The Isma'ilis*, p. 359.
5. Kennedy, *Crusader Castles*, p. 84.
6. Fedden and Thomson, *Crusader Castles of the Levant*, p. 80.
7. Burns, *The Monuments of Syria*, p. 32.
8. For more information on the Aga Khan Trust for Culture and its activities, see the website of the Aga Khan Development Network at www.akdn.org.

CHAPTER 15

Badakhshan and Hunza

I have frequently mentioned the name of Naser Khosraw, and I would like to devote this chapter to him and his influence, as well as my search for his tomb in Badakhshan – which to the best of my knowledge has never been precisely identified or described. My visit to this tomb in the remote village of Jurm also led me on to the valleys around Hunza in northern Pakistan, near the present Chinese border. The majority of people in Hunza, Gilgit and Swat are Nizari Ismailis who owe the origin of their faith to Naser Khosraw. There are no great Ismaili fortresses in Afghanistan and Pakistan. But the valleys around Hunza, an important administrative centre in the days of the British Raj, contain some of the most beautiful and evocative scenery I have seen and seems to reflect the peace and tranquillity of mind which is also part of the Ismaili tradition and Naser's legacy.

Naser Khosraw was a learned Ismaili theologian, philosopher, traveller and poet of the highest integrity and sensitivity, revered as a truly saintly man in many parts of Iran, Afghanistan, Central Asia and Pakistan to this day. He was born in 1004 near Balkh, one of the great cities of medieval Islam which was at that time in Khorasan and later completely destroyed by the Mongols. He came from a well-to-do family of government officials and landowners, and after obtaining his advanced education he entered government service as a financial administrator. But over the years he became increasingly discontented with his life of ease and luxury, and when he was about 42 years old experienced a spiritual crisis that resulted in his conversion to Ismailism. In 1047 Naser resigned his official post and went on a pilgrimage to Mecca and then travelled on to Cairo, the capital of the Fatimid empire, where he stayed for three years and was trained as a *da'i*. He returned to his native Khorasan where he commenced his Ismaili mission. We must remember that this was almost fifty years before Hasan Sabbah established himself in Alamut. But the success of Naser's teaching provoked great hostility from some Sunni clerics who denounced him as a heretic and called for his death. They destroyed his house in Balkh and obliged him to flee to the remote mountainous region of Badakhshan, which is now divided between Afghanistan and Tajikistan. Naser loved his Iranian homeland and bitterly resented his exile which continued until his death around 1072. Naser is regarded by all Ismailis in Badakhshan and the areas around Gilgit and Hunza as the great saint who converted them to their true faith. He is referred to as a *Pir* (Master), *Hakim* (Sage) and given the honorific title of *Sayyid* (a descendant of the Prophet). His grave in Yumgan (now called Hazrat Sayyid) is regarded as a shrine and many people, Ismailis as well as Sunnis, go there to offer prayers and honour his memory.

It was during his exile in Yumgan that Naser Khosraw wrote most of his prose and poetical works, which are considered among the best expressions of Persian literature. He is the author of one of the most celebrated prose works of Persian literature the *Safarnameh* (*Book of Travels*), a vigorous, straight-forward and fascinating account of the scenes and events he witnessed during his seven-year long journeys. In his fluid narrative style and accurate observations, Naser is certainly one of the great travel writers. His description of Cairo during the Fatimid empire, its palaces, gardens and markets, is compelling. He was undoubtedly greatly impressed by the Fatimid system of government and the Fatimid Imam-caliphs are mentioned in terms of the warmest praise. His poetry collection, the *Diwan*, is rich, sonorous, full of wisdom and also invectives against his enemies. E.G. Browne, in his *A Literary History of Persia*, commended Naser's poetry for its 'combination of originality, learning, sincerity, enthusiastic faith, fearlessness, contempt for time-servers and flatterers, and courage rarely to be found, as far as I know, in any other Persian poet.'[1]

I had, of course, learnt and read much about Naser Khosraw during my earlier travels to Iran, but my chance to visit Badakhshan came in 1968, the year in which I was awarded a Winston Churchill Fellowship in Exploration. I had as my travelling companion a former student of mine from Wellington College, David Chaldecott. We bought a new landrover and set out through Hungary, Greece and Turkey to Iran. From Tehran we first drove through Afghanistan to Pakistan and visited Ismaili centres in Gilgit and Hunza before returning to Afghanistan. From Kabol we took a plane and travelled to Tashkent, Bukhara, Samarkand and Doshanbe, the capital of Tajikistan, where I was able to talk with members of the Russian Academy of Sciences. Although they could not help me with Ismaili artefacts, they insisted that at the time of Naser Khosraw there had been a very definite Ismaili community embracing the areas of the old province of Badakhshan before it was split into Russian and Afghan zones, the Wakhan, the Hindu Kush, Gilgit and Hunza in Pakistan, and Sinkiang in China. The Soviet academics referred to it as the Pamir state. This could not be conceived as a 'state' as in Iran, but it was united in allegiance to the Ismaili Imams and their reverence for Naser Khosraw.

It was while I was in Doshanbe that I was able to talk to Mr Ziyuddin Khan, the then Mufti of Middle Asia. He told me that there were about three million Shi'a Muslims in Tajikistan and Uzbekistan, and approximately 500,000 Ismailis who acknowledge the Aga Khan as their Imam. He said that it was very difficult to be a Communist and a Muslim at the same time. The older generation were certainly practising Muslims, but most of the younger generation were atheists, though they nominally called themselves Muslim.

Our most useful contact, however, was a diplomat and a poet living in Kabol, Professor Khalili. He told us exactly how to get to Yumgan and where to commence our search for the tomb of Naser Khosraw. The village is 50 km south of Jurm and west of Seyhak. In the course of our conversation, the professor expressed much appreciation of the Ismaili thinker. He said that Naser Khosraw always believed that the Qur'an must be studied from a spiritual and not exclusively a literal point of view. The search for knowledge and the life of the spirit were at the heart of Naser's teachings. The soul must always travel closer to God, despite the disappointments and frustrations of its earthly existence. To this end everyone must seek to live honourably and righteously in keeping with the ethics of Islam. Naser felt profoundly the contradictions of life. For him human existence was problematical, transitory and doomed to decay. Life ought to be lovely, joyous and happy, but instead it is full of disappointment, corruption and deception. Naser felt this keenly and was therefore often angry and pessimistic in his poems. But he was deeply devoted to the Ismaili Imams and took great comfort from the fact that there is a spiritual reward after death for the good and righteous.

Although we were now well provided with information about the exact whereabouts of Naser Khosraw's tomb, we still had to obtain a permit from the Afghan government to travel to Fayzabad and Jurm. At first we were advised to apply to the general commanding the gendarmerie, who approved our request. We took his letter of consent to the Deputy Minister of the Interior and were told that we must first have the approval of the Ministry of Information. An influential Afghan friend then advised us to go to the Foreign Minister whom he described as 'a man of power'. When we saw the Foreign Minister he said quite frankly that he disapproved of the Ismailis, but as he liked the British he would try to help me. He suggested that in the meantime we should spend a few days at the great Buddhist shrine at Bamiyan (now sadly destroyed by the Taliban regime that came to power following the expulsion of the Russians from Afghanistan). This we did and surreptitiously on the way spoke to members of the Ismaili community. They received us in a friendly way and assured us that although the Aga Khan was their Imam they were also good Afghans. To our surprise they said that their ancestors had originally been converted by *da'is* of Hasan Sabbah and they showed me a holy book containing his maxims which their leader kissed.

When we returned to Kabol nothing, of course, had been settled. We were even told that there was something wrong with our tourist visas and we must hand our passports to the police. There could be no question of permission for us to go to Fayzabad as this was forbidden territory. There followed a frustrating period of ten days but we were able to watch the country's independence celebrations called Jeshen. The celebration was in fact a commemoration of Afghan independence from British supremacy. There was a great military parade watched by most of the citizens of Kabol. The parade was led by tanks commanded by Russian officers who stood stiffly to attention.

Eventually after this period of waiting the foreign minister was as good as his word. He brought our case up before a full cabinet meeting who agreed to let us go to Fayzabad provided we took a guide with us. I told the foreign minister that this request was unacceptable. I feared that a guide would probably be more of a hindrance than a help, and in any case he would probably be someone from the Ministry of the Interior. Fortunately the foreign minister laughed and said that he just wanted to be rid of us. He would have the Interior Ministry send letters of approval to the towns we wanted to visit, but he cautioned us that no record of our visit to Badakhshan must ever be put on paper. He wished us good luck and with a great sigh of relief we left Kabol the next day.

On to Badakhshan

Our journey to Badakhshan took us first along the great military highway superbly engineered by the Soviets to enable their armour to reach Kabol as quickly as possible. The first part of the climb to the Salang pass is gentle and passes the high pastures or *yalak*s, which Robert Byron once described as the essence of green, though in summer they are dotted with yellow and blue flowers. Rivulets of clear water ran down each side of the road. The hills were terraced with fields of corn, all very different from Iran and Syria. We passed two camel caravans looking incongruous on the tarmac road. Gradually the vegetation receded and the road twisted and turned as we approached the pass. A series of concrete galleries enclose the road just below the pass carrying mountain streams over their thick concrete roofs. These galleries act, too, as a safeguard against landslides and avalanches. The ceiling of the galleries was arched like a gothic church and we felt as if we were driving through the precincts of a cathedral. The road continued ever upwards and towards the top we could see that it had been blasted out of the solid rock.

The height at the entrance to the final gallery and tunnel is 3,150 metres and in 1968 the highest tunnel in the world. Before you enter the tunnel you can see the original mule-track ascending the last metres of bare rock covered with snow. On both sides of the tunnel great gold and red letters proclaim in Farsi and Pashtu, the two main Afghan languages, that the tunnel was built in 1968 with the help of 'our Russian friends'. The road still rises inside the tunnel until a few green lights and a slight dip herald the end. As we left the tunnel behind our altimeter was reading 3,365 metres.

The descent towards Doshi, our first objective, was not nearly so dramatic. Its only hotel cannot have seen many visitors as all the chairs were covered with a thick layer of dust. News of our arrival soon spread and various prominent local Ismailis came to pay their respects. When we showed them our book containing the late Aga Khan's memoirs, they were highly impressed and kissed the portrait of him. We were given a lot of information about the Ismaili communities in the district. The hotel owner, Sayyid Kayan, told us that he had six sons, but four of them were in prison or under house arrest, another son was a member of parliament and the youngest was still at school. These figures seemed to indicate eloquently the complex and often hostile relations between the Shi'a and Sunni Muslims, which deteriorated further under the intolerant rule of the Taliban regime.

At Doshi we were very near the Oxus river at Termez, but as special permission from Kabol was needed to get there and this would have taken weeks of negotiation to obtain, we decided to take the more direct but very tortuous and dangerous road to Khamabad and Talogan. Afghanistan must be one of the few countries in the world in which there are no railways. In 1968 the only main roads were the perimeter highways running round the borders on the west, south and east of the country and a very bad but passable track through the middle. The northern road scarcely deserved the name of highway. We banged and clattered our way through Khamabad, the luggage at the back of our landrover rising in a great heap and thudding down on the floor at each bump. Sometimes the whole vehicle would be tossed to and fro like a ship in a storm, the occupants hitting the roof, clouds of dust swirling up from the floor and all our belongings being hurled to the floor. We were now in Bactria and had our first glimpse of Bactrian camels, with only one hump, passing arrogantly by. Before long we reached the oasis town of Talogan. As we approached Keshem we saw horsemen proudly riding their beautiful strawberry-coloured, well-groomed mounts. Bactrian horses are fine animals, renowned in history and Alexander is said to have reinforced his cavalry here. We were uncertain as to which road to take out of town, but a friendly Russian in a jeep spotted our difficulty and put us on the right road to Keshem. Here we were received by Mr Dekhan for whom we had a letter of introduction from Professor Khalili. He had been to Yumgan and had seen Naser Khosraw's tomb. He said the tomb had been built 900 years ago and restored 250 years ago. It used to be a regular place of pilgrimage, but had been visited less frequently recently, perhaps because of the government's hostile attitude towards the Ismailis. Mr Dekhan told us that Pir Naser, as he is called, is officially considered a Sunni and not an Ismaili. Naser's brother is buried at Keshem, which was their family home. Mr Dekhan believes that the Pir lived in exile at Yumgan for 25 years. Legends say that his real tomb lies in a cave 40 metres below the top of the hill which was built over it

Keshem is on the provincial border to Badakhshan. We were allowed to pass over and followed a barren, steeply inclined road past hills which jutted up in great diagonal lines. Trees clung starkly to the hillside and the predominant colour was slate-grey. At rare intervals bridges anchored in stone and wood carried the road across the boiling river. Normally most bridges were on the point of collapse, and at one site we saw an iron winch which was almost permanently in use for hoisting buses and lorries out of the stream.

The capital of Afghan Badakhshan is Fayzabad. This is a bustling town and the bazaar sold cotton cloth, brass and tinware, modern ceramics, food, fruit, clothes, guns, agricultural implements, hats, yak brushes and all manner of other goods. By the roadside were a number of tailors working with old-fashioned Singer sewing machines. I decided to buy two silk dressing gowns, shirts and trousers which cost very little. To the amusement of the crowd who gathered round us, I was measured up in the street and the clothes were ready an hour later. Our first job was to present our passports at police headquarters. We anticipated little trouble, but after looking at our passports the police commandant told us we did not have the correct papers and must return at once to Kabol. In vain we protested and told the commandant of our high-up connections in Kabol. But we were not believed and he started to lecture us on the necessity of obeying the laws of a country in which we were guests. Suddenly he spotted some letters on his desk which bore the seal of the Ministry of the Interior. He opened them and began to smile. They informed the local *wali* (governor) and chief of police of our arrival. 'Please, excuse me,' said the commandant who had just called us liars, and sent us on our way, armed with another certificate.

We now followed the Fayzabad river until at length it flowed into the valley of Jurm. Shortly afterwards we reached the hamlet of Eskan. Just outside the village was a beautifully cultivated field of opium poppies with white and dark purple flowers. We smiled at the villagers who were with us. They smiled back and said 'tarok' (opium). Shortly afterwards we noticed a number of similar tarok fields and as we drove up the valley we realised that the cultivation of opium poppies was the staple industry of the valley.

After about 50 kilometres we came to another fertile patch of opium poppies and asked if we were near Hazrat Sayyid, as the village of Yumgan is now called. We were told that we had indeed arrived and we first asked to see Mr Dekhan, whose brother we had met at Keshem, and who had given us a letter of introduction. Mr Dekhan received us very hospitably, although he only spoke a few words of English. Soon we were joined by a group of villagers, among whom was the headmaster of the village school. When he heard why we had come he said we were doubly welcome. Very few foreigners came to the valley. Some Germans had wanted to visit the area the previous year but they had been stopped at Fayzabad. He then went on to say that Naser Khosraw was not only a poet, philosopher and religious leader, but also a good scientist, biologist, astronomer, physicist and chemist, rather like the great Muslim scholar Avicenna.

He talked to us too about the village of Yumgan. There were 1,000 inhabitants and a new school had been built that year called the Naser Khosraw School. There were five teachers and 178 pupils, who were taught the three R's. The district of Jurm has about 30,000 inhabitants. The main products were apricots, tarok, walnuts, barley and potatoes. The cattle were healthy and the milk plentiful. Their needs were simple: breakfast consisted of bread dipped in tea with milk and sugar; for lunch they had fruit and bread, and for supper soup into which they broke bread to make a paste. Sometimes they had meat. The houses contained little furniture apart from carpets on the floor and the quilts and cushions on which people slept. The only 'consumer goods' were some kitchen utensils, a hurricane lamp set on a little wooden stool, a piece of calico on which food was placed, a water ewer and a basin for washing hands.

We lived for three days as the guest of the Ismaili schoolmaster and I much enjoyed my conversations with him. He was quite widely read and had a lively mind. One evening after supper he surprised me greatly by asking my views on the empirical philosopher John Locke who wrote his *Essay Concerning Human Understanding* in 1690. We went on to discuss Cartesian philosophy and the respective merits of the inductive and deductive methods of reasoning. I suppose, in retrospect, that I should not have been so surprised. The search for knowledge has always played a large part in the intellectual life of Ismailis and my village schoolmaster had shown that it still does.

These villagers are very devout. Unlike some other parts of Afghanistan, the Ismaili and the Sunni communities get on well together. Both believe that Naser Khosraw converted them to Islam and it seemed to make little difference to them whether they went to a *masjid* or a *jamatkhana*. There are no doctors in the area and I found myself having to dress an open ulcer on a man's leg and even suturing very unskilfully, I must confess, some deep wounds. I had practised before in the approved traditional manner on an apricot.

The shrine of Naser Khosraw

I do not know whether I am the first European to visit the tomb of Naser Khosraw, but I am sure that I am the first traveller to have described it in detail (Plate 29). The tomb itself is set against a green hill just above Mr Dekhan's house. Mr Dekhan is 'guardian of the shrine' and keeps the keys. The tomb complex is small, built on a natural mound of compressed conglomerate about 14 metres high. To reach it you climb through a charming orchard of apricot trees, where mules, donkeys and horses graze and goats scamper. The complex consists of the shrine chamber in front of which is a small covered balcony; a small devotional room adjoining the shrine; an open cobbled courtyard; and facing the shrine a small mosque with a covered courtyard on one side. All the buildings are white-washed and well cared for.

The shrine chamber built on the compact conglomerate is no more than 7.5 metres wide, 9 metres long and 4.5 metres high with a shallow cupola in the roof. There is a narrow space around the shrine and through two small openings you can get one of the best views of the valley, especially at sunset when the mists begin to rise over the Hindu Kush mountains. The meadows round the shrine are covered with flowers and the building is almost overshadowed by a gigantic and very old plane tree. Two great branches reach out over the open courtyard and cover it and the shrine. The outer balcony is about 6 metres long and 3 metres wide, open on the eastern side facing the plane tree. It is surrounded by a low wooden railing and the wooden sloping roof rests on six carved pillars. There are the remains of plain stucco work on the southern wall and on the eastern wall is an enlarged representation of an opium poppy in full flower! There are two low tombs near the eastern wall, one of which was the tomb of our teacher's grandfather.

A short low passage leads into the shrine, which is lit by three narrow windows, almost just slits. The shrine itself is in the south-east corner and is covered with a green cloth. A metal grille surrounds the shrine covered with a red, green, blue and white cotton and silk cloth. Two incense burners are suspended from the low ceiling, which are said to have belonged to Naser but give the impression of being considerably more recent. There are also curious decorations which look for all the world like decorations on a Christmas tree and had come from England. Three wooden walking sticks with long pointed metal ferrules are placed beside the shrine. They are supposed to have belonged to the Pir and they are wrapped in linen. Three good white and pale yellow carpets cover the floor. They were gifts from the Ismailis of Sinkiang in China given about 150 years ago.

There are two other tombs in the shrine room, but we could not obtain much information about them. These tombs have their own wooden grilles. The roof of the shrine is supported by further wooden poplar pillars engraved with inscriptions from the Qur'an. Four wooden chests covered with circular geometric bronze decorations have been placed in front of the shrine. The lower two are badly damaged but the top two are in good condition. We were told that they were gifts from Bukhara and given 450 years ago when the tomb was restored. Inside one of the chests is a wallet rather like a briefcase and, wrapped in silk, Naser Khosraw's own copy of the Qur'an, according to legend. On the wall the opium poppy appears again with other flowers and landscape scenes.

The devotional chamber next to the shrine is open on one side. Some of the villagers were tempted to say that this was Naser Khosraw's cell, but were contradicted by others who maintained that his home and tomb were 40 metres below. Leaning against the outer courtyard of the shrine were two curious long flagpoles with split steel heads. Strips of cloth were tied to one end and we were told that these represented the Pir's flag of authority. They clearly had not been used for years. The horns and skulls of Marco Polo sheep were hung on the door leading to the shrine. These were said to have been brought as gifts by Ismailis from the Wakhan region of north-eastern Afganistan.

The shrine is well-kept and the atmosphere is one of great reverence, but unlike other shrines I have seen elsewhere in this part of the world there are no crowds of beggars or miracle workers. The small mosque in the courtyard was of no great significance. A sign said that it had been restored 30 years ago and was originally erected 88 years before that. In an outhouse in the courtyard there is a huge brass cooking pot. An inscription says it was donated in 1276/1859 in the name of the King of Afghanistan and intended to provide food for the poor pilgrims who came to the shrine. I wonder how often it has been used and whether it had ever stood on the embers of a fire. It was so large that I doubt if there was enough food in the whole district of Jurm to fill it! Having said that, it was obvious to us that the villagers were quite at home there, the children played happily, and the animals grazed amongst the profusion of blue forget-me-nots and yellow flowers called *gorushka*.

During our stay at Yumgan the schoolmaster and I often sat under the great plane tree talking about religion and Naser Khosraw's philosophy of life. It was harvest time, and perhaps helped by the sounds and scents of the harvest, this was such a peaceful and idyllic scene that I had the impression that even Naser would have felt that the burdens of his exile were now dissolved into something approaching the heavenly paradise for which he yearned.

Before we left Yumgan the schoolmaster insisted that we must visit his school. He, the teachers and all the pupils were dressed in their best clothes, and I and my team felt embarrassed at our bedraggled appearance, even though some of our dirtiest clothes had been washed by the kindly villagers. All the classes were held out of doors, the pupils (boys only) sitting on dry earthen terraces in long rows with a blackboard at the end. We had seen their textbooks before. They were modern and contained pictures of Western schools. The pupils were taught to read and speak correctly by repeating the necessary sounds together and there was a lively chatter as we approached. Someone must have given a signal as suddenly the children stopped their recitation, turned towards me and saluted. They continued to stand as stiff as pokers until I made a little speech. More salutes, cheers, embraces and handshakes. I tried to take photographs of this momentous occasion, but alas I was not very successful in getting the children or their teachers to relax. Then to waves and shouts we started on our return journey. I think all of us felt very privileged to have located and spent a little time at the shrine of one of the great thinkers and poets of Islam and indeed of the civilised world.

The fort of Baltit in Hunza

The most pleasing and aesthetically certainly the most attractive Ismaili castle I have seen is the fort of Baltit in Hunza. The Hunza valley is situated in the Northern Areas of Pakistan, close to the border with China. The nearest town is Gilgit and shortly before you approach Gilgit by road, you pass a stone guidepost pointing to the spot where the three great mountain ranges of the Karakorams, the Hindu Kush and the Himalayas all meet. Hunza is one of the most spectacular of mountain valleys, dominated by the white-washed almost fairytale fortress of Baltit standing proudly as it has for over 700 years in a commanding position on a white marble bluff 600–700 metres above the main river.

I first visited this remarkable valley in 1968. I returned there for over a month in 1982, when I surveyed with my team the rapidly deteriorating fort. My last visit was with Adrianne Woodfine in 2000 after the fort had been skilfully rehabilitated by the Aga Khan Trust for Culture Historic Cities Support Programme. These two places have therefore played a large part in my own research programme and consequently have a special significance for me.

My interest in this part of the Subcontinent had first been aroused by Major-General Shahid Hamid, who had been private secretary to Field-Marshal Sir Claude Auchinleck when he was Commander-in-Chief in India at the time of

Partition. Shahid and I became great friends and when Shahid heard that I had
been awarded a Winston Churchill Fellowship he suggested that David Chaldecott
and I should stay for a time at his house near Rawalpindi. He urged me to go to
Hunza where all the inhabitants were Ismaili and said that he would introduce us
to his friend, the Mir. The Ismailis of Hunza, Chitral, Gilgit and Swat have been
ruled for many generations by their Ismaili dynasties of *mir*s or *nawab*s, centred
at the castle of Baltit.

Naturally I was delighted and at once accepted his kind invitation. Shahid had
already written a book about Hunza and knew the region well. He also suggested
that we should leave our landrover at his home and go to Hunza by air, as the
Karakoram Highway had not then been built and our vehicle was too wide for the
primitive tracks in Hunza. Accordingly we arranged to fly by a Fokker Friendship
aircraft from Rawalpindi to Gilgit. After ten minutes we were over the superb
peaks of the Karakorams glistening white in the snow. The sun was shining on
them and the flight was a breathtaking experience, especially flying close to Nanga
Parbat (height 8,135 metres) which dominates the Hunza valley. The journey is
not without its perils. It is in fact one of the world's most dangerous flights, as the
plane has to constantly avoid touching two great mountains. If the weather is not
good the flight has to be aborted. Fortunately all was well this time, we landed
safely and were warmly greeted by members of the Ismaili community at Gilgit.

We found our discussions with the Ismaili leaders at Gilgit very informative.
In Iran and Afghanistan we were meeting members of a persecuted minority. In
Pakistan, especially in Hunza and Gilgit, the situation was completely reversed.
The Ismailis kindly provided us with a Chinese jeep, a driver and a guide and we
set off for Karimabad, the main town in Hunza. It was only 103 kilometres away,
but in 1968 the journey on the old road which followed the ancient Silk Route took
us six hours. Our journey was one of the most romantic, most beautiful and most
hair-raising I have ever undertaken. At first the road was comparatively gentle, but
as we went further up the valley the landscape became wilder and more majestic.
Great snow peaks and glaciers sparkled in the sun. Glacial streams of water cas-
caded down the mountain sides. The road became ever steeper and was at times
no wider than the jeep. The angle of incline was often over 45 degrees and then the
guide had to sit on the bonnet to keep the four wheels of the vehicle on the track!
Hairpin bends at impossible angles, daunting overhangs, overheating so that the
engine had to be flushed out with ice-cold water were all taken by the driver in
his stride. A hole in the sump was discovered which had to be filled with mud
and slime. At times we could see the outside edge of the track crumbling beneath
our wheels. But in the end we, or rather the driver, won through and we arrived
at Karimabad. We were told that the Mir was spending the night at the old fort, a

message had been sent to him to warn him of our arrival and that we were invited to stay at the guest house. We were given a delicious omelette for supper, washed down with good Hunza wine or *pane*, a mixture of wine, *arak* and sand.

The next day we were admiring the glorious spectacle of the great 7,620 metres peaks when an official invitation arrived in the following terms:

> His Highness the Mir and Her Highness the Rani of Hunza State request the pleasure of Mr P.R.E. Willey and family (or party)'s company for lunch today on 18th June at 13:00 hrs (1 p.m.) at Jand Palace, Karimabad.

We arrived punctually at 1 o'clock and the Mir's secretary hurried down the steps to greet us. We walked into the new modern palace, unpretentious but furnished in good taste. The Mir and the Rani greeted us and took us round the palace. The first thing we noticed was the obvious Chinese influence, good Chinese porcelain, wall-prints and carpets, followed, of course, by the influence of the British Raj: fine silver, good shotguns and pleasant furniture. We drank some excellent Hunza wine before lunch. The Mir and the Rani smoked cheroots during the whole of lunch, as did their guests for the day. Shahid Hamid had clearly sent the Mir a telegram announcing our arrival as we were treated with great deference. It was difficult to talk over lunch, which consisted of soup, *hors d'oeuvres*, curry, cream caramel and green tea, and so I asked His Highness if I might return and talk later and ask him some questions about the Ismailis. He willingly agreed and he was a mine of information. He was a member of the Aga Khan's Supreme Council and was responsible for Ismaili interests in Afghanistan, China and Russia as well as Pakistan. He said that he thought that the Ismaili strength lay in their concept of Imamate and their modern approach. He said that the state of Hunza had existed for at least 900 years. Even when it formed part of Kashmir, the Maharajah (a Hindu) allowed Hunza its own self-government. There were no untouchables in the community and money was not wasted on vain ceremonies. The duty of a ruler was to care for those committed to his charge. The Hunzakuts, as they are called, have their own special language and live to a ripe old age. They help one another to build houses, irrigate the land and tend to their crops. The population is 40,000 and some Hunzakuts claim to be descended from the armies of Alexander. In 1968 Hunza was granted a self-governing status within Pakistan, apart from defence, foreign policy and communication. The Mir's law was absolute and accepted by everyone. There was little crime in Hunza and no police force. Anyone with a grievance came to him. The Mir claimed that there was really no opposition to his rule and from my own observation I could not disagree.

The next day we set out with some pomp and ceremony to visit the old palace or castle called Baltit. It was from there that the Mir's ancestors first ruled this tiny state 900 years ago. We were escorted by the mayor of Karimabad, the *mukhi*, an alert and intelligent man wearing baggy brown pyjama-like trousers and the Hunza flat woollen cap, and the Mir's butler who carried the necessary provisions. He had dyed his moustache with henna. We passed the new school built of brick and stone proudly flying the Ismaili flag of red and green with the earthen polo field in front of it. The game of polo is said to have originated in Hunza and has always been popular among the men in this area. One village had a turf polo ground which seemed as green and smooth as Smith's Lawn at Windsor in England. Hunza is well known for the excellent wood carving on the houses. In the centre of Karimabad there is a magnificent open wooden *jamatkhana* with outstanding carving and traces of the original red and brown colouring, which was founded several hundred years ago when the Hunzakuts converted to Ismailism. The houses are tidy and clean and everywhere the roofs covered with apricots ripening in the sun.

We were given various dates for the foundation of the Baltit castle, which had been the home of all the Mirs of Hunza until 1945 when the present modern palace with its garden and swimming pool was built. There is no groundfloor, but a rickety wooden staircase leads from the entrance to the first floor. The whole palace is small and without any trace of luxury. Most of the old furniture had been removed to the new palace, so inevitably there was a certain air of dilapidation and neglect. Most of the 'state-rooms' were really nothing more than large common rooms with an open hearth in the centre. The smoke escaped through a hole in the roof. Wooden benches ran round the wall in traditional style. An adjoining bedroom had a brick hearth, a wooden bed and built-in cupboards. Occasionally the Mir would leave the comfort of his modern palace and spend a night here. The most 'modern' room was a charming small Victorian drawing room with tinted glass windows. The room had been enlarged beyond the outside walls and was supported by stout wooden beams which somewhat spoilt the symmetry of the rectangular castle. But from these windows which opened wide were the most exhilarating and marvellous views of the valley and the great Karakoram mountains beyond. This was a landscape without parallel and the balcony enabled the traveller to enjoy some of the most breathtaking views which exist anywhere in the world.

The walls of the drawing room were hung with portraits of 19th-century Mirs or early photographs of them standing beside the British Resident at Gilgit. The most amusing exhibit was a coloured reproduction of Queen Victoria, which also served incongruously as an advertisement for Mellin's baby food 'untouched by human hands'.

We were then taken up the rickety staircase to the roof on which was placed the Mir's official throne. This was really just a bench under the horns of a Marco

Polo sheep. Here the Mir would hold court and adjudicate disputes. Above the throne was an inscription in Arabic which said 'There is no hero like 'Ali, there is no sword like Zulfiqar'. These are the words uttered by the Prophet Muhammad when he presented his own double-edged sword to 'Ali, the first Shi'i Imam, after a famous victory on the battlefield.

The castle of Baltit was a perfect gem – part Central Asian, part Victorian, part Hunza. I found it a happy monument to the partnership of the Ismaili state of Hunza and the British Raj.

I returned again to Hunza in 1982 with a small expedition to make a closer inspection of Hunza and the castle and to visit the neighbouring valleys. By now the great Karakoram Highway had been built which was a joint achievement of the Pakistan and Chinese governments. It was still possible to fly by Fokker Friendship plane to Gilgit but the journey on the Karakoram Highway presents few difficulties. In Hunza valley, stretches of the old road which was part of the classical Silk Road still exist, and as I looked at them memories of our challenging journey in 1968 came flooding back to me. But even the new Highway has its own problems. Landslides often block the road in the mountains and swirling dust storms still block out visibility in seconds, presenting a constant menace to drivers of lorries and cars.

Our survey of the castle at Baltit went well. But with an interval of 14 years since my last visit the fabric had deteriorated alarmingly. It was clear that the structure itself was no longer sound and the floorboards and stairs were anything but safe. In fact my team was constantly in danger from crumbling stonework and as we moved we were showered with falling pieces of plaster. We often put our feet through the floorboards and suffered cuts and abrasions. When we returned home we informed the Pakistan Embassy in London of our alarm at the imminent collapse of this historic monument, and the High Commissioner assured us that he had urged his government to take immediate action to prevent any further deterioration to the fort.

It was not until some years later that I learnt that in 1985 the Aga Khan Trust for Culture had commissioned a survey to draw up proposals to save the fort from further decay, and to formulate a long-term programme for the full-scale conservation of the site. In order to implement the conservation plans a new trust was formed, known as the Baltit Heritage Trust, which would transfer the fort from private to public ownership. In their fascinating report on the Karimabad and Baltit Project Development, the Trust outlines the techniques used to restore the fort, which included the necessity of inserting new concrete foundations below the walls as well as restoring the retaining walls at the foot of the fort. During the period of restoration discoveries were made and artefacts uncovered which enabled the archaeologists to determine the different stages of building. The appearance of the fort had been altered several times in its long history with the addition of various towers, a second storey and culminating in the 'gentrification' of the top floor to transform it into a palace with many features drawn from the British colonial buildings in the Punjab. The restorers showed commendable sensitivity in keeping untouched many of the 19th-century rooms, especially the women's area, the Mir's bedroom and the reception rooms which are some of the finest in the fort.[2]

When we returned to Baltit in 2000, Adrianne and I were able to see for ourselves and sincerely admire all that had been achieved by the Trust (Plate 30). We were shown around at the Mir's request by a young man who spoke excellent English which he had learnt at the local school. He evidently shared the pride of everyone associated with the project. We also noticed all sorts of imaginative details the Trust had made to give a genuine atmosphere to the fort. Some of the Mir's private possessions were on display, including the beautiful black and gold cloth of estate which used to cover his throne. Some of his uniforms were on show together with some lovely old carpets, ceremonial robes, swords and weapons. Gratings had been let into the floor, so that you could look down into the cellars and dungeons. The woodwork was particularly impressive. The Baltit Heritage Trust wanted the fort to be a museum and cultural centre and it has achieved its objectives admirably. The Trust hoped, of course, that the fort would bring about an increase in tourism and that it would be recognised as an important cultural centre. Both these objectives have been achieved with corresponding advantages to the village, which is now a wealthy town. Instead of the sleepy, somewhat shabby Hunza I first knew, Karimabad is now a warm, vibrant centre with many shops and other facilities. New houses have been built and a modern water supply, sanitation and electrical systems installed.

In our conversation the Mir told Adrianne and me that the population of Hunza was a close-knit community, tourism was encouraged and most of the goods offered for sale were products of local cottage industries. The Mir appointed two officials to run the day-to-day administration, but he continued to be the final arbiter in the case of disputes. The valley was nearly self-sufficient in foodstuffs and potatoes were a speciality. It had its own doctors and medical services. There were both government and Ismaili schools. He was clearly proud of his family tradition stretching back hundreds of years. His mother, whom I met when I first came to Hunza, was still alive, aged ninety. The Mir struck me as a highly intelligent man with a very modern outlook.

At the end of our conversation the Mir asked us if we had visited the castle of Altit, a few kilometres away. It was pouring with rain but we hired a jeep and found our visit very worthwhile. Altit is of even earlier construction than Baltit. It was built around 1200, and most of the building can still be visited. After Baltit, Altit was very much like stepping back to the Middle Ages. Most of the castle is original, but the stairways and steps are treacherous. The rooms are largely intact, though stripped of any furnishing. There is a special prayer room. The central feature is the great tower which has an uninterrupted view of the main approach. While Baltit became a residential castle, almost a palace, Altit was always meant to be a fortification of some strength as well as an observation post.

Hunza, like Badakhshan, has no great military tradition, despite occasional wars between rival Mirs. Under the leadership of the Aga Khan, the local population, both Ismaili and Sunni, have embarked on a major programme of rural development that has transformed the valley into a fertile and prosperous region. We noticed many tractors, fields of potatoes, wheat and barley, and orchards of walnut, apple and apricot trees. The Ismailis have established many medical clinics and new schools for both boys and girls with a modern curriculum, including English, and equipped with the latest computers. There seem to be many places catering for tourists, including a small teashop near the Hoppa Glacier called the Hilton Hotel! The Aga Khan Development Network has recently opened a first-class hotel in Gilgit, the Serena, to cater for the growing numbers of tourists, especially Japanese, visiting the Northern Areas of Pakistan. Despite its rapid modernisation, this is the land that reflects the peace and tranquillity of Naser Khosraw, on the surface at least, and sheds a peaceful balm in contrast to the turbulence in many parts of the Muslim world.

Notes

1. E.G. Browne, *A Literary History of Persia* (Cambridge, 1902–1924), vol.2, p. 271.

2. The restoration of the Baltit fort won the Award for Excellence from the UNESCO Asia-Pacific Heritage Awards in 2004. For more information on this project, see the Aga Khan Trust for Culture, *Historic Cities Support Programme: Karimabad and Baltit Project Development* (Geneva, 1996).

CHAPTER 16

Epilogue

We know that after the fall of Alamut in 1256, the Mongols massacred a great number of Ismailis throughout Iran. In addition to killing the garrisons of various castles who had surrendered on promise of safe custody, the Mongols put to the sword entire communities in towns and villages. In one incident alone reported by Juwayni the Mongol commander of Khorasan, Otegu-China, summoned the Ismailis of Qohistan to a public gathering and slaughtered all the men. Their women and children were sold as slaves in the markets and their properties confiscated. It is impossible to estimate how many perished in the immediate aftermath of the collapse of the Ismaili state and the following decades of Il-Khanid rule. But it is not unreasonable to suppose that out of a pre-Mongol conquest population of 250,000 Ismailis, nearly half this number may have lost their lives.

It was for long assumed by Persian and Western scholars, following Juwayni, that the Ismaili community of Iran was virtually exterminated by the Mongols, but now we know this not to be the case. In spite of the appalling massacres, many Persian Ismailis survived the horrors of the Mongol conquest, going into hiding in southern Iran or into exile in Afghanistan, Central Asia and the Indian subcontinent, where there already existed substantial Ismaili communities. For those Ismailis who remained in Iran, destitute and demoralised, the doctrine of *taqiyya* or dissimulation was often a lifeline enabling them to assume the guise of Sufis, Twelver Shi'is or even Sunnis in order to avoid further persecution, while at the same time preserving their faith in secrecy.[1] As such they were able to rebuild their shattered lives, the Ismaili mission was reactivated and gradually its *da'i*s became active once again in Daylaman, Qohistan and other areas. Indeed, they made several attempts to recapture Alamut and even succeeded in occupying it for a year in 1275–76 before it was lost again to Hulegu's sons. There is much evidence in local histories to show that although their political power had been broken, the Ismailis continued to be a strong presence in the south Caspian region well into the 14th century.[2]

As we have seen, the last Ismaili Imam of the Alamut period, Rokn al-Din Khurshah, was brutally murdered by his Mongol guards in 1257. Juwayni's assertion that 'He and his followers were kicked to a pulp and then put to the sword; and of him and his stock no trace was left,' was both arrogant and absurd. According to Ismaili tradition, one of Rokn al-Din's sons escaped his father's fate and was never handed over to the Mongols. This son, Shams al-Din, was smuggled out of Maymundez before it fell to the Mongols and escorted to Azarbayjan where he settled down in Tabriz. He succeeded to the Imamate of his father and through him the Nizari line of Ismaili Imams continued. These Imams lived in the greatest secrecy for several generations, and it was not until the 15th century that they re-emerged in Iran. Having established their residence in Anjudan, a small village in central Persia, they began to reorganise their community in Iran, Central Asia and the Indian subcontinent. In the 19th century the Ismaili Imams acquired political prominence in the courts of the Qajar dynasty and were honoured with the title of Aga Khan. This title has been maintained in the family to the present time.

The present Imam of the Nizari Ismailis, His Highness Prince Karim Aga Khan IV, was born in 1936 in Geneva and educated in Switzerland and at Harvard. In this year, 2005, he has been Imam for 48 years, during which he has established an impressive record, both as a spiritual leader of the Ismailis and as a world statesman. Under his leadership, the Ismailis have transformed themselves into a highly organised, modernised and prosperous Muslim community. There are an estimated 15–20 million Ismailis in the world, established in many countries of Asia, Africa and the Middle East, as a well as growing numbers in Europe and North America.

Whenever I travelled in the Middle East, Africa and Asia, I have taken the opportunity to meet Ismailis of all classes and conditions, and I have been struck by their practical idealism and intelligent approach to the problems of modern life. They are singularly devoted to their Imam, whose guidance touches upon virtually every aspect of their worldly and spiritual lives. They take considerable pride in their history and hold fast to the spiritual and ethical tenets of their faith. But unlike many religious communities, Muslim and Christian, the modern Ismailis are refreshingly free of dogmatism and fanaticism, and they no longer seek to convert others to their persuasion. They place great importance on humanitarian and developmental projects in the Third World, which they regard as a fundamental aspect of their faith. These projects are implemented through an impressive number of development agencies, institutions and programmes grouped under the Aga Khan Development Network (AKDN). The AKDN constitutes, in fact, the world's largest private philanthropic organisation. Its services are not restricted to the Ismailis but made available to all people in the poorest parts of the world, especially Asia and Africa, regardless of their origin or faith. The present Aga Khan is anxious to demonstrate that Islam has contributed and continues to enrich the intellectual and cultural heritage of the world. The Ismailis are also well aware of the need to heal the deep breach that still exists between many people of Christian and Islamic persuasions.

I hope that I have given the reader convincing proof that the Ismailis of the Alamut period were anything but the fanatical terrorists, brigands and hashish-eaters of legend. Without doubt the pejorative use of the word 'Assassin' throughout the centuries has blinded us to the real achievements of the Ismailis. The reality is far more extraordinary than the fictions which were circulated about them. To quote Marshall Hodgson:

> That this handful of villagers and small townsmen, hopelessly outnumbered, should again and again reaffirm their passionate sense of grand destiny, reformulating it in every new historical circumstance with unfailing imaginative, power and persistent courage – that they should be able so to keep alive not only their own hopes but the answering fears and covert dreams of all the Islamic world for a century and a half – this in itself is an astonishing achievement.[3]

My research over the last forty years has shown that the Ismaili state in Iran did not depend on a few isolated castles in Daylaman and Qohistan, but that it covered a much larger area in eastern Persia, extending in Khorasan as far as the border with Afghanistan. The Ismailis were highly skilled military architects and exceptionally competent in organising the limited resources at their disposal. Remarkable too were their practical achievements in irrigation and agriculture in mountainous areas.

In the West we traditionally consider a castle to be a strongly defended fortress controlling an important trade route or stretch of land, capable of sustaining a siege of limited duration and giving protection during the siege to inhabitants living in the immediate neighbourhood. We normally think of a Norman type castle, consisting fundamentally of a keep and outer defence works or perhaps the larger castles such as Caernarvon built by King Edward I in the 13th century. A large Ismaili castle was in fact a fortified city, with a substantial military and civilian population, and often containing an important library. The complex was stocked with supplies and provisions which were intended to feed the garrison and a considerable number of people from the surrounding countryside for many years during a siege. A sophisticated water system consisting of diverted springs and catchment areas provided a continuous source of water for men and animals.

The valleys surrounding the fortress produced all the food that was required in time of peace.

The strength of these Ismaili fortresses was essentially due to the following factors:

- The inaccessibility of the chosen site, for example in Alamut, the Rudbar, Qohistan and the Jabal Bahra in Syria, and the difficulty of taking the fortresses by storm. Most of the fortresses were situated on the top of very high crags or even mountain peaks. Many of the sites had, of course, been fortified before, and after the Ismailis had taken possession of these strongholds, they were considerably strengthened and enlarged. The final approach to the defended position was often up sheer rock or scree which precluded any mining or sapping. The only possibility of reducing the fortress was by prolonged siege, but, as we have seen, this involved the attackers in considerable difficulty because the local food supplies had all been destroyed before the siege began.
- The strength of the defences and the advanced military architecture. Many fortresses, such as Soru in the south Caspian region, had triple defensive walls and exceptionally well built and designed gate-towers. The curtain walls were of great strength and amply provided with strong towers, so sited as to bring supporting fire to each other. The slope leading to the fortress was often so steep that it was impossible for the attackers to set up their mangonels within effective range.
- Lastly and most importantly was the high morale of the garrison, which had been evident throughout the construction of the fortresses. Building these elaborate fortresses demanded a huge supply of manpower, equipment and material, and even quarrying the stone was a considerable feat. The organisational ability of the Ismailis must have been outstanding. They were a competent, imaginative and far-seeing group, and the strong conviction of the righteousness of their cause provided them with the inner strength which enabled them to build and defend their castles so successfully.

I have now come to the end of my narrative and I shall feel content if at least I have succeeded in correcting some of the many historical errors that still persist. In addition, I hope I may have thrown some light on a hitherto obscure period of history. I also feel that it is very important that we in the West should evaluate correctly the abilities, skills and achievements of other people in the world. Our cultural and political judgements are still clouded by the after-rays of Empire. Why is it that so many people in the West still tend to believe that the height of civilisation and culture is to be found in the glories of European Christendom and are so ignorant of the great achievements of the Islamic world? This is all part of the somewhat blinkered attitude of many people in the West to the achievements of earlier civilisations of the Eastern world in the arts and sciences. The great Buddhist temples of the Khmer dynasty in Cambodia, culminating in their chief masterpiece at Angkor Wat, is another striking example.

I was originally drawn to my study of Persia and the Orient when as an undergraduate at Cambridge I read the *Westöstlicher Divan* by the German poet Goethe, in which he expresses his sincere admiration for the great Persian poet Hafez, whom he calls his twin brother. Hafez lived in 14th-century Shiraz, when it was ruled as part of Khorasan by a descendant of the Mongol conqueror Hulegu. Goethe's main purpose in writing his *Divan* was to show that true creativity of the spirit transcends all national boundaries and forms a corpus of what he calls *Weltliteratur* (world literature). He stresses that knowledge must always be accompanied by understanding, otherwise it will be sterile. The search for this knowledge and understanding of the Ismailis and their castles has occupied me for more than forty years. I hope that I have shown how lacking this knowledge has been in the past, and that this book will shed new light on a period of history and an important Muslim community which is playing a strategic role today in bringing about greater understanding between the civilisations of Islam and the West, as well as using its unique position to improve the well-being of the disadvantaged in the developing world.

Four decades have now passed since I began my love affair with Iran. It has been a turbulent period. These years of archaeological and historical research have been a time of great richness, despite the hazards, frustrations and hurdles put in my way by the more zealous officials of government, which always accompany enterprises of this kind. I started my research when the Iranian monarchy was still strong. I worked through the beginnings of the Islamic Revolution and felt the hostility that was directed at Westerners, especially Christians, and I finished my work almost twenty years later despite the opposition of the present theocratic régime in Iran. I feel I know the country very well and that my work and acceptance there, especially by the Ismailis, has been a great privilege. Of course, we are all satisfied when we have accomplished, even if not completely, the task we have set ourselves. I am sure that others will take on where I have left off. We must all acknowledge that very little can be achieved without the help and unstinting support of others. I have learnt much during all this time and remember with affection and gratitude those who have taught and helped me. The lesson of history is to value what is good, reject all that is false and to judge aright. And this demands patience and persistence, and even at times obstinacy, coupled with a tint of optimism. Above all, I have learnt the power of faith, of faith that is genuine and sincere and which is used to benefit humanity. Faith and truth should be the keystones of our lives, as should social justice and our duty to protect and help the poor and needy.

In summary, as I wrote in my concluding sentences of *Castles of the Assassins*: 'It is not power that rules the earth, for power is, in the long run, neither strong nor holy. It is the rich warmth of human emotions, friendship and respect for others that builds and sustains.'

This, I still believe.

Notes

1. For more details see Nadia Eboo Jamal, *Surviving the Mongols: Nizari Quhistani and the Continuity of Ismaili Tradition in Persia* (London, 2002), pp. 50–53.

2. Virani, 'The Eagle Returns', cited earlier in Chapter 7, note 6.

3. Hodgson, 'The Isma'ili State', in *The Cambridge History of Iran*, Volume 5, p. 482.

Research Expeditions led by the Author

Archaeological and historical research expeditions led by Peter Willey from 1959 to 2000 to locate and describe Ismaili castles and other sites in the Middle East, Pakistan and Central Asia. Also included is the author's research into human rights abuse for Anti-Slavery International, the United Nations Human Rights Commission and the European Parliament.

1959   Oxford University expedition to the Alborz Mountains. First visit to Alamut and location of the site of Maymundez.

1960   Alamut valley expedition. Investigation of Samiran castle, followed by approach to the Alamut valley from the Caspian. Preliminary examinations of Lamasar, Alamut castle, Nevisar Shah and a detailed investigation of Maymundez. Made film for Anglia TV on Samiran and Maymundez.

1961   Article in *The Times* announcing the location of Maymundez and other research findings. Expedition sponsored by the BBC to film the ascent and interior of Maymundez for their 'Adventure' programme.

1963   Second expedition to investigate Samiran. Publication of *The Castles of the Assassins*.

1965   Expedition to Isfahan to examine the castle of Khanlanjan.

1966   First expedition to Khorasan. Investigations of Gerdkuh, Birjand, Tabas, Ferdaws, Esfedan, Afin and Zuzan. Publication of article 'Assassin Forts' in *Geographical Magazine*.

1967   Second expedition to Khorasan and Qohistan to study Ismaili sites in greater detail. Publication of 'Persian Odyssey' in *Explorers Remember*.

1968   Sir Winston Churchill Fellowship Expedition.
        Research into Ismaili sites in Syria, Pakistan and Afghanistan.

Discussions with Russian Academy of Science in Doshanbe, Tajikistan.

Visit to the tomb of Naser Khosraw in Badakhshan, Afghanistan. Further research in Khorasan and Qohistan. Investigations of Furk, Mo'menabad, Shahdez and Alamut.

Publication of article on 'Assassins of Qa'in' in *Geographical Magazine*.

1969	Resarch at request of Anti-Slavery Society on the problems of narcotics, slavery and other issues of human rights in Afghanistan.
1970	Expedition to Syria. Investigation of Masyaf and other sites. Comparison of Ismaili and Crusader castles.
1971	Investigation of forced prostitution for Anti-Slavery International and the United Nations Human Rights Commission in Turkey. Publication of *Drugs and Slavery in Afghanistan* by the Anti-Slavery Society (London, 1971).
1972	Led 50–strong expedition to Alamut, supported by British and Iranian armies. A detailed investigation into all aspects of the Ismaili state in Alamut and Taleqan Valleys.
1973	Second visit to Turkey continuing research into forced prostitution.
1978	Expedition to Qohistan to prepare a map of as many Ismaili sites as possible. The Iranian Revolution of 1979 prevents further research in Iran for the next 17 years.
1982	Expedition to Hunza and the Northern Areas of Pakistan.
1984–85	Expeditions with young Europeans to Iceland and Africa.
1990–91	Human Rights expeditions to Turkey.
1993	Publication of *Forced Prostitution in Turkey* by Anti-Slavery International, (London, 1993).
1994	Further research in Turkey, accompanied by Adrianne Woodfine.
1995	Visits Tehran to discuss continuation of research on Ismaili castles.
1996	Research work with Adrianne Woodfine at Alamut, Gerdkuh and northern Khorasan.
1997	Further detailed research work in Khorasan and Semnan. Discovery of Soru and adjacent fortifications.
1998	Joint research work in Syria. Investigation of Kahf. Comparison of Ismaili, Crusader and other castles.
2000	Joint research work in Hunza, Chitral and Swat in the Northern Areas of Pakistan.
2001	Publication of the American edition of *The Castles of the Assassins*.
2004	Article on 'Isma'ili Monuments' in *Encyclopaedia Iranica*.

APPENDIX II

List of Ismaili Castles and Fortifications

This Appendix gives the names and approximate positions of various Ismaili sites in Iran and Syria visited by the author with Adrianne Woodfine and his research teams, as well as the dates of their initial location. The list includes a number of sites reported by other sources, but it is by no means exhaustive[1] For ease of reference, all sites are listed according to region and in alphabetical order.[2] The following nomenclature has been used in categorising the size and importance of the sites:

Major fortress	An important Ismaili centre, as well as being strongly defended. It may often cover a large area, but not necessarily so as in Alamut.
Castle	A strongly defended site, guarding a strategic point, but not a major centre.
Fort	A military site, well defended, but not of special strategic importance.
Watchtower	A small defended site whose primary purpose is to give warning of the approach of hostile forces, and also used as a communications centre.

Alamut Valley and the Rudbar

Alamut	Major Ismaili fortress and headquarters of Hasan Sabbah near Gazorkhan.	1959
Amameh	Castle, south-east of Alamut (reported by W. Kleiss).	
Andej	Two castles, east of Alamut, a ceramic centre.	1960
Ayin	Fort, near Dikin, west of Maymundez.	1972
Bahramabad	Subsidiary castle of Lamasar.	1972

Bidelan	Strong castle, also called Badasht, south-west of Alamut, defending approach from Taleqan valley.	1960
Borj/Barak	Two forts built halfway up each side of the entrance gorge.	1960
Dozdaksar	Castle opposite the village of the same name. Also a pottery site.	1972
Dikin/Wastah	Two forts guarding the approach routes to the Alamut valley from the north-west on the old road from Lamasar to Shams Kelayeh.	1959
Garmarud	Castle of considerable size near the western village of Garmarud, but there are no remains of walls or buildings.	1959
Ghutinar	Castle, south-west of Alamut (reported by W. Kleiss).	1972
Hasanabad	Subsidiary fort of Samiran, near Menjil.	1960
Hazarchan	Fort and watchtower in the upper Taleqan.	1966
Ilan	Castle, north-west of Nevisar Shah.	1960
Keya Kelayeh	Subsidiary castle of Lamasar.	1972
Key Ghrobad	Castle, 14.5 km south-west of Nevisar Shah, in the Taleqan valley.	1972
Koch-e Dasht	Watchtower, near Garmarud.	1966
Lal	Fort, north of Shirkuh, above the Shahrud Bridge.	1972
Lamasar	Major fortress, north of Shahrestan Bala, with subsidiary castles.	1960
Mansuriyya	Castle in the Taleqan valley, south-west of Nevisar Shah.	1972
Maymundez	Major fortress, near Shams Kelayeh north-west of Alamut	1959
Nevisar Shah	Major fortress, above eastern Garmarud.	1960
Qal'eh Asara	Castle, south-east of Alamut (reported by W. Kleiss).	
Qal'eh Dokhtar	Castle, west of Samiran, on the road to Tabriz (reported by W. Kleiss).	
Qal'eh Sang	Castle in the Taleqan valley, south-west of Nevisar Shah.	1972
Qal'eh Zohak	Castle, west of Samiran, on the road to Tabriz (reported by W. Kleiss).	
Sa'adatkuh	Castle, in the Rudbar.	
Samanghan	Subsidiary castle of Samiran.	1960
Samiran	Major castle, west of Menjil.	1960
Sanamkuh	Castle, near Abhar, west of Qazvin	

	(reported by F. Daftary).	
Sarjahan	Castle in the district of Tarum.	1960
Saveh	Castle, near Qomm.	1960
Shahrud	Remains of many other forts on the Shahrud.	1960
Shirkuh	Large fort at the western entrance to the Alamut valley.	1959
Taleqan	Remains of several other forts.	1960
Tashvir	Castle, north-west of Samiran.	1960
Tvishehey Semeh	Subsidiary castle of Lamasar.	1972
Zavarak	Watchtower, west of Nevisar Shah.	1960

Qumes and the South Caspian region

Cheshmeh	Castle.	1997
Firuzkuh	Major castle. Remains of many other castles, forts and watchtowers in the area.	1997
Gerdkuh	Major fortress complex surrounded by its ring of defensive forts.	1966
Jironsefid	Castle, near Cheshmeh (reported locally).	1997
Kelar Khan	Watchtower, near Firuzkuh.	1997
Lajevardi	Substantial castle, near to Firuzkuh.	1997
Mansurehkuh	Large castle, near Gerdkuh. A Mongol castle is nearby.	1997
Mehrin	Castle, 20 km from Damghan, also known as Mehr Negar.	1997
Ostunavand	Castle near Gerdkuh on the road to Mashhad (reported locally).	1997
Qa'leh Biar	Castle at Biajormand, north of Shahrud (reported locally).	1997
Sara Anza	Castle, near Firuzkuh.	1997
Shahmirzad	Two castles, 20km from Semnan.	1997
Shir Qa'leh	Castle, near Shahmirzad.	1997
'Soldiers Castle'	Fortified barracks, near Firuzkuh.	1997
Soru (Greater)	Major fortress, 17 km north of Semnan.	1997
Soru (Lesser)	Subsidiary fortress, 2 km north-east of Greater Soru.	1997
Vehel	Castle, near Cheshmeh	1997
Zaydar	Castle, between Firuzhkuh and Mashhad (reported locally).	1997

Qohistan (north of Qa'in)

Ahangaran	Castle, north-east of Esfedan.	1967
Ayask	Watchtower, north-west of Qa'in near Sarayan.	1967
Bidokht	Castle, near Gonabad.	1997
Bihud	Castle, on Sarayan road, 30km west of Qa'in.	1967
Dezbad	Two or three castles. Pivotal centre of communications to Gerdkuh and Khorasan.	1996
Faruth	Small castle, near Gonabad (on old road between Ferdaws and Qa'in).	1967
Kalat	Castle, south-west of Gonabad.	
Kandar	Castle, near Nishapur.	1997
Khayrabad	Castle, near Ahangaran (reported locally).	1967
Khaf	Castle, 120 km south-east of Torbat-e Haydarieh.	1997
Khargerd	Large castle, near the *madrasa*.	1997
Khazri	Small castle between Qa'in and Gonabad north of Sarayan.	1967
Khusf	Castle, north-east of Khargerd.	1966
Mahsuk	Castle, south-west of Sedeh.	1968
Mazar	Castle, north of Ferdaws near Bagestan.	1967
Qal'eh Dokhtar	Large fortress, 13 km south of Ferdaws.	1966
Qal'eh Gholam	Small castle, near Ferdaws and Sarayan.	1966
Qal'eh Hasanabad	Medium sized castle, north-west of Ferdaws. Also called Qal'eh Kuh.	1966
Salameh	Large hill fort, north of Khaf.	1966
Shahli	Fort, west of Qa'in on Sarayan road. Also called Qal'eh Dokhtar.	1967
Tabas	Castle, south-west of Ferdaws.	1966
Torbat-e Haydarieh	Large watchtower, seen in 1966, disappeared in 1997.	1966
Tun (Ferdaws)	Numerous castles and forts.	
Tus	Substantial ruins of Mongol character, with some indications of Ismaili occupation.	1996
Zaydar	Castle, south of Mashhad (reported locally).	1997
Zuzan	Castle, 30 km south-west of Khargerd.	1997

Qohistan (south and east of Qa'in)

'Afin	Two castles, south-east of Esfedan.	1966
Asadabad	Subsidiary fort, close to Furk.	1997

Aviz	Two castles, 70 km east of Qa'in.	1972
Birjand	Many castles and forts in the area.	1966
Chardeh	Underground castle of 40 rooms, north-west of Sehdeh (reported locally).	
Chehel Dokhtar	Fortress, south-east of Qa'in.	1997
Darmiyan	Castle, close to Furk.	1968
Dorokhsh	Castle, 30km south of Zordu.	1966
Esfedan	One castle, 50 km east of Qa'in.	1967
Fayzabad	Castle, east of Birjand.	1967
Furk	Strong castle, 80 km south-east of Birjand.	1968
Gazik	Castle, east of Birjand close to the Afghan border.	1967
Gholam Kosh	Strong castle, at Dareh, 16 km south-east of Birjand.	1997
Jangal	Castle, 20km west of Birjand.	1966
Khoshk	Castle, north-east of Sedeh.	1997
Khoshareh	Castle north of Nehbandan (reported locally).	1967
Khunik	Walled city and castle, north-east of Birjand.	1997
Khunik	Fort, near Nehbandan.	1997
Kuh-e Shaken	Castle near Birjand (reported locally).	1967
Mud	Castle and walled estate, 30 km south of Birjand.	1997
Mo'menabad	Major fortress and walled city, south-east of Birjand, now inaccessible.	1967
Nasrabad	Two adjoining castles, both major structures, at Garsak near Tabas Masina.	1966
Nawghab	Castle near Mo'menabad. Also know as Qal'eh Dokhtar.	1967
Nehbandan	Major fortress, probably the site of the ancient settlement of Neh, now largely 'mongolised'.	1997
Nik	Observation posts, mostly underground, near Birjand.	1997
Qa'in	Major fortress and centre of Ismaili Qohistan.	1967
Qa'lat-e Sayeh	Remains of a castle, south of Qa'in.	1967
Qa'leh Nasr	Castle, 80 km south of Birjand.	1997
Sangan	Castle, south-west of Sedeh.	1968
Sarab	Small castle, north-west of Sedeh.	1967
Sarbisheh	Large castle, 80 km south of Birjand. Of early Islamic period, occcupied by the Ismailis. .	1978
Sedeh	Three small castles, 50 km south of Qa'in.	1967
Shahanshah	Major fortress, near Nehbandan. Also known as Shahdez.	1967

Shardeh	Three small forts, near Birjand.	1997
Shusf	Two small castles, 60 km north of Nehbandan, both of Sasanian origin, occuppied by the Ismailis.	1978
Tabas Masina	Castle, north-east of Mo'menabad.	1966
Unik	Two castles, north of Dorokhsh.	1966
Zordu	Large castle, south-west of Afin.	1972

Isfahan, Arrajan and other regions

Beriz	Castle, near Bandar Abbas (reported by W. Kleiss).	
Kerman	Castle, north of Kerman (reported by W. Kleiss).	
Khanlanjan	Fortress, near Isfahan, also called Kuh-e Boz.	1965
Lar	Castle, near Bandar 'Abbas (reported by W. Kleiss).	
Qala't Haldan	Castle, 50 km north of Arrajan, also known as Dez Kelet (reported by H. Gaube).	
Qala't-e Jess	Castle, 15 km north-east of Arrajan, close to modern Behbehan (reported by H. Gaube).	
Qala't-e Nizar	Castle, 30 km north of Arrajan (reported by H. Gaube).	
Shahdez	Major fortress, near Isfahan.	1966

The Jabal al-Summaq in Syria

Afamiya	Strong castle in northern Syria.	1970
Azaz	Castle, north of Aleppo (reported by B. Lewis).	
Bab Buza'a	Castle, between Azaz and Aleppo (reported by B. Lewis)	
Inab	Castle, south of Ma'arrat Misrin.	1970
Kafarlatha	Fortified town, west of Inab.	1970
Ma'arrat Misrin	Castle, south of Bab (reported by B. Lewis).	
Qala'at Jabar	Fort east of Aleppo, overlooking the Euphrates.	
Qala'at al-Mudiq	Castle, north of Shayzar (reported by A. Mirza).	
Sarmin	Fortifications, near Ma'arat Misrin.	1970

The Jabal Bahra (Jabal Ansariyya) in Syria

Abu Qubais	Small round castle, north of Khariba.	1998
Baniyas	Ismaili centre and castle, in modern Lebanon.	
Hasbayya	Ismaili centre, in modern Lebanon.	
Hisn al-Sharqi	Castle, south of Khawabi (reported by A. Mirza).	
Kahf	Major fortress and Sinan's palace.	1970

Khariba	Castle, north of Qadmus.	1970
Khawabi	Strongly fortified town, quite near the coast.	1970
Maynaqa	Castle, near Ullayqa.	1970
Masyaf	Major fortress and centre of Ismaili power.	1970
Qadmus	Strong castle in the centre of the Jabal.	1970
Qulay'a	Castle, near Krak des chevaliers (reported by A. Mirza).	
Rusafa	Castle, near Masyaf, with subsidiary castle nearby.	1970
Shayzar	Strong castle, west of Khariba.	1970
Ullayqa	Castle, east of Khariba.	1970
Wadi al-Yun	Castle, south of Khawabi.	

Notes

1. More information on Ismaili castles and their locations in Iran can be found in Manuchehr Sotudeh, *Qela'-e Isma'iliyya dar reshteh-ye kuha-ye Alborz* (Tehran, 1996), and Faruq Furqani, 'Ismailis' in *Historical Atlas of Iran* (Tehran, 1999), pp. 82–86.

2. I would like to thank very warmly Anna Enayat, Farhad Mortazaee and Kutub Kassam for their assistance in finalising this Appendix.

Ismaili Pottery from the Alamut Period

Rosalind A. Wade Haddon[*]

The Nizari Ismailis of the Alamut period and their secretive society have captured the imagination of many researchers and writers. For example, in the 1970s there was a Japanese team of archaeologists surveying much the same areas of Iran as Peter Willey and his team. The only testimony to this is a report, written in English, in the Cultural Heritage Central Archives in Tehran, which I chanced on in October 2003, when searching for a report on Nishapur ceramics by an Iranian archaeologist. The Japanese report, dated 1972, entitled *Report on the Study of Ismaili Castles*, was written by a Dr M. Honda of Hokkaido University, Sapporo. This covered the Qohistan and Damghan areas over a period of three months, in which they recorded twenty Ismaili castles, starting in Qa'in, and the castle of Qal'ehkuh (*sic*), which he saw as one of the most important Ismaili sites in Khorasan. He appeared to cover much the same area that Peter Willey had in his two reports of 1967 and 1969, which were also produced for me. At this stage I was unaware of the fact that I would be invited to contribute to this volume. There was a promise of a book to be published in 1974, which would include the Japanese study of the Alamut area carried out in 1970, but subsequent enquiries have established that this was never published, and Dr Honda passed away in 1991.[1]

Although the Nizari polity in Persia lasted over 150 years,[2] we do not, as yet, have any pottery defined as 'Nizari' or 'Ismaili'. This does not mean that they did not manufacture their own diagnostic wares; it simply means that insufficient archaeological work has been carried out in their known strongholds and settlements to establish such a fact. Indeed, we will see below that Peter Willey's team may well have identified a typical Nizari product. It is to be hoped that this picture will gradually change as both national and international teams work at these numerous sites. Three seasons have already been carried out at Alamut, under the direction of Madam Chubak of the Cultural Heritage Department, and the preliminary report is now available; unfortunately I was unable to obtain a copy before going to press. The picture is no clearer in Syria, although the Levantine Crusader castles are better studied, and some of the Syrian strongholds such as Qala'at Jabar and Shayzar. This is why Peter Willey's past surveys are so important and his determination to publish his findings is a great credit to him. While they cannot positively define anything, they provide a small, completed corner of a vast jigsaw puzzle. He also has the good fortune to possess information on the excavated remains of a small kiln, something that has eluded many archaeological missions on Muslim sites in the Middle East. He has already touched on this in the main text and it will be discussed below.

Before discussing the pottery finds, a few points should be made with regard to the current state of research into medieval Islamic ceramics. The greatest problem is that of the use of coin dating for archaeological contexts. This was first noted by Miles in the 1950s, based on the American excavations at Istakhr,[3] and amplified by Northedge who indicates that there is an absence of copper coinage for the 9th–11th centuries, from excavated levels at most Middle Eastern sites.[4] In consequence, after 800 CE dating is relative to the excavated sequences, up to the mid-12th century, which accounts for the rather fluid dating found in museum catalogues. Furthermore, on many of the sites, because these medieval levels are uppermost, they have been greatly disturbed by both natural and human intervention, which has destroyed archaeological evidence. In north-west Iran the sites of Takht-e Sulayman[5] and Sultaniyya[6] have been excavated and produced comparative material for the Ismaili castle finds; I have seen material from these two sites in the pottery storage of the National Museum in Tehran. At many of the key sites there are also imported Chinese and South-east Asian wares, which assist these relative sequences, and conversely some of the luxury Abbasid lustre wares have been found in datable contexts in South-east Asia.

Because of this relative sequencing, the reader will find wide variations in the dating of some of the glazed wares which are more distinctive and easier to identify than the everyday utilitarian unglazed coarse wares. When we reach the late 12th/early 13th centuries, we arrive at some dated, finer, stonepaste or composite-bodied, tablewares and tiles to assist us. Perhaps at this point I should just stop to explain the terminology here. In the literature you will find many terms for these whiter wares, which the medieval potter evolved to imitate Chinese porcelains. The process of creating this quartz-based body was fortunately documented by the Persian bureaucrat Abu'l Qasim, who came from a famous Kashan pottery family, in his treatise dated 700/1301, and modern scientific analysis has confirmed the accuracy of his description.[7] The technology was introduced to Europe in the 15th century, where it was styled 'softpaste porcelain'. There is no such standardisation for works on Middle Eastern ceramics though, and you will see 'fritware', 'faience', 'stonepaste' or 'composite-bodied' used. Stonepaste has been coined from the modern Farsi *sangineh-saz* or 'stonepaste potter'.[8] When you handle the material you see so many different variants that I prefer the term 'composite-bodied', because it is not always instantly recognisable as a quartz-based body, as opposed to earthenware with a sandy temper.

The most relevant ware for us to pursue in this study is those lead-glazed, slip-painted, earthenware vessels decorated with incised designs, which cut through the slip through to the reddish body to accentuate the designs, commonly known by the Italian term *sgraffiato*. Even here, by the 14th century potters were using the same decorative technique on some composite-bodied, underglaze-painted wares. In eastern Iran these *sgraffiato* wares developed from the slip-painted wares, but those found in western Iran had no such transition.[9] Rudolf Schnyder, the ceramicist for the German archaeological team at Takht-e Sulayman sees early production commencing at the end of the 10th century,[10] and a later, unpublished German report, cited by Morgan, indicates that these wares form the largest part of the glazed ceramic assemblage up to around 1300. Returning to the Ismaili castles we will see the relevance of this diversion.

In 1972 Peter Willey's team archaeologist, Tony Garnett, reported that their most important discovery was at Andej, a small attractive village near Alamut, the site of Hasan Sabbah's headquarters before his occupation of the citadel at Alamut. Describing the site location he states:

> The pottery site was discovered on a rounded poplar covered hilltop, 75m above the valley floor, and about 2 km south-west of the village. The hilltop was formed by a resistant outcropping sill of vesicular basalt, containing large amygdales, part of a much larger geological feature which stretched for some miles along the Alamut valley. Behind it and around it rose to a much greater height the typical coarse conglomerates of the area. The arenaceous nature of these conglomerates preclude the possibility of clay beds forming, whereas the igneous basalt rock contains the felspars essential for the formation of clay. Very small quantities of a fine textured greyish coloured clay were found in some of the irrigation channels which intersected this fertile hilltop, but the exploratory pits which were dug to try and locate larger deposits revealed only deep topsoil covering solid rock. It was concluded that

the clay deposits may have been exhausted or that they are now heavily concealed by recent cultivation.

The actual pottery site was located by the scattering of sherds lying in profusion in the cultivated fields around the sides of the hill. These sherds were more numerous in the small gullies of the irrigation channels and increased in density towards the hilltop which was crowned by a small level field, surrounded by poplar trees and a thick bramble hedge. In the roots of these bushes thickly condensed layers of kilnwasters were found, and on the slopes immediately surrounding this field many fragments of vitrified kiln fabric and other sintered material pointed to earlier kiln structures.[11]

Garnett continues to describe a structure that was excavated on the eastern slope, which he interpreted as a kiln, and is better described in an abbreviated article he published in the *Bulletin of the Experimental Firing Group*:

The kiln followed the pattern of many other medieval Islamic pottery kilns, but was smaller than most examples. It measured 64cm across, was constructed of a fired clay wall, cylindrical in shape and approximately 25cm high and 5cm thick. It was supported on three quite large stones. It had been partially exposed and destroyed by water action in a small gully. Surrounding it was a 5cm thick layer of white ashy soil, while inside, in layers, were varying levels of charred ash and burnt earth. In front of the kiln there was a group of stones which may have been a support for an air duct. To the side of this was a fire-hardened rectangular area, which may have been the bottom of the entry to the fire-box. Inside the bottom of the kiln was similarly fire-hardened, leaving in softer unfired earth the typical curved protruding shape of the kiln-floor support.

Inside the kiln itself was a variety of pottery, including the large fragment of a complex decorated dish, several tripod stilts, pieces of other glazed dishes and unglazed cook-pot ware, heavily textured with inclusions. On other parts of the kiln site were found two glazed oil-lamps, part of a basalt quern-stone, several small bowls, and many pieces of sintered kiln fabric and over-fired kiln wasters, together with large quantities of decorated dish fragments.[12]

He goes on to describe the wares as being:

...relatively unsophisticated, lead-glazed, sgraffiato ware decorated with scroll-like arabesques incised through a white covering slip, and then additionally painted with brush-strokes of copper, iron and manganese oxides. The whole was then covered with a transparent glaze, mostly honey in colour, but tingeing grey-green in areas of greater reduction in the kiln. The dishes were wide-rimmed which was where the incised and brush-applied decoration was located, and had well-turned foot-rings.

They also found large quantities of unglazed water-pot fragments. He describes the fabric as being '... usually of a fairly fine-textured buff coloured body, mostly light in colour and well oxidised in the firing. However, some of the glazed bowl fragments were of a much darker colour, indicating a reducing atmosphere in the kiln, and many showed distortion through over-firing'. These were all illustrated in line drawings in his report, but unfortunately we have no photographs of these fine decorated rims, and no examples were found in either the British Museum stores or Peter Willey's private collection. There are a few fragments from Alamut that I assume are Andej ware. I did find two of Garnett's photographs in an article written by James Allan in 1974.[13]

The only positively identified Andej-fabricated material available is a few base sherds, one with the tripod-stilts still attached in Peter Willey's collection. Other finer, luxury-ware fragments, possibly from Kashan, found in the village indicate that it had once been a wealthy community.

A puzzling fact in this discovery is the kiln itself. In his report Garnett included line drawings of the Siraf, Takht-e Sulayman, Nishapur and Afrasiyab kilns to compare with his own. He states that they are all of similar construction, but an overriding fact cannot be ignored – the Andej kiln is considerably smaller, with much thinner walls. The others are all two metres plus in diameter. Unfortunately he did not appear to excavate a section of it before clearing the debris to reveal the remaining structure, or to demonstrate that the base had once been below ground level. The nearest structures comparable in size are the two small glazing ovens in the pottery complex at Siraf.[14] It is tempting to propose that this is what Garnett excavated. Some of the dishes he discovered were apparently over 30 cms in diameter, so it is hard to imagine how they could have been stacked and fired successfully in such a small structure, whose actual kiln chamber diameter was unlikely to have measured more than one metre, extrapolating from information supplied by the other kilns. With all the debris that they found littered over a wide area, there is no denying that there was a pottery complex; we just need to positively identify the kiln's usage. Garnett estimated that this kiln material 'suggested that there may have been a dozen or so kilns in different parts of the hilltop'. Apparently all evidence has now been removed by the agriculturalists, so unless there is more material below the present-day fields, unfortunately we may never have a fuller picture. Garnett was able to identify a pottery series in these *sgraffiato* wares, examples of which he states were found at all the Ismaili sites in the Alamut area. Thus, it is of utmost importance to bring this material to a wider audience.

In what follows, I have attempted to match up fragments from the Willey collection in the British Museum[15] and those from his personal collection to

Garnett's 'Record of Finds from Castles and Other Sites' listed at the end of his report (sherds unless stated otherwise), but due to the generalised labelling it has been rather conjectural. Unfortunately there are very few unglazed cooking wares and water pots in these two available collections.

Ayin (a fortress near Dikin, behind Maymundez)

Hand-made cooking pots; unglazed water pots; slip decorated ware; fine red cooking-pot ware (Lamasar type); Kashan underglaze-painted ware; underglaze bowl (*sic*), coarse type with clear glaze.

Alamut

Lead-glazed Andej ware; unglazed water pots; fragment of lusterware, possible part of an oil lamp; piece of Safavid blue and white ware (Mashhad?) with black slip design (Plate 31).

Andej

Lead-glazed slip and *sgraffiato* wares; two almost complete oil lamps; quern; unglazed water pots; cooking pots, kiln fabric and kiln tripod stilts (Plates 32 & 35).

Qal'eh Sang (a castle in the Taleqan valley)

Large decorated water pots and glazed Andej ware.

Chillisdari

Red ware, hand-made cooking pots; glazed Andej wares (plain and decorated); blue glazed coarse pottery; fragment of blue and white tin-glazed pottery.

Dozdaksar (a fortress site opposite the village)

A cooking pot, in fragments, but half complete, found in a gravel promontory 20 feet (*sic*) above the valley floor; glazed Andej ware; unglazed cooking pots and water pots.

Hanarak

A fragment of Safavid blue and white underglaze-decorated ware; blue glazed water pot with a red fabric; a white slip decorated and incised water pot; glazed Andej ware, with a fine untypical design. See Plate 33 for an illustration of glazed water pot fragments found in the British Museum collection. Although I would describe this colour as turquoise blue, it is the only glazed water pot preserved. Later Garnett uses 'cobalt blue,' so it is probably safe to conclude that this illustration is the Hanarak pot. Unfortunately the registration numbers only indicate that they are from the Alamut region. The vessel has a red body and is also tempered with coarse black grits.

Kay-Ghrobad (a castle in the Taleqan valley)

Fired pottery cistern, probably for water storage fed with connecting interlocking pipes, three extant (pipes measuring 38cm by 15cm, illustrated in both the report and Garnett's 1984 article). He comments that there was no kiln material in the vicinity, so was definitely not connected with a pottery workshop. In addition they found fragments of a decorated blue bowl and an unglazed sprinkler top (this could also be interpreted as a filter and was illustrated by a line drawing in the report).

Lal (a castle above the Shahrud Bridge)

Handle of a dark red-bodied cooking pot; other cooking pot fragments; glazed Andej ware, both fine and decorated; and coarse plain ware.

Lamasar

Two pieces of Chinese celadon ware; a fragment of tin-glazed pottery; many pieces of blue underglaze decorated pottery, some Safavid *circa* 17th century; plain cobalt blue fragments; glazed Andej wares; cooking pots; various decorated unglazed water pots; and turquoise and cobalt blue glazed tiles.

Mansuriyya (a castle in the Taleqan valley)

Fine white fabric water pots; underglaze decorated turquoise glazed wares; large unglazed water pots with handles; lead glazed bowl with copper and manganese design, not made in Andej; bright green glazed wares; and a fragment of a white unglazed water pot with a stamped design.

Nevisar Shah

Pieces of iron ore; glass fragments; pierced foot of an unglazed bowl – when this occurs in glazed wares, commentators report that these holes are for display purposes, but I think that there is a more practical use: in the absence of cupboards, most utensils had to be suspended around the walls for convenience, and therefore the hole is for storage purposes; cooking pot rim and lug; unglazed jug handles; fine textured red fabric ware; superb fragment of lusterware with cobalt blue exterior; underglaze-painted turquoise glazed wares (Kashan?); clear glazed pottery over a white slip and underglaze design; tin-glazed pottery with blue decoration; piece of tin-glazed blue decorated ware; tin-glazed wares (Plate 34).

Samiran

Garnett lists this collection without indicating that Samiran is considerably further west, situated 'some 12 miles to the west of Menjil and lies on the Qizil Uzun, a tributary of the Sefid Rud'.[16] He cites in the collection: plaster stamp with incised design; pieces of alkaline blue pottery; clear glazed wares with a blue design on a white slip (this could be the wares illustrated as possibly being from Nevisar Shah); Andej ware fragments and some green glazed pottery. Garnett does not mention the almost complete *sgraffiato* bowl, now in Peter Willey's collection (Plates 37 & 38). It was found incorporated into one of the defensive walls. It measures 27 cm in diameter, 14.7 cm in height and the foot diameter is 11.2 cm. Its red earthenware body I assume to be diagnostic Andej ware, but I did not find any similar vertical rimmed bowls in Garnett's profiles, or the distinctive vertical ridges around the exterior – there are four extant, and most probably six originally. It is partially coated with a white slip and glazed with the typical honey-coloured glaze. The incised decoration is schematic, with a band of roughly drawn circles on the exterior rim, with vertical lines dividing them in half; the interior has two bands of scrolls below the rim, and four teardrops with diagonal crosses suspended from the lower band, separated by schematic 'Y' shapes, the space at the top infilled with crosshatching. The incised lines reveal the red body contrasting strongly with the glaze and slip. There are tinges of green indicating iron in the glaze. The conical profile with the high vertical rim and applied exterior ridges is distinctive, and there was one identical green-glazed rim fragment #S35 or OA+15257 (its incised exterior decoration is a more elegant foliated scroll, under a green glaze, and the interior an undecorated mottled yellow glaze) in a group collected from Samiran by Professor Michael Rogers and Mr Ralph Pinder-Wilson, now housed in the British Museum storage in a box labelled 'Northwest

Iran'.[17] It can be compared with a similarly shaped bowl excavated by the German team at Takht-e Sulayman and illustrated in their 1976 exhibition catalogue,[18] dated to the 12th/13th century. This Samiran collection included Timurid sherds too, and would seemingly indicate more continuous occupation.

Shirkuh (a castle in the Alamut valley)

Glazed Andej wares; unglazed water pots; white slip tailed pottery on unglazed red fabric.

Shrine site (near Lamasar)

Tile fragment, tin-glazed with blue design; and finely decorated Andej sherds.

Khorasan and Qohistan finds

Garnett did not include the pottery from these surveys in his report. Box 45 in the British Museum contains four bags of Khorasan wares, but not all are from Ismaili castles. For example there is a collection from a Saljuq tower at Karat. From personal observations this is certainly located on a *tepe* or occupation mound, which would have been occupied during the Alamut period. Peter Willey has more material stored at home, and we looked through material from Firuzkuh (Qohistan), Gerdkuh (Damghan), Furk (southern Khorasan) and Ayiz (Khorasan). The material from Ayiz was an almost complete Ilkhanid underglaze painted so-called Sultanabad T-rim bowl, decorated in a series of alternating geometric panels in cobalt and black on a fine white composite body (Plates 39–40). However, it showed the tell-tale signs of local restoration using a fine gypsum plaster, and incorporating rogue sherds from another similarly decorated vessel; so I can only conclude that it was purchased during the course of the survey. It is a fine example, but its provenance is a little doubtful for our purposes. There is an almost identical bowl on display in the Birjand Museum, and we should not discount a Khorasanian manufacture for these wares; so from this viewpoint it is useful to add to the corpus.

There would appear to be a difference between the eastern and western wares, with many more plain, coarse turquoise, and turquoise and black wares in Khorasan. A coarse buff body seems to predominate in Khorasan, contrary to the distinctive red body in the west. When much of the ongoing archaeological work is published, I think we will find many clearer definitions of these wares, and hopefully the Iranian archaeologists will soon be able to identify typical regional wares and establish the provenance of the more widely distributed luxury wares.

Kahf (a Syrian castle near Masyaf)

There were no Syrian sherds in the British Museum collection, but we did find one bag in Peter Willey's collection. The sherds from Kahf (Plate 38) were all heavily abraded and consisted of white slipped, red bodied *sgraffiato* wares similar to those in Box 128 of the Alamut collection in the British Museum (Plate 35). This completes our brief survey of the pottery information culled from Peter Willey's surveys. This was pioneering work and will certainly assist in defining the Islamic pottery sequence in Iran.

Notes

*Rosalind A. Wade Haddon is currently a PhD candidate at the School of Oriental and African Studies, University of London, focusing on Iranian underglaze-painted wares of the 14th century. She has an MA degree in Islamic Art and Architecture from the American University in Cairo and was for several years archaeological adviser to the National Museum in Sana'a, Yemen. All photographs for this article (in the Plate section) were taken by the author and remain her copyright. Thanks to Drs Venetia Porter and Sheila Canby at the British Museum, and Dr Massoud Azarnoush and Mr Reza Mirkhalaf of the Cultural Heritage Department in Tehran.

1. I am grateful to Dr Yuka Kadoi at the University of Edinburgh for this information on Dr Honda.
2. Azim Nanji, 'Nizariyya,' *Encyclopaedia of Islam*, 2nd ed.,vol. 8, p. 84.
3. G.C. Miles, *Excavation Coins from the Persepolis Region* (New York, 1959).
4. Alastair Northedge, 'Friedrich Sarre's Die Keramik von Samarra in Perspective,' in *Continuity and Change in Northern Mesopotamia from the Hellenistic to the Early Islamic Period*, ed. K. Bartl and S. Hauser (Berlin, 1996), p. 230.
5. Excavated by a team from the German Archaeological Institute in the 1960s and 1970s. See the catalogue written by Rudolf and Elisabeth Naumann entitled *Takht-i Suleiman: Ausgrabung des Deutschen Archäologischen Instituts in Iran* (Munich, 1976).
6. These were from the excavations of Dr Saeed Ganjavi, carried out before 1989. The site is currently being excavated by Professor Sa'id 'Ali Asghar Mirfatah, but at the moment he is clearing architectural features on the citadel and is nowhere near the purported workshops.
7. J.W. Allan, 'Abu'l Qasim's Treatise on Ceramics,' *Iran*, 13 (1973), pp. 111–120.
8. Hans E. Wulff, *The Traditional Crafts of Persia* (Cambridge, MA, and London, 1966), p. 151.
9. Peter Morgan, 'Sgraffiato. Types and Distribution,' in Ernst J. Grube, ed., *Cobalt and Lustre: the First Centuries of Islamic Pottery* (London, 1994), p. 120.
10. Rudolf Schnyder, 'Mediaeval incised and carved wares from North West Iran,' in *The Art*

of Iran and Anatolia from the 11th to the 13th Century AD (London, 1974), pp. 85–95.

11. Unpublished report submitted to Peter Willey.

12. Tony Garnett, *Bulletin of the Experimental Firing Group*, 3 (1984–85), pp. 115–127, at p. 122.

13. James W. Allan, 'Incised Wares of Iran and Anatolia in the 11th and 12th Centuries', *Keramos*, 64 (1974), pp. 15–22.

14. David Whitehouse, 'Excavations at Siraf', *Iran*, 9 (1971), p. 15.

15. Stored in box number 128, 167–176 and 369, with registration numbers OA+14456–15232.

16. Willey, *Castles of the Assassins*, p. 83.

17. This holds accession numbers OA+15233–15305, which are pottery and glass sherds collected in Samiran and Qala'at.

18. Nauman, *Takht-i Suleiman*, note 5: pl 4 (#90); it has six medallions around the cavetto, below some scrolling bands, and is 32 cms in diameter and 13.5 cms in height.

Ismaili Coins from the Alamut Period

Hussein Hamdan and Aram Vardanyan*

Introduction

For a period of about 120 years the state of the Nizari Ismailis produced its own coinage, of which around sixty specimens can be traced today in collections outside Iran that were available to the authors. The first isolated coins were published in 1859 by Bartholomae and Soret. Subsequently, Paul Casanova (1893), George Miles (1972) and Igor Dobrovol'skiy (1980) attempted to give an overview of the material. Compared to what is known now, these studies presented fragmentary insights which did not clarify the monetary history of the Nizari state. While it seems today that the general outlines of this history have become well-known, it has to be borne in mind that, even with the multiplied material of today, major gaps remain. Not a single coin has been found that could be dated securely to the second quarter of the sixth century AH. New dates and new coin types continue to turn up and will modify and extend the picture.

The first attempt to organise a coinage in the Nizari-controlled state was made by the da'i Bahram in Baniyas, which he had received as a fief from the Burid Tughtikin (497–522 AH), the lord of Damascus. At first glance these coins (see no. 43 of catalogue below) appear to be ordinary black dirhams of the Burid atabeg of Damascus with the main sentences of the creed and names and titles of Tughtikin and his son Buri. However, at a closer look, the lack of the obligatory Abbasid caliph's name as well as the inclusion of the Shi'i addition to the creed "Ali is the friend of Allah' point to its origin. Finally, clarification comes from the unusual marginal legend 'Aid comes from Allah and victory is near' (Qur'an, 61:13), which is occasionally found on earlier Islamic coins issued in historical situations under military pressure,[1] to which the words *li-mawlānā* or 'For our mawla' are added. Mawla, 'our lord', referred to the Nizari Ismaili Imams. However, as Baniyas lost its backing from Damascus and was soon uprooted, its coinage remained merely an episode.

It was only in 536/1141 that the third lord of Alamut (Muhammad b. Buzurg-Ummid) took the initiative of starting to mint in Alamut itself, which continued to the times of the Mongol conquest. A major gap in the surviving coinage during the second quarter of the sixth century AH may either represent a break in minting activity or only a lack of hoards as a result of a comparatively peaceful period. For the first eighty years until 618/1221, only gold coins were struck.

These gold coins from Alamut were relatively small coins of apparently very high purity. Their weight was random, as was customary for many types of eastern Islamic gold coins from the third to eighth centuries AH. Weights around one gramme are most frequently found. When used in payments, such coins had to be weighed. In this way the fraudulent use of clipped coins in commerce could be avoided. They represent a regional coinage distinct from their neighbours. In the Syrian Jabal, the last Saljuqs and their successors produced dinars during the second half of the sixth century AH that were much more alloyed and of poor technical quality and higher weight, generally between 1.5 and 2 grammes.[2] To the west in Azarbayjan no gold but in some mints copper coins and in other mints heavily alloyed silver were minted, while foreign gold circulated alongside the copper.

Only at the beginning of the Nizari Imam 'Ala' al-Din Muhammad's reign in 618 AH were silver coins introduced. Coins of fine silver had been virtually non-existent in Saljuq Iran. However, during the second half of the sixth century AH some sort of regional gold coinage in Kerman and Khorasan became so heavily debased that they were virtual silver coins. On the other side, in Syria proper silver dirhams of classical weight (2.97g) had been reintroduced by Salah al-Din in 571 AH, and the Saljuqs of Rum had followed that model. Both Ayyubid and Rum Saljuq dirhams circulated in Armenia and Azarbayjan by the time of the Mongol invasions, and they were systematically overstruck by the first Mongol coinage in this region from 631 AH onwards. The Nizari Ismailis seem in this respect to have been influenced by eastern Iranian development as the dirhams of Alamut, as well as the Ghurid and Khwarazmshah dirhams, varied in weight like the gold coins. The introduction date 618 AH of the silver points to a likely direct linkage to the Mongol invasion under Genghis Khan in 617 AH, which caused waves of fugitives to come from eastern Iran and Central Asia westwards, presumably carrying with them a large stock of coined silver.

Next to gold and silver coins, copper coins are also said to have been minted in the Nizari state, but none could be traced in available collections.[3] This would be plausible as copper was widespread in Azarbayjan.

The mint was never called by the name 'Alamut' but by its honorific name *Kursi al-Daylam*, in later years often extended by the epithet *Baldat al-iqbal*, the 'City of Good'. This use of an official rather than the popular name may be paralleled by the Abbasid practice, where coins minted in Baghdad from the origins invariably name the mint as *Madīnat as-salām*, and in the third century AH the mint of Samarra was always named *Surra man ra'a*.

No other mints can be named, although towns in Qohistan under Ismaili control may also have had a second mint. A slightly doubtful dinar of crude style and base gold struck under the Nizari Imam Jalal al-Din al-Hasan (no. 24), may well explain its differences from the coinage of Alamut with a Khorasani origin.

The inscriptions of Nizari coins are primarily religious as on all medieval Islamic coins. They follow the Fatimid coinage with the addition of the phrase *'Alī walī Allāh* to the basic contents of the *shahāda*. Furthermore, in the early coinage of Alamut, the recognition of the Fatimid Nizar with his caliphal titles was essential. But when Jalal al-Din al-Hasan attempted his rapprochement with the Abbasid caliph al-Nasir li-Din Allah around 611 AH, his name and caliphal title replaced Nizar's. Unfortunately, none of the few surviving coins of this period reveal legible dates. A splendid large gold coin (no. 30) of uncertain attribution with the name of Muhammad b. al-Hasan bears the phrase *lā imām illā amīr az-zamān Nizār*, 'There is no Imam except the Commander of the Age, Nizar'. This has been regarded by the authors as an early donative coin of the Imam 'Ala' al-Din Muhammad, whose legend stresses the reason for his reversion to Nizari doctrine in 618 AH. The coin remains problematic as the date is illegible and the style resembles most strongly the few known coins from the early reign of Nur al-Din Muhammad (equally a Muhammad b. al-Hasan), struck nearly half a century earlier. But a stylistic reversion may have been part of the religious programme in itself, and if so it would not contribute to the dating. However, on all other late coins the religious statements become irregular: Nizar is almost never and 'Ali only rarely mentioned. Only the systematic omission of the Abbasid caliph's name points to the Ismaili origin after 618 AH.

The titulature of the lords of Alamut as mirrored by their coins underwent a drastic evolution. Initially, Muhammad b. Buzurg-Ummid presented his name devoid of any titles, while the subsequent lords of Alamut (who were all recognised as Imams) were, at least until 574 AH, unpretentious and allowed only the name of Nizar on the coinage. However, with the rapprochement with the Abbasid caliphate, the lords of Alamut adopted worldly titles and styled themselves *as-sulṭān al-a'ẓam*, 'the great sultan'. This can be regarded as an arrogation of the position which had passed from the Saljuq sultans to the Khwarazmshahs, whose reputed dinars of Nishapur had a very similar appearance. Occasionally the title was replaced by the lower ranking *al-sulṭān al-mu'aẓẓam*, 'the powerful sultan'. A similar fluctuation appears also on the contemporary coins of the Khwarazm-shahs; these changes seem to have been of little importance, but the Rum Saljuqs retained the lower ranking title as long as the Khwarazmshahs continued to govern the old Saljuq empire.[4] At various times the later lords of Alamut replaced the sultanic title with their proper religious title of *al-mawlā* (nos. 27, 35, 40), but they never used the designation of *Imam* on the coins. It is not quite clear whether these changes represented political conditions or whether the different titles addressed different groups of their followers.

Some of the Nizari silver coins bear figural representations, such as birds or lions formed out of the names of Imams (nos. 38, 41, 42). Although this is unusual for Islamic coinage in general, it cannot be regarded as a peculiarity of Shi'i or Ismaili coinage. Representations of animals and weapons appear frequently on coins minted in the Islamic East from the mid-sixth century AH for one century, and in Khorasan even until about 690 AH.

Finally, we wish to express our gratitude to those people and organisations which assisted us with providing numismatic materials. We would like to thank the Library of The Institute of Ismaili Studies, and Mr Muhammad Limbada of London, for putting at our disposal the images of some Ismaili coins, as well as Dr Ariel Berman of Qiriyat Tiveon, Israel, for giving some valuable information on early Nizari coins known to him.

Our special thanks must be given to Dr Lutz Ilisch, the Director of the Forschungsstelle für Islamische Numismatik, University of Tübingen, without whose scientific assistance and support this catalogue would have never been prepared.

Notes

* Hussein Hamdan is a student of Islamic sciences and Iranian studies at Eberhard-Karls-University in Tübingen. Aram Vardanyan is undertaking PhD studies on Islamic coins at the University of Tübingen. The preparation of this catalogue was facilitated and supervised by Dr Lutz Ilisch, the Director of the Forschungsstelle für Islamische Numismatik at the University of Tübingen.

1. See G. Miles, *The Numismatic History of Rayy* (New York, 1938), pp.151, 161.

2. L. Ilisch, 'Goldmünzen aus dem Gibal um 600 H.', Jahresbericht 2000, *Forschungsstelle für Islamische Numismatik* (Tübingen, 2001), pp. 14–16.

3. E. Zambaur, *Münzprägungen des Islams* (Wiesbaden, 1968), pl. 12, lists a copper coin struck in Rudbar in 604 AH with a reference to the Fonrobert collection which seems to be erroneous, perhaps a confusion with an Ayyubid issue of al-Ruha, the mint which forms the neighbouring column to Rudbar. However, the numismatist Mohammad Limbada (London) informs us that he once saw in the coin trade a Nizari copper coin of this period with the representation of a bird.

4. N. Aykut, *Türkiye Selcuklu Sikkeleri* (Istanbul, 2000), vol. 1, pp. 158–162.

Bibliography

ANS Annual Report, no. 2. New York, 1966.

Artuk, I. *Istanbul Arkeoloji Müzeleri Teshirdeki Islami Sikkeler Katalogu*, vol. 1. Istanbul, 1971.

Aykut, N. *Türkiye Selcuklu Sikkeleri*. Istanbul, 2000.

Bartholomae, I. 'Lettre à M. Soret sur des monnaies koufiques inédites rapportées de Perse,' *Revue Numismatique Belge*, 3 (1859), pp. 432–434.

Casanova, Paul. 'Monnaie des Assassins de Perse,' *Revue Numismatique*, 3 série, (1893), pp. 343–352.

——*Catalogue des Pièces de Verre. Collection Fouquet M. Miss.*, vol. 6, Fasc. 3. Cairo, 1893.

Centuries of Gold. The Coinage of Medieval Islam, ed., E. Draley-Doran. London, 1986.

Dobrovol'skiy, I. 'O monetakh ismailitov Alamuta,' *Soobscheniya Gosudarstvennogo Érmitazha* (Leningrad), 45 (1980), pp. 66–68.

Ilisch, L. 'Goldmünzen aus dem Gibal um 600 H.' *Jahresbericht 2000, Forschungsstelle für Islamische Numismatik* (Tübingen, 2001), pp. 14–16.

Markov, A. *Inventarny Katalog Musulmanskikh Monet Gosudarstvennogo Imperatricheskogo Ermitazha*, vol. 1. Saint-Petersburg, 1896.

Miles, George C. *The Numismatic History of Rayy*. New York, 1938.

——'The Coins of the Assassins of Alamut,' *Orientalia Lovaniensia Periodica*, 3 (1972), pp. 155–162.

Qingxuan, D. and J. Qixiang. *Xinjiang Numismatics*. Hong Kong, 1991.

SNA-Sylloge Nummorum Arabicorum, vol. 6, Palästina, ed., F. Schwarz. Tübingen, 2001.

Vasmer, R. 'Spisok monetnykh nakhodok,' *Soobschenija Akademii Istorii Material'noy Kul'tury*, 1 (1928), pp. 287–308.

Zambaur, E. *Münzprägungen des Islams*. Wiesbaden, 1968.

Museums and Collections

ANS: The American Numismatic Society, New York, USA.
BNF: Bibliothèque Nationale de France, Paris, France.
IIS: The Institute of Ismaili Studies, London, UK.
IAA: Israel Antiquities Authority, Jerusalem, Israel.
SII. State Hermitage, Saint-Petersburg, Russia.

SHMA: State History Museum of Armenia, Yerevan, Armenia.
Tübingen: Forschungsstelle für Islamische Numismatik, Universität Tübingen, Germany.
Azami Collection: Ch. A. Azami Collection, Tehran, Iran.
Mohammad Limbada, London, UK.

Auction Catalogues and Price Lists

Album S., *Price List*, 1992, no. 91, Santa Rosa, CA, USA.
Album S., *Price List*, 1993, no. 96, Santa Rosa, CA, USA.
Album S., *Price List*, 1994, no. 104, Santa Rosa, CA, USA.
Album S., *Price List*, 1994, no. 112, Santa Rosa, CA, USA.
Morton & Eden: Ancient, *Islamic, British and World Coins, Historical Medals* (in association with Sotheby's), London, 2004.
Spink Zürich, *Catalogue of Coins of the Islamic World*, Zürich, 1988, 1991.
Peus: Auktion Katalog von Dr. Busso Peus Nachf. Münzhandlung (Frankfurt), 2004.
Sotheby's: *Coins, Medals and Numismatic Books*, London, 1991.
Münzen und Medaillen A.G. Basel, *Jean Elsen Auction Catalogue*, Brussels, 1986, 1988.

Catalogue

Muḥammad b. Buzurg-Ummid (532–557/1138–1162)

(1)   Kursī al-Daylam, 53(6?) AH (gold)

Obv: *Lā ilāh / illā Allāh / Muḥammad / rasūl Allāh*

Marginal legend: *Bismillāh ḍuriba hādhā al-dinār bi-Kursī al-Daylam sanat (sitt?) wa thalathīn wa khamsmiʿa*

Rev: *ʿAlī walī Allāh / al-Muṣṭafā / li-dīn Allāh / Nizār*

Marginal legend: *Amīr al-muʾminīn ṣalawāt Allāh ʿalayhī wa ʿalā abāʾihī al-ṭāhirīn wa abnāʾihī al-akramīn*

Ref.: Spink Zürich 27, 1988, p.69, no.370 (1.13).

(2)   Kursī al-Daylam, 536 AH (gold)

Obv: *Lā ilāh / illā Allāh / Muḥammad / rasūl Allāh*

To the left: *Buzurg-Ummīd.* To the right: *Muḥammad ibn*

Marginal legend: *Bismillāh al-raḥmān al-raḥīm ḍuriba hādhā al-dinār bi-Kursī al-Daylam sanat sitt wa thalathīn wa khamsmiʿa*

Rev: *ʿAlī walī Allāh / al-Muṣṭafā / li-dīn Allāh / Nizār*

Marginal legend: *Amīr al-muʾminīn ṣalawāt Allāh ʿalayhī wa ʿalā abāʾihī al-ṭāhirīn wa abnāʾihī al-akramīn*

Ref.: Münzen und Medaillen A.G. Basel 69, 1986, p. 18, no.107 (1.76; 18); Münzen und Medaillen A.G. Basel 73, 1988, p.53, no.423 (2.47; 18).

(3) Kursī al-Daylam, 536 AH (gold)
Obv: *Lā ilāh / illā Allāh / Muḥammad / rasūl Allāh*
To the left: *Buzurg-Ummīd.* To the right: *Muḥammad ibn.*
Marginal legend: *Bismillāh ḍuriba hādhā al-dinār bi-Kursī al-Daylam sanat sitt wa thalathīn wa khamsmi'a*
Rev: *'Alī walī Allāh / al-Muṣṭafā / li-dīn Allāh / Nizār*
Marginal legend: *Amīr al-mu'minīn ṣalawāt Allāh 'alayhī wa 'alā abā'ihī al-ṭāhirīn wa abnā'ihī al-akramīn*
Ref.: SHMA, no.6337 (0.97; 14,9); Peus 369, 2001, p. 96, no.1756 (0.76).

(4) Kursī al-Daylam, 537 AH (gold)
The same type as no. (3).
Ref.: Miles, 1972, p.156, no. 1 (1.01; 14) = BNF (acq. in 1969).

(5) Kursī al-Daylam, 538 AH (gold)
The same type as no. (3).
Ref.: Spink Zürich 31, 1989, p.59, no.318 (1.05); Peus 343, 1995, p.68, no.1025 (1.06) = Peus 348, 1996, p.77, no.1145.

(6) Kursī al-Daylam, 538 AH (gold)
Obv: *Lā ilāh / illā Allāh / Muḥammad / rasūl Allāh*
To the left: *Buzurg-Ummīd.* To the right: *Muḥammad ibn*
Marginal legend: *Bismillāh ḍuriba hādhā al-dinār bi-Kursī al-Daylam sanat thamān wa thalathīn wa khamsmi'a*
Rev: *'Alī walī Allāh / al-Muṣṭafā / li-dīn Allāh / Nizār*
Marginal legend: *Amīr al-mu'minīn ṣalawāt Allāh 'alayhī wa 'alā abā'ihī al-ṭāhirīn wa abnā'ihī al-akramīn*
Ref.: Sotheby's, 1985, no. 442.

(7) Kursī al-Daylam, 541 AH (gold)
The same type as no. (3).
Ref.: Tübingen, no. FE4 D3 (0.90; 16).

(8) Kursī al-Daylam, 542 AH (gold)
The same type as no. (3).
Ref.: Bartholomae, 1859, pp.432–4; Casanova, 1893, pp.343–52; Markov, 1896, p.403, no.1 (0.83; 15,5) = (SH, no.1292); Miles, 1972, p.156, no.4 (1.01; 15).

(9) Kursī al-Daylam, 548 AH (gold)
The same type as no. (3).
Ref.: Casanova, 1893, pp. 344; Miles, 1972, p.156, no. 4 = BNF, no. 3561 (1.01; 15).

(10) Kursī al-Daylam, 548 AH (gold)
The same type as no. (6).
Ref.: Artuk, 1971, p. 341, no. 1042 (0.80; 15); Miles, 1972, p.156, no. 3 (1.12;17); Sotheby's, 1987, p.61, no. 868 (1.34); BNF, no.3559.

(11) Kursī al-Daylam, 549 AH (gold)
The same type as no. (3).
Ref.: Peus 333, 1992, p.76, no. 1111 = IIS, (1.02; 16).

(12) Kursī al-Daylam, 551 AH (gold)
The same type as no. (2).
Ref.: Casanova, 1893, pp. 343–344; Vasmer, 1928, pp. 287–308; Miles, 1972, p. 157, no. 6 (1,19; 16); BNF, no. 3560.

(13) Kursī al-Daylam, 553 AH (gold)
The same type as no. (6).
Ref.: ANS Annual Report 1966, no. 2 = Miles, 1972, p.155 (0.63; 14); Sotheby's, 1988, p. 31, no. 284 (0.76).

(14) Kursī al-Daylam, 555 AH (gold)
The same type as no. (2).
Ref.: Vasmer, 1928, pp. 287–308; Miles, 1972, p. 157, no.7 = Azami Collection (16mm).

(15) Kursī al-Daylam, 556 AH (gold)
The same type as no. (6).
Ref.: SH, no. 3139 (0.97; 16); *Centuries of Gold*, 1986, p. 46, no. 134 (1.06; 15,5).

(16) Kursī al-Daylam, 5XX AH (gold)
The same type as no. (2).
Ref.: Sotheby's, 1981, no. 373 (1.67).

(17) Kursī al-Daylam, 5XX AH (gold)
The same type as no. (2).
Ref.: Peus 333, 1992, p.76, no. 1112 (0.90).

al-Ḥasan (557–561/1162–1166)

(18) Kursī al-Daylam, 560 AH (gold)
Obv: *Lā ilāh / illā Allāh / Muḥammad / rasūl Allāh*
Marginal legend: *Bismillāh ḍuriba hādhā al-dinār bi-Kursī al-Daylam sanat sittīn [wa khamsmiʿa]*
Rev: *ʿAlī walī Allāh / al-Muṣṭafā / li-dīn Allāh / Nizār*
Marginal legend: *Amīr al-muʾminīn ṣalawāt Allāh ʿalayhī wa ʿalā abāʾihī al-ṭāhirīn wa abnāʾihī al-akramīn*
Ref.: Artuk, 1971, p.341, no. 1042 (0.80; 15); Sotheby's, 1986, p.46, no.579 (1.10).

(19) Kursī al-Daylam, 561 AH (gold)
The same type as above no. (14).
Ref.: Tübingen, no. FE4 D5 (1.40); Peus 374, 2003, p.72, no. 1256 (0.95).

Nūr al-Dīn Muḥammad b. al-Ḥasan (561–607/1166–1210)

(20) Kursī al-Daylam, 56 [4/7/9] AH (gold)
The same type as no. (18).
Ref.: CIS.

(21) Kursī al-Daylam, 5[70] AH (gold)
Obv: *Lā ilāh / illā Allāh / Muḥammad / rasūl Allāh*
Marginal legend: *Bismillāh ḍuriba [hādhā al-dinār] bi-Kursī al-Daylam sanat [sabaʿīn wa] khamsmiʾa*
Rev: *ʿAlī walī Allāh / al-Muṣṭafā / li-dīn Allāh / Nizār*
Marginal legend: *Amīr al-muʾminīn ṣalawāt Allāh ʿalayhī wa ʿalā abāʾihī al-ṭāhirīn wa abnāʾihī al-akramīn*
Ref.: Sotheby's, 1984, no. 134 = *Centuries of Gold*, 1986, p. 46, no. 133 (1.31; 15); Spink Zürich 31, 1989, p. 59, no. 319 (3.07).

(22) Kursī al-Daylam, 57[4] AH (gold)
Obv: *Lā ilāh / illā Allāh / Muḥammad / rasūl Allāh*
Marginal legend: *Bismillāh al-raḥmān al-raḥīm ḍuriba hādhā al-dinār bi-Kursī [al-Daylam] sanat [ar]baʿ wa sabaʿīn wa khamsmiʾa*
Rev: *ʿAlī walī Allāh / al-Muṣṭafā / li-dīn Allāh / Nizār*
Marginal legend: *Amīr al-muʾminīn ṣalawāt Allāh ʿalayhī wa ʿalā abāʾihī al-ṭāhirīn wa abnāʾihī al-akramīn*
Ref.: Spink Zürich 31, 1989, p. 59, no. 320 (0.60).

Jalāl al–Dīn al-Ḥasan b. Muḥammad (607–618/1210–1221)

(23) Kursī al-Daylam, date illegible, (gold)
Obv: *Lā ilāh illā Allāh / Muḥammad rasūl Allāh / [al]-Nāṣr li-dīn Allāh / amīr al-mu'minīn*
Marginal legend: *Bismillāh al-raḥmān al-raḥīm ḍuriba hādhā al-dīnār bi-Kursī [al-Daylam] al-hijjra*
Rev: *Al-sulṭān al-a'ẓam / Jalāl al-dunyā wa / al-dīn Abū al-Fatḥ / al-Ḥasan ibn Muḥammad*
Marginal legend: *Bismillāh huwa al-ladhi arsalahu rasūlahu bi'l-huda wa dīn al-ḥaqq liyuẓhirahu 'alā al-d[īn]*
Ref.: Tübingen, no. FE4 E2 (3.97; 20,5).

(24) Mint and date illegible (gold)
Obv: *Lā ilāh illā A / llāh Muḥammad ra / sūl Allāh an-Nā / ṣr li-dīn Allāh*
Rev: *Allāh / as-sulṭān al-mu'aẓẓam / Jalāl al-dunyā wa / al-dīn Abū al-Fatḥ / al-Ḥasan ibn Muḥammad*
Ref.: Tübingen, no. FE4 E3 (3.86; 25).

(25) Mint and date illegible (gold)

Obv: *Al-Imām / Lā ilāh illā Allāh / waḥdahu lā sharīk lahu / an-Nāṣr li-dīn Allāh / amīr al-mu'minīn*

Marginal legend: *Unread.*

Rev: *[Muḥamm]al rasūl Allāh / ṣalla Allāh / al-mawlā al-mu'ayyad Abū / Muḥammad al-Ḥasan*

Marginal legend: *hādhā al-di[nār]*

Notes: In the word 'Allāh' between the letters the word "aliya' placed.

Ref.: Tübingen, no. 92–44–13 (pale gold, 2.63; 21).

'Alā' al–Dīn Muḥammad b. al-Ḥasan (618–653/1221–1254)

(26) Kursī al-Daylam, 650 AH (gold)

Obv: *Lā ilāh illā Allāh / Muḥammad rasūl Allāh / 'Alī walī Allāh*

Marginal legend: Arsalahu bi'l-huda wa dīn al-ḥaqq liyuẓhirahu 'alā al-dīn kullihi wa lau kariha al-mushrikūn

Rev: *Al-ṣulṭān al- / a'ẓam 'alā al-dunyā / wa al-dīn Muḥammad ibn / al-Ḥasan*

Marginal legend: *Ḍuriba hādhā al-dīnār bi-Kursī al-Daylam fī sanat khamsīn wa sittami'a*

Ref.: Sotheby's, 1986, p. 47, no. 580 (3.43).

(27) Kursī al-Daylam, 651 AH (gold)

Obv: *Al-mawlā / al-aʿẓam*

Marginal legend: *Ḍuriba hādhā al-dīnār bi-Kursī [al-Daylam]*

Rev: *Muḥammad ibn / al-Ḥasan*

Marginal legend: *sanat aḥda wa khamsīn wa sittamiʾa*

Ref.: Tübingen, no. 94–33–5 (1.69; 14); Album, 1992, 91, p.2, no. 68 (1.6); Album, 1993, 96, p.2, no. 53 (0.8); Album, 1994, 104, p.1, no. 31 (1.5); Album, 1994, 112, p.1, no. 36; Morton & Eden, 2004, n. 517 (1.40).

(28) Kursī al-Daylam, 651 AH (gold)

Obv: *As-sulṭān / al-aʿẓam ʿalā / al-dunyā wa / al-dīn*

Marginal legend: *Ḍuriba hādhā al-dīnār bi-baldat al-iqbāl bi-Kursī al-Daylam*

Rev: *Abū / al-Muẓaffar / Muḥammad ibn / al-Ḥasan*

Marginal legend: *[Fī shuhūr sanat aḥda] wa khamsīn wa [sittamiʾa]*

Ref.: Casanova, 1893, pp. 343–4; Vasmer, 1928, pp. 287–308; Spink Zürich 31, 1989, p. 59, no. 322 (1.54); Peus 369, 2001, p. 96, no. 1757 (1.50); BNF, no. 3560 (1.19; 16); IIS; Tübingen, no. 94–33–7 (0.82; 13); Limbada (1.12; 13).

(29) Kursī al-Daylam, 6XX AH (gold)

Obv: *Lā ilāh illā Allāh / Muḥammad rasūl Allāh / ʿAlī walī Allāh*

Rev: *Al-sulṭān al- / aʿẓam ʿalā al-dunyā / wa al-dīn Muḥammad ibn / al-Ḥasan*

Marginal legend: *[Bismillāh ḍuriba hādhā al-dīnār] bi- Kursī al-Daylam fī sanat... sittami'a*

Ref.: Sotheby's, 1987, p. 61, no. 869 (1.70).

(30) Kursī al-Daylam, date illegible (gold)

Obv: *Lā ilāh illā Allāh / Muḥammad rasūl Allāh / 'Alī walī Allāh / Fāṭima Sayyidat/ nisā' al-'lamīn / Sayyid ashbāb / ahl al-janna*

To the left: *Muḥammad ibn al-Ḥasan*

To the right: *al-Ḥasan wa al-Ḥusayn*

Inner marginal legend: *Al-Ḥusayn ṣalawāt Allāh 'alayhim*

Outer marginal legend: *Bismillāh al-raḥmān al-raḥīm ...wa law karih al-mushrikūn*

Rev: *Lā imām illā amīr al-zamān / 'Abd Allāh wa walīhi Nizār Abū al-Manṣūr / al-Imām al-Muṣṭafā li-dīn Allāh / amīr al-mu'minīn*

Inner marginal legend: *Ṣalawāt Allāh 'alayhi wa 'alā abā'ihi al-ṭāhirīn wa abnā al-akramīn*

Outer marginal legend: *Bismillāh al-raḥman al-raḥīm ḍuriba hādhā al-dīnār bi-baldat al-iqbāl bi-Kursī al-Daylam...*

Ref.: Spink Zürich 27, 1988, p. 70, no. 372 (8.92).

(31) Mint and date illegible (gold)

Obv: *Lā ilāh illā / Allāh Muḥammad / rasūl Allāh / 'Alī walī Allāh*

Rev: *Al-sulṭān / al-aʿẓam ʿalā / al-dunyā wa al-dīn / Muḥammad ibn al-Ḥasan*

Ref.: Tübingen, no. FE4 E1 (base gold, 2.68; 18).

(32) Mint and date illegible (gold)

Obv: *[Lā ilā]h illā / Allāh Muḥammad / rasūl Allāh / ʿAlī walī Allāh*
Marginal legend: Unread.
Rev: *Al-sulṭān al-aʿẓam ʿalā / al-dunyā wa al-dīn / Muḥammad ibn / al-Ḥasan*
Marginal legend: Unread.
Ref.: Qingxuan, Qixiang, 1991, p. 36, no. 131 (26mm), Hoard of Bole (Turkestan, China).

(33) Mint and date illegible (gold)

Obv: *Allāh / Lā ilāh illā Allāh / Muḥammad rasūl Allāh / ʿAlī walī Allāh / [al-Muṣ]ṭafā li-dīn*
Marginal legend: Unread.
Rev: *Al-sulṭān al-aʿẓam / ʿalā al-dunyā wa al-dīn / ṣāḥib qirān al-zamān / [Muḥammad ibn] al-Ḥasan*
Marginal legend: Unread.
Ref.: Spink Zürich 31, 1989, p. 59, no. 321 (4.40).

(34) No mint and date (gold)

Obv: *Lā ilāh illā Allāh / Muḥammad rasūl Allāh / ʿAlī walī Allāh*

Rev: *Al-sulṭān al- / a'ẓam 'alā al-dunyā / wa al-dīn Muḥammad ibn / al-Ḥasan*

Ref.: Tübingen, no. 94–33–8 (1.34; 14).

(35) No mint and date (gold)

Obv: *Al-mawlā / al-a'ẓam*

Rev: *Muḥammad ibn / al-Ḥasan*

Ref.: Tübingen, no. 94–33–6 (0.99; 14,8); Spink Zürich 31, 1989, p. 59, no. 323 (0.83); IIS; Limbada, (0.85; 12).

(36) Without mint, 618 AH (silver)

Obv: *Lā ilāh illā Allāh / Muḥammad rasūl A / llāh*

Marginal legend: *Ḍuriba hādhā al-dirham shuhūr sanat thamān wa 'ashara wa sittami'a*

Rev: *Muḥammad / al-sulṭān al-a'ẓam / 'alā al-dunyā wa al-dīn / al-Ḥasan*

Marginal legend: *Arsalahu bi'l-huda wa dīn al-ḥaqq liyuẓhirahu 'alā al-dīn kullihi wa lau kariha al-mushrikūn*

Ref.: SH, no. 13110 (1.96; 21).

(37) Baldat al-Iqbāl (Kursī al-Daylam), 619 AH (silver)

Obv: *Lā ilāh illā Allāh / Muḥammad rasūl A / llāh*

Marginal legend: [*Bismillāh ḍuriba*] *hādhā al-dirham bi-baldat al-iqbāl sanat tisʿ wa ʿasharat wa sittamiʾa*

Rev: *Muḥammad / al-sulṭān al-aʿẓam / ʿalā al-dunyā wa al-dīn / ibn al-Ḥasan*

Marginal legend: *Arsalahu biʾl-huda wa dīn al-ḥaqq liyuẓhirahu ʿala al-dīn kullihi wa lau kariha al-mushrikūn*

Ref.: Spink Zürich 27,1988, p. 69, no. 371 (3.02); Tübingen, no. FE4 E6 (3.36; 20); Tübingen, no. FE4 F1 (3.45; 20).

(38) No mint and date (silver)

Obv: *Muḥammad ibn / al-Ḥasan*

Rev: Two lions.

Ref.: Tübingen, no. 97–27–4 (0.70; 10).

(39) No mint and date (silver)

Obv: *Al-sulṭān / al-muʿẓẓam*

Rev: *Muḥammad ibn / al-Ḥasan*

Ref.: Spink Zürich 27, 1988, p. 69, no. 371 (0.88).

(40) No mint and date (silver)
　　　Obv: *Al-mawlā / al-aʿẓam*
　　　Rev: *ʿalā al-dunyā / wa al-dīn*
　　　Ref.: Tübingen, no. 96–37–28 (1.91; 13).

(41) Mint and date illegible (silver)
　　　Obv: Bird formed out of the words – '*al-sulṭān / al-muʿazzam*'
　　　Marginal legend: Unread.
　　　Rev: *Muḥammad ibn / al-Ḥasan*
　　　Marginal legend: Unread.
　　　1. *Spink Zürich 34, 1990, p. 58, no. 352 (1.05).*

(42) Mint and date illegible (silver)
　　　Obv: *Lā ilāh illā Allāh / Muḥammad / rasūl Allāh*
　　　Marginal legend: Unread.
　　　Rev: *Al-sulṭān / al-aʿẓam / ʿalā al-dunyā / wa al-dīn*
　　　Around the words *ʿalā al-dunyā* a bird formed out of the words '*Muḥammad ibn al-Ḥasan*' placed.
　　　Marginal legend: *Ḍuriba hādhā al-dirham ...*
　　　Ref.: Limbada (2.01; 21).

Bahrām al-Dāʿī (520–522/1126–1128)

(43) Baniyās, 521 AH (billon)

Obv: *Lā ilāh illā Allāh / Muḥammad rasūl Allāh / ʿAlī walī Allāh / Fatḥ*

Marginal legend: Bismillāh al-raḥmān al-raḥīm Naṣr min Allāh wa Fatḥ qarīb li-mawlānā

Rev: *Ẓahīr al-dīn / tughtakīn atābak / tāj al-mulūk bū / rī*

Marginal legend: *Bismillāh ḍuriba hādhā al-dirham bi-Baniyās sanat aḥda wa ʿashrīn wa khamsmiʾa*

Ref.: SNA, p. 28, no. 258, (2.85); IAA (Two other specimens of the same dies. Found in the excavations of Baniyās. Information from A. Berman, Qiriyat Tiveon, Israel).

Bibliography

Aga Khan Trust for Culture. *Historic Cities Support Programme: Karimabad and Baltit Project Development.* Geneva, 1996.

Allan, James W. 'Abu'l Qasim's Treatise on Ceramics,' *Iran*, 13 (1973), pp. 111–120.

—— 'Incised Wares of Iran and Anatolia in the 11th and 12th Centuries,' *Keramos*, 64 (1974), pp. 15–22.

Boase, T.S.R. *The Castles and Churches of the Crusading Kingdom.* Oxford, 1967.

Boyle, J.A. 'Dynastic and Political History of the Il-Khans,' in *The Cambridge History of Iran*: Volume 5, *The Saljuq and Mongol Periods*, ed., J.A. Boyle. Cambridge, 1968, pp. 303-421.

Braune, Michael. *Untersuchungen zur mittelalterlichen Befestigung in Nordwest-Syrien: Die Assassinenburg Masyaf.* Damascus, 1985.

Browne, E.G. *A Literary History of Persia.* Cambridge, 1902–1924.

Brugsch, H. *Reise der k. Preussischen Gesandschaft Nach Persien.* Leipzig, 1860-1861.

Burns, Ross. *The Monuments of Syria: An Historical Guide.* London, 1994.

Corbin, Henry. *Cyclical Time and Ismaili Gnosis*, trans. Ralph Manheim and James W. Morris. London, 1983.

Daftary, Farhad. *The Isma'ilis: Their History and Doctrines.* Cambridge, 1990.

—— *The Assassin Legends: Myths of the Isma'ilis.* London, 1994.

—— 'Hasan-i Sabbah and the Origins of the Nizari Isma'ili Movement,' in F. Daftary, ed., *Mediaeval Isma'ili History and Thought.* Cambridge, 1996. pp. 181–204.

—— *A Short History of the Ismailis: Traditions of a Muslim Community.* Edinburgh, 1998.

—— 'The Isma'ilis and the Crusades: History and Myth,' in *The Crusades and the Military Orders: Expanding the Frontiers of Medieval Latin Christianity*, ed. Z. Hunyadi and J. Laszlovszky. Budapest, 2001, pp. 21–41

—— *Ismaili Literature: A Bibliography of Sources and Studies.* London, 2004.

Deschamps, P. *Les Châteaux des croisés en Terre Sainte, I. Le Crac des Chevaliers.* 2 vols. Paris. 1993.

Fedden, Robin and John Thomson. *Crusader Castles of the Levant.* London, 1957.

Fitzgerald, E. *The Rubaiyat of Omar Khayyam.* London, 1955.

Forqani, Faruq. 'Ismailis,' in *Historical Atlas of Iran* (Tehran, 1999), pp. 82–86.

Garnett, Tony. *Bulletin of the Experimental Firing Group*, 3 (1984–85), pp. 115–127.

Gaube, H. 'Arrajan,' in *Encyclopaedia Iranica*, ed. E. Yarshater. London-New York, 1987 vol. 2, pp. 519–520.

Halm, Heinz. *The Fatimids and their Traditions of Learning*. London, 1997.

Hammer-Purgstall, Joseph von. *Die Geschichte der Assassinen aus Morgenländischen Quellen*. Stuttgart-Tübingen, 1818; English trans., O.C. Wood, *The History of the Assassins*. London, 1835.

Hanna, Zakieh. *The Castles and Archaeological Sites in Syria*, trans., B. Khoutry and R. Botrus. Damascus, 1994.

Haqiqat, Abu'l-Rafi. *Tarikh-e Qumes*. Tehran, 1370/1991.

Herzfeld, E. 'Reisebericht,' *Zeitschrift der Deutschen Morgenländischen Gesellschaft* (1926), pp. 226–283.

Hillenbrand, Carole. *The Crusades: The Islamic Perspective*. Edinburgh, 1999.

Hodgson, Marshall G.S. *The Order of Assassins: The Struggle of the Early Nizari Isma'ilis Against the Islamic World*. The Hague, 1955.

—— 'The Isma'ili State,' in *The Cambridge History of Iran*, Volume 5: *The Saljuq and Mongol Periods*, ed. J.A. Boyle. Cambridge, 1968, pp. 422–482.

Honda, M. *Report on the Study of Ismaili Castles*, produced for the Cultural Heritage Central Archives. Tehran, 1972 (unpublished).

Hourcade, Bernard. 'Alamut,' *Encyclopaedia Iranica*, vol. 1, pp. 797–801.

Hunsberger, Alice H. *Nasir Khusraw, the Ruby of Badakhshan: A Portrait of the Persian Poet, Traveller and Philosopher*. London, 2000.

Ibn al-Haytham, Abu 'Abd Allah Ja'far. *Kitab al-munazarat*, ed. and trans. W. Madelung and P.E. Walker as *The Advent of the Fatimids: A Contemporary Shi'i Witness*. London, 2000.

Ivanow, Wladimir. 'Alamut,' *Geographical Journal*, 77 (1931), pp. 38–45.

—— 'Some Ismaili Strongholds in Persia,' *Islamic Culture*, 12 (1938), pp. 383–396.

—— *Alamut and Lamasar: Two Mediaeval Ismaili Strongholds in Iran*. Tehran, 1960.

Jafri, S. Husain M. *Origins and Early Development of Shi'a Islam*. London, 1979.

Jamal, Nadia Eboo. *Surviving the Mongols: Nizari Quhistani and the Continuity of Ismaili Tradition in Persia*. London, 2002.

Juwayni, 'Ata-Malik. *Tarikh-i jahan-gushay*, ed. M. Qazvini. Leiden-London, 1912–37; English trans., J.A. Boyle, *The History of the World-Conqueror*. Manchester, 1958.

Kennedy, Hugh. *Crusader Castles*. Cambridge, 1994.

Kervran, M. 'Une Forteresse d'Azerbaidjan: Samiran,' *Revue des Études Islamiques*, 41 (1973), pp. 71–93.

Kleiss, Wolfram. 'Assassin Castles in Iran,' in Robert Hillenbrand, ed., *The Art of the Saljuqs in Iran and Anatolia*. Costa Mesa, CA, 1994, pp. 315–319.

Lewis, Bernard. *The Middle East*. New York, 1995.

—— *The Assassins: A Radical Sect in Islam*. London, 1967.

Lockhart, L. 'Hasan-i Sabbah and the Assassins,' *Bulletin of the School of Oriental (and African) Studies*, 5 (1928-1930), pp. 689-696.

—— 'Some Notes on Alamut,' *Geographical Journal*, 77 (1931), pp. 46–48.

Maalouf, Amin. *Samarkand*. London, 1992.

Marshall, Robert. *Storm from the East: From Gengis Khan to Khubilai Khan*. London, 1993.

Matheson, Sylvia. *Persia: An Archaeological Guide*. London, 1972.

Minasian, Caro O. *Shah Diz of Isma'ili Fame: Its Siege and Destruction*. London, 1971.

Mirza, Nasseh A. *Syrian Ismailism*. Richmond, Surrey, 1997.

Mitha, Farouk. *Al-Ghazali and the Ismailis: A Debate on Reason and Authority in Medieval Islam*. London, 2001.

Monteith, W. 'Journal of a Tour through Azerdbijan and the Shores of the Caspian,' *Journal of the Royal Geographical Society*, 3 (1833), pp. 15–16.

Nanji, Azim. 'Assassins,' in *Encyclopedia of Religion*, ed. M. Eliade. New York-London, 1987, vol. 1, pp. 469-471.

—— 'Nizariyya,' *The Encyclopaedia of Islam*. New ed., vol. 8, p. 84.

Naser Khosraw. *Naser Khosraw's Book of Travels (Safarnama)*, ed. and trans. Wheeler M. Thackston, Jr. Costa Mesa, CA, 2001.

Naumann, Rudolf and Elisabeth. *Takht-i Suleiman: Ausgrabung des Deutschen Archäologischen Instituts in Iran*. Munich, 1976.

Petrushevsky, I.B. 'The Socio-Economic Conditions in Iran under the Il-Khans,' in *The Cambridge History of Iran*: Volume 5, *The Saljuq and Mongol Periods*, ed. J.A. Boyle. Cambridge, 1968, pp. 483–537.

Pope, Arthur Upham. *Persian Architecture*. London, 1964.

Phillips, John. 'Assassin Castles in Syria,' *The Connoisseur*, 191, no. 770 (1976), pp. 287–289.

Rawlinson, H.C. 'Notes on a Journey from Tabriz, through Persian Kurdistan, to the ruins of Yakhti-Soleiman, and from there by Zenjan and Tarom, to Gilan, in October and November, 1838,' *Journal of the Royal Geographical Society*, 10 (1841), pp. 1-64.

Runciman, Steven. *A History of the Crusades*, Volume 1: *The First Crusade and the Foundation of the Kingdom of Jerusalem*. Cambridge, 1951.

Shiel, J. 'Itinerary from Tehran to Alamut and Khurrem-abad in May 1837,' *Journal of the Royal Geographical Society*, 8 (1838), pp. 430–434.

Silvestre de Sacy, A.I. 'Mémoire sur la dynastie des Assassins et sur l'étymologie der leur Nom,' *Mémoirs de l'Institut Royal de France*, 4 (1918), pp. 1–84; English trans., 'Memoir on the Dynasty of the Assassins, and on the Etymology of their Name,' in F. Daftary, *The Assassin Legends: Myths of the Isma'ilis*. London, 1994, pp. 136–182.

Sotudeh, Manuchehr. *Qela'-e Isma'iliyya dar reshteh-ye kuh-ha-ye Alborz*. Tehran, 1966.

Stark, Freya. *The Valleys of the Assassins and other Persian Travels*. London, 1934.

Stern, Samuel M., E. Beazley and A. Dobson, 'The Fortress of Khan Lanjan,' *Iran*, 9, (1971), pp. 45–57.

Tusi, Nasir al-Din. *Akhlaq-i Nasiri*, trans. G.M. Wickens as *The Nasirean Ethics*, London, 1964.

—— *Sayr wa Suluk*, ed. and trans. S.J. Badakhchani as *Contemplation and Action: The Spiritual Autobiography of a Muslim Scholar*. London, 1998.

—— *Rawda-yi taslim*, ed. and trans. S.J. Badakhchani as *Paradise of Submission*. London, 2005.

van Berchem, Max. 'Épigraphic des Assasslus de Syrie,' *Journal Asiatique*, 9 série, 9 (1897), pp. 453–501; repr. in idem, *Opera Minora*. Geneva, 1978, vol. 1, pp. 453–501.

Virani, Shafique N. 'The Eagle Returns: Evidence of Continued Isma'ili Activity at Alamut and in the South Caspian Region following the Mongol Conquests,' *Journal of the American Oriental Society*, 123 (2003), pp. 351–370.

Wasserman, James. *The Templars and the Assassins: The Militia of Heaven*. Rochester, VT, 2001.

Watt, W. Montgomery. *The Majesty that was Islam: The Islamic World 661–1100*. London, 1974.

Whitehouse, David. 'Excavations at Siraf,' *Iran,* 9 (1971), p. 15.

Willey, Peter. 'New Finds in Valleys of the Assassins,' *The Times*, London (25th Feb., 1960).

—— 'The Valley of the Assassins,' *Royal Central Asian Journal*, 48 (1961), pp. 147–151.

—— *The Castles of the Assassins*. London, 1963; repr. Fresno, CA, 2001.

—— 'Further Expeditions to the Valley of the Assassins,' *Royal Central Asian Journal*, 54 (1967), pp. 156–162.

—— 'Persian Odyssey,' in Odette Tchernine, ed., *Explorers Remember*. London, 1967, pp. 79–101.

—— 'Assassins of Qa'in,' *The Geographical Magazine*, vol. 11 (1968), pp 1294–1303.

—— 'The Assassins in Qohistan,' *Royal Central Asian Journal*, 55 (1968), pp. 180–183.

—— 'The Assassins: Brutal Myth or Living Sect?' *The Traveller*, 16, 3 (1986), pp. 42–46.

—— 'The Land of Cyrus the Great, the Assassins and Omar Khayyam,' *Christ's College Magazine*. Cambridge, no. 222 (1997).

—— 'Castles of the Assassins,' *The Geographical*, 70, no. 2 (1998), pp. 34–39.

—— 'The Ismaili Fortresses in Semnan and Khorasan 1100–1250,' *University Lectures in Islamic Studies*, London, 1998, vol. 2, pp. 167–181.

—— 'The Order of Assassins and Modern Iran,' *Balliol College Annual Record*. Oxford (1998), pp. 81–84.

—— 'Ismailism: Ismaili Monuments', in *Encyclopaedia Iranica*, vol. 13 (forthcoming).

—— 'The Castle of the Assassins,' *The British Army Preview*, 137 (2005).

Willey, Peter with N.R. Jones, A.C. Garnett and Rosalind Jones. 'The 1972 Assassin Expedition,' *Asian Affairs*, 61/5 (1974), pp. 60–70.

Yavari, Neguin. 'Nizam al-Mulk Remembered: A Study in Historical Representation,' Ph.D. thesis, Columbia University, 1992.

Index

Abbasid dynasty, Abbasids 4–5, 6, 7, 9, 10, 14, 15, 24, 38, 56, 61, 77, 278, 288, 290
'Abd Allah II, first Fatimid caliph 9–10
'Abd Allah the Elder 8
'Abd al-Malek b. 'Attash, Ismaili *da'i* 24, 207, 208
Abiz, Qohistan 185, 312
Abu'l-Hasan al-'Ashari, theologian 6
Abu Bakr, first caliph 2
Abu Hamza, Nizari *da'i* 206, 213
Abu Mansur Nizar b. al-Mustansir, Nizari imam 16–17, 25, 26, 56, 63, 64, 213, 290
Abu Qubais, castle in Syria 240, 275
Abu Tahir al-Sa'igh, Ismaili *da'i* 42, 43, 240
Achaemenid Empire 38
Acre, Syria 38
Afamiya (Qal'at al-Mudiq) castle in Syria 42, 43, 240
al-Afdal b. Badr al-Jamali, Fatimid vizier 16
Afghanistan, Afghans 167, 168, 182, 201, 246, 247, 250, 252, 254, 256, 257, 262, 264, 268, 269
Afin, Qohistan 178, 183, 184–185, 268
Afriz, Qohistan 178
Aga Khan IV, H.H. Prince Karim, current Nizari imam 8, 205, 206, 213, 245, 248, 249, 250, 257, 261, 263, 264
Aga Khans 84, 213

Aga Khan Development Network (AKDN) 261, 263
Aga Khan Trust for Culture 221, 245, 259; Historic Cities Support Programme 255
Aghlabid dynasty, Aghlabids 10
Ahangaran, site of castle in Qohistan 185, 203
Ahmad b. 'Attash, Ismaili *da'i* 31, 34, 59, 208–209, 210
'Ala al-Din Mohammad, Nizari imam 67, 76, 114, 289, 290
Alam family 169, 190, 192, 193, 195, 198
Alamkuh *see* Takht-e Sulayman
Alamut fortress and seat of Nizari state, in Daylaman 21, 26, 27, 28, 29, 30, 31, 34, 35, 37, 41, 42, 43, 44, 49, 59, 60, 61, 63, 64, 65, 66, 67, 68, 69, 70, 71, 76, 77, 78, 89, 90, 95, 96, 98, 99, 100, 101, 103, 115–128 *passim*, 129–146 *passim*, 147, 148, 153, 154, 163, 165, 167, 168, 169, 171, 172, 175, 180, 187, 198, 207, 208, 209, 212, 214, 219, 227, 235, 246, 262, 264, 265, 268, 269, 270, 271, 272, 277, 278, 279, 281, 282, 283, 285, 286, 288, 289, 290, 291; description 106–114; Ismaili capture of; 22–24; life of 52–58; fall of 80–84
Alamuti, Mr 121
Alamut period 14, 55, 171, 198, 214, 263, 264, 277, 285
Alborz mountains 21, 26, 30, 72, 95, 104,

108, 122, 148, 152, 167, 217, 268

Aleppo, Syria 12, 31, 38, 41, 42, 43, 44, 47, 50, 57, 58, 219, 220, 229, 238, 240, 243

Alexander 24, 38, 250, 257

Alexandria 12, 16, 25

'Ali Mahmet 226

'Ali b. Abi Talib, first Shi'i imam and fourth caliph 2–6 *passim*, 10

'Ali b. al-Husayn, Zayn al-'Abidin Shi'i imam 6

Aliabad, Qumes 148, 150, 151

Allan, James 143, 281

Alp Aralan, Saljuq sultan 39, 43

Altit, nr Hunza 261

Amid, Turkey 94, 95

Anatolia 39, 94

Andej 23, 53, 124, 125; pottery and kilns 107, 141–144, 279, 281–285

Anjudan, Mahallat 213, 263

Antioch, Syria 38, 40, 42, 43, 48, 50, 240

Anushtagin, Turkish *atabeg* 129

Arabia 1, 2, 7, 9, 12, 47

Armenia, Armenians 16, 25, 60, 94, 168

Arrajan (Argun), Iran 31, 34, 96, 204, 205, 206, 209, 212, 213, 214

Asadabad, Qohistan 182, 195

Asia Minor 38, 39

Askavar river 124

Assassins, assassination 36, 50; as a method of warfare 61–63; legends of 49, 55–56, 62, 84, 154, 214, 234; origin of name 57

Assassin Legends, The (Farhad Daftary) 55

Auchinleck, Field-Marshal Sir Claude 255

Avicenna (Ibn Sina) 252

Aviz, Qohistan 274

Ayin, fort in Daylaman 124, 270

Ayn Jalut 221

Azarbayjan 25, 135, 263, 289, 290

Azaz, Syria 219

al-Azhar, mosque and university in Cairo 13

al-'Aziz, Fatimid caliph 12

Ba'arin, castle in Syria 226

Bab Buza'a, Syria 219

Bactria 250

Badakhshan, Afghanistan 178, 246, 247, 249, 251–253 *passim*, 261, 269

Badakhshani, 'Abbas 155, 169, 170, 176, 189, 201

Badasht, Daylaman 22, 105

Badr al-Jamali, Fatimid vizier 16, 25

Baghdad 4, 5, 10, 12, 14, 15, 24, 31, 32, 38, 72, 75, 77, 290

Bahram, Nizari *da'i* 43, 288, 307

Bahramabad, castle nr Lamasar, Daylaman 270

Bahrayn 9

Baku 92

Balkh 71, 74, 94, 172, 246, 247

Baltit, castle nr Hunza, Pakistan 245, 255–260, 261

Baltit Heritage Trust 259, 260

Baluchistan 167, 205

Bam, south-east Iran 93, 204, 205

Bandan, Sistan 203

Bandar 'Abbas, south-east Iran 205

Banyas, Syria 43, 220, 227, 230

Barmiyan, Afghanistan 248

Barqiyaruq, Saljuq prince 32

batin (esoteric) 9, 57

Baybars I, Mamluk sultan 218, 220, 226, 231, 238, 240, 242

Bazghash, Saljuq amir 168, 182

Beazley, Elizabeth 211, 212, 215

Behbahan, Khuzistan 213

Beirut 38

Biajarmand, Khorasan 164

Bidelan (Badasht), castle in Daylaman 104, 105–106, 107, 115, 124, 141, 145, 146, 270

Bihud, Qohistan 185, 186, 187, 273

Birjand, Qohistan 101, 168, 172, 185, 189, 190, 191, 192, 193, 194, 195, 202, 268, 285

Boase, T.S.R. 90

Bohemond IV, Frankish ruler 50, 238

Bozorg-Ommid (Buzurg-Ummid) Kiya, head of Nizari state 30, 35, 59, 65, 98,

114, 120, 129, 132, 133, 289
Braune, Michael 225, 226
Brown, Joe 119, 120
Browne, E.G. 247
Bukhara, Central Asia 71, 204, 247, 254
Burkett, Mary 211, 212
Burns, Ross 90, 216, 218, 221, 233, 234, 239, 243
Buyid dynasty, Buyids 5
Byron, Lord George Gordon 249
Byzantium, Byzantines 1, 3, 10, 12, 13, 39, 90, 91, 92, 93, 94, 97, 98, 99, 218, 220, 225, 231, 240, 241, 243

Cairo 12, 13, 14, 15, 17, 24, 25, 26, 29, 31, 56, 64, 89, 94, 144, 245, 246, 247, 286
caliphate 2–3
Cambridge History of Iran 172
Caspian Sea 30, 94, 104, 108, 124, 135, 147, 152, 165, 263, 268
castles: European and Crusader 90–92; Ismaili 95–102, 262–263; Oriental and Middle Eastern 92–95 *see also* under individual castles
Castles of the Assassins (Peter Willey) 103, 107, 122, 143, 267
Central Asia 1, 3, 5, 15, 64, 75, 168, 204, 210, 246, 262, 263, 268, 290
Chahar Kesht, Qohistan 190
Chaldecott, David 247, 256
Chastel Blanc, castle in Syria 92
Chateau Gaillard, France 91
Chehel Dokhtar, Fortress, Qohistan 173, 174, 176
Chenesht, Qohistan 192–193
Cheshmeh, Qumes 162, 164, 165
China 12, 38, 71, 72, 74, 144, 147, 247, 254, 255, 257, 262, 303
Chitral, Pakistan 256, 269
Christianity, Christians 1, 12, 13, 50, 217, 218, 266 *see also* Crusades
Conrad of Montferrat, Crusader King of Jerusalem 48
coins 3, 54, 199, 288–307

The Connoisseur 216, 233
Constantine, Byzantine emperor 1, 38
Constantinople 39, 91, 93
Coon, Carlton S. 193
Cordoba, Spain 1
Crusades, Crusaders 13, 31, 38, 39–51 *passim*, 57, 59, 61, 72, 77, 82, 96, 97, 99, 102, 122, 210, 216–219 *passim*, 224, 225, 229, 232, 233, 234, 238, 240, 241, 242, 243, 245, 269, 278; castles of 90–92
Ctesiphon, Sasanid capital 158

da'i, *da'is* 8, 9, 10, 14, 15, 24, 25, 26, 28, 31, 43, 44, 53, 56, 59, 63, 64, 65, 167, 204, 206, 213, 246, 249, 262
da'wa 8, 9, 14, 17, 24, 26, 56, 59, 63, 64, 207, 208
Daftary, Farhad 7, 36, 42, 46, 48, 49, 55, 179, 207, 208, 213, 220, 240
Damascus 3, 6, 31, 38, 41, 42, 43, 47, 50, 57, 216, 221, 225, 229, 238, 288, 289
Damavand, Mt. 104, 163, 164
Damghan, Qumes 30, 58, 89, 95, 147, 148, 152, 163, 164, 172, 277, 285
Darband, Northern Iran 134, 135
Dareh, nr. Birjand, Qohistan 28, 29, 157, 158, 159, 161, 192
Dar al-'Ilm 14
Dar al-Hikma 14
Darmiyan, Qohistan 195
Dasht-e Kavir (Great Salt Desert) 95, 167, 182
Daylaman, Daylamites 21, 22, 26, 30, 31, 60, 65, 135, 208, 262, 264
Dehkhoda, 'Ali Akbar 158
Delhi 1, 71
Deschamps. P. 218
Diyarabakir, Anatolia 94
Dobson, Andrew 180, 211
Dome of the Rock 93
Doshambe, Tajikistan 247, 248
Doshi, Afghanistan 250
Dozdaksar 282
Dugmore, Captain Roddie 103, 108, 119

Edessa 40

Edward I, King of England 91, 264

Egypt 1, 5, 10, 12, 13, 16, 17, 25, 39, 40, 41, 43, 47, 50, 51, 59, 60, 63, 64, 72, 89, 94, 98, 144, 205, 208, 213, 218, 221

Encyclopaedia Iranica 213

Esfedan, Qohistan 183–184, 185, 268

Eskan, Afghanistan 251

Eskureh, nr Sirjan, Iran 205

Fath 'Ali Shah, Qajar monarch 213

Fatimid Dynasty, Fatimids 9–17 *passim*, 24, 25, 26, 38–43 *passim*, 47, 56, 59, 60, 63, 64, 68, 89, 94, 98, 144, 205, 208, 213, 246, 247, 290

Fayzabad, Qohistan 195, 248, 249, 251, 252

Ferdawsi, Persian poet 169

fida'is 46, 48, 49, 54, 55, 59, 62, 77, 115, 119, 133, 212

Fiorani, V. 173

Firuzabad, Fars 158

Firuzkuh, Qumes 165; castle 162–164

Frederick II of Germany 38, 39, 41, 49

Fitzgerald, Edward 29,

Furk, castle in Qohistan 182, 193, 195–198, 201, 210, 269, 285

Garmarud, castle in Daylaman 104, 120, 121, 122, 123, 125

Garnett, Tony 140, 142, 279, 280, 281, 282, 283, 284, 285

Gazorkhan, Daylaman 22, 23, 52, 53, 106, 107, 109, 110, 145

Genghis Khan, Mongol Great Khan 71, 74, 172, 289

Gerdkuh, castle in Qumes 30, 31, 35, 52, 54, 55, 58, 60, 67, 75, 76, 78, 82, 83, 84, 90, 96, 98, 100, 101, 140, 147–154, 158, 162, 163, 164, 165, 175, 181, 197, 202, 218, 219, 268, 269, 272, 273, 285

al-Ghazali, Abu Hamid Muhammad, Sunni scholar 57

Gholam Kosh (Dareh), castle in Qohistan 190–192, 197

Gilgit, Pakistan 246, 247, 255, 256, 258, 259, 261

Goethe, Johann Wolfgang von 266

Gonabad, Khorasan 187, 188, 273

Graube, H. 213

Great Salt Desert *see* Dasht-e Kavir

Gujarat, India 17

Guyuk, Mongol Great Khan 72, 77

Habashi, Saljuq *amir* 30, 148

Hafez, Persian poet 266

al-Hakim, Fatimid caliph 12, 13, 14

Halm, Heinz 13, 64

Hama, Syria 47, 220, 226

Hamid, Major-General Shahid 255

Hammer–Purgstall, Joseph von 36

Hanna, Zakieh 231, 236

Häntzsche, Julius Caesar 134

Haqiqat, Abu'l-Rafi 158

Harun al-Rashid, Abbasid caliph 4

Hasan Sabbah 10, 14, 15, 17, 21–36, 41, 49, 52–65 *passim*, 69, 70, 82, 84, 89, 95, 98, 100, 103, 108, 114, 124, 125, 129, 135, 140, 148, 162, 167, 168, 182, 199, 207, 208, 234, 246, 249; achievements 34–36; capture of Alamut 22–24; early life 24–26; and Nizari state 34–36

Hasanabad, castle in Qohistan 179, 180, 181

al-Hasan 'Ali b. Abi Talib 6

Hasan *'ala dhikrihi'l-salam* (Hasan II), Nizari imam 44, 65, 67, 198

Hasan 'Ali Shah, Nizari imam 213

Hattin, Palestine 40, 48, 216, 241, 242

Helmut, Leopold 234

Henry of Champagne, Crusader King of Jerusalem 48, 49

Herat, Afghanistan 74, 171

Herzfeld, E. 168, 172

Hillenbrand, Carole 40, 51, 168

History of the World Conquerer (Juwayni) 100

Hodgson, Marshall 35, 36, 47, 62, 66, 67, 79, 90, 172, 182, 264

Homs (Hims), Syria 220, 226

Hosayn Qa'ini, Nizari *da'i* 28, 59, 167, 169

Hospitallers, Frankish military order 44, 46, 50, 92, 218, 220, 231, 241

hujja 8, 14, 65

Hulegu Khan, Mongol ruler 68, 69, 70, 71, 72, 73, 75, 76, 77, 78, 79, 80, 81, 82, 83, 101, 114, 115, 118, 119, 123, 129, 154, 169, 179, 262, 266

Hunza, Pakistan 246, 247, 255, 256, 257, 258, 259, 260, 261, 269

Hunzakuts 257, 258

al-Husayn b. 'Ali b. Abi Talib, Shi'i imam 4, 6, 8

Ibn Hawqal, historian 205

Ibn Killis, Fatimid vizier 12

Ibn Shadad, geographer 40

Ibrahim Pasha 229

Il-Khanid dynasty 181, 262

Ilan, castle in Daylaman 106, 124–125

Imamate 6, 9, 25, 64, 82, 84, 208, 257, 263

Inab, castle in Syria 219, 275

India 1, 7, 12, 17, 38, 71, 92, 255

Iraq 1, 2, 4, 5, 7, 8, 9, 15, 16, 25, 31, 39, 47, 56, 93, 207

Isfahan, Iran 14, 24, 25, 31, 32, 34, 36, 57, 58, 95, 96, 129, 148, 177, 201, 204, 206–214 *passim*, 268

Ismailis: early history 7–10 *see also* Fatimids, Nizari Ismailis

Isma'il b. Ja'far al-Sadiq, Ismaili imam 7, 8

Italy 93

Ivanow, Wladimir 112, 115, 120, 122, 130, 133, 189, 192

Izzard, Ralph 119

Ja'far al-Sadiq, Shi'i imam 6, 7, 8, 9

Jabal Bahra (Jabal Ansariyya) 43, 44, 46, 47, 58, 217, 219, 220, 221, 227, 229, 231, 233, 234, 238, 240, 241, 265, 275

Jabal al-Summaq 42, 219

Jalal al-Din Hasan, Nizari imam 290

Jambaz, Mr 190, 192, 195, 198

Jerusalem 13, 39, 40, 41, 43, 46, 48, 51, 93, 94, 176, 182, 234, 241

Jeshen 249

Jesus 2, 13, 47, 66, 177

Jews 1, 12

Jironsefid, castle in Qumes 164

Jones, N.R. 145

Justinian, Roman emperor 218

Juwayni, 'Ata-Malik, historian 24, 27, 34, 36, 55, 59, 66, 74, 75, 76, 77, 79, 80, 81, 82, 83, 84, 97, 100, 101, 107, 114, 115, 119, 120, 122, 123, 129, 155, 163, 164, 172, 179, 182, 191, 200, 214, 262, 263

Kabol 247, 248, 249, 250, 251

Kafarlatha 219

Kahak, Mahallat 213

Kahf, castle in Syria 44, 46, 48, 49, 217, 219, 220, 226, 229, 233–237, 238, 240, 241, 244, 269, 286

Karakoram, Mongol capital in Central Asia 71, 72, 76, 83,

Karakoram Mts 256, 258, 259

Karbala, Iraq 4, 6

Karimabad, Pakistan 256, 257, 258, 260

Karimabad and Baltit Project Development 259

Kashan, central Iran 144, 279, 281, 282, 284

Kassir, Sayf al-Din 244

Kausambi, nr Aliabad, India 92

Kavir-e Lut 204

Kay-Ghrobad, castle in Daylaman 124, 282

Kay Khosraw (Chrosroes) I, Sasanid ruler 187

Kazakhstan 170

Kelar Khan 164, 165

Kennedy, Hugh 218, 241

Kerman, south-east Iran 31

Keshem, Afghanistan 250, 251, 252

Ket-Buqa, Mongol general 75, 76

Khaf, Khorasan 171, 273

Khalili, Professor 248, 251

Khan, Ziyuddin 248

Khanlanjan (Kuh-e Boz), castle nr Isfahan

31, 34, 95, 208, 211–213, 268, 275
Khargerd, Qohistan 171
Khariba, castle in Syria 44, 219, 220, 229, 240, 275, 276
Khawabi, castle in Syria 44, 46, 50, 217, 219, 220, 229, 238–239, 244
Khayrabad, Qohistan 203
Khayyam, Omar, Persian poet and mathematician 29, 140
Khorasan, Iran 5, 14, 26, 28, 29, 31, 58, 66, 74, 76, 89, 94, 95, 98, 99, 147, 153, 167, 169, 170, 171, 172, 179, 182, 211, 246, 262, 264, 266, 268, 269, 277, 285, 289, 291
Khoshareh, castle nr Nehbandan 202
Khoshk, Qohistan 178, 183, 185, 186
Khunik, Qohistan 193, 194, 203, 274
Khunik, Sistan 203, 274
Khuzistan 31, 58, 213
Khwarazm, Iran 71
Kerman, south-east Iran 93, 204, 205, 289
Krak des Chevaliers, Crusader castle in Syria 44, 46, 90, 92, 97, 99, 122, 217–220, 221, 225, 233, 241, 243
Kublai Khan, Mongol ruler 54, 71, 72
Kufa 2, 6, 24
Kuh-e Boz *see* Khanlanjan
Kurdistan 25, 138, 207

Lajevardi, castle in Qumes 164, 165
Lal, fort in Daylaman 124, 283
Lamasar, castle in Daylaman 30, 35, 55, 58, 78, 80, 83, 98, 103, 106, 112, 126, 128, 129–133, 141, 145, 146, 153, 197, 227, 268, 283, 285
Latakia, Syria 38, 220, 241
Lawrence, T.E. 90, 99, 220
Lebanon 7, 47, 219
Lewis, Bernard 47
Literary History of Persia, A (E.G. Browne) 247
Locke, John 252
Louis IX, King of France 39, 50, 51, 72, 218, 234
Ludwig of Bavaria 48

Mahallat, Iran 213
the Mahdi, messiah 8, 65
Mahdi, Lord of Alamut 21, 22, 23
al-Mahdi bi'llah 'Abd Allah II, first Fatimid caliph 9, 10
Malekshah, Saljuq sultan 15, 21, 22, 26, 29, 30, 32, 40, 141, 191, 206, 207, 208, 210
al-Malik al-Zahir Ghazi, Ayyubid prince 243
Mamluk dynasty, Mamluks 60, 218, 221, 231, 234, 240, 241, 242
Maniqa (Maynaqa), castle in Syria 44, 46, 219, 220, 229, 230–232, 238
al-Mansur, Fatimid caliph 10, 16, 49, 162
Mansurbagh, Daylaman 129
Mansurehkuh, Qumes 31, 35, 272
Mansuriyya, castle in Daylaman 124, 283
Marco Polo 49, 54, 55, 57, 259
Margat 46, 92, 219, 220, 243, 245
Mashhad, Khorasan 95, 155, 164, 167, 168, 169, 170, 171, 183, 186, 282
Masjed-e Jomeh 214
Masyaf, castle in Syria 44, 46, 47, 49, 51, 61, 64, 99, 216, 217, 218, 219, 220–227, 229, 233, 237, 238, 239, 244, 245, 269, 286
Matheson, Sylvia 193
Mayhan 203
Maymundez, fortress in Daylaman 35, 54, 58, 70, 80, 81, 82, 96, 97, 103, 106, 107, 114–120, 122, 123, 125, 128, 129, 134, 141, 145, 146, 148, 263, 268, 282; siege of 75–79
Mecca 1, 2, 5, 12, 93, 176, 182, 240, 246
Medina 1, 2, 6, 12, 177
Mehrin (Mehr Negar), castle in Qumes 35, 163, 165, 272
Menjil, Daylaman 134, 140, 271, 284
Merv 71, 74, 75, 94
Mikmameh, Mohammad 'Ali 186, 187
Minasian, Caro 207, 209, 210, 212
Minorsky, Wladimir 115
Mirshahi, Isa 155, 157, 158, 159, 165
Mir of Hunza 256, 257, 258

Mo'menabad, palace-fortress in Qohistan
  29, 64, 65, 101, 195, 198–200, 201, 219
Mongke, Mongol Great Khan 72, 77, 83
Mongols 24, 27, 55, 68, 69–85, 90, 97, 99,
  100, 101, 112, 113, 114, 115, 116, 118, 120,
  121, 123, 129, 136, 143, 148, 150, 151, 153,
  154, 156, 161, 163, 169, 171, 172, 179, 181,
  200, 203, 207, 214, 218, 220, 243, 246,
  262, 263 methods of warfare 72–75;
  rise of power 71–72; conquest of Ismaili
  strongholds 75–85
Monuments of Syria (Ross Burns) 221
Moradi, 'Ali 156, 159, 163, 165, 183
Morocco 10, 12
Mostofi, Bagher 190, 204
Mu'awiya b. Abi Sufyan, first Umayyad
  caliph 2, 3, 6
Muhammad, the Prophet 1, 2, 3, 4, 5, 6, 8,
  10, 14, 38, 56, 64, 176, 177, 247, 259
Muhammad al-Baqir, Shi'i imam 6
Muhammad Tapar, Saljuq sultan 32, 34, 43,
  207, 208, 211
al-Mui'zz, Fatimid caliph 10, 12
Muqaddam al-Din, Mongol commander
  70, 80
Musa al-Kazim, Twelver imam 7
al-Musta'li, Fatimid caliph 16, 25, 26, 43
Musta'lis 17, 41
al-Mustansir Abbasid caliph 77
al-Mustansir, Fatimid caliph 12, 16–17, 25,
  26, 56, 63, 64

Nader Shah, Afsharid monarch 170
Na'inarud 128, 129, 132, 197
al-Nasafi, Muhammad b. Ahmad, Ismaili
  (Qarmati) *da'i* 204
Naser Khosraw, Ismaili *da'i* and author 13,
  94, 95, 178, 187, 213, 246–247, 248, 251,
  252, 261, 269; tomb of 253–255
Naser al-Din Mohtasham, Ismaili governor
  of Qohistan 67, 76
Naser al-Din Shah, Qajar monarch 154
al-Nasir li-Din Allah, Abbasid caliph 290
Nasratabad, Sistan 205

Nehbandan, Sistan 151, 167, 184, 189, 192,
  194, 201–204
Nevisar Shah, castle in Daylaman 78, 83,
  84, 104, 106, 115, 120–124, 126, 128, 140,
  141, 212, 216, 219, 268, 284
Nezam al-Molk, Saljuq vizier 15, 21, 23, 24,
  29, 30, 61, 141, 206
Nishapur, Khorasan 29, 58, 71, 74, 94, 142,
  277, 281, 291
Nizari Ismailis 8, 10, 49, 56, 57, 59, 62, 71,
  84, 147, 263, 266, 277, 288; in Badakhshan and Hunza 246–261; intellectual
  and religious life 63–67; in Iran 21–24,
  26–34, 52–60, 63–68, 184, 205–206;
  military organisation 59–63; origins
  15–17; state 52–58; in Syria 40–47; *see
  also* Alamut; Hasan Sabbah; Rashid
  al-Din Sinan
North Africa 4, 9, 10, 25, 40, 56
Nur al-Din Muhammad, Nizari imam 290
Nusayris 41, 229

Orontes 240
Ostunavand, castle in Qumes 31, 272
Otegu-China, Mongol commander 262
Ottomans 41, 221, 229, 244
Oxus river 71, 250

Pakistan 7, 167, 168, 245, 246, 247, 255, 256,
  257, 259, 261, 268, 269
Palestine 10, 12, 13, 16, 25, 39, 48, 50, 77, 93,
  94, 221
Paris 213
Payghamberan, Qumes 156
Persepolis 93, 134, 204, 206
Petrushevsky, Ilya P. 172
Phillips, John 216, 222, 223, 233, 235
Phoenicians 241
Pinder-Wilson, Ralph 140, 143, 284
Poitiers 1
pottery 53, 54, 112, 118, 119, 123, 124, 126,
  133, 138, 141, 142, 143, 144, 161, 163,
  164, 170, 176, 191, 193, 194, 197, 211, 271,
  277–287

Qa'in, Qohistan 28, 54, 64, 67, 95, 97, 101,
    168, 169, 171–177, 182, 183, 185, 186, 189,
    192, 194, 195, 201, 210, 219, 269, 277
Qa'inat 168, 171, 172, 176, 185
al-Qa'im, Fatimid caliph 10, 66
Qadmus, castle in Syria 44, 217, 219, 220,
    226, 227, 228–230, 231, 232, 233, 240, 244,
    276
al-Qaher, castle in Syria 226
Qajar dynasty, Qajars 154, 193, 213, 263
Qal'at 170, 240
Qal'at al-Jess, Arrajan 213
Qal'at Haladan (Dez Kelet), Arrajan 213
Qal'at Marqab *see* Margat
Qalaun, Mongol ruler 220
Qal'eh Dokhtar (Qal'eh Kuh), nr Ferdaws,
    Qohistan 179–181
Qal'eh Gholam, nr Sarayan, Qohistan 178
Qal'eh Hasanabad, nr Ferdaws, Qohistan
    179, 180
Qal'eh Sang, castle in Daylaman 282
Qarmatis 9
Qazvin, Daylaman 21, 22, 23, 26, 27, 28, 30,
    72, 83, 103, 104, 105, 107, 114, 124, 128, 271
Qohistan, Iran 26, 28, 29, 30, 31, 32, 35,
    55, 58, 62, 63, 64, 65, 67, 68, 75, 76, 77,
    83, 95, 96, 98, 99, 100, 101, 153, 167–172,
    176, 178, 179, 182, 186, 189, 193, 194, 198,
    201–204, 207, 209, 210, 214, 217, 219, 220,
    262, 264, 265, 268, 269, 273, 274, 277,
    285, 290
Qomm, central Iran 24, 213
Qulay'a, castle in Syria
Qumes, Iran 28, 30, 31, 35, 58, 75, 96,
    147–166, 207, 214
Qur'an 1, 2, 6, 9, 54, 63, 81, 236, 248, 254,
    289, 254
Quraysh 5
Qezil-Uzun 134, 136

Ra'is Mozaffar, Saljuq official 23, 30, 147
Ramla, Palestine 10
Raqadda, North Africa 10
Rashid al-Din Sinan, Nizari leader in Syria

38, 41, 44–49, 50, 51, 55, 62, 65, 66, 216,
    218, 220, 224, 225, 226, 227, 229, 231, 233,
    234, 237, 238, 241
Rawalpindi, Pakistan 256
Rawlinson, Sir Henry 134, 135, 136, 138
Raymond de Saint-Gilles 220
Rayy, Iran 24, 26, 135, 144
Richard I, King of England 48, 91
Ridwan, Saljuq *amir* 42, 240
Robert of Saone 241, 242
Rokn al-Din Khurshah, Nizari imam 70,
    77, 78, 79, 80, 82, 83, 84, 114, 118, 123, 263
Rome, Romans 1, 38, 39, 74, 91, 220
Rudbar, Daylaman 21, 26, 28, 29–34
    passim, 35, 58, 68, 77, 90, 96, 98, 99, 114,
    128, 129, 141, 144, 147, 153, 168, 197, 207,
    214, 265, 270, 271
Runciman, Steven 13
Rusafa, fortress in Syria 44, 46, 219, 220,
    226, 227, 238, 276

Sa'adatkuh, castle in Daylaman 35
Safarnameh (Naser Khosraw) 13, 94, 247
Safavid dynasty, Safavids 54, 93, 108, 158,
    176, 178, 189, 195, 197, 205, 214, 282, 283
Saladin (Salah al-Din), founder of the
    Ayyubid dynasty 17, 40, 47, 48, 50, 61,
    92, 216, 222, 225, 241, 242, 243, 289
Salamiyya, Syria 8, 9, 40, 216, 244
Saljuq dynasty, Saljuqs 5, 15, 16, 21, 22, 23,
    25, 26, 28–34, 36, 37, 39, 40, 41, 42, 43, 55,
    56, 57, 59, 61, 62, 68, 69, 84, 89, 90, 94,
    129, 141, 143, 147, 148, 167, 168, 182, 191,
    206–214 *passim*, 240, 244, 285, 289, 291
Samarkand, Central Asia 71, 245, 247
Samiran, fortress in Daylaman 58, 106,
    134–141, 268, 284
Sanamkuh, Daylaman 28
Sangar, nr Baku 92
Sanjar, Saljuq sultan 32, 34, 35, 168, 182
San Vitale 93
Saone (Qal'at Salah al-Din), Crusader
    fortress in Syria 92, 241–243
Sarab, castle in Qohistan 185, 215

Sara Anzar, castle in Qumes 164, 164
Sarbisheh, Qohistan 194, 195, 201, 210
Sargudhasht-i Sayyidna 24
Sarmin, Syria 219
Sasanid dynasty, Sasanids 1, 93, 158, 159, 163, 187, 206,
Sedeh, Qohistan 168, 169, 182
Sefidrud, Daylaman 134, 135
Seleucid dynasty, Seleucids 220, 240
Semnan, Iran 58, 89, 95, 147, 148, 152, 155, 156, 157, 158, 162, 164, 269
Shahanshah, castle at Nehbandan, Qohistan 77, 78, 200, 201–203, 204
Shahdez, castle near Isfahan 31, 32, 34, 36, 58, 95, 100, 201, 206–211, 212, 213, 269, 274, 275
Shahkuh, castle near Birjand, Qohistan 203
Shahmirzad, Qumes 164, 165
Shahrak, Daylaman 22, 103, 115, 124
Shahrud, Khorasan 21, 27, 103, 128, 129, 141, 146, 152, 166, 283
Shah Abbas I 176, 214
Shah Dez of Isma'ili Fame (Caro O. Minasian) 207
Shalforushan, Mehdi 155, 157
Shams al-Din, Nizari imam 263
Shams-Kelayeh, castle in Daylaman 119
Shayzar, castle in Syria 43, 226, 229, 240, 278
Shi'ism, Shi'a, Shi'i: early Shi'ism 5–7; Twelver Shi'ism 7, 12, 24, 41, 43, 64, 171, 262; Ismaili Shi'ism 7–10 *see also* Fatimids, Nizaris
Shiraz, south west Iran 204, 206, 266
Shirkuh, castle in Daylaman 21, 27, 104, 105, 106, 125, 141, 285
Shotorkhan, Daylaman 22, 52, 109, 110
Shusf, Qohistan 202
Sijilmasa, Morocco 10
Silk Road 93, 147, 259
Sirjan, Kerman 178, 204, 205
Sistan 58, 95, 167, 195, 201, 202, 203, 204, 205, 214

Soru, castle in Qumes 58, 83, 84, 98, 99, 140, 147, 154, 155–162, 163, 164, 165, 175, 176, 181, 216, 217, 235, 265, 269, 272
Spain 1, 4
Stark, Freya 107, 121, 123, 125, 128, 130, 132, 133
Stern, Samuel M. 115, 168, 212
Stoppard, Tom 119
Sunni Islam, Sunnis 2, 4, 5–6, 7, 9, 12, 15, 17, 26, 30, 32, 36, 38, 40, 41, 42, 43, 44, 46, 47, 48, 50, 57, 62, 64, 65, 66, 67, 68, 72, 76, 77, 81, 205, 207, 208, 209, 211, 214, 216, 220, 225, 238, 240, 247, 250, 251, 252, 261
Swat, Pakistan 246, 256, 269

ta'wil 9
Tabas, Qohistan 28, 32, 58, 95, 168, 179, 182, 185, 195, 200, 268
Tabas Masina, Qohistan 182
Tajikistan 247, 248, 269
Taj al-Din, Ismaili *da'i* 50
Takht-e Sulayman (Alamkuh), Daylaman 27, 93, 104, 121, 278, 279, 281, 285
Taleqan, Daylaman 21, 27, 30, 70, 78, 104, 105, 106, 109, 121, 123, 124, 126, 128, 141, 143, 144, 146, 250, 269, 271, 272
Tancred, Frankish prince 42, 240
taqiyya 7, 8, 14, 262
Tartus, Syria 227, 238
Tashkent 247
Tehran 24, 103, 134, 140, 144, 155, 156, 157, 165, 168, 169, 183, 185, 187, 192, 206, 216, 247, 269, 277, 278, 286
Templars, Frankish military order 44, 46, 50, 92
Thomson, John 90, 242
Thousand and One Nights, A 4
Tikrit, Iraq 31, 207
Torbat-e Haydarieh, Khorasan 170, 176, 182, 273
Tortosa, Syria 50, 220, 238
Transoxiana 1, 71
Tripoli 10, 38, 40, 43, 44, 92, 218, 220, 238

Tughtikin Saljuq amir 42, 43, 288
Tun (Ferdaws), Qohestan 28, 76, 95, 151,
     168, 169, 172, 177–182, 185, 189, 201, 202,
     268, 273
Turkey 38, 93, 94, 247, 269
Turkmans 218
Tus, Khorasan 58, 66, 76, 169–171
al-Tusi, Naser al-Din, Shi'i scholar 66, 67,
     101, 169, 172

Ullakeh, Nizar 221
Ullayqa, castle in Syria 46, 219, 229,
     230–231, 233, 276
'Umar b. Khattab, second caliph 2, 29
Umayyad dynasty, Umayyads 2, 3–4, 6, 7,
     10, 38, 61
Uniq, Qohistan 185, 275
Urartians 92
Urban II, pope 39
Uzbekistan 248
'Uthman b. 'Affan, third caliph 2

Valleys of the Assassins (Freya Stark) 123
Valliolah, Mr 205
Vom Kriege (Karl von Clausewitz) 61

Wakhan, Afghanistan 247, 254

Wellington College 144, 247
Whittaker, Jim 155, 157
William of Rubrick 72, 77
William of Tyre 46, 51
Winston Churchill Trust 168
Woodfine, Adrianne 103, 107, 144, 147,
     150, 155, 156, 159, 163, 165, 168, 169, 172,
     181, 182, 185, 186, 187, 189, 190, 192, 193,
     194, 197, 198, 201, 202, 212, 215, 217, 219,
     221, 230, 236, 238, 242, 244, 255, 260,
     269

Yemen 1, 9, 12, 17, 93, 286
Yumgan, Afghanistan 247, 248, 251, 252,
     254, 255

Zabol, Baluchestan 176, 203, 204
Zagros mts 60, 167, 213, 214
Zahedan, Baluchestan 193, 202, 204, 205
zahir (exoteric) 9
Zangid dynasty, Zangids 47
Zanzibar 245
Zavarak, Daylaman 121, 125
Zaydar, castle in Qumes 164
Zayn al-'Abidin 6
Zordu, Qohistan 185, 274, 275
Zuzan, castle in Qohistan 28, 170, 268